# *Selection &*
# *Recruitment*

## The Open University course team

Sylvan Bentley, *Picture Research*

Pam Berry, *Compositor*

Sue Carter, *Staff Tutor, Faculty of Social Sciences*

Stephen Clift, *Editor*

Lene Connolly, *Print Buyer*

Barry Cripps, *Author, Study Guide/Statistical Concept Refresher*

Jonathan Davies, *Graphic Designer*

Mark Embleton, *External Consultant*

Wilf Eynon, *Audio Visual*

Janis Gilbert, *Graphic Artist*

Andy Gudgeon, *External Consultant*

Celia Hart, *Picture Research*

Wendy Hollway, *Critical Reader, Faculty of Social Sciences*

Jonathan Hunt, *Co-publishing Advisor*

Jane Sturges, *Critical Reader, Open University Business School*

Martin Le Voi, *Critical Reader, Faculty of Social Sciences*

Thaiquan Lieu, *Course Manager*

Marie Morris, *Secretary*

Winifred Power, *Editor*

Linda Preston, *Secretary*

Elaine Richardson, *Secretary*

Rosalind Searle, *Course Team Chair and Lecturer, Occupational Psychology, Faculty of Social Sciences*

Joanne Silvester, *External Assessor, Goldsmiths College, University of London*

Gail Whitehall, *Audio Visual*

Chris Williams, *Production and Presentation Administrator*

# Selection & Recruitment

## a critical text

## Rosalind H. Searle

in association with

This publication forms part of an Open University course, D842 *Psychometrics: Selection and Assessment.* Details of this and other Open University courses can be obtained from the Course Information and Advice Centre, PO Box 724, The Open University, Milton Keynes MK7 6ZS, United Kingdom: tel. +44(0)1908 653231, e-mail general-enquiries@open.ac.uk

Alternatively, you may visit the Open University website at http://www.open.ac.uk where you can learn more about the wide range of courses and packs offered at all levels by The Open University.

To purchase a selection of Open University course materials visit the webshop at www.ouw.co.uk, or contact Open University Worldwide, Michael Young Building, Walton Hall, Milton Keynes MK7 6AA, United Kingdom for a brochure. tel. +44 (0)1908 858785; fax +44 (0)1908 858787; e-mail ouwenq@open.ac.uk

The Open University
Walton Hall, Milton Keynes
MK7 6AA

First published 2003

Edited, designed and typeset by The Open University.

Printed and bound in the United Kingdom by The Alden Group, Oxford.

ISBN 1-4039-2146-6

1.1

# Contents

**To Paul**

## Acknowledgements

This book could not have been written without the help and support from a number of people. I would particularly like to thank Andrew Gudgeon, Wendy Hollway, Thaiquan Lieu, Joanne Silvester and Jane Sturges for their very helpful comments and suggestions. I would also like to thank Sylvan Bentley, Sue Carter, Stephen Clift, Lene Connolly, Barry Cripps, Jonathan Davies, Mark Emberton, Sarah Gamman, Celia Hart, Alma Hales, Jonathan Hunt, Martin Le Voi, Margaret McManus, Marie Morris, Lynda Preston, Elaine Richardson and Chris Williams. Finally, my gratitude and appreciation must go to my editor Winifred Power.

# CHAPTER 1

# Introduction to selection and recruitment

## 1 Overview

There has been a resurgence in confidence in selection and recruitment systems since the 1990s. The field has the potential to undergo a rapid change as developments in new technology and assessment begin to present novel opportunities and mediums for assessing potential job applicants. In some cases, the speed of change is so fast that there has been insufficient opportunity to evaluate and consider its impact and value. This book explores the key tools and techniques that are used in selection and recruitment today. It examines the development process and assumptions that underpin these tools. It identifies how they are being used in practice, reviews their strengths and potential weaknesses in a selection context, and suggests how they can be used more effectively in organizations.

## 2 Impetus for the book

Since 1990 I have worked in the field of recruitment, selection and assessment. This has involved developing selection systems for all levels – from apprentices, team leaders, graduates, managers and directors. It has included using psychometric tests to help identify and plan the development of senior managers and directors. I have also lectured to post- and under-graduate psychologists and business students about the different methods and techniques used in selection and recruitment. Psychometrics also featured in my research, which involves examining team composition and processes. These processes are at the heart of the work I (and many other work psychologists and human resources (HR) practitioners) undertake.

In my career, studying and using these tools and techniques, I have found that there has been a wide constituency who have been touched by them. These are the line operators who – despite their enthusiasm and desire – are still on the line as they did not pass the selection programme; the student who tearfully told me after a graduate-assessment test that she 'was not leadership material'; or the older woman who was too scared to apply for a job because part of the selection process involved using a computer. I have encountered the company director who found it gave him a means of identifying and de-selecting those who saw the world differently and therefore 'won't fit in'. These are the other side of selection processes: people who have been labelled by the process and have had their dreams taken away, or those who now have a new tool in their armoury to perpetuate their biases and support their discrimination.

I have been fortunate in my career to have been trained and challenged by some very eminent scholars and individuals. As a student of **occupational psychology** at The University of Hull, I was given a good grounding in the theory and practice of psychometrics, which expanded later into specialist training in various instruments. My first job after university was working for Vauxhall Motors. This gave me the opportunity to put my training into practice to develop and implement a selection programme for a new engine facility. My successes there allowed me to develop selection processes and train assessors in these new skills at all the Vauxhall UK sites. One vital lesson that working in the car industry taught me was to respect the huge talent and under-used resources of those who worked on the track. I recall with wonder seeing chess played by operators across the line, who would store their moves in their heads until they had a chance to move their pieces on the board. I also witnessed the staff-management talents of trade-union officials. I felt there were many people with potential that remained unrealized. I wondered why.

Embarking on an MBA allowed me to step back and put my psychology into a wider strategic context that my previous studies had not been concerned with. I found that many of the new models I studied did not consider the impact of selection on an organization's success. Through my studies, I developed my understanding of the importance of integrating and devising consistent HR policies and practices. Without this synergy, confusion reigned.

Through my MBA dissertation, I became even more aware of some of the *weaknesses* of psychometrics: I found participants who could not understand the questions given in tests and so while a response was provided it did not reflect what they told me in an interview. My factor analysis did not replicate the structure the instrument's authors had intended. Through my in-house consultancy work, I also began to see how selection decisions influenced employees' future careers and how organizational maturity was an important factor in ensuring their fair use. Selection data were highly sensitive information and I was very concerned with the impact of their potential misuse.

Over the last nine years as an academic and consultant, I have witnessed the emergence of different ways of thinking about and understanding organizations. In the main, I have been most challenged by non-psychologists. My assumptions of effectiveness have been contested; my understanding of the impact of selection and assessment has been broadened to include society's and sociological concerns such as institutionalization and surveillance; and my appreciation of subtle forms of discriminatory practices has increased. My Ph.D. involved comparing and contrasting how organizations' culture affected HR practice. This revealed the different assumptions and approaches organizations' cultures bring to selection processes, changing the impact.

Starting a new job at The Open University gave me the opportunity I had sought to research and develop a more *critical* exploration of psychometrics and selection and recruitment. The new millennium presented a unique opportunity for academics to reflect and comment critically on selection processes. Although many wrote on the subject, the time-scale they considered was very truncated and there has been limited consideration of how psychometrics has come to arrive at its current position. Before starting to write I talked to colleagues who also teach in the area, and they suggested I write a book that was critical and also looked at new developments. After examining other texts I decided to create a text that could be used to support students completing the British Psychological Society's competence in occupational testing. I also wanted to examine how selection tools were developed, discuss the assumptions that underpin them and consider critically the new developments in the field.

The net result is this ten-chapter book.

## 3   Introduction

This first chapter begins by defining some of the key terms used in selection and recruitment processes. I then move on to consider the processes in terms of their wider organizational strategy and human resource context. Currently, organizations are undergoing changes in response to the expansion of horizons – beyond the local to national and international frontiers. For many organizations, such as the health service, as well as private firms, an increasingly important source of their labour lies outside Europe. I shall consider why, since the 1980s, the use and importance of selection and recruitment processes within organizations have increased. It became clear when researching for this book that the selection and recruitment processes used by organizations are becoming more prolific and sophisticated. One reason for this is the change in the position and confidence of HR systems within organizations (Legge, 1995). From synthesizing the literature in this field, eight overarching assessment topics are discussed which emerge in different guises throughout the book. These create some key questions for readers and researchers alike. The chapter closes with a brief overview of the nine further chapters.

## 4   What is selection and recruitment?

This book focuses on selection and recruitment, but what do we mean by these terms? **Selection** is when a firm chooses an applicant for a post from a pool of applicants already employed by the organization while **recruitment** involves filling a post from a pool from outside the firm. (The terms 'firm' and 'organization' are used interchangeably to describe public, private and not-for-profit organizations.) The aim of selection and recruitment processes is to assess psychological differences between individuals and their relationship to subsequent job performance. Research in this field varies in terms of the breadth of selection activities considered: in this book I explore the basis of both the measurement of individual differences and their relationship with performance. Selection and recruitment are a process (see Figure 1.1). The selection and recruitment process includes two main elements: **attraction** and **assessment.**

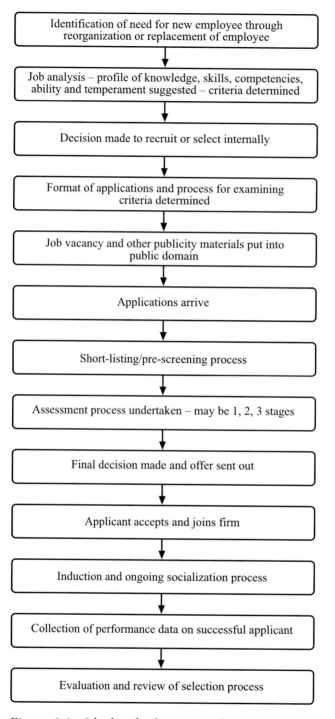

*Figure 1.1 Idealized selection and recruitment process*

### 4.1 Attraction

The first process I consider is attraction to an organization, which is concerned with how individuals become applicants. Here, I consider attraction, pre-screening and the applicant's decision-making. This is an important and often under-researched area but it is vital that it is borne in mind by organizations as it illustrates the **two-way power relationship** involved in selection. Most texts tend to focus solely on the power of the firm in selection decisions, but it must be kept in mind that an applicant *chooses* the firm just as much as the firm chooses the applicant. Research has indicated that the media exposure of a firm is a sign of its reputation (Newell and Shackleton, 2001). So it is not surprising that organizations spend in excess of £1 billion on recruitment advertising. Moreover, newer technologies are changing how active job seekers and more passive potential applicants hear about and become attracted to a firm. New **media** also allow the screening of would-be applicants by providing a conduit for screening work previews and delivering organization-fit questionnaires. Because of this, firms can reduce the cost of their selection and recruitment processes as applicants can be rejected in a more positive way early on in the selection process. Important privacy and discrimination issues are at play here that link into many of the later selection practices used by firms (Searle, 2003). This is an area where there is much critical investigation and evaluation to be done.

### 4.2 Assessment

The second aspect – assessment – is considered in far greater detail in this book. I look at the analysis of job vacancies to determine the job requirements and examine the various tools and techniques used to evaluate an applicant's suitability. These tools include **references, curriculum vitaes (CVs), autobiographical application blanks (biodata), interviews, ability** and **personality psychometric tests** and **work-sample methods**. In different chapters the development and application of each method is discussed in more detail. Although many of the techniques could be used in measuring educational attainment, the focus here is on the application of assessment within a work context. Assessment in this book is located in the identification of potential to fill a work vacancy.

The integration and internal consistency of HR systems is important for organizational success (Legge, 1995). Selection and recruitment processes are the *first* part of finding and identifying potential. It must be noted however that the identification of potential is different from its realization: the complete success of these processes depends on the subsequent integration and retention of the candidate by the organization. Although part of the evaluation of the effectiveness of selection and recruitment processes can include subsequent job performance, there is not the space in this book to examine in depth these subsequent processes. Organizations may use the selection of new staff as a means of creating an organizational change, with these new employees hired on the basis of their distinct attitude and skills. Often these organizations can become myopic in their attention to change once they have identified these new recruits, forgetting that their new recruits have to work with their existing staff. Thus, selection and recruitment should be regarded as just one tool within a coherent HR strategy.

Organizations need to offer a receptive context in which an individual is given the opportunity to display and increase their skills and abilities. Research (Heilman *et al.*, 1992; Small, 1991) shows that many new selection systems – those which, for example, encourage minority ethnic groups through targeted selection (in the USA termed '**affirmative action**' or '**positive discrimination**') often fail because of the discrimination faced by these new recruits after joining the organization. The cost of this is not just to the organization, in having to recommence recruitment, but can take a huge toll on successful applicants by reducing their self-esteem and increasing stress levels. Change through selection is a difficult thing to achieve and should not be treated lightly by firms seeking a quick transition in culture. It is important that selection is recognized as part of an overarching HR process.

### Box 1.1   Lessons of diversity for a high-street bank

Early in the 1990s a high-street bank decided that they wanted to recruit more applicants from minority ethnic groups to work for them, especially in areas of London that had a large number of minority populations.

The bank looked at the low number of applicants from these minorities and assumed that part of the reason these applicants were not coming forward was because they did not have basic skills. It deliberately targeted this group in advertising and developed pre-selection numeracy and literacy workshops for anyone from a minority ethnic group. The number of applicants from this group rose for the bank, but so did their subsequent turnover. Why?

A study was conducted which identified that minority ethnic recruits were being stigmatized by their fellow workers who perceived that they all had basic skills problems. Line managers did not feel part of the recruitment process and saw these new staff members as having reduced levels of competence, and as foisted upon them.

The bank began to recognize it had a problem with the assumptions that had been made. It stopped the programme and gained commitment and support from top management that highlighted diversity as a key issue for the bank's ongoing success. It still used the workshops but as part of a wider community-based initiative. Now the workshops were open to anyone seeking to develop their key skills. Turnover of this type of recruit fell and new markets opened up for the bank.

## 5   Setting HR in the business context

It is important that anyone interested in selection and recruitment regards **HR processes** as a reflection of the wider context. They are developed to enable an organization to achieve its strategy and are not stand-alone systems. An **HR strategy** may be flawed: for instance, it may fail if the goals and aspirations of the organization's leader are changed, or distorted, as it becomes operationalized down the organization. **Middle managers** are often engaged and empowered to operationalize the strategy, but they can also inadvertently (or deliberately) change the wishes of their leaders. Despite the importance of synergy between strategic intent and organizational action, this is sometimes not achieved. Unfortunately, an area where there is often evidence of a mismatch is in organizations' selection and recruitment practices (Searle and Ball, 2003). This may be due to limitations in the skills and abilities of those developing the system, or through deliberate pursuit of their own different and personal goals. This distortion is a cause for ongoing concern in organizations and a topic that resonates throughout this book. Selection processes, as you will see, can be distorted by both assessors and candidates, or through incomplete measurement tools.

Whether producing cocoa beans or developing new software, the strategic aim of most commercial organizations is to improve their long-term viability. Often, their strategy focuses on improving their competitive advantage and developing their competencies to sustain and develop their place in the market. Of course, not-for-profit organizations also have strategic aims. They too have stakeholders, such as governments, or users to whom senior managers are accountable to for the organization's performance. These organizations often show the same, if not more, concern and sensitivity for equal opportunity issues and their inclusion than their commercial counterparts. HR processes are thus also a tool for them to deploy.

In the 1980s, major changes occurred within organizations in regard to their HR practices. HR became more assertive as to its role in organizations (Legge, 1995). This was due to an increasing awareness and evidence of the impact HR had in the viability of firms. For example, work by economists and psychologists has examined the economic performance of firms and suggested that HR policies, previously considered as important but largely unconnected to economic viability, in fact played a major role in organizations' success (Patterson *et al.*, 1997). HR policies emerged through this period as significant levers for assisting organizations in repositioning, or consolidating, their place within the sector. As part of the resultant changes, selection and recruitment processes were recognized as critical components in successful change management (Iles and Salaman, 1995, p.203). They were a means of introducing those with a new attitude, as well as new skills and abilities, to the organization.

To reflect this change, many authors of strategy, HR and organizational behaviour began to re-evaluate the relationships between strategy and the operation of HR policy. An example is Purcell's 1989 model (Figure 1.2), which built on earlier work by Chandler (1962) to identify three levels of strategic process in organizations. The model shows how HR strategy emerges directly from decisions about the firm's long-term direction and its organization. It also indicates the important links between all levels of strategy to their wider environment: firms exist within a context.

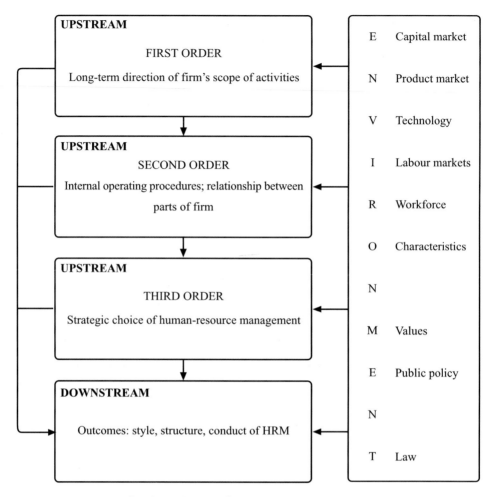

*Figure 1.2   Purcell's three levels of strategic decision-making*

At the same time, other authors were examining the processes of HR themselves. In the early 1980s the Harvard Business School had a major impact in shaping HR policy as we currently know it. In particular, Beer *et al.* (1984) developed a model that showed the relationship between inputs, processes and outputs of HR strategy for a firm (as you will see in Figure 1.3). The outcome of these HR practices was firmly connected with improved organizational effectiveness (Illes and Salaman, 1995), but they also benefit the individual and the wider society.

Four key policy choices are at the heart of the model. The first aimed at improving the **competence** of employees and focused on competence and ability measurement and their change over time. The second choice highlighted commitment and identified issues such as **turnover**, or more subtle indications of dissatisfaction. The third area pointed to the importance of '**fit**' and was concerned with the congruence between the worker and the organization's goals. Much attention has focused on the '**utility**', of selection systems: the final issue highlighted in the model was the cost-effectiveness of HR systems. Such studies have claimed that the cost of good selection is quickly recouped through resultant productivity gains. The utility of selection tools and techniques is a theme addressed in subsequent chapters. This model shows the breadth of HR processes and, by expanding the stakeholder group, shows the link between practices, processes and outcomes.

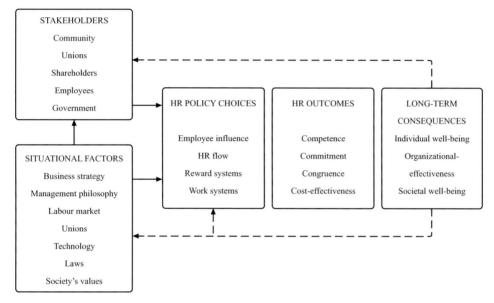

*Figure 1.3   'Map of the HRM territory'*

(Beer *et al.*, 1984, p.16)

## 6   Globalization

### Box 1.2   *Globalization of selection: a case study*

An Argentinean candidate is looking for work as an operations manager for a US-based multinational. The local recruitment agency manages to secure the candidate an interview. The selection system used was developed in the US headquarters – a Washington office – but the vacancy is in Singapore. The Singapore office identifies a senior manager (who is Australian) to conduct the structured interview using a video-conferencing link. She has no psychometric interpretation skills for the tests used. The Washington office asks the local site to administer the ability and personality tests. They have no expertise in interpretation and so a consultant is hired. The consultancy, a UK-based firm, developed the psychometric tests used. The test results are sent to their top consultant, a Belgian psychologist, who is working at the consultant's Irish offices. He sends the interpretation back to the interviewing manager. After weighing up the evidence she decides that the candidate is not suitable for the job. The candidate is unhappy with the decision and feels, as a Black person, that they have been unfairly discriminated against. They want to legally challenge the decision: Whom do they sue? And which country's legal system do they use?

The context in which organizations are now operating is changing significantly. One reason is the increasing influence of **globalization** on the application of selection systems. Many organizations – from multinationals to health-service trusts – are searching for suitable employees from across the world and applying the same selection criteria with limited attention to the effectiveness of these processes in assessing applicants from different cultural backgrounds. Many have little insight into how local context and climate may affect the effectiveness of their selection criteria. This is an area where practice is far ahead of research and comment. However, it will not be long before legal challenges begin to force us to question and evaluate what is occurring. The case in the box above is an example of what is already happening in selection practice and poses a dilemma for both the organization and applicants.

One way firms are trying to manage their operation within this new global context more effectively is by using sophisticated selection assessment practices. If the underlying basis for their assessment is flawed, then these more high-powered tests and assessments will inevitably be a further waste of resources. Nonetheless, selection tools are becoming increasingly popular in organizations: given the concerns about distortion, this begs the question, why?

## 7  Increasing use of selection and recruitment techniques

There are two primary reasons for the growth in the application of selection and recruitment systems: first, improved methods of assessment and, second, the increasing influence of multinational companies. Improved methods of assessment reflected the changes in how tools are evaluated for effectiveness. In the 1960s and 1970s, research challenged the quality of the techniques used and suggested that they were not robust. The development and use of meta-analysis from the 1980s as a means of evaluating selection systems has alleviated some of the earlier problems caused by small sample sizes. This resulted in the re-confirmation and enhanced standing of many of the tools as valid and reliable selection processes, as Figure 1.4 shows.

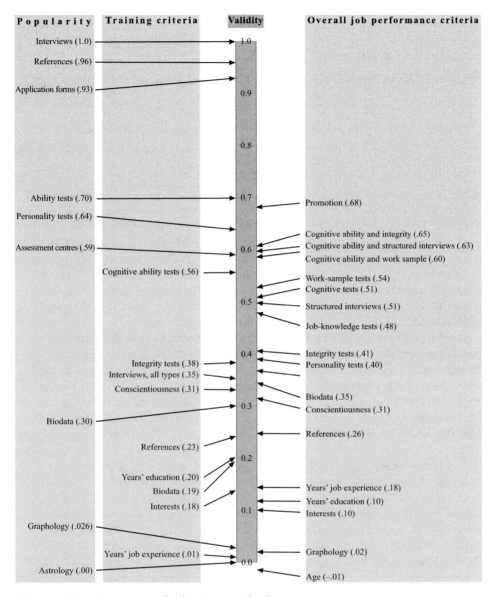

*Figure 1.4   Accuracy of selection methods*

(adapted from Robertson and Smith, 2001, p.443 and
Anderson and Shackleton, 1993, p.30)

The second change was the growing influence of multinationals. During
the late 1980s academics began to study the impact of '**Japanization**' and
'**Americanization**' as multinationals from these countries began to export
their home practices into radically different contexts. In HR terms, it is
arguably Americanization that has had the greatest impact through the
exporting of psychometric-based models and practices. Whilst there are
differences *across* countries in the application of selection tools (Shackleton
and Newell, 1994, 1997), Iles (1994) suggests that multinationals play a key

role in the erosion of such cultural differences. Many of the tools and techniques studied in this book were developed for, and evaluated in, a US context, and there is little interest shown in exploring whether they are as effective in an overseas context.

In contrast, the influence in the HR area from Japanese multinationals has been far more limited. Their focus on standardized operations and on co-operative working practices has served to reinforce the importance of attitudinal components in selection and recruitment (Forrester, 1994, 2000). Japanese firms regard attitude to work as a more important selection criteria (Delbridge and Turnbull, 1992) and consider relevant skills as trainable.

The influence of the USA has also been magnified by the dominance of US-based journals (such as *Personnel Psychology* or *Journal of Applied Psychology*) within HR research. This has had two consequences: an overemphasis on the psychometric view and a disinterest in the re-validation of selection tools. In the USA, the psychometric model of assessment dominates research. As a result, selection is reduced to the measurement and identification of criteria by the organization. This dominant approach has marginalized the impact of alternative views, such as a European-led emphasis on **social processes** and **social construction** views, which indicate a more prominent role in these processes for the applicant and highlight the emergent negotiation between the parties.

Second, there has been limited interest or concern for the application of these US-derived systems within new contexts such as Europe, Africa and South-East Asia. Non-US based academics such as Shackleton and Newell (1994/1997), Ryan *et al.* (1999) and Newell and Tansley (2001) have pioneered research assessing cultural differences in the use of selection processes, but there is still a dearth of interest in the impact on validity of different cultural contexts of such tools. As this book will reflect, changes in context can have a significant impact on their effectiveness. Meta-analytic studies have contributed to diminishing the importance of context differences in selection processes (Hunter and Hirsch, 1987). However, interest in identifying sources of measurement error and the creation of global tests have caused these concerns to re-surface and it is hoped that this will lead to further study.

## 8   Eight key themes: important concerns and challenges to selection and recruitment paradigms

In researching this book, eight key themes emerged which are important to those seeking a more critical understanding of the field of selection and recruitment. They reveal some key challenges and concerns to the dominant paradigms in this area. We shall consider each in more detail now.

### 8.1 Irrational decision-making?

Few books on selection consider the premise of rationality of decision-making involved in selection processes. The traditional emphasis in selection literature has been on the employing organization's decision-making process. This stresses an organization's power in setting the selection criteria, working conditions and remuneration packages for each post. The applicant's power in this process is rarely considered. In addition, there is an assumption of rationality in the decision-making process for both the organization and applicants: selection is seen as a sequence of prescribed steps that are followed in a set order before a decision is made. (These are typified in the idealized processes shown in Figure 1.1.) Evidence from psychology and organizational behaviour, however, indicates that human beings have a problem following such a sequence, with recent evidence confirming that applicants are as poor as organizations (Highhouse and Hoffman, 2001).

Research indicates that despite the best of intentions, decisions are based on a 'bounded rationality' (an incomplete search) (Simon, 1960). This involves a partial search through all of the options available: there is neither the time nor the mental resources to do a complete analysis, so instead a satisfying, or 'good enough', solution is sought and found. Studies show this behaviour is often based on previous experiences: we prefer to focus on what we know and understand. Agor (1986) showed in his study that data were used to support, rather than provide the basis for, decisions. Thus, the assumption of rationality in selection decisions must be questioned.

As part of this theme, in this book I explore the development of each of the tools commonly used in order to expose the underlying philosophy or assumptions that lie behind each and identify the problems that result. I am also interested in how these tools are applied in practice and so I show how the results produced by these tools can be contaminated – either wittingly, or unwittingly – by either the assessor, or the applicant. This brings into question the assumptions of the rationality implied by these processes.

A further underlying concern that influences the enactment of many of the selection processes is that they often involve a *group* of assessors. Research on teams has shown that groups are just as fallible – if not more so – than individuals in their decision-making (Janis, 1972; Steiner, 1972). **Group dynamics** and power issues can reduce effectiveness significantly. Limited attention has been paid in the selection literature to the issue of rational decision-making and its effect on the quality of selection decisions (Zedeck, 1986).

Related to this is the wider dimension of perception and distortion: for example, **stereotyping** and **bias** by assessors or impression management by candidates. Again, traditional texts show a paucity of work here within the more applied field of selection and recruitment. Few authors consider the role of perception and distortion in decision-making, or indeed in shaping how we present ourselves. Evidence shows that assessors misattribute the causes of events by paying too much attention to negative information (this will be explored in more detail in Chapters 5 and 8). What happens to the selection processes if individuals also do this and fail to recognize and adequately describe their own talents? This book attempts to explore how distortion and bias can enter and contaminate selection processes and decisions.

## 8.2  If it moves, test it?

Psychometrics often presents a façade of objectivity for both the test and the user. The outcomes of some tests provide over-simplistic results that mean that the applicant is either accepted or rejected. There is limited consideration for a more appropriate expression that places the individual along a *continuum* of suitability. Nor is there attention paid to rejection in terms of that context. So, for example, a rejected graduate trainee is unlikely to succeed as a leader in one context, but could succeed as a leader elsewhere. In the book, I reveal degrees of, and deviation from, a scientific measurement rational for each tool. I also consider the implications of this. In Chapter 2, the issue of criteria identification is challenged; elsewhere, problems of criteria contamination are highlighted and the underlying assumption of their stability disputed (see Chapters 3, 4, 5, 7, 8 and 9). The implications of these concerns and recommendations for the future are discussed throughout.

At the heart of criticism of psychometric-based measurement is the question of whether the results obtained are in fact an artefact of the test items themselves, rather than indicative of a psychological phenomenon of the applicant. For example, there can be a huge variation in the number of items included in tests claiming to measure constructs such as 'intelligence' or 'dominance'. A key assumption is that the underlying construct the test is purporting to measure is 'normally distributed'. Some challenge this assumption and argue for instance that personality and intelligence are not normally distributed and that such an assertion is a deceitful product of **factor analysis** (Laming, 1997). Cartell (1978) argues for a more pragmatic view, which holds that it is possible to proceed as if intelligence is normally distributed until we are forced to abandon such a hypothesis. The problem is that few studies have sought to examine and challenge these underlying premises.

The assessment and testing of **psychological constructs** assumes it is possible to measure internal processes and attributes. Their quality varies depending on the precision and nature of the measurement. Stevens (1951) highlighted the unchallenged expansion of psychological assessment processes. He argued that the basis for many psychometric instruments involves an arbitrary assignment of a number to any object or event based on a rule; any rule regardless of whether it has a theoretical basis or not. Michell (1951) took up this view to suggest that many tests are flawed, and there is rarely any attempt made to demonstrate the existence of their structure *before* measurement is undertaken. Second, he suggested that in natural sciences proof is required that the attribute has a quantitative structure. Thus, the claims by natural science are provisional. He postulated that the hypothesis that any attribute is quantitative is a contingent, empirical hypothesis that may, in principle, be false. Yet this view is rarely entertained in social science.

Throughout this book, I explore the issue of measurement within a high-stakes environment. The hallmarks of quality psychometric measurement are identified, namely the tools' **reliability** and **validity**. Reliability is, however, not a product of the measurement *per se*, but a property pertaining to the scale score. Similarly, validity depends on the purpose for which the scale is used and the sample who completed it. Thus, the context in which these tools are applied is critical: tests that show high validity in one context might not be valid in another. Moreover, these concerns become magnified when selection begins to occur on a global basis.

Measurement systems that depend on **self-report** can also be challenged. These pose the question of how well we know ourselves? For many of the tools suggested here, evidence indicates that self-report is a poor response process and that in fact others who know the applicant well may provide a better basis for assessment. However, how many applicants would be comfortable with such a process? Particularly if they were rejected?

## 8.3  A marginal view of individual differences

The application of testing and assessment has, from its inception in the 1880s, focused on improving performance by the identification of differences *between* human beings. Early applications of work psychology from the 1900s onwards focused on enhancing organizational efficiency by identifying and selecting those individuals who had the skills, talents and inclination suitable to an organization. For example, Hull (1928) showed that the systematic selection of spoon-polishing workers could result in a five-fold increase in their productivity.

This approach to individual differences involves two central assumptions: stability and predictability. The first assumes that individual differences are stable over time, that there is a consistency to the ability level, personality traits and behaviour of individuals. Thus, change in these aspects is assumed to be limited. This view will be challenged a number of times in the book; for example, in Chapter 8, where we look at personality assessment and how individuals make contradictory assertions about their own personality. The second assumption is that previous behaviour influences our propensity to behave in the same way in the future. This limits the possibility of individual change and development, and therefore is at odds with research looking at learning and development processes.

Moreover, these views of individual difference fail to consider four key factors that influence behaviour. First, as we shall explore in Chapters 3, 4, 5, 8 and 9, they ignore the role of context in shaping and changing individuals' behaviour. Second (as discussed in Chapter 7), they do not incorporate the influence of motivation or volition in shaping behaviour. Motivation is not stable and *can* change over time. Third, as Smith (1994) highlights, they omit any consideration of 'life-space', which considers the proportion of time an individual is prepared to devote to their work. This links with current considerations of work–life balance. Finally, as we shall examine in Chapters 5 and 8, there is no place indicated for **efficacy** or self-belief, which have a major role in shaping our behaviour (Newell and Shackleton, 2001). By failing to consider these influences, it is only possible to gain a partial and static view of the individual differences that influence work performance.

## 8.4  Biased population and restriction of range

As I noted earlier, the accurate measurement of differences related to variance in performance is at the heart of all selection and recruitment processes. The range of applicants applying to the firm can influence selection decision quality. This is often biased to particular population groups, such as Caucasians.

A further problem from a research perspective is the over-reliance on students, rather than workers, as participants in studies. Findings of research in psychometrics tests can be compromised if they are conducted with students who are not representative of the working population. Limited consideration is given to the generalizability of results found for this specific student population to a broader working one.

The traditional paradigm of assessment and selection involves the accurate identification of the **criteria** by the selection method so that only those who pass the criteria are accepted. As Figure 1.5 shows, selection systems need to minimize those who achieve a false pass, or who are rejected incorrectly. Instances are a student who randomly answers a multiple choice test and gains a higher score than they would normally, or a candidate who is rejected as nervousness stops them from being able to think of more pertinent examples in an interview. The evaluation of these systems, however, focuses on a population that may differ significantly from the initial sample. At the very least, the sample is incomplete: what happens to those who are *not* successful is never examined. This creates a statistical problem by restricting the range.

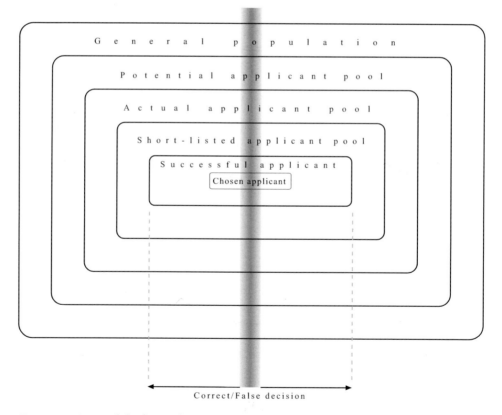

*Figure 1.5   Model of populations*

In Chapter 9, I look at evidence from Kandola (1995) which reflects the challenge created by those from non-traditional backgrounds in selection criteria generation. These groups challenge traditional employers' (White males) implicit assumptions of what constitutes effective job performance. For example, recent questions across Europe have questioned the ongoing domination of white males on company boards. Some selection practices discriminate unfairly against particular groups, and, as a result, the range is erroneously curtailed.

Newell and Shackleton (2001) posit an action-oriented perspective to selection. This challenges the more commonly held deterministic view by recognizing the subjectivity of the process. However, they argue that such recognition could also result in the condoning of unfair practice, rather than its reduction. Instead, an acceptance and awareness of the likelihood and the impact of discriminating practices in any selection process is required. Few firms have embraced this view, or undertake a regular review of their practices.

Related to this work, psychologists have been challenged for holding a myopic view, for not being interested in the wider context, nor concerned with the impact of their processes (Iles and Salaman, 1995). Hollway (1991, p.7) contends that knowledge neither can, nor should be, separated from its effects. All too frequently our examination of selection practices appears to do both. This book aims to identify the paradox of successful testing: meta-analysis after meta-analysis identify that the general cognitive ability factor ($g$) and the personality factor 'conscientiousness' are the best predictors of job success. However, evidence shows that cognitive ability tests have an adverse impact on Black people. So why are they still used?

Discrimination (or 'adverse impact' as it is called in the US literature) is an issue that has been slow to attract the attention of either academics or practitioners. Controversially, the groups most often discriminated against are those representing lower socio-economic minority constituencies, and they therefore have limited power in organizations. These groups are under-represented in senior organizational positions. Indeed some countries – for instance, Norway – are taking active legal steps to ensure better representation of women at director level. Increasingly, however, demographic changes have reduced the availability of the traditional White male applicants, creating a fresh impetus to diversify workforces. The 1990s saw this demographic 'time-bomb' emerge as a key concern.

New developments are also perpetuating these previous discriminating practices. The impact of new technology, such as the use of the internet in assessment practice, threatens to reinforce earlier patterns of discrimination favouring white males from higher socio-economic backgrounds. This group appears to be more comfortable with this medium than older, female and minority ethnic applicants. What is of particular concern for these minority groups is that frequently those organizations that prefer to use these new media are also those offering very high levels of remuneration. These include financial and banking firms who see this new media as providing an invaluable screening process to remove unsuitable applicants. In this book, I assess the impact of new developments to see how far discrimination is emerging in new guises.

Through the inclusion of a brief history of the development of each tool, the book shows that the institutionalized nature of many of these selection tools has provided a means of de-selecting minorities and reinforcing existing stereotypes. As a corrective, I highlight the role of selection tools developed from robust psychological constructs. Through these processes, real performance differences would be revealed instead of merely perpetuating unsubstantiated and biased results that continually and adversely influence the same population groups.

There is relatively little legal protection for individuals from such discrimination. UK law in the areas of the Sex Discrimination Act (1986), Race Relations Act (1976, and amendment 2000) and the disability discrimination Act (1995) are outlined and their limitations described in detail. However, it is important that selection system developers, users, and takers are aware of these problems, their long-term consequences and how their effects can be ameliorated.

## 8.5  The psychometric versus the social process paradigm

More and more, selection and recruitment criteria involve the identification of one best way of performing a task. Contrasts are made throughout this book between traditional scientific psychometric models and those that suggest an alternative social process approach. This alternative view identifies that there is a two-way social process involved in selection (Herriot, 1987; Hollway, 1991). This proposes that both the individual and the outcome are a construction of the measurement process. For example, a criterion such as leadership focuses on particular types of behaviour to the exclusion of others that might achieve the same outcome whilst the individual applicant is asked to demonstrate these skills in a contrived environment. This challenges the psychometric process by suggesting that paradoxically this measurement is not concerned with uncovering potential, but in defining and constructing it in its own terms. The alternative view sees the recruitment process as a manifestation of the organization, revealing its values, culture and strategic mission; the applicant is not a passive databank, but a co-constructor of the outcome. The individual therefore is regarded as a powerful actor and partner in the process who can change and affect it.

The book discusses these different paradigms. In Chapter 5, I show that although the social process view is equally valid for other selection techniques, it is only in interviews that such a discussion has been developed.

## 8.6  Faking a desired response?

Both assessor and applicant are potential contaminators of selection processes. Many researchers in selection and recruitment have considered only the assessor as the contaminator of the process: for example, misattributing an outcome to luck rather than skill, or through holding stereotypical views of people who wear white socks, or who have red hair. This view of the assessor as the only contaminator is increasingly being challenged. The falsification of information by applicants has always been a cause for concern by organizations since the advent of more formalized selection processes began in the UK with the civil service exam in 1855.  It is important to recognize that both parties can be potential sources of distortion. For example, applicants may deliberately make up examples of their work experiences; firms may attempt to present themselves in the most favourable terms, with interviewers conveying a positive culture and set of values of the organization to applicants (Highhouse and Hoffman, 2001).

Goffman (1959) identified the importance of self-presentation that has underpinned our current interest in impression management. Selection and recruitment decisions are high-stakes environments in which the applicant's future is reviewed and decided. It is simplistic to regard applicants as passive participants in the process: they are trying to present themselves in the best light possible. This can either be indirectly in the application form, or in an item in a personality test, or more directly, for example, during the interview. Arnold *et al.* (1997) identified common **impression-management** techniques that applicants use. These include ingratiation, selective descriptions of events and positive self-descriptions (this is explored in more detail in Chapters 5 and 8). We also examine the research pertaining to distortion and **faking** for every selection technique and ways to reduce it are suggested.

Many applicants, particularly for graduate and managerial posts, have had a great deal of experience of assessment processes. Any job applicant will attempt to show themselves as worthy, often at the expense of their fellow candidates. It is naïve to assume that they have no ingenuity in trying to guess the selection criteria and will not try and present themselves accordingly. In Chapter 9, I look at the research that shows that providing candidates with details of the real criteria can have positive benefits for both the organization and the applicant.

Psychologists have tended to focus on a pejorative view of such impression management, with studies of manipulation, or 'faking'. It is equally myopic, however, to view attempts at favourable distortion as illegitimate or deceptive. The juxtaposition of this view regards this behaviour as creating a desired self-identity (Scklender and Weigold, 1990). Such presentation cannot be simply disregarded as superficial, nefarious, or machiavellian. In Chapter 8, we look at recent research which suggests that favourable self-presentation may be indicative of high applied intelligence and sensitivity to context.

## 8.7 Selection: a three-way dynamic?

During the 1980s, the British psychologist Herriot (1987) spearheaded a re-evaluation of the power dynamics of selection. As Chapter 5 shows, he argued that selection was a two-way process and that would-be employees also have power in situations. Herriot showed that applicants with the skills the organization needed were able to significantly change the balance of power and demand different conditions and look for higher rewards. Subsequent research by Highhouse and Hoffman (2001) confirms that the two-way power of applicants is present from the outset of the process. Thus, the candidate emerges as a powerful stakeholder in selection processes.

In this book I identify a third stakeholder. This is a new departure, which emerges from the current changes in the balance of power within recruitment processes and decision-making (Searle, 2003). The third stakeholder is the test-developer, of whom little is written. Barritz (1965) termed such consultants 'the servants of power'. I will argue that test-developers have their own agendas within selection processes and that this can be at odds with the goals of applicants and organizations. In the past, test-developers have provided firms with the materials to assess individuals. The firms then used the materials as they wanted, and so test-developers had limited control over their use and restricted access to results. The advent of technology changes has revolutionized test procedures and in so doing has elevated the power of this group. The methodology underpinning these tests is also undergoing a transition. In Chapters 6–10, I will argue that the combination of these two influences has shifted the potential status of the contractor group so that they now have far more power over both the individual applicant and the organization.

## 8.8  New applications and considerations

Each chapter in this book identifies new developments in theory, methods and application. Each development is important and is examined to assess how far repetition of previous mistakes and problems is being minimized. One of the major developments in selection is the largely neglected role of **volition**. For example, enthusiastic applicants will apply themselves more readily to finding out rules underlying an electronic systems test. Some work has been done indicating its importance in ability and personality test performance (Ackermann, 1997).

There is also a review of how new media such as the telephone and the internet have changed selection processes.

# 9  Overview of forthcoming chapters

Chapter 2 examines job-analysis techniques: these play a critical role in identifying the criteria used in selection. This is a topic that has been much neglected at a time when the nature, location and place of modern work is in flux. I review eleven commonly used **job-analysis** techniques and discuss the assumptions of **stability** and the role of past job performance in underpinning these techniques. The two key challenges emerging for job analysis are the issue of **error** and the necessity for identifying one best way of performing a job. The ongoing problems caused by the separation of the worker from the work context are also reviewed. I identify future developments in this area, including the expansion of criteria identification to incorporate pro- and anti-social as well as task-related activities, attempts to identify skills needed to perform new and yet to become known job roles, the relevance of social construction theory to job analysis, and the under-utilization by organizations of existing electronic data-collection sources.

In Chapter 3, two issues that are hallmarks in assessing the value of any selection process – reliability and validity – are examined. I discuss the main types of validity and major aspects of reliability. The contribution of two forms of distortion are identified and assessed within the selection context. These include external distortions (which may have been inadvertently introduced by the test) and internal effects, which focus on the behaviour of test-takers. While it is clear that selection test-users cannot control these, we need to be more aware of how practice and motivation factors can distort final raw scores. The impact of discrimination is a topic which has not received the attention it deserves: I review fairness in selection, concentrating in particular on racial discrimination. The subtle variation produced by changes in job type, organizational climate or situation for selection validation is also examined. Chapter 3 lays the ground for clarifying technical details discussed in subsequent chapters.

In Chapters 4–9, I scrutinize the most commonly used selection and recruitment methods. The historical development behind each is reviewed in order to gain an insight into their current use; critical strengths and problems are discussed and new developments identified and assessed.

Chapter 4 is the first 'tools' chapter, exploring those used at the *start* of the selection process. The chapter explores the role of résumés or CVs, which are often the first point of contact between the applicant and the organization. The chapter then focuses on biographical data (biodata), which has received a great deal of research attention. This is used to illustrate the problems of an **atheoretical** approach to selection. The chapter ends with a brief look at references – a method still favoured by many employers. Again this is an area where new technology is enabling the information candidates provide to be checked more thoroughly. This leads to a discussion of associated privacy concerns.

Interviews are the focus of Chapter 5. These are the most ubiquitous of all selection processes. Issues of power and perception in selection are addressed. This is illustrated by contrasting two different paradigms: the psychometric and the social process model. The role of impression management in interviews is also assessed. This is a topic which exemplifies the distortion of selection processes by introducing bias and contamination. Recent developments such as the growth of telephone interviews as a response to globalization are addressed. Finally, the impact of candidates' and assessors' training is discussed.

Chapter 6 explores psychometric test construction. I identify the different techniques used to develop and construct tests and show how these methods can be used for both ability and personality tests. Distinctions are made between tests of typical and maximal performance. The focus is on how psychological-measurement techniques can be devised.

The role of ability testing is examined in Chapter 7. The chapter begins by surveying the historical development of the field to illustrate how assessment has evolved. We look at the development of theories of intelligence to show their links to psychometric tests. The paradox that ability tests show the highest validity of any selection tool but also have a significant adverse impact is discussed, and the new role of the internet in cognitive testing is considered and concerns are raised about the repetition of discrimination.

Personality is the focus of Chapter 8. Here, I explore the development of personality theory and discuss its role in the development of psychometric instruments. The increasing application by organizations of these tools outside selection processes is also examined. There is a paradox between the different perceptions of personality by lay audiences and psychologists:

the reasons for this are reviewed. The topic of personality reveals concerns about consistency and fakeability, and we shall explore these in detail. Recent work has indicated that personality and motivation play a key role in both selection results and subsequent job performance. The impact of these studies of psychometrics is discussed.

In Chapter 9, job-related tools for selection are assessed: these instruments aim to assess an individual's abilities from their performance in a job simulation. These simulations are shown to vary enormously in their complexity: they range from simple dexterity tests to complex multi-method, multi-criteria assessment centres. Many of the methods deployed have not changed since the 1920s, but their application is shown to have broadened and increased dramatically to include managerial-level jobs. I discuss why job-related tools can be important in reducing discriminatory effects of testing. New applications of these techniques in assessing professional skills and abilities are explored and their part in extending behavioural measurement to include interpersonal and team-working skills is highlighted. Concerns are raised about '**attenuation**': the increased reduction in the validity of these scores over time and the reasons behind this and its impact are explored.

Chapter 10, the final chapter, explores two competing perspectives for selection and recruitment: the psychometric and alternative views. Future developments in the field of assessment and recruitment are identified regarding technology and globalization. These developments point to the new opportunities offered as well as the challenges to be overcome. It suggests the ongoing importance of taking discrimination into account in the future and the need to ensure internet and other new technologies do not replicate our previous errors.

## 10  Summary

I began this chapter by discussing my motivation for writing the book. I identified the place of selection and recruitment within a wider organizational context and highlighted the relationship between organizational strategy and human resource policy and procedures. Key changes in method and practice were identified as being responsible for the increased attention and use of selection systems across organizations. These included the enhanced confidence in HR processes with the application of techniques, such as meta-analysis. There is also a growth in process-oriented research, which highlights an alternative view of selection and recruitment and is at odds with the dominant psychometric approach. The book considers selection to be a process and is mainly concerned with the assessment of applicants. Eight overarching topics that will feature throughout the book were then highlighted. These include the irrationality of decision-makers in selection; different paradigms of selection, individual differences, a new re-conception of impression management, the problems of unfair and discriminatory selection processes, the importance of test-developers as a distinct stakeholder in the process, the façade of objectivity and the assessment of new developments to see how far previous discrimination is being repeated. Finally, a brief synopsis of each of the subsequent chapters was outlined.

# CHAPTER 2

# Defining work and jobs

## 1  Overview

Job analysis is one of the most widely used techniques for collecting information about the roles that people undertake in organizations. Pivotal to any good selection system, it is nonetheless a topic that receives limited attention – other than criticism – from researchers. Our understanding about the nature, location and place of modern work is in flux: some workers have more than one job, and in fact juggle a portfolio of different activities, while for others the distinction between home and work has blurred as home-based working has increased.

Work is no longer the centre of many people's lives as it was for their parents. Instead, working life is now a balance between travel, new experiences and family commitments, or a series of career changes interspersed with new learning. A key problem with traditional approaches to job analysis is an assumption of stability in jobs and roles. As a result, traditional rationalistic approaches are being challenged as outmoded, irrelevant and time consuming (Bridges, 1994). They can be seen as inflexible and failing to capture socially oriented skills which are becoming increasingly important in the knowledge era (Newell, 2000).

Paradoxically, it is becoming clear that as jobs are changing rapidly to incorporate more knowledge-based requirements, the necessity for interpersonal skills is growing, in order to enable information to be elicited from disparate sources. Related to this, many organizations are beginning to consider not only the person requirements or the behavioural competencies for performing a job but also the final **output**, but they pay limited attention to how this can be achieved. In the past, performance and its effectiveness have been regarded as distinct entities, with attention concentrating on how the task was carried out. This has shifted attention away from the current trend towards the identification of emerging competencies. As a result, far more focus needs to be placed on understanding and identifying which aspects of a job are enduring. Alternative techniques that involve more interpretative approaches are emerging (Sandberg, 2000). Whilst these may be more competent at capturing the *meaning* of work for those who experience it, they may not assist those who are developing recruitment and selection processes for organizations as they do not provide usable information. The tension within work psychology is between the practical utility of these new techniques and their psychometric robustness.

In Chapter 2, I discuss two key tensions. The first is the ongoing separation of workers from their context, which results in a focus on generic skill and tends to emphasize only one way of doing a job. The second tension can be found between techniques that are easy to use in contrast to those that have more robust psychometric properties.

The chapter begins by examining the pivotal role of job analysis in organizations. I show how these techniques have moved from being the remit of engineers to psychologists and discuss the distinction between task and personal skills, demonstrating the contrast between task-based and worker-oriented data-collection techniques. Following this, ten commonly used techniques are reviewed and the distinctions between ease of use and psychometric robustness considered. Then I examine the accuracy of job-analysis data by depicting how the results can become contaminated. Another related question – the issue of job stability – will be explored in detail, and the key changes that challenge the premise of stability will be identified. I then consider the impact of these issues for organizations. Finally, future developments in the assumptions and techniques of job analysis will be discussed.

## 2   Introduction

Job analysis has traditionally been regarded as one of the 'building blocks' of an organization (Schein, 1980): it reveals a blueprint for how an organization works, identifying different jobs and how they fit together. It plays a pivotal role in HR and personnel departments and can be seen as the foundation for virtually all other HR systems (Butler and Harvey, 1988). Job analysis includes a family of techniques, which are critical from an administrative systems perspective in ensuring sound information for HR processes. These techniques assist in the evaluation of jobs to ensure equity in salary and grading across different posts within organizations. They play a role in **appraisals** and in defining the criteria used in the recruitment of new staff. They can help to identify **development**, **training** or **rehabilitation plans** for existing workers and underpin potential **career paths** and **promotion routes** for an organization's 'high-flyers'. Finally, they can aid those involved in labour-relations disputes in ensuring equity between different roles.

In addition, job-analysis techniques are a vital tool for gathering information that can be used to develop more robust selection systems. As I shall show in Chapter 3, they also play a crucial role in ensuring that the content of any selection process is valid. Evidence indicates that the validity of selection tools, such as psychometric testing and structured interviews, increases when they are based on a job analysis (Wiesner and Cronshaw, 1988). In Chapter 9, I shall discuss how the job-analysis process is also useful for determining the weight to be assigned to different selection tools when developing an assessment centre (Arthur *et al.*, 1996). Such techniques can form the basis of later validation studies to ensure selection systems are performing effectively (Harvey, 1991; Goldstein *et al.*, 1993).

Finally, job analysis is a legal requirement in many parts of the world. For example, in the USA it is a prerequisite to recruitment (Albermarle Paper Co. *vs* Moody, 1975). It provides the data for a sound legal argument that ensures selection processes can be defended in court (Harvey, 1991). In the UK, individuals are also protected from discrimination through the Sex Discrimination Act (1975), Race Relations Act (1976), Equal Pay Act

(1970) and the Disability Discrimination Act (1995) (we shall discuss these in more detail in Chapter 6).

Outside the HR function, job-analysis techniques can have a wider role within other departments in organizations. They can be used by those involved in the designing of jobs, or they can help ensure staff are not overworked. They can help identify the safest and most efficient way of carrying out a task, thus reducing later litigation for organizations. The data produced by these techniques are also useful to those *outside* an organization for informing the work of vocational guidance for young people and other career changers.

## 3   Historical development of techniques

Taylor (1911) in the USA was the first to use simple job-analysis techniques to understand the distinct tasks that underpinned different jobs. This assisted in skills-training programmes: analysing jobs within a predominantly static environment, his methods were used to identify the smallest unit of a task, which was termed an 'element'. For instance, a job element might be 'removing a saw from a tool box'. From these individual elements, distinct tasks involved in any particular job could be identified and families of related jobs created. These job data were predominantly the preserve of the 'time and motion engineer', who could be found on shop floors assessing workers with a stop watch and measuring precisely how long each element of their work took. Today, many of these practices still exist (for example in manufacturing and call-centres) and assist in balancing workloads, to ensure that the demands of each role do not overwhelm workers, and monitoring average rates to ensure productivity.

What is striking about the 'Tayloristic' approach to job analysis is the separation of the *worker* from the *context*. Workers become a generic part of an organization, fitting in with its demands, rather than having specific skills of their own. They become easily substitutable commodities in the process. Little attention is paid to the worker as a unique human being with a wide range of skills and abilities that may – or may not – be required to perform their current role. This removal of the individual from the process obscures issues such as the individuality or artistry involved in work. The task becomes reduced to simple stages, omitting any 'magic'. Simplifying jobs in this way may also reduce the commitment and motivation of workers.

An instance can be found in the sweet-manufacturing industry where job analysis has resulted in the exclusion of subtle talents. To make sweets, the raw ingredients of sugars, heat, cooling levels and pressures from extruding processes must be combined with subtle influences (such as changes in local climate) to create complex interactions. This makes it difficult to define key aspects of the role that need experience and particular expertise from operators. These expertises are difficult to pin-point as local climates and contexts can vary enormously. In the past, the skills involved in sugar-based manufacturing were seen as mysterious. Now these roles have been reduced to a series of standard operations that disregard the small changes required to take into account variations in local conditions (Ball and Searle, 2002).

As work psychologists adopted the engineers' techniques, they began to identify a broader range of skills. They added cognitive factors, such as reasoning, verbal fluency or numerical and spatial abilities, to the existing physical skills levels. Psychologists expanded the previous prescriptive and simplistic approach to job analysis to include the wider skills and abilities required. The techniques have been adopted in selection systems, through to training strategies and change-management processes. They also form the basis for adult education and training processes; for example, policies such as the UK's National Vocational Qualifications (NVQs) are developed from job-analysis techniques that define the skills and competencies required for a whole range of different jobs.

## 4   Type of job descriptor

Traditionally, job analysis can be divided into two main topics: '**work-oriented analysis**' (focusing on the job itself) and **worker-oriented analysis** (focusing on the worker). The first technique provides a list of the essential activities involved in a job, which generate a detailed and concrete description for the job (an example is given in Box 2.1).

---

### Box 2.1 Job description

- **Post:** Accountancy administration, print section
- **Grade:** Clerical level 4
- **Salary:** Up to £19,000
- **Reports to:** Management accountant
- **Responsible for:** Preparing financial accounts and management accounts in print section.
- **Summary responsibilities:** Preparation of financial accounts and management accounts as per group system for print section.
- Gathering necessary data.
- Analysis of financial information and preparation of reports for print-section manager and management accountant.
- **Professional qualifications:** In process of completing examination for membership of appropriate accountancy body, e.g. Association of Cost and Management Accountants (ACMA), or Association of Chartered Accountants (ACA). Must be part way through.
- **Academic qualifications:** A-level or equivalent, e.g. BTEC in business and finance.
- **Work experience:** A minimum of 3 years direct comparable experience as an accountancy administrator preparing and submitting financial accounts in small to medium organization.
- Evidence of understanding of current cost-accounting practices.

## Box 2.2 Person specification

**Essential**
- **Physical make-up:** Smart appearance

**Attainments**
- **General ability:** Top 45 per cent of the general population
- **Special aptitudes:**  Numerical reasoning, top 35 per cent of general population
- **Ability to organize information, e.g. spreadsheet**
- **Attention to detail**
- **Good oral communication**
- **Desirable aspects:** Experience in an office environment
- Robust health
- Experience of using spreadsheet package, WP/keyboard skills
- Flexible to changing priorities
- Car driver

# 5    Work-oriented job analysis

Work-oriented job analysis has been sadly neglected, and this has detracted from its important contribution to job analysis in supplying less subjective criteria than its worker-oriented counterpart. The group of techniques used in work-oriented analysis can include checklists, questionnaires, observations, activity diaries/log books and hierarchical task analysis. The rationale of these techniques is to establish concrete aspects of the role, such as 'once a week re-oil the machine'. These task-related aspects of the role are less likely to fluctuate with psychological processes. Problems can occur when these techniques produce so much detail concerning precisely what the job involves that an analysis becomes too unwieldy to be of any practical use.

Most of the recent research in work-oriented analysis was conducted in the early 1990s, for example Sanchez and Fraser (1992). An important distinction was made by Borman and Motowidlo (1993) and later by Campbell (1994) in differentiating between the traditional focus for job analysis on task, or **in-role behaviours**, and those additional aspects of performance that are more context-dependent. These are termed '**extra-role' behaviours**, and have included such factors as good citizenship behaviour or supporting colleagues outside their traditional sphere of operation. This development extended the scope of the task to include both those directly and indirectly related to successful job performance. Further distinctions have been made to extra-work dimensions (Coleman and Borman, 1999) to distinguish between three sets of extra-role behaviours: namely, those that (1) benefit the employee, (2) the organization and (3) the work itself (such as task conscientiousness). This is a significant departure from previous research to emphasize how organizations can profit from both formal job and extra-role behaviours. It widens what might be considered as a role function.

Increasingly, organizations are defining the roles of workers more in terms of outcome. Thus, a target is specified and the employer leaves it up to the job incumbent how to achieve this. While this is a welcome departure from the previous focus on achieving the task in one specific way, this new approach is not without its problems. It is the complete antithesis of traditional job analysis because it separates what needs to be done from how it is achieved. The definition of outcome effectiveness may become problematic: for example, a sales agent could achieve all of their sales targets by taking them from his/her colleagues, rather than from outside competition. This attention on targets may also represent a short-term view of business and so while an agent may have achieved sales today, they might not have managed client relationships effectively and ensured repeat business for the firm. Although the focus may appear to be on achieving objectives, more subtle tacit and extra-role aspects of the work may also be important.

## 6   Worker-oriented job analysis

The second focus of job-analysis techniques concentrates on identifying attributes that workers themselves need to possess. These include techniques such as interview, **critical incident technique, repertory grid, position analysis questionnaires (PAQs)** and **work-profiling systems.** There has been significantly more work done in this area, concentrating on establishing 'competencies' or worker-oriented attributes. Boyatzis (1982, p.21) defines a competence as 'an underlying characteristic of a person in that it may be a motive, trait, skill, or aspect of one's self-image or social role, or a body of knowledge that he or she uses'. One approach to competencies is to regard them as generic facets which can be translated into other contexts. For example, Spencer and Spencer (1993) reviewed 200 different jobs to identify the competencies of superior job performers. These included competencies such as achievement orientation, information-searching, conceptual formation and flexibility, impact, self-confidence, pro-active orientation. Part of the difficulty for those seeking to use generic competencies as a means of identifying job requirements is that they may be too general and abstract to be of any practical use. This problem diminishes if competencies are defined as specifically focused on a particular role.

More and more, analysts are falling back on using '**KSAs**' – knowledge, skills and abilities (US version), or knowledge, skills and attitudes (UK version) – to define the characteristics of effective workers in a role. In the past, practitioners have used a task analysis to identify these KSAs, but increasingly this initial step is bypassed and those with knowledge of a job are being asked to identify the competencies required. There is, however, limited information concerning the psychometric properties, such as reliability and validity, of this more direct process (Robertson and Smith, 2001, p.446).

Mr. Hewitt possesses a nurturing
management style.

*Figure 2.1   'A good manager?'*

The identification of KSAs has been assisted by the development of
analysis tools that distinguish the relevant personality traits for job roles
(Veres *et al.*, 1990). Many systems build on existing personality models: two
have been devised that are based on the **big five personality model** (we
will look at this model in more detail in Chapter 8). These are Rolland and
Mognent's (1994) **ipsative** tool, and Raymark *et al.*'s (1997) questionnaire.
These tools can be useful both in suggesting personality variables that
might be good predictors for the role, and in assisting with the
development of selection-criterion measures. Other personality-derived job-
analysis measures include Hogan and Rybicki's (1998) system using the
Hogan personality test, and more recently Westoby and Smith's (2000)
16PF-derived questionnaire. There has been very little assessment of the
predictive powers of such tools but the use of a structured and systematic
approach to data collection and multiple informants should increase their
reliability and validity. However, their value depends in part on the
underlying models of personality on which they are based.

An implicit assumption behind the worker-oriented group of job-analysis
methods is that the worker is a tool of the organization who can be easily
substituted for another who possesses the same competencies. This
suggestion has two important limitations. First, it ignores the influence of
the organization's culture or local climates in the enactment of such

competencies; instead the worker is simply chosen for, and hopefully displays, their KSAs. For example, many organizations are recognizing the need to be more innovative in order to sustain themselves within the market-place. How would an organization that is risk-averse cope with a new hire who has been deliberately recruited because of their innovation and pro-active orientation? It is likely that this will result in a tension between the organization's approach and that of the individual, which ultimately may restrain the new recruit from being fully able to demonstrate their skills within that organization.

Second, the assumption tends to reinforce the idea that there is one style and one approach to undertaking the job, with the consequence that workers are easily substitutable. For instance, techniques may be inherently biased and favour one, perhaps Western, style of behaving within a role and fail to consider the transferability of these worker-oriented elements for the same job roles across different national cultures and organizations. There has been limited exploration of this important and emergent issue as practice creeps ahead of research, and the implications of cultural differences and their impact on how a job might be performed have not been considered.

Let us examine now the ten most common techniques used in job analysis.

## 7    Ten job-analysis techniques

The techniques I will now briefly describe provide different insights into a job, varying in their sophistication and sensitivity. The first five focus predominantly on identifying the work-oriented elements, or the tasks that underlie a job, whilst the latter five are more sensitive to the type of workers and their skills. This is by no means an exhaustive list.

### 7.1 Questionnaires and checklists

One of the most popular ways that jobs can be analysed is through a structured questionnaire or checklist. These checklists are derived from a taxonomy of tasks. Krzystofiak et al. (1979), following an analysis of 814 different jobs at a power station, developed a 754-item questionnaire. The questions concentrated on the frequency with which 600 tasks were performed by employees in their jobs. The most significant modern progress in job-analysis questionnaires has been developed in the USA by Petersen et al. (1999) who devised the O*net. This is a flexible database which contains occupational information on the attributes of both work and workers. Identifying aspects of both the task and the person marks a significant departure for such tools. O*net collects information on four sets of attributes and behaviours including personality, cognitive, behavioural and contextual variables. The inclusion of contextual aspects is in response to earlier problems of this group of techniques. O*net is used extensively in the USA and large databases are being established for the results (see Figure 2.2).

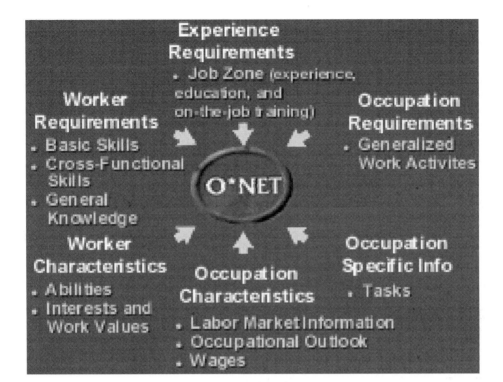

| Job Zone Component | Job Zone Component Definition |
| --- | --- |
| Overall Experience | A minimum of two to four years of work-related skill, knowledge, or experience is needed for these occupations. For example, an accountant must complete four years of college and work for several years in accounting to be considered qualified. |
| Job Training | Employees in these occupations usually need several years of work-related experience, on-the-job training, and/or vocational training. |
| Job Zone Examples | Many of these occupations involve coordinating, supervising, managing, or training others. Examples include accountants, chefs and head cooks, computer programmers, historians, pharmacists, and police detectives. |
| SVP Range | (7.0 to < 8.0) |
| Education | Most of these occupations require a four-year bachelor's degree, but some do not. |

Figure 2.2   Example of O*net extract for the job of an accountant

Overall, such methods can be flexible in identifying different aspects of jobs, but are constrained by the underlying taxonomy that is used to define the question domains. As these tools generate numerical values, properties such as their reliability can be easily assessed by comparing the responses of different analysts. Who collects the data can also vary, with both workers and analysts completing the questionnaires. A problem can emerge, however, as some questionnaires demand higher cognitive skills in order to understand and successfully complete the items. Care must be taken to ensure that whoever is completing the questionnaire *understands* the questions: otherwise, the value of their responses will be compromised. It can also be difficult to transport the results obtained in one context into another. For example, an administrator in one organization is not necessarily the same role in another.

## 7.2 Observation

Observation is a simple task-oriented job-analysis method, and offers three different variants for data gathering. The simplest and most straightforward is through the direct observation of the task. This may not, however, pinpoint the importance of any particular task above another, nor will it necessarily provide an insight into the level of difficulty. In some occupations, the tasks undertaken change at different times; for example, the role of a fire-fighter or air-traffic controller would vary dependent on the task they were performing. Observations of handling a fire, or averting a disaster would present a different insight. The second type of data gathering involves an interview, either while the task is being observed or as a later follow-up. The interview can provide this previously omitted data. The third variant focuses not on *what* is being done, but on *how* it is being done. Thus, the observation is targeted at behaviours, not tasks in themselves. This technique is frequently used to devise a checklist of important job criteria.

The data collected can also be used to identify the sequencing of actions. Observations are frequently made with a stop-watch to collect information regarding the duration of each task. In addition, the observation may be videoed in order to capture different aspects of the task.

Problems can emerge for this method if the observer does not understand what they are watching and, as a result, may not see all the actions as meaningful. This will affect the reliability and validity of the analysis. Differences can also be found across observers, where each is focusing on different parts of the job. Additionally, the task can be carried out in subtly different ways by different role holders, creating artificial distinctions in how the task is done.

*Figure 2.3   Hawthorn wiring room*

The technique can be easy to use in selection and recruitment. A key to its success lies in ensuring adequate training for the analysts so they can distinguish where it will, and will not, be a suitable tool. It can be difficult to use for those involved in tasks which have high cognitive demands, such as computer-programming or architecture. In such cases, the analysis can ask the job incumbent to narrate the mental processes they are undertaking. Training helps analysts standardize their approach and thus increases the reliability of the instrument. Research has indicated that being observed can also change the way a task is done (termed the 'Hawthorn effect'). It gives the job incumbent attention from someone potentially more senior in the organization and they may have a vested interest in deliberately distorting their performance of the task and sabotaging the reliability of the results. It is important therefore to gain their commitment and support for the process. This may be difficult. For example, if the organization is undergoing a change and recruiting new staff, whilst also making some existing employees redundant. Feeding results back and gaining the interpretations of the post-holder can be a useful but time-consuming checking mechanism to ensure that everything of value has been recorded.

### 7.3  Self-report: diaries and logs

Another task-oriented method involves role holders themselves collecting information about the tasks they have performed through diaries and simple logs. This can offer an insight into common tasks the role involves and their duration. For example, diaries were used to analyse the tasks of pub landlords and their tenant directors (Pearn and Kandola, 1993). This revealed considerable duplication across both roles, with the directors providing direct supervision for the tenants, rather than taking a more removed strategic role. This is a good example of how a job analysis can also assist in strategic organizational development.

The analyst needs to give initial attention to the type and frequency of the data required. For example, is it everything the incumbent does, or just specific types of activity? As a group, self-report methods can be difficult to manage; incumbents will often cheat and typically complete logs at the end of the day or week, rather than at the designated time. This can affect their reliability significantly. Moreover, deliberate sabotage, or bias, can be a problem if the incumbent fears the outcome.

An alternative – which can provide similar data – is simply to ask incumbents to recall a typical day. This will provide a narrative of their role, but may inevitably involve some recall problems. The approach can be subjective if the job holder does not understand the reasons why the data are being gathered.

## 7.4 Participation

Participation is one way of trying to bypass some of the potential contamination issues the job incumbent can introduce. By becoming a participant in the task and gathering data from their perspective, the analyst can be given a unique insight into the job. This does, however, require them to have sufficient mastery of the task themselves. For obvious reasons, this technique is restricted to the simplest of tasks.

## 7.5 Hierarchical task analysis

The final work-oriented method I describe is hierarchical task analysis, which was developed by Annett and Duncan in the 1960s. Here, the task is defined in terms of its *outcome*. The process focuses on the planning of how to get to the outcome and is designed to deconstruct any job into a hierarchy of tasks, sub-tasks and plans. Working with the job incumbent, the analyst identifies an ordered series of sub-plans, or tasks that are required to achieve the eventual outcome. The analyst is required to follow a specific set of rules to ensure a clear and unambiguous analysis of the activity. In addition, attention has to be paid to establishing the level of performance required and the conditions under which the task should be carried out.

As a result of these restrictions, the process can appear rigid and defines only one definitive way of performing a task. Nonetheless, it can be a very useful technique in identifying training requirements. In the aluminium-manufacturing industry, for example, this approach has dramatically reduced training for smelting staff from two years to a few weeks by pinpointing the key parts of the process. The final outcome, which is a very detailed and hierarchical description of the task, may be simply too detailed to be of use (see Figure 2.4). The technique does require initial training for the analysis.

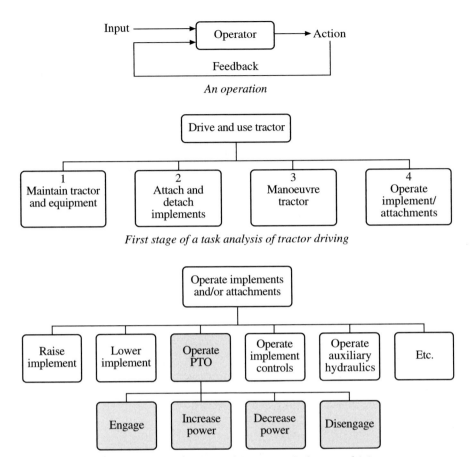

*An operation*

*First stage of a task analysis of tractor driving*

*Partial further breakdown of Operation 4 of tractor driving*

*Figure 2.4   Example of hierarchical task analysis for driving a tractor*

(Stammers and Patrick, 1975, p.53)

## 7.6 Interviews

For *worker*-oriented data collection, a number of techniques are used. One of the most common is an interview. Interviews are a flexible technique: they can take the format of either a structured interview with predetermined items, or a more freewheeling version. It is obviously easier to compare responses using a structured format. They can be readily applied to all levels of jobs and conducted to fit in with the role holder. Note that training *is* required for the analyst to get the most out of the session and to ensure that sensitive information is gathered. It can prove difficult to combine the results of the interviews from different analysts. The process can become contaminated by biases from both the interviewer and the interviewee. We will look at these problems in more detail in Chapter 5.

## 7.7  Critical incident technique

A variation to the interview format is the 'critical incident technique' (Flanagan, 1954), which involves identifying the most important parts of a task. This method was developed to assess aviators during the Second World War. The technique requires someone who knows the job well to identify critical aspects of the role. The job is analysed in terms of effective and ineffective behaviours, and so a critical incident can be something with either a positive or negative impact. The person involved must have a clear insight into both the intention and consequences of their action (see Box 2.3). This technique is very sensitive in identifying critical aspects of a task and can be used in either an individual, or group, situation. The results can be computer analysed, enabling the comparison of multiple responses.

Drawbacks include a reliance on the accuracy of the role holder's memory. This can be subjective in its focus and may thus be prone to bias. As with other techniques, the incumbent may inflate the importance of their role.

### Box 2.3 An extract from a critical incident interview

Can you give me an example of an occasion when you did something extremely badly which meant you didn't meet an objective?

Well, there was a situation where I was running a workshop for staff. It was a difficult course looking at the change programme we were about to undergo. There were lots of tricky questions as staff were scared about the whole thing. Well, there were two people in particular who wanted to hijack the whole thing and use it as a chance to get at management. I wasn't having any of it and told them not to bother coming back after the break if they were not going to be more constructive. It really put a dampener on the rest of the workshop and I realized I had been responsible for potentially making the situation worse.

Can you tell me what you think you did that was poor?

I lost my temper with them. The most important thing I had to do was to enable people to think about the future and to ask questions. I should have used the group more to shut them up. But I didn't. I tried to do it by myself and that just alienated everyone from me and made the trouble-makers heroes in the end.

## 7.8  Repertory grid technique

A similar technique that is used to identify good and bad performance dimensions is the repertory grid technique. This was developed for use in clinical psychology by Kelley (1954) and is based on personal construct theory. Like the critical incident technique, this provides a subjective view of the role. The data must be gathered from someone who knows the role well. The analysis focuses on what is involved in the role (see Box 2.4 for an illustration of a grid and interview).

The technique comprises an ongoing and exhaustive comparison of elements. The elements can be anything, as long as they belong to the same family of items. For example, they may compare good, average and poor role holders, or distinct parts of the task. Through comparing three of these elements at a time, bi-polar (two ended – a positive and a negative) 'constructs' are produced which can then be assessed to determine their importance to the role. The job analyst's skill lies in probing or 'laddering' to ensure that the constructs are expressed in their most simple form.

## Box 2.4 Example of repertory grid to identify the differences between the best and worst sales representatives for a firm

Purpose: to identify the difference between the behaviours of its best and worst sales representatives.

The elements would be people: good, average and poor reps.

### Example of interview for the grid

INTERVIEWER: Can you tell me what two of these have in common that differs from the third? *(Taking Sandra, Claire and Harry cards.)*

RESPONDENT: Oh now let me see, well both Sandra and Claire are really good at keeping on top of things, they rarely let the paperwork mount up, even when they are on the road. Whereas Harry is just hopeless. It takes me all my time to get his expenses from him.

INTERVIEWER: Is there anything else that two have in common from this group that differs from the third?

RESPONDENT: That's a hard one – they are very good sales staff. But well, Claire and Harry, they can really pick themselves up if a sale hasn't gone well, but Sandra finds it a bit tougher. She spends a lot of time thinking about what she could have done to have changed the situation. I tell her it is just one of those things, but she won't have it, especially if she gets a run of them – then she's really in a bad mood for a long time.

INTERVIEWER: Going back to the first point you made about paperwork, can you look at the others on the list and indicate whether they are more like Claire and Sandra or Harry in their style?

| Positive construct ✓ | Sandra | Harry | Claire | Martin | John | Negative construct x |
|---|---|---|---|---|---|---|
| Quickly completes relevant paperwork | ✓ | x | ✓ | ✓ | x | Leaves paperwork to mount up |
| Picks self up after rejection | x | ✓ | ✓ | ✓ | ✓ | Unable to respond positively after rejection |
| Highly attentive interpersonal skills | ✓ | ✓ | ✓ | x | x | Lacks confidence in new social situations |
| Establishes personal relationship with clients | ✓ | ✓ | x | ✓ | ✓ | Good first impressions with clients |

The technique has a number of strengths. It is sensitive to less obvious aspects of the task, such as styles of decision-making or relationships. It is also very flexible as the elements can be easily adapted for any job role. The only prerequisite is that they come from the same family, such as all people or all tasks. In addition, the same data can be re-analysed in a number of ways. It is common for the technique to produce a large volume of data from interviews from a small number of people. There are a range of computer packages that make the comparison of results far easier. Problems arise where there is inadequate probing, for example, by taking at face value what is said rather than exploring in detail each and every aspect of behaviour. Training of the analyst is vital to ensure that they have been exhaustive in their use of laddering techniques.

## 7.9  Position analysis questionnaire (PAQ)

A variation on the interview method typically involves using a verbally delivered checklist to provide the structure for the interview. The position analysis questionnaire (PAQ) (McCormick *et al.*, 1972) is a common example. The PAQ comprises some 200 items and was developed from an analysis of more than 62 jobs. It examines a job in terms of six factors. These include information input, mental processes, work output, relationships with others, job context and other characteristics. The analysis is undertaken by the job holder, or someone who knows the role well enough to be able to rate the different aspects. The technique, like the questionnaire technique, can be a more robust tool in terms of its psychometric properties, as the resultant numerical data can be easily collated and comparison made across respondents. There are also databanks of more than 2,200 jobs from US analysis to enable easy comparison with jobs in other organizations. Although research indicates that the questionnaire has high reliability (0.79), no specific work activity is described in detail. As a result, this may obscure genuine task differences between roles which receive similar ratings. You can find examples of PAQ analysis for fire-fighters' roles in Tables 2.1–2.3.

**Table 2.1 Example of extract PAQ results for a fire-fighter's role (items with the highest percentile scores)**

| Name | Rating | Percentile |
|------|--------|------------|
| First aid cases | 47 | 99 |
| Long-handle tools | 4.0 | 99 |
| Signalling | 4.0 | 99 |
| Balancing | 4.8 | 99 |
| Temporary disability | 4.2 | 99 |
| Non-precision tools/instruments | 4.5 | 99 |
| Operating equipment | 3.0 | 99 |
| Improper illumination | 2.7 | 99 |
| Man-made features of environment | 4.2 | 98 |
| Body balance | 4.3 | 98 |
| Non-job-required social contact | 5.0 | 97 |
| Awkwardness of confining work space | 2.3 | 97 |
| Physical handling | 4.5 | 96 |
| Assembling/disassembling | 4.0 | 96 |
| Touch | 3.8 | 96 |
| Personal sacrifice | 3.7 | 95 |
| Air contamination | 2.8 | 95 |
| Estimating size | 3.7 | 94 |
| Hand–arm steadiness | 4.0 | 94 |
| Level of physical exertion | 4.0 | 93 |
| Vigilance: infrequent movements | 4.2 | 93 |
| Body movement sensing | 2.0 | 93 |
| Visual displays | 4.2 | 92 |
| The public | 3.3 | 92 |
| Permanent partial impairment | 2.5 | 92 |
| Precision tools/instruments | 4.2 | 92 |

(Pearn and Kandola, 1993, p.60)

**Table 2.2 Job analysis (PAQ) interviews. The fire-fighter's job is *extreme* in its demands in comparison to other jobs**

| Dimension no. | | Percentile |
| --- | --- | --- |
| 5 | Being aware of environmental conditions | 98 |
| 22 | Being in stressful/unpleasant environment | 94 |
| 24 | Being in hazardous job situations | 94 |
| 10 | Performing activities requiring general body movements | 93 |
| 32 | Being alert to changing conditions | 90 |
| **Overall dimensions** | | |
| 44 | Working in unpleasant/hazardous/ demanding environment | 97 |

Extreme = 90th percentile or higher

(Pearn and Kandola, 1993, p.61)

**Table 2.3 Job analysis (PAQ) interviews. The fire-fighter's job is *above average* in its demands in comparison to other jobs**

| Dimension no. | | Percentile |
| --- | --- | --- |
| 16 | General physical co-ordination | 87 |
| 29 | Working an irregular schedule | 77 |
| 13 | Performing controlled manual and related activities | 76 |
| 11 | Controlling machine/processes | 71 |
| 23 | Engaging in personally demanding situations | 68 |
| 1 | Interpreting what is sensed | 65 |
| **Overall dimensions** | | |
| 41 | Engaging in physical activities | 84 |
| 40 | Being aware of working environment | 77 |

Above average = 60th percentile

(Pearn and Kandola, 1993, p.61)

## 7.10   Work-profiling system (WPS)

Finally, the work-profiling system (WPS) was developed by SHL[TM] (1990) as a structured job-analysis expert system. It comprises three separate questionnaires which correspond with different job types. These include professional/managerial, administrative/service and technical/manual. The system gathers two distinct sets of data. The first focuses on the main tasks of the job and collects detailed information including ratings of the importance of main tasks, and their proportion and frequency of occurrence. The second set is concerned with training and qualification levels requirements, the responsibility given, the physical environment and the remuneration package (see Figure 2.5).

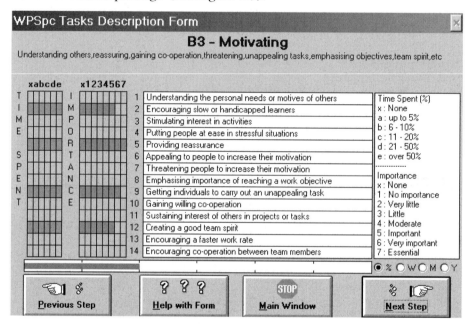

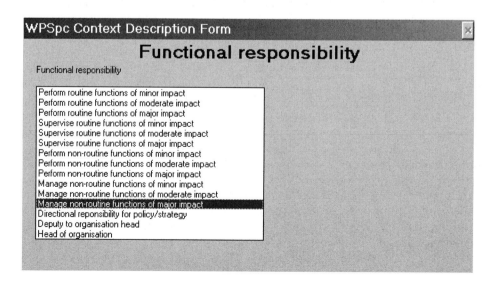

# PMC·PROFILE·¶

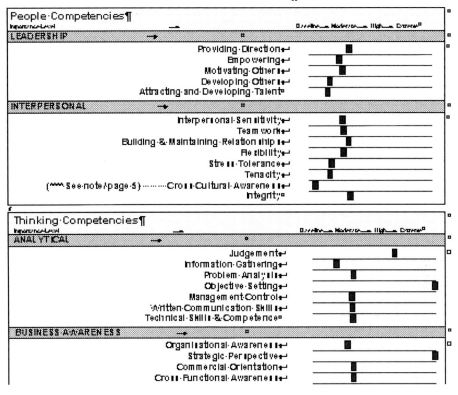

*Figure 2.5   Example of the work-profiling system*

These data can be analysed in four distinct ways. The first indicates the relative importance of the distinct task in the role (job description). The second shows the precise details of what the role involves (competency specification), whilst the third is an attribute analysis indicating personality requirements, such as style, and level and type of skills. Finally, it provides an indication of the most relevant assessment methods for each aspect.

Some flexibility is created through the use of the three distinct questionnaires. It can also be used as a self-report tool, with the job incumbent completing it alone, and so does not require an analyst to collect the data. The resultant analysis is only as good as the underlying model on which it is based and some care is required in interpreting the results (Pearn and Kandola, 1993, p.56).

Job analysts will frequently use a number of these different techniques to gather data on both work- and worker-oriented aspects of a job they are profiling. It is clear that some overlap and can be augmented, for example including an interview into observations, or checklists. They differ in their focus either considering a pre-determined range of issues or generating more emergent aspects of a job. There will be an inevitable trade-off between the ease of use, the level of detail required, the skills of the analyst and the context.

We shall turn our attention to identifying some overarching issues that may affect the accuracy and stability of job-analysis data.

# 8 Potential problems for job analysis

In examining job analysis there are two key problems that emerge. These relate to *accuracy* and *stability*. These are issues which are often overlooked but can have a critical impact on the value of job analysis to the resultant selection and recruitment systems.

## 8.1 Accuracy

The first problem found in job-analysis data is what I have termed 'accuracy'. This term, however, includes four distinct issues, involving the informant, context, underlying processes and measurement effects that can influence the quality of the information gathered by job analysis. Whilst some attention has been given to the impact of cognitive factors in other parts of selection systems, limited research has examined the influence of identical processes in this crucial initial process. It is paradoxical that neither the validity nor the reliability of job analysis have received much interest from researchers despite the pivotal role it can play in a large number of subsequent HR processes. Inaccuracy in this key process can have a profound human and financial impact (Morgeson and Campion, 1997). Part of the problem for those concerned with the quality of job analysis is that no 'true score' exists (Sanchez, 2000); most evaluations concerning the quality of job analysis are based on inter-rated agreement of human judgements. Many of the techniques outlined earlier rely on the subjective interpretations of the job analyst about the role, or may not provide access to more inferred cognitive components. Job analysis cannot necessarily be considered a reliable and valid measurement if it is not apparent what discrepancies are revealed. Are differences indicative of a meaningful variance in role enactment by different job incumbents, or an error in the measurement system itself?

Implicit for many of these tools is the truthfulness of job holders not to distort their descriptions or enactment of the task, or in their completion of a questionnaire. There is no means of checking for faking as in some other questionnaires. Further, it may be difficult for job analysts to have sufficient expertise of the job to be able to realize if/when distortion occurs. Errors therefore can be introduced to the process from a number of distinct quarters (Maxwell and Abraham, 1985). Although attempts can be made to control these problems by collecting data from multiple job holders, they may collude together, for example to 'go slower' – in which case comparative verifying procedures may not detect any error. Error factors may be difficult to remove from the analysis, but will affect the longer-term validity of the results. They are also more immediate sources of contamination which affect the accuracy of job-analysis data. Researchers have neglected to consider the ways in which errors may arise in the job-analysis process, thereby reducing the accuracy of the data obtained. We now look at four influences that create errors and exacerbate inaccuracy.

### 8.1.1 *Different perspective factors*

Job-analysis data are collected from a variety of different sources; most notably the job incumbents. Whilst they may appear to be the best people, paradoxically, at times they may not be sufficiently familiar or experienced with the job to provide adequate detail (Borman *et al.*, 1992; Landy and Vasey, 1991; Madden, 1962, 1963; Prien and Saleh, 1963). Neither may they have reached a sufficient level of performance to be able to show mastery of the role (Aamodt *et al.*, 1982; Borman *et al.*, 1992 ). Role-holder competency perceptions are continually revised and re-constructed as their skill level develops from novice through proficiency to mastery.

The information role holders provide will reflect their distinct conceptions and perspectives of the role. A key factor which influences perceptions and therefore the job analysis is demographic variations. Studies reveal that variance in age, sex and race all affect job analysis (Aamodt *et al.*, 1982; Schmidt and Chan, 1989; Veres *et al.*, 1991). Education and cognitive ability levels will also shape insights (Ash and Edgell, 1975; Cordery and Servastos, 1993). As a result, different job informers may have very different views of the same role. The analyst may be forced to identify whose responses are most valid where large discrepancies emerge.

More radically, Sanchez (2000, p.208) argues that 'those who perform the job may not necessarily be the best qualified to report the job'. He suggests that data can sometimes be gathered from a job analyst because they see the role differently. (He indicates how analysts might more usefully take this position; I will discuss this in more detail in this chapter's penultimate section which looks at future developments.) However, inadequate training and skill levels of analysts may not necessarily result in any improvement in the process, nor may they actually discern the relevant features. Hahn and Dipboye (1988) suggest that the most accurate job raters are those with both rater training and full job information. A number of the techniques outlined earlier require additional skills and training so that the analyst collects the data in a consistent and accurate way.

### 8.1.2 *Context factors*

In addition to the specific job incumbent-based influences, the organizational context will inevitably shape how the job can be performed. Organizational structures and cultures can significantly influence what a job involves and how it is done. For instance, organizations vary in the amount of job autonomy they permit, which will influence the variety of ways a task can be performed. This can be clearly seen in jobs such as trainee accountancy.

Strategic job analysis is undertaken for a specific purpose within an organization. Here the focus is on selection, but as noted earlier, the tools can also be used to define compensation and grading systems, or training and development needs. It would be naïve to suggest that the underlying purpose does not influence the data obtained from these instruments. Where the purpose of job analysis can significantly influence the current job holder – such as in remuneration – the propensity for distortion, manipulation or biased responding increases.

Given the influence of organizational context on the reliability and validity of job analysis, caution should be exercised when transporting any analysis into a different context (Goldstein *et al.*, 1993). Those creating selection systems for jobs in multinationals that involve different operating contexts would therefore be well advised to check to ensure that any global job descriptions and person specifications are accurate representations of the job in each and every location. It is clear, however, that a balance will be struck between the practical and political realities of the situation of this checking process.

### 8.1.3   *Process factors*

Any job-analysis tool involves a process that entails two important underlying psychological components: social and cognitive factors. Social elements, such as normative pressures, self-presentation and social influences, can compromise the accuracy of a job analysis. Indeed, these concerns inform a social constructionist perspective which would argue that traditional conceptions of 'accuracy' are as a result meaningless. Cognitive psychology also reveals the distortions which arise due to the biases and limitations of our information processing. These factors affect the interrater agreement levels and reliabilities of job-analysis tools. They can distort the data for a particular role and provide only partial data for the job. In addition, they can reduce the discrimination between different jobs and their dimensions, resulting in a homogenized generic result which cannot be usefully deployed.

Social factors can become a contaminant where group data-collection methods are used. Data collected in a group context are more affected by social conformity pressures (Deutsch and Gerard, 1955; Hackman, 1992), particularly when an unanimous decision is required (Kaplan and Miller, 1987) or where time constraints are applied (Benson and Hornsby, 1988). Groups do have more knowledge and insights than any single individual, and present a more considered view of the role which may or may not improve its accuracy by diminishing many of the aforementioned single informant contaminants (McGrath, 1984).

Job analysis can present an opportunity for the role incumbent to influence organizational policy and decision-making. The process can provide contact with higher status members of the organization. This presents an opportunity for the incumbent to maintain – or even enhance – their standing in the firm. This type of impression management will inevitably affect the quality of the data. Common manipulations include the descriptions of roles and their relative importance in the firm, which can escalate where there is role ambiguity. Evidence indicates that these distortions are more likely to occur for those jobs in which direct accountability is a factor (Tetlock, 1985), or where KSAs data rather than task-based information is being collected (Morgeson and Campion, 1997). As noted earlier, the temptation to finesse these important job details is dependent on the final purpose of the analysis; the benefits of impression management can be considerable where job analysis is determining remuneration levels. This was clearly seen in the early stages of the 2002 fire-fighters strike where it could be argued the job was portrayed as more complex than it is.

Many of the techniques in job-analysis instruments involve the identification of critical work incidents, or the listing of knowledge, skills, attitudes and abilities for a role. Following this process, an incumbent is frequently asked to evaluate in some way the information they provide, either through ranking or rating to indicate their importance, duration, frequency or difficulty. This evaluative process can be a complex cognitive undertaking, which may result, through cognitive overload, in more arbitrary and, thus, error-prone judgements being made. Cognitive processes are stretched where the individual is being asked to recall data, or where the task being described is complex. Further, a typical strategy used by job incumbents is to simplify the information, which may result in a reduction in its accuracy. For example, Smith and Hakel (1979) in their study of PAQ analysts found almost perfect intercorrelations for the job dimensions, suggesting that far from analysing the job, the assessors were measuring a simplification or a stereotype of the role.

Through studies of decision-making heuristics, cognitive psychology reveals the common distorting mechanisms which both analysts and incumbents use when faced with complex issues (Morgeson and Campion, 1997). People tend to overemphasize the similarities, instead of the differences, between two stimuli. For example, if two jobs have similar job-analysis ratings but different pay rates, an analyst might assume they should be the same and be more inclined to move one up, rather than the other down. We tend to confuse recent, or important, experiences with those that occur more frequently. This can distort our recall of critical incidents. We also anchor our decision in particular ways, for example in giving higher job evaluations to those with higher status job titles (Smith *et al.*, 1989). Thus, there can be a lot to be gained by the individual through the use of titles, such as 'vice president', or 'director'. Biases can creep into analysis based on different effects, such as the order of presentation or the attractiveness of the job incumbent. More details of common cognitive biases are reviewed in Chapter 5 in the context of the interview process but they apply equally to job analysis.

### *8.1.4   Measurement formats and precision*

The earlier range of job-analysis techniques included some that were derived from a model of work. These more structured formats restrict the attention of the analysis to a predetermined number of areas. This restriction of the range of issues that the job analysis explores may exclude other emergent or important elements. As a result, as we shall explore in Chapter 3, the content validity of the tool can be compromised.

The approach used to gather job data may exacerbate the inaccuracies by creating a high level of abstraction in identifying the tasks. For example, task-based surveys, used in conjunction with a 'relative time spent' measure, typically maximize within-job differences, whilst more abstract rating systems, such as 'importance' or 'difficulty', used with apply/not apply ratings, appear to find fewer differences (Morgeson and Campion, 1997). These formatting issues may influence the validity of the measurement. Some of the techniques result in a generic list of tasks or attributes that could apply in any context, or to any job. Often they fail to distinguish the unique parts of the job and become so broad as to be meaningless. There can almost be a banality to the results obtained from job analysis.

Little research has considered the level and impact of these accuracy issues within a selection context. More awareness is required both by individual analysts and HR practitioners, who use the resultant data to recognize that these instruments can provide a partial and potentially biased and inaccurate view of the actual job role.

A further problem, which I have highlighted earlier, is that a 'job' is not a fixed construct. It can be performed differently by different people. They are subject to change. This makes the issue of the reliability and validity of a job-analysis technique problematic. Therefore what exactly is job analysis doing? Given these difficulties, a more important question arises concerning the purpose of job analysis, i.e. is it perspective of the job or an in-depth description? Through focusing on the purpose, rather than the outcome *per se*, the issue of accuracy is under question.

## 8.2  Stability

The second significant problem is the underlying assumption of stability inherent in analysing any job. Yet it is clear that the whole nature of work and the resultant job description and person specification are changing with increasing rapidity over time. Job-analysis tools assume that jobs are relatively stable and subject to limited or no change. There are four reasons to challenge this assumption.

### *8.2.1   Seasonal changes*

Some roles are subject to time-determined changes. These might include seasonal changes, such as working as a fruit picker or a life-guard. They also include small changes in technology over time, such as a new version or upgrades of software. Many of these changes in jobs can be anticipated and therefore are the easiest for organizations to tackle.

### 8.2.2   Technology changes

Technology developments can offer automation of many procedural aspects of work and have created significant changes in organizations. Although these may have a seasonal dimension (for instance, upgrades), information technology has fundamentally changed the nature of many roles. The knock-on effect of this is an evolution in the different types of working practices employees need to adopt in order to perform their roles satisfactorily within a firm. For example, the introduction of bar codes in retail has reduced the skill level required of check-out staff. Paradoxically, however, technology, such as the internet, has also increased the autonomy and decision-making for some roles through the introduction of new delivery services. Information systems departments have become more involved in designing new retail environments, rather than merely creating new IT solutions as they did in the past.

New technology has also brought about a re-consideration of distribution systems in order to manage new delivery processes. Some retailers have in fact re-structured to build new warehouses to capitalize on the existing skills of their warehouse staff; others have set up small-scale delivery systems using their existing store structure as the warehouse. This has as a result affected the work of some supermarkets' retail assistants by, for example, introducing driving as a competence and requiring them to work outside the store.

In addition, technology is creating massive changes in how work is performed. There has been an exponential growth in information repositories, from the internet through to journals and books. As a result, the influence of knowledge management (although considered by some as a current management fad) has paradoxically re-emphasized the importance of social skills for workers, highlighting those that are necessary for forming and sustaining networks (Newell, 2000). These social skills are critical in facilitating access to dissipated knowledge pools required by the post-holder but held by other people.

### 8.2.3   Employee-determined changes

A third challenge to stability are 'employee-determined' changes – those introduced by job incumbents themselves. Psychologists were the first to recognize the interaction between the worker and the role, with post-holders developing their jobs to reflect their own particular interests and skills, and perhaps in the process altering their latitude or changing their focus. These are important elements in enhancing satisfaction and increasing perceptions of control. The opportunities for this type of change are commonly found in work that involves some autonomy, such as research, teaching or sports-coaching. In order to identify the effect of this, Dunnette (1966) argued that job analysis should not just gather data from one person, but assess a range of job-holders in order to report generic aspects. This is important in ensuring the validity of the results of job analysis.

### 8.2.4   *Environmental changes*

Environmental changes are a fourth category of influences that have significantly changed job roles. These are considered the most difficult to anticipate, as such changes are determined by those outside the organization, such as customers or competitors. One key transition has been the increased importance of the 'customers' in every type of job. This has emphasized customer-service skills and developed an ethos that focuses on ensuring their satisfaction. Many jobs now involve the identification of customers, who in the past would have been just part of the organization, not those whose expectations have to be considered and managed. This change is reflected in selection criteria that may now include 'customer sensitivity'. For example, a job analysis recently revealed that successful retail assistants attributed customers' purchase decisions to their own behaviour, such as showing and helping them to decide on a product (Silvester *et al.*, 2003).

There are other examples of how short-term environmental changes have required different skills from employees. For example, if there was a fire at work, employees might be required to become fire-fighters in addition to their usual role. These *ad hoc* roles often include competencies that job incumbents bring to their work from an external interest and only come to bear on particular situations. For example, computer skills gleaned from playing computer games at home. These changes are therefore difficult to predict in terms of when they will occur or their duration.

While job analysis is important as the basis for selection and recruitment processes for identifying the main elements of a job and the attributes that successful job incumbents require, these four dimensions highlight that change is the only certainty in any organization. This underlines that it is vital that HR practitioners and those involved in creating selection and recruitment processes recognize the limited time-spans of any job analysis. Equally, however, it is naïve to try and suggest an appropriate 'shelf-life' for any such analysis. Judgement is required to ensure that selection criteria are checked so that they reflect any transition in the role and if there are major transitions, that the job is re-analysed.

Whilst other HR systems, such as appraisal, may provide a useful indication of the appropriateness of the selected candidates in performing their work, these systems may be contaminated. Often, they do not review job-holders' performance in using the same criteria they were selected for; they are biased towards the positive by managers to ensure that their fiefdoms are protected, or inaccurate due to the speed with which they are completed to fit the HR calendar. This is an on-going contamination problem encountered when evaluating selection processes. These issues will be discussed in more detail in Chapter 3.

## 9   The future?

In researching this area it is very clear that this is a topic which has received little attention of late. There are four striking issues that merit further discussion and point the way for new developments.

## 9.1 A re-focus on work performance

Information about work in many sectors is in flux as organizations attempt to cope with the velocity and volume of change expected from them. The first emergent issue presents a direct challenge to the static assumptions that have underpinned job analysis in the past. It involves a re-classification of the domain in order to address the more dynamic nature of jobs. This new domain re-defines jobs in much broader terms – such as 'work analysis' (Sanchez and Levine, 1999). This signifies the removal of traditional, more rigid definitions of roles, and emphasizes instead the incorporation of change and innovation.

Two examples emerge. Campbell *et al.* (1990, 1993, 1994) propose a multi-dimensional theory of job performance. This makes a distinction between job *performance* and the *results* of performance. They identify three contextual factors that affect individual's performance: declarative knowledge, which concerns factual knowledge; procedural knowledge, which focuses on interpersonal or cognitive skills; and finally **motivation**, which involves choices about whether to extend effort, and the level and persistence of that effort. The identification of these factors is important in revealing differences between different employees' performance. In this model, the worker and work are still, however, seen as distinct and separate entities. Thus, individual differences become situated in terms of the fit between worker's knowledge, skills, abilities and personality and the context in which they work.

A second important model by Viswesvaran and Ones (2000) builds on the distinction made by Borman and Motowidlo (1993) between *task* and *context* in order to devise a wider view of work performance. The model distinguishes between the formal, informal and counterproductive dimensions of work. 'Informal' dimensions include pro-social behaviours and good citizenship activities, while 'counterproductive' dimensions highlight deviant and negative behaviours that threaten the well-being of the organization and/or its members. One strength of this model is that it pinpoints dimensions that are generic and those that are more applicable to specific occupations, such as managers, military or entry-level service industry. The inclusion of such a wide array of work behaviours extends the scope of relevant aspects to include personal and organizational issues. The model highlights the link between task-specific dimensions and wider organizational elements.

Some criticisms can be made of the use of tautological or vague phrases in this model and the limit to their variety (Robertson and Smith, 2001). The model does extend the scope of worker behaviour to include personal aspects. It places a huge demand on the individual to behave in a way that benefits the wider organization. I wonder what organizations will give back in return for such advantages? These pro-social behaviours have evident advantages for the organization, but are very one-sided.

## 9.2 Future transition

Traditionally, job analysis assumes that job information should be available and that change is limited (Schneider and Kinz, 1989). Increasingly, organizations are having to anticipate what the future will bring and adapt jobs accordingly. One response is the identification of new knowledge, skills and abilities that jobs require (Hough and Oswald, 2000; Newell, 2000). Another response is to use existing job-analysis techniques in a different way. Some suggest that these techniques provide an important initial starting-point by giving information on current work activities and organization. This can be used to create a baseline from which change and development can be identified (Sanchez, 2000).

Landis *et al.* (1998) take this idea one stage further and suggest that any current analysis should be future-orientated, and predict the skills that organizations will require. They used these techniques in an insurance company that wanted to adapt to a rapidly changing electronic world. Traditional job-analysis techniques were first used to gather information about the current processes and role. Then a future-oriented group-based approach was used to assist in predicting what jobs would be like in the future. The process had a number of advantages. It created a robust analysis that ensured a legally defensible, content-valid selection system could be developed. It also provided data that allowed an ongoing comparison between the current and future-oriented KSAs. However, the speculative criteria this process generated is inherently at odds with the scientific reductionism underlying job analysis that requires current and not emergent criteria.

Sanchez (2000, p.207) has extended this future-oriented method and suggests the sole use of *non*-job incumbents as job-information sources. He argues that incumbents do not in fact have a superior insight into the role – especially where change is an issue. In addition, they are expensive to release, may not understand what is required, nor be sufficiently motivated to rate their roles effectively. Through using trained job analysts, who are not job incumbents, he argued that a more radical and strategic review of work could be undertaken. This would result in the development of a more effective model of future tasks and a reduction in the time and cost of analysis.

Critically, this latter approach overlooks the challenge for organizations in gaining workers' insights, or co-operation for future change in which they have played no part. Change can create considerable labour unrest at the best of times. The inclusion of some role-holders may minimize the potential of later unrest and gain workers' support.

Future-oriented analysis does have some advantages over traditional approaches for organizations. It is particularly relevant for organizations who are struggling to keep abreast in a dynamic market. It can be used to provide feedback on wider organizational changes (Scheider, 1991). It can provide a forum for reflecting on the future design and structure of job roles, for encouraging consideration of technology developments and help to identify the emergent training requirements of staff (Landis *et al.*, 1998). In addition, it can offer advanced warning of organizational communication problems. It signals whether employees have understood the changes that are required of them and also provides a forum for discussion between different stakeholders, which will assist change and development of the organization. The predictive value of such processes, nonetheless, has yet to be established.

## 9.3  New electronic formats

In reviewing recent developments, what is particularly striking is that novel approaches to analysing work have been slow to utilize new electronic performance data that are currently available within many organizations. By virtue of information systems, data such as time spent on the task, total number of tasks completed and idle time are collected automatically. Whilst such data are frequently used by some organizations as a performance-monitoring tool, they remain under-utilized in defining jobs within a selection context. Sanchez (2000, p.212) argues that a plethora of 'cookie files' and electronic records are increasingly available for a wide variety of jobs which would assist in the collection of robust performance data and could be used in future job analysis. This is an area where new electronic data-collection processes are likely to emerge.

Although these data could be deployed for selection purposes, it is worth noting that using this type of information is a potential invasion of privacy and thus care must be exercised in the escalation of any such 'surveillance' practices.

## 9.4  The worker–context interaction

Few current job-analysis processes and techniques consider the role-holder as an active creator of their job. Current techniques still regard the job incumbent as passive in relation to organizations. Despite attention from some psychologists and sociologists highlighting the importance of fit between the worker and the organization, it remains a neglected issue for those interested in selection and recruitment. Over time, employees adapt themselves to their work, through 'socialization'. Organizations have limited reflexivity regarding their role in the implementation of their selection criteria actually being exercised; what is evident in some workplaces is that despite identifying the necessary role competencies which are important to the cultures they are trying to create they may, paradoxically, stifle these new behaviours. This is critically important for firms seeking to change and develop. For example, the focus since the 1990s has been on innovation and teamwork. Organizations may select new types of employees with new criteria important for innovation, but then prevent them, through their aversion to risk and organizational processes, from using these KSAs. Similarly, despite the growth of team-based working, there has been little consideration of the problems of defining roles within a team context.

Sandberg (2000) is the first to present an alternative view of work from a social constructionist perspective. This demonstrates important and different ways in which the same job can be performed and re-emphasizes the interplay between role-holder and context. The dilemma he presents to those involved in selection policy is how to turn this insight into a process that will inform the human resource processes that job analysis has traditionally supported in the past. Work psychology is only beginning to have its paradigms challenged through a social constructionist perspective. This is likely to be an ongoing and significant trend.

Such critiques offer a challenge to those adopting the reductionist scientific approach which underpins many job-analysis tools. This approach reflects a move to create more integration between the workers and the context in which they work that has been so neglected by researchers to date.

## 10 Summary

Chapter 2 highlights the importance of job analysis for organizations, particularly in underpinning the development of robust selection processes. Job-analysis techniques have been taken from engineering and re-applied by psychologists to identify both task and worker-oriented dimensions. The distinction between task and personal skills was raised to show the contrast between work-based and worker-oriented data-collection techniques. Then ten commonly used job-analysis tools were outlined, which require different levels of training and provide distinct types of information about a role. What is often overlooked is the potential contamination of this data.

The errors produced through measurement inaccuracy were reviewed and potential for errors arising from the informant, the context, the process and the instruments themselves were identified. Indeed, a paradox emerged as job-analysis techniques are based on the premise of there being one 'right' way of performing a job, rather than several potentially different approaches. Therefore, within-job variance emerges as an error rather than a consequence of people at work. The problem of the dynamics of work was highlighted and distinct types of change process were outlined. This included a discussion of the potential for organizations to predict such role modifications.

Four areas for future development were suggested: the wider definition of job to work performance, which enlarges worker KSAs to include pro- and anti-social behaviours; the emergence of future-oriented analysis to assist organizations in coping with work dynamics; the under-utilization of electronic data-collection; and attempts to address, through a social constructionist paradigm, the ongoing separation of the worker and their context. This previous distinction disregards the important interrelationship between both the worker and the organization in the creation of satisfactory job performance.

---

### *Exercise*

*The life of a student – using job-analysis tools to define the job of a student*

In groups, select two contrasting approaches to job analysis. Taking a role with which you are familiar use the two approaches and compare and contrast the outcomes.

Undertake an internet search and see how your findings compare with O*net or another job-analysis database.

---

# CHAPTER 3

# Selection assessment: reliability and validity

## 1   Overview

The process of assessment for selection purposes can be judged through two key aspects: validity and reliability. Both are pivotal to the development of robust selection tools. In Chapter 3, I examine the main types of validity and the major aspects of reliability, and look at the implications of these for *fairness* in selection, and concentrate in particular on the issue of 'race'. The part 'race' plays in selection processes has not received the attention it deserves and, as you will see throughout this book, it is where many selection tools in fact show bias. When we consider selection and assessment in its *global* context, it is clear that this issue is very important for developers, users and takers of tests. Chapter 3 then discusses the technical issues concerning the different selection tools featured in the following chapters.

## 2   Introduction

Selection tools are designed to assess a candidate's suitability for a job role. The decision to employ someone (or not) is frequently based on the results of their performance in these tools. Clearly then, it is vital that assessments measure the candidate in sufficient breadth for the role and that the results are accurate and trustworthy and not prone to fluctuating over time. Selection and assessment tools measure elements that are not immediately obvious: we cannot walk up to someone and read their numerical ability meter by looking at their hair colour; we cannot judge a person's level of interpersonal skills by looking at their eyes.

Selection measurements are developed in different ways – some derive from theory; others emerge from statistical relationships. I will explain their background in detail in the forthcoming chapters. In order to choose which tool to use we need to know what it is actually being measured, and how well this is being done. Put simply, validity concerns the *appropriateness* of what is being measured, whilst reliability focuses on its *accuracy*. These two concepts will now be explored in more detail and it will be shown that although they are related, they have separate characteristics and properties.

## 3   Validity

The validity of a test is concerned with what is being measured. A standard textbook definition considers it to be 'the agreement between a test score or measure and the quality it is believed to measure' (Kaplan and Saccuzzo, 2001, p.32). It is important that you note that this definition focuses on the fit between what a test purports to measure and what it actually measures.

Vernon (1963), however, added an interesting modification to this, suggesting that validity may vary depending on the purpose it is put to. For example, the Myers Briggs Type Indicator (MBTI®) is a personality-assessment tool and is argued to be a valid test, but for development purposes only. The test developers themselves acknowledge that it is not valid as a selection tool, because it does not include a faking measure that would indicate whether a person was trying to lie. It is, therefore, not considered useful in a high-stakes environment such as selection, as its purpose is to facilitate greater self-insight and understanding. It is valid only in a development context. This is an interesting example of how the purpose of measurement affects what is measured, or how it can be used.

Some, such as Kline (1998, p.34), argue that the inclusion of this context specificity dimension is a sop and that 'a truly scientific psychometric test would be valid per se'. The problem for selection tool developers is that validity can be a problematic issue to prove and does not rest, as I shall show, on a simple measure. What is being measured may be multifaceted and often has to be inferred. There are four ways such validity can be identified: face validity; content validity; construct validity and criterion-related validity.

## 3.1 Face validity

The first and most obvious means that test validity can be established is by simply looking at whether it measures what it claims to. This is termed the 'face validity' and is concerned with the *appearance* of the test. For example, a test of verbal comprehension that contains only mathematical equations would measure what it sets out to. There is, however, some dispute as to how far this can actually be regarded as a form of validity. For example, in their classic study of US army cook selection, Vernon and Parry (1949) found that, despite the high face validity of the test used which included recipe and method information, what was actually being tested was reading ability and not cooking skills.

The face validity of a test is important, particularly to test-takers. They have invested time and effort in trying to get the job and therefore want to feel that they have been assessed by something that is relevant for the role. For example, a word-processing test may be challenged when used to select a crane driver as opposed to a personal assistant. The applicant will feel disgruntled (especially if they do not get the job) if the assessment process appears to bear no relation to the role. If sufficiently aggrieved with the process, they may even seek legal redress and sue.

A problem for those developing selection tools emerges when test-takers look at the test and pick up cues – however irrelevant – based on the appearance of what they perceive is being assessed and distort their responses accordingly. Guildford (1959) argues that a result of this unwelcome additional process is that paradoxically the face validity of a test may in fact be detrimental to the overall validity because it can distort a test's true validity.

Face validity can also exert an inappropriate influence on test-users who are deciding which tool to use. At times, face validity may override other issues, so that instead of reading the test manual and finding out what the test is designed for, the test-user may simply look at the items and make a decision based on how it appears. Face validity may therefore offer false validity. Its part in validity may be a distraction.

## 3.2  Content validity

The **content validity** of a selection tool is concerned with the adequacy of coverage of a conceptual domain. It is most commonly found in **attainment** or ability tests when an individual is required to demonstrate their knowledge or skill in a particular area. For instance, a test assessing competence as a medical doctor would be expected to include items taken from the General Medical Council's syllabus. If this was not the case, its content validity would be questionable.

As we shall explore further in Chapter 6, content validity is pivotal to attainment testing. It is important for this type of testing because, other than face validity, it is the only form of validity based on logical rather than statistical information. The key issue is the adequacy of coverage for the domain. As a result, this form of assessment is often constructed by a panel of experts to ensure sufficient breadth of coverage.

In addition to simply looking at the content, an index of content representation can be produced using judges to rate the test items in terms of the content. Two problems can be readily identified through using this system. The first, '**content under-representation**', occurs when an important component relevant to the conceptual domain has been omitted. For example, a test would be invalid if it was measuring numerical skills for managers but failed to include any testing of percentages. The second issue involves contamination by factors which are not relevant to the domain and is termed '**construct-irrelevant variance**'. For example, a test of numerical ability might require reading comprehension. The cookery test I mentioned previously inadvertently tested reading rather than practical skills.

### *Dilemma box 3.1 International selection*

A psychologist is putting together a selection process for an international finance director for a logistics firm. The vacancy will attract a considerable number of overseas applicants. The main language of the job is English, but it would be beneficial to have someone who spoke other languages, particularly Spanish. In choosing the ability tests the psychologist notices that some of the tests are also available in a range of other languages. Should they choose one test, the English version, or one that is in the candidate's first language? What will give the most accurate assessment of the candidate's ability?

## 3.3  Construct validity

The concept of '**construct validity**' was first introduced by Cronbach and Meehl (1955) when they suggested that underlying each test is a construct that is being assessed. Construct validation assumes that we can define and measure anything. As noted before, we cannot read someone's intelligence metre. Therefore, a hypothetical construct defining what **intelligence** is has first to be created in order to measure it. What the domain of intelligence includes must be defined and a measurement process devised in order to test that hypothesis. There has been criticism of this as a basis for measurement within the human sciences. For example, Stevens (1946) argued that the **null hypothesis** ('that it is not the case') is rarely considered; Kline (1998) also critiques this measurement issue.

In terms of construct validity, the adequacy of the original definition and the availability of appropriate comparison measures are critical. A key concern of test-developers is to show the relationships between their instrument and other established tests which are assessing a similar domain. They also need to find discrimination with other tests of *unrelated* domains. This distinction will indicate the unique domain the test is assessing. It is not a question of a simple dichotomy –'yes or no' – as to whether this construct is being measured. What is more important is the degree to which it is being measured. For example, if we were developing a test to measure the personality dimension 'openness', our hypothesis would be that, as 'openness' is related to intelligence, our test should show a correlation of at least 0.5 with other intelligence tests. We would expect it to diverge from other personality factors, such as extroversion or neuroticism and indicate a lower correlation. In addition, we would expect a positive correlation with academic and subsequent job success, but that this would be more important in some occupations than others – for example those that include enquiry and novelty. It is therefore clear that in developing such a test the suitability of the initial definition and the availability of suitable comparison measures are critical.

All the information regarding the definition of the domain that is being assessed and the development process for the test should be included in a test manual. This part of the manual is often overlooked but it holds critical information for anyone trying to decide whether to use a test or not. It shows the composition of the test and the populations used for comparison. This is particularly important where the population varies in terms of 'race' or gender. Legal cases have been lost through the use of inappropriate tests for recruitment.

## Dilemma box 3.2 Validation information from test manual: choosing appropriate norm tables

You are in charge of recruiting a new marketing manager for a major high-street bank. You look through the manual for the tests you want to use and find the following norm groups. Which do you use: the general manager, or the financial service manager?

A strength of recognizing construct validity is that it is based on a theory: the tool occupies a specific conceptual domain. It is evident, however, that problems can easily arise. First, as we shall explore in Chapter 7, it can be easier to identify underlying constructs for some tools than others – for example intelligence versus more problematic aspects of personality or volition. Second, the results can be difficult to interpret if only partial correlations between the test and the other measures are found, so it is questionable whether the test does, or does not, relate to the hypothesized construct. Third, in the context of the growth of international selection, organizations are obliged to ensure tests are devised which reveal performance and not cultural differences. As Figure 3.1 shows, there is often bias against minority groups.

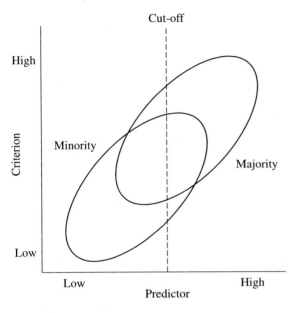

*Figure 3.1   Restriction of range differences for minority ethnic groups*
(Cook, 1998, p.230)

Modern test construction methods, such as those used to create adaptive and on-line testing, use **Item Response Theory** techniques (IRT). This method assumes construct validity by specifying that a test must measure an underlying construct, and that it must be uni-dimensional, but it does not specify either what that construct is or what it must be (Schmidt *et al.*, 2000). What is of more concern is that in some cases the wrong construct is used, but the response data still fit the underlying construct. Item Response Theory does not attempt to address this question in any formal way. I shall return to this in more detail in Chapter 6.

### 3.4  Criterion-related validity

The final form of validity, '**criterion-related** validity', relates what is being measured to an *external* criterion. Similar in some ways to construct validity, it focuses instead not on the relationship of the new instrument with another established test, but on an external measure, such as job success. Individuals' abilities are set within a 'real-world' context. The key to this form of validity is the adequacy of the identification and assessment of the external standard. The measure chosen needs to be relevant and uncontaminated by the collection process. (Criteria contamination is an important but overlooked concern.)

Problems arise with regard to criterion-related validity in a number of ways. Frequently, the external measure is chosen based on its convenience rather than its relation to the dimension to be assessed (Murphy, 2000). In addition, it needs to include sufficient scope of performance to allow deficiencies to emerge. An example of this type of validity is a driving test where the individual's ability to perform particular manoeuvres is assessed. Test-takers pass if they can perform an emergency brake, reverse round a corner, drive safely on the road and manoeuvre round a roundabout. A suggestion, for instance, that driving on motorways should be included in the test is an attempt to increase the breadth of situations being tested. However, can it be said that those who have just passed their test are good drivers?

Criterion validity can be assessed in two distinct ways: **concurrently** or **predictively**.

### 3.4.1 Concurrent validity

Validity can be measured by assessing the test-taker's performance in the test at the same time as they undertake another assessment, for example a job-sample test. For example, a paper and pen version of a test measuring filing skills and a practical test measuring the same skills. This form of criterion-related validity is concerned with the current level of the individual's performance. It presupposes assessment of validity is based on the correlation between these two simultaneous assessments. Obviously, such an assessment is based on the validity of both tests and assumes that the criterion is valid. Kline (1998) disputes how far this can be achieved as there are few suitable benchmark tests available, such as the **Wechsler scale for intelligence**, or the **Eysenck personality questionnaire**.

A central debate here concerns the strength of the **correlation** between the two forms of assessment. Convention holds that 0.70 is the usually accepted level, but it must be noted that at this level a large proportion of the variance between the tests is still not shared. This can be compounded by further contamination by the choice of items where the second test mimics the items of the benchmark. This process can create an ossification of some variables within tests, so that although a statistically satisfactory outcome is produced, the outcome is not necessarily a good scientific result. This returns to the question of the development of conceptually coherent assessment tools.

### 3.4.2 Predictive validity

Predictive validity, in contrast with concurrent validity, focuses on the future and assesses the individual at two separate points to reveal the relationship between the initial test result and some later outcome. This aspect of validity is particularly important when looking for tools to identify those promotable to senior roles. For example, there is a predictive relationship between gaining an Oxbridge degree and success in legal examinations (Dewberry, 2001).

It is sometimes difficult to identify suitable criteria (see Table 3.1 for examples of common measures). Assessments of performance are a multiple process. First, the assessor may not be directly aware of the individual's performance and have to infer it. The assessor needs to have sufficient time to gather relevant information. All too frequently, assessments are undertaken with insufficient data by someone too removed from the individual's activities to be able to make a meaningful or insightful evaluation. Second, performance assessment is a political process. The performance being evaluated is not merely that of the individual, but an indirect comment on the department and its management. Therefore, any manager who gives a low assessment is reflecting their own low competence and the criteria can become contaminated. Most data of this form of validity are collected during annual appraisal processes. There is frequently a positive skew to any such performance-rating information. Again, this reflects behaviour which may be more akin to political protectionism than to objective assessment and evaluation. The criterion used in job-performance assessment may not be the same as that used in the initial selection. This makes direct comparison between selection and performance more difficult.

## Table 3.1 Examples of types of performance measured

| Type of objective | Example of measure |
| --- | --- |
| Productivity | Unit production levels, throughput of patients, sales performance, research patent submission, quality attainment, waste levels, customer satisfaction. |
| HR | Attendance and sickness record, promotion rate, performance appraisal results, 360° feedback. |
| Training | Speed of learning, final level achieved, mistakes vs. correct responses. |
| Financial | Salary, level, bonus or commission rates, savings created for the firm. |
| Professional status | Membership of professional bodies, 'fellowships'. |
| Survival | Organizational tenure. |

Care also needs to be taken when looking at financial information. Many of these remuneration-based measures may reflect existing and institutionalized human resources practices. They are, therefore, susceptible to 'racial' and gender-based discrimination and bias. Promotion, reward and performance differences have been found with white employees benefiting in comparison to other ethnic groups (Robertson and Block, 2001). Predictive validity can inadvertently promote discriminatory practices because it is based on *previous* success. For instance, the validity coefficients of biodata range from 0.3 to 0.5 for predicting performance, tenure, salary progression, person–organization fit and achievement-oriented activities (Elkins and Phillips, 2000).

Intelligence is arguably one of the easiest criteria to assess, but often it is difficult to identify suitable criteria to measure it against consistently over time. Other performance measures produce a clear-cut response: they are present or they are absent. However, some involve interpretation or additional insight. For example, if we had a selection process designed to identify senior managers and we were trying to measure predictive validity after eight years, within a few months of the assessment, those who had not passed might leave as they would feel promotion was now not an option for them. This would create 'shrinkage' or **attenuation** of data. More commonly, throughout the study's eight-year period, re-organizations would occur, such as outsourcing departments containing successful applicants. As a result, the data on these applicants might be removed from the study. In addition, HR changes might occur, such as the introduction of a new competency-based appraisal system to reflect new organizational concerns, and these might completely remove some of the performance criteria the study required.

In undertaking a predictive validity study, a range of factors outside the control of the researcher can also have an impact on the validity assessment. The previous example showed how shrinkage can occur (termed '**restricting of range**'), when those with lower scores are removed artificially from the research. As a result, we do not know what has happened to candidates who *were not* successful in the assessment centre. In an ideal world, both those who had passed and those who had failed the assessment would be retained within the firm in order to monitor whether the assessment anticipated their subsequent success. More commonly, they are removed through organizational or self-selection. There are a number of ways this range of problems can be corrected, but often the very correction further distorts the results by artificially inflating the variability (Hartigan and Wigdor, 1989; Hunter and Schmidt, 1990; Viswesvaran *et al.*, 1996).

The development of a validity coefficient is vital to determining the value of a test because it reveals the strength of the relationship between the tool and a criterion. Validity is important as it provides an indication of the value of the tools. High validities above 0.6 are rare in practice, indicating that a large amount of variance is still not accounted for by most tests. Dunnette (1967) provided compelling evidence of the savings to the US tax-payer that could be made through the adoption of a simple questionnaire for military selection, resulting in thousands of dollars being saved. In another example, a valid test for keyhole surgery for medics has been shown to improve success rates of patients and reduce accident levels (**Arthur, 1998**).

New statistical processes, such as meta-analysis, have revolutionized selection testing. In the past, selection results had low validity which favoured the creation of **bespoke tools** for every new role or for use in a different organization (Ghiselli, 1966). Meta-analysis, or validity generalization analysis, was pioneered by Schmidt and Hunter (Schmidt and Hunter, 1996, 1998, 1999; Hunter and Schmidt, 1990; Schmidt *et al.*, 1979, 1992). They argued that although validity does vary with context and role, it is nevertheless relatively stable. Based on this argument, selection tools could be transferred across different contexts and roles and retain their predictive validity. This creates potentially huge savings for firms as generic tools can now be used instead of devising expensive bespoke instruments. As we shall see in Chapters 7 and 8, these meta-analytic studies have also assisted in the development of personality and other cognitive theories, identifying and supporting the existence of broad underlying dimensions of ability and personality (Hunter and Hunter, 1984; Schmidt and Hunter, 1999).

This form of analysis has been important in substantially raising the validity of selection tools and procedures overall. It has provided robust scientific support for their use in a selection context. Schmidt and Hunter (1999) reviewed 85 years of validity research and found evidence that biographic data tools, cognitive ability tests, work sample and assessment centres were valid measures of job performance and training. Other researchers have added personality and interviews to the list of valid tools (Robertson and Smith, 2001). This result indicates that both **generalizability** and consistency of validity are retained regardless of setting (Murphy, 2000).

## Dilemma box 3.3 Selection and cost

You are asked to recommend a selection process to recruit a director for a computing firm. The firm is facing a financial crisis and asks you to propose the most cost-effective process for them. Look at the validity of the various selection processes. Does it significantly change as more assessment tools are added? What do you recommend?

## 4    Critique of meta-analysis approach

Validity generalization theory is not without its critics and it is important that some of the underlying problems of this approach are highlighted. Meta-analysis is based on the collection and re-analysis of comparable studies of tools, such as the situational interview. I do not intend to go into the minutia of the process here (others such as Schmidt [1992], and Murphy [1994; 2000] offer more detail). Instead, I identify four key problems that you need to be aware of before accepting the new higher validities these meta-analytic studies report: poor study design, small sample sizes, use of inadequate performance assessment data and context specificity.

First, in their initial form, the studies showed a lower validity for selection tools. This might have occurred for a variety of reasons. It could be the result of an inadequate test being used, possibly reflecting a poor underlying design to the study. Different versions of a given test produce subtle differences, so that the results which are combined in meta-analysis may not necessarily be identical measures. Subtle variations are common, such as a validity meta-study of the same tool, but which comprised different sub-factors. Therefore, as we shall see in Chapter 8, it can not measure the same thing.

Second, until the advent of meta-analysis studies, many good pieces of research examining validity were blighted by small sample sizes, which reduced the power of the statistical analysis that could be undertaken. Nevertheless, sample problems can still be an issue for meta-analysis, as variances occur when using population samples that differ in terms of sex, age, ethnic background and experience levels. Individuals with different backgrounds use different approaches to tackle the same problem (Anastasi, 1990). Thus, highly valid tools in one context may not be the same in another. Sample heterogeneity can affect studies. For example, Burnham's (1965) study of selection for top US university places found changes in the validity between the commonly used students' high-school grades and their final university results. Over a 30-year period the correlation between the two was reduced from 0.71 to 0.52. On closer inspection, the reason for this drop was due to changes in the sample type; the later students were more homogenous than the earlier cohort in both their predictor and criterion performance levels. This finding is important as it aptly demonstrates that validity is not fixed and can change over time, situation and sample.

Third, the criteria against which the selection tool is assessed frequently use individuals' subsequent job performance appraisal ratings. As noted earlier, there are a number of problems associated with this. The subsequent performance measurement focuses only on those who have passed the test. Moreover, job appraisals, on which these data are based, are often unreliable, revealing leniency and skewed use of the rating system, where for political reasons ratings are restricted to the higher part of the scale provided (Jawahar and Williams, 1997).

A fourth problem of meta-analysis studies results from the removal of **situational specificity**. While the original validity research on which they are based might show substantially different validities for the tests because of different job roles, settings or organizations, these variations are assumed to be due to simple sampling error and therefore treated as statistical artefacts. As a result, they are removed during meta-analysis and true differences that emerge across different contexts are discounted. This is important if tests are to be used on a global basis. Expatriate management failures are increasingly identified as resulting from ineffective selection processes which have overemphasized technical and managerial skills above family and spouse adjustment and cultural insensitivity (Elkins and Phillips, 2000).

The cumulative effect of these issues is two-fold, raising the studies' means and shrinking the variance. For example, McDaniel et al. (1994) combined 16 studies in their meta-analysis study of selection interviews. When corrected for statistical artefacts, the mean rose from 0.27 to 0.5 and the standard deviation dropped from 0.14 to 0.05. The final corrected validity was 0.43. As a result, any real variation was removed. For example, the assessment centre method emerged 'as at least minimally valid in virtually all reported applications, but the level of validity was not consistent across studies' (Murphy, 2000, p.198). This reveals important assumptions, suggesting that job characteristics, the local employment settings, organizational distinctions and the specific type of assessment centres exercises *do not* affect the validity of a selection tool. Validities become generalizable, but they are not consistent, offering more value in some roles or organizations than others. This meta-analysis process removes such valuable variation. For example, evidence indicates that, for job roles with high cognitive complexity, general ability tests emerge as the most valid predictive tool. However, some researchers have argued that this type of finding has simply removed situational variance and instead more relevant questions should be asked (Murphy, 1989, 2000; James *et al.*, 1992).

The current application of meta-analysis studies removes the possibilities for us to understand why situational differences emerge. They prevent us from identifying what makes a situation unique. For example, they hide aspects such as job roles, or local climate and the processes by which these changes emerge. Situational variations are subtle issues that affect our ability to create valid tests. Organizations currently operate in turbulent global environments, and evidence suggests that there are important relationships amongst task type, technology and the external environment that meta-analysis studies do not assist us in exploring. As a result of their dominance, we cannot improve our selection designs to help organizations in these contexts. Evidence suggests that local working conditions where the climate does not restrict the role-holders' autonomy show higher validity than those where autonomy is more limited (James *et al.*, 1992). Under the current generalizing procedures used in establishing validity, these factors become at best obscured, and at worst 'corrected for'.

On the other hand, validity studies, particularly meta-analysis-based ones, have played an important role in improving the credibility and professionalism of human resource practices and applied psychology. They have helped us combine small-scale studies to show a high generic validity of selection tools. They have offered organizations access to more robust and cost-effective selection systems. Figure 3.2 demonstrates how validity assessment has enabled human resource professionals to identify which selection tests are suitable and to confirm correct selection decisions and validate rejections and acceptances. The key to this process is the setting of suitable cut-off points for tests. Those using selection tools need to assist in determining an appropriate cut-off for the job criterion, which will indicate an adequate level of performance, but also a corresponding assessment score cut-off point that will maximize their valid acceptances. It is therefore a balance between identifying a selection tool and suitable performance levels that will not result in more people being rejected than could have undertaken the task, nor accepting those unsuitable for the task. Care must be taken when establishing cut-offs to ensure that they are appropriate. For instance, London Underground was found to have used cognitive tests for train drivers with cut-offs that did not reflect the job requirements. As a result of this action, they were found to have unfairly discriminated against Afro-Caribbean applicants and was deemed unlawful. This reflects the importance of ensuring that an adequate job analysis has been undertaken to avoid an arbitrary cut-off point being made.

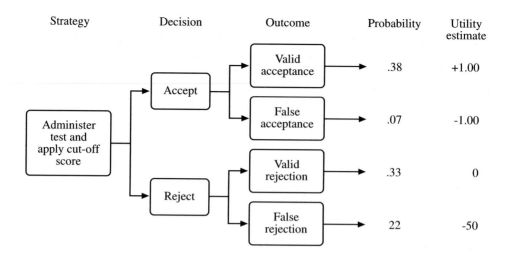

| Strategy | Decision | Outcome | Probability | Utility estimate |
|---|---|---|---|---|

*Figure 3.2   Selection decision-making*

(Anastasi, 1990, p.179)

Schmidt *et al.* (1979) assessed the value of selection systems for US federal computer programmers and using a computer aptitude test that had a validity of 0.76 calculated the productivity increases for one year. They identified that, in comparison with random selection, the gains ranged from $97.2 million if the selection ratio was 0.5, and $16.5 million if the ratio rose to 0.80. Thus, a valid tool can have a huge impact on an organization's ongoing viability.

In addition, validity studies have enhanced our understanding of which personal attributes and personality traits are important in predicting general performance, and have consequently influenced our understanding of personality and ability. In particular, as you will read, they have revealed the importance of general ability and the personality trait 'conscientiousness' in contributing to high job performance. In the future we have an opportunity to turn our attention towards gaining further understanding of how to improve the way selection tools are used in organizations.

We now turn our attention towards the second key issue for any selection tool: its reliability.

## 5   Reliability

A test might produce a measure that is valid for one person, but the results may not be reproducible for another. This brings into question the issue of reliability – another important consideration for those developing assessment tools. Tests can often have high reliability, but at the expense of validity. The two are distinct and are both vital considerations when choosing assessment tools.

Reliability concerns the accuracy of the tool. Any measurement procedure is subject to some level of error. Test reliability gives an indication of how much weight, or importance, should be attached to the score. As we shall explore in Chapter 6, there is always some error in measurement so that the score achieved will not be the same as the 'true' score. This is the central premise behind **classical test theory** and will be discussed in detail later. Reliability, however, is concerned with minimizing the unsystematic errors, so that those taking the same test a number of times always show the same result. This consistency is a key issue for measurement accuracy. Therefore, a reliable test would be one in which a very high correlation (perfect = 1) would be found between the results over time.

Increasingly, reliability is an issue which is becoming a legal requirement for selection tests. An unreliable test is an instrument that has a questionable role in selection because it is not clear precisely what its results mean. A number of governments across the world demand that a test's reliability is demonstrated before it can be used in assessment (Huebert and Hauser, 1999). It is worth checking with your national psychological organization regarding local guidelines as these vary across the world. The **British Psychological Society** website allows you to download such details for work-based testing (http://www.bps.org.uk/docdownload). Establishing the reliability of a selection tool involves three main elements: stability, consistency and equivalence of the results (or parallel form). We shall examine these in more detail now.

## 5.1 Stability

Stability is the most obvious means of measuring reliability and involves the repeatability of a test outcome over time. This can be done by getting the same person to complete the same measure on two separate occasions. This is termed '**test–retest reliability**'. In this case, stability is the difference between the two scores over the period.

A central assumption behind this form of reliability is that the trait being measured does not change with time. For example, we do not assume that people become more, or less, intelligent over time. As a result, this form of reliability assessment is only applicable for stable traits. For example, a test measuring dimensions such as emotion (a fleeting expression) are changeable and thus not amenable to stability of measurement.

In undertaking this form of re-testing, the duration of gap between the first test experience and the follow-up is crucial. If the gap is insufficiently long then the second score can be artificially raised through what are termed '**carry-over effects**', where the test-taker remembers the questions and their responses or completes more answers. These effects are of concern if they are random, but not if they occur systematically across the whole sample, in which case the results will be uniformly affected.

A second cause for concern is the '**practice effect**', which looks at how performance levels change as a result of practice. By taking the first test the test-taker can be sensitized to the topic. For instance, if the test is concerned with numerical ability and the test-taker had not done percentage calculations for a long time, doing the test provides an opportunity to rehearse and practice these skills. As a result, when the test is repeated they are much better prepared. Practice effects are particularly common for those doing manual dexterity tests.

Finally, practical problems associated with this form of test reliability arise due to **attrition**: test-takers can sometimes fail to attend the second session. Retaining the original sample is important. Test-developers often over-recruit in order to anticipate and minimize these negative impacts.

Considerable attention has been given to the time needed between test sessions. Kline (1993) recommends that a gap of no less than three months is sufficient for re-testing adults. **Test manuals** provide details about the length of gap between the test and re-test sessions. It must be noted that low reliability between the two scores may not be an indication of an unreliable test, but rather an indication of a change in the test-taker, for example indicating changes in motivation level, or a new life experience. These factors are difficult to access.

## 5.2 Consistency

Measuring reliability also needs to take account of consistency of the measure. This is concerned with reliability through the internal consistency of a test, rather than the temporal change and learning of the test-taker. Measurement consistency is important in order to ensure that variations in scores are not a result of external factors, such as the choice of item, but a reflection of the underlying domain being measured. There are two ways consistency can be measured: **split-half testing** and the **Kuder–Richardson reliability** or **coefficient alpha.**

### 5.2.1 Split-half testing

One of the easiest methods of assessing reliability is split-half testing: this involves dividing the test into two and comparing the results from each half. There are two ways this can be done. First, the test can be simply divided in half at the midpoint. Problems, however, can emerge as often assessment tests are designed to begin with easier questions and become progressively more difficult. The results on the two may therefore differ as a result of item differences. A second, and more common, method attempts to control for difficulty aspects by splitting the test in two with one half comprising all the odd number and the other the even numbered items. This ensures that the difficulty is comparable.

Split-half testing can create a problem in that the test which is completed is only half its correct length. Reliability increases with the number of items due to improvements in the content sampling; stability is not affected by test length. Using these methods, the newly created mini-tests may be artificially deflated reliabilities. To amend this, **Spearman–Brown's formula** can be used to correct the results, enabling the correlation to be done as if each were a full-length test.

*Spearman–Brown's formula*

$$r = \frac{2rhh}{1 + rhh}$$

where *rhh* = the correlation between the two halves.

### 5.2.2 Kuder–Richardson reliability or coefficient alpha

The second, and arguably the best, measure of internal consistency is Kuder–Richardson's method devised in 1937. This is far simpler to carry out and is based on results of only one administration of the test. It assesses the *inter-item* consistency of the test by looking at two error measures: the adequacy of the content sampling and the heterogeneity of the domain being sampled. This form of reliability is based on the assumption that reliable tests contain more variance and are therefore more discriminating. The more heterogeneous the test, the lower the inter-item consistency will be.

This original measure was designed for use with simple right/wrong response formats and was further developed by Cronbach in the 1950s for use with tests such as personality tools that use a more complex rating system.

*Coefficient alpha formulas*

For right/wrong scores, that are non-dichotomous items:

$$Rkk = k/k{-}1(1{-}\Sigma\sigma^2 i/\sigma^2 t)$$

> Where:
>
> *Rkk* = the alpha coefficient of the test
>
> *k* = number of items
>
> $\sigma^2 i$ = the item variance
>
> $\sigma^2 t$ = the test variance

The preceding formula indicates that the greater the individual variance of the items, the smaller the covariance. Anastasi (1990, p.123) argues that in mathematics this formula is the mean of all split-half coefficients. The resultant mean is not based on the systematic splitting of the items and, thus, unless the items are highly homogeneous, the alpha measure found will be lower than those found for split-half reliabilities.

This measurement system can be widely applied and is used to assess the reliability of behavioural rating systems which, as you will see in Chapter 9, are more commonly found in the assessment centre selection format. In addition, the kappa statistic, which assesses agreement levels between assessors, can also be used as a means of showing the reliability of an observation-based assessment system.

## 5.3  Equivalence of results (parallel form)

The third means by which reliability can be measured is based on the equivalence *between* tests (also called the parallel form). This looks at reliability by comparing different versions of the same test. Thus, the measurement domain (in terms of broad content) is the same, but different items are used. Just as in split-half testing, the results from each version of the test are compared.

This process has advantages over the test–retest method as test sessions can be completed in the same day, which reduces the practical problem of test-takers dropping out. There are concerns, nonetheless, regarding the gap between tests. Some argue that the two versions of the test can be taken far sooner than tests comprising of the same items as practice effect will be more random. Often the ordering of the two versions is varied to try and control this effect.

In some cases, the creation of two versions of the same test can be expensive and this has undoubtably contributed to reductions in the use of this method. The increasing sophistication of computers has allowed items to be cloned far more easily and as a result it has become quicker to create parallel versions of tests. Indeed, the advent of non-supervised internet testing has seen the increasing use of parallel tests as a means of controlling potential cheating by test-takers. To devise these parallel versions, as I will show in Chapter 7, test-developers create huge databases of items.

Cartell (1973), in a dissenting voice against this form of reliability, has warned that very high internal validity is actually antithetical to validity, because the breadth of coverage may be reduced. Through the creation of what are termed '**bloated specifics**', the test can be manipulated so that it comprises items with small variations on the same theme. Thus, there can be a trade-off in some ways between the reliability and validity, so a test with high reliability may not have high validity. High internal consistency may reduce the content validity of a test, making it a less than meaningful measure. It must be noted, however, that not all highly reliable measures consist of bloated specifics. Although Kline (1993) argues that it is very difficult to devise a test in which the items correlate only with the criteria and not with each other, this is an objective to which test-developers aspire.

**Parallel versions** can be important for some samples, such as new graduates attending post-university 'milk-round' job searches. Frequently, this group will have done the same version of a test several times in short succession without the organization's knowledge. The use of equivalent versions of the same test can be important for organizations employing graduates because it minimizes the unfair advantages obtained through practice and carry-over effects.

A primary consideration in ensuring equivalence of tests is that the test result is not affected by who is taking it. Research has shown that for some tests different scores are obtained by different sample groups. This results in unfair discrimination against particular population categories, and in the US is termed '**adverse impact**'. An area of most concern, as we shall see in Chapters 5 and 6, is the unfair discrimination of Black people by cognitive ability tests. Studies suggest that the more transparent the assessment process, the lower the discrimination for this group. As I suggest in Chapters 6 and 9, this may be why there is lower discrimination found in work sample tools than in cognitive ability tests for this group. This equivalence is a critical issue for the generation of global tests.

If discrimination is found, test-developers can devise new scoring systems for tests to enable them to be used in different countries. For example, a commonly used personality tool, which originated in the USA – the Myers Briggs Type Indicator (MBTI™) – was redeveloped in the 1990s for the UK market after poor equivalence was found for a number of items. In some cases, the redevelopment process can involve minor changes to the wording and scoring systems; in other cases the test has to be completely redeveloped for a new context. Details of the samples on which tests have been carried out can be found in test manuals. The information is important because it ensures that the test is suitable for the proposed population, particularly when tests are being used on a global basis.

Each of these aforementioned types of reliabilities can be artificially enhanced by making items in each mini-test similar to each other. Reliabilities of around 0.9 should be expected and should never be less than 0.7 (Kline, 1993, p.11). As the reliability of a test increases, so the standard error of measurement of a score decreases, indicating that the accuracy of the measurement has improved. (This effect will be discussed in more detail in Chapter 5.)

As I show in Figure 3.3, reliability can be affected by a number of factors. In addition to test-content issues – such as ambiguity or insufficient coverage of the domain – there are six procedural aspects that can affect the reliability of a test. These include:

1   Conditions under which a test is taken may result in different scores. They may make the candidate uncomfortable, or they may be the perfect forum for the cheat.

2   Inconsistent administration practices, such as changing the time for test-takers to complete a test, or failing to stick to the formal instructions can all create conditions that may discriminate against some or unfairly assist others.

3   Test-scoring, misusing **scoring keys**, sloppy test-marking practices. Test-developers pay particular attention to trying to ensure that they have the correct ergonomics for the test. They will try and maximize the legibility for the test format, with clear instructions and examples.

4   Application of an inappropriate **norm group** will also reduce the reliability of the result.

5   Internal state of the test-taker will affect how a test is taken: lower reliability can be produced by candidates who are feeling unwell, or upset, or fatigued.

6   Experience level. Although I have indicated that practice effects are important in the test–retest condition, it is clear as you will see in Chapter 5 that test experiences do alter how we undertake this form of assessment, providing us with strategies that may enhance our performance.

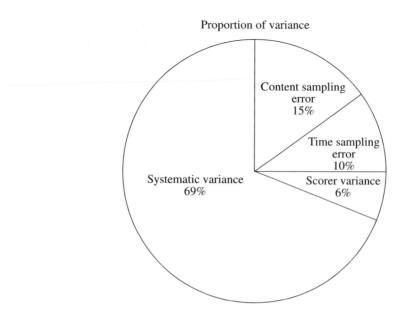

Figure 3.3   *Sources of reliability variance*

## 6   Summary

Both the reliability and validity of an assessment tool can change over time. They are affected by changes in context or in the population being recruited into the firm. Validity studies therefore need to be undertaken on an ongoing basis and test reliabilities checked.

I have outlined in Chapter 3 the different ways in which the reliability and validity of tests can be measured and how these results are affected by situational and sample changes. We can consider the processes of reliability and validity in terms of external distortions, which may have been inadvertently introduced by the test, or internal effects from test-takers themselves. Test-users cannot control them all, but they need to be aware of how practice effect and motivation will alter the score obtained.

It is clear that more consideration needs to be given to examine how the test-taker can distort – consciously or unconsciously – their responses (this will be discussed in more detail in Chapter 7). This is a subject where interest is growing. Research has focused on issues such as deliberate response sabotage, or unconscious response biasing in which the test-taker wishes to appear better, or in some cases worse, than they are. These will all influence the reliability of the test. I will explore in Chapters 6 and 8 the effect of test-takers' response patterns, particularly in personality and interest tests, and show how test-presentation factors, such as reversed items, can be used to break up potential patterns. At this point it is sufficient to indicate that reliability will be affected. It does however raise important questions about our conception of error.

More commonly, problems enter the assessment process through the test itself. I have already suggested how content and construct validity may affect performance if the test does not adequately cover the domain. Validity and reliability provide different indications of a test's value, but they are different issues. I have shown how test validity can be established but have warned of the impact of meta-analysis studies in this area which may be to hide important and subtle variations produced by job type, organizational climate and situation. The correction of error undertaken in these studies may obscure important differences. This is an area about which we need to understand more if we are to develop tests that can be used on a global basis. These issues are pertinent to all selection and assessment instruments.

## *Exercise*

Choose a psychometric test and find out about its reliability and validity. Identify if it could be used in the selection of managers, engineers, personal assistants and apprentices. Comment on any potential problems you might need to be aware of: in particular, consider the issue of population sample.

Think about a graduate recruitment for the pharmaceutical industry. Which forms of validity are important for test-takers? If an organization is seeking to avoid litigation, consider each of the forms of validity and discuss how procedural and distributive fairness will be perceived. What recommendations would you make to HR teams?

# Selection tools 1: curriculum vitae, biodata and references

## 1 Overview

Chapter 4 focuses on selection tools that tend to mark the start and final stages of recruitment and selection processes: curriculum vitae, biodata and references. It could be argued that it is in these application and reference-taking stages that the applicant has most control over their selection.

I begin by assessing the impact of the curriculum vitae (CV) as an influencing mechanism. There is limited (but growing) research in this topic. The little research that has been done highlights the applicant's power in effectively influencing the organization through the use of CVs and other application information, and emphasizes the cognitive processes that underlie the short-listing process by assessors and the role of impression management in creating bias. A two-way dynamic appears to be in operation. It is also important to note that all three tools involve the collection of data, in the most part, concerning applicants' *past* behaviours. In the case of CVs and biodata, this is provided by the candidate about themselves, whilst references are requested from a third party.

The chapter moves on to look at application forms; I review the considerable research around a specific type of application form – namely biographical data, or 'biodata' as it is more commonly called. This is by far the biggest section (reflecting the volume of research that has been undertaken). I discuss the emphasis from researchers on this tool in contrast with its more limited uptake by practitioners. I highlight the pseudo-psychometric advantages biodata offers and its increasing role in helping organizations manage high-volume recruitment processes. I also look at the growing role of new technology in providing online applications, and show that this is an area where *practice* is leading and where limited critical work has examined the impact of this novel medium. Concerns of note include underlying discrimination issues.

Finally, the chapter examines the reference process and reviews the paucity of attention this topic has received from researchers, in contrast to its overwhelming endorsement by recruiters. This suggests a division between psychological research evidence and a more intuitive focus adopted by users. I highlight distinctions between practice and research evidence in selection systems and reveal the need for ongoing education and research in the field.

## 2   Introduction

Any recruitment and selection process begins with the applicant formally indicating their interest in a position. This is usually done in two ways: either by submitting a CV or by completing an application form. In the first, applicants have more control over how they present themselves to their potential future employers; the second places control more firmly with the organization. In either case, the goal of the applicant is to cast themselves in a favourable light. This brings into question the increasingly important role of *impression management* in selection systems, which I will go on to discuss in more detail. I will also highlight the two-way dynamic in the application process.

Research into these initial selection stages is unbalanced with far more work looking at the organization-led pseudo-psychometric application process (in particular the role of biographical data) rather than on the impact of applicants' CVs. This balance is just starting to change. I will highlight recent work examining CVs and discuss the reasons behind biodata popularity amongst researchers later in the chapter.

It is also worth noting that the application process is currently experiencing considerable change through the advent of new technologies: these have increased the use of novel **attraction**, search and selection facilities (Searle, 2003). Here, practice is ahead of research and there has been little examination of the impact of 'e-recruiting' for organizations or applicants. Studies examining the impact of these technology-led tools on privacy and discrimination are only starting.

More often than not, the recruitment and selection process concludes with the taking-up of references concerning the applicant. While references remain one of the most popular tools used by practitioners, they attract limited research interest and are frequently seen as having limited utility unless more standardized information is requested. Yet few organizations would employ someone without one. This is another part of the process in which applicants have some control in how they present themselves, and so the issues of impression management and the two-way nature of power in selection and recruitment emerge again.

Let us now begin by looking at recent evidence concerning the CV, before we look at application forms, in particular biodata, and finally the reference process.

## 3   Starting the application process: curriculum vitae (CV)

The CV, or **résumé** as it is termed in the USA and Australia, is a principle tool for the applicant in the selection process. This is often the first contact between the applicant and their prospective employers. Given its evident importance in the selection process, it is surprising that it has received so little attention from researchers regarding its reliability and validity to the selection process. Robertson and Smith (2001) argue that it has a disproportionate effect on recruitment decisions as errors in this initial contact can have disastrous consequences for applicants, resulting in their premature removal from the process. Limited study has examined how such errors can occur in this part of the process, in contrast to the well-documented parallel positive ('**halo**') and negative ('**horns**') effects for interviews (these will be discussed in detail in Chapter 5).

CVs play an important part in the two-way selection process. For candidates, they represent an important opportunity to create a positive impression, a chance to market themselves, indicate their job fit and impress the reader with their skills and abilities. In this way, impression management helps determine whether a candidate will proceed in the selection process.

For the organization, they are the basis on which short-listing decisions are made. Managers use these statements to inform their decisions – but only if they trust the applicants. Candidates who are perceived to be dishonest in any of the information they include will find it counted against them (Bright and Davies, 1999). Recent developments in CV practices have seen an increase in the use of 'competency statements' in which candidates provide short positive summaries of their competencies for the job (see Box 4.1). For example, a candidate might write that she is an 'innovative, organized manager with good team-working skills and proven track record in delivering targets to tight deadlines'. It must be kept in mind that statements of competency are *self*-evaluations and as a result are potentially illusionary. Bright and Hutton (2000) point out that such claims are also difficult to verify in the same way that qualifications or employment histories can be.

## Box 4.1 Example of a CV for the role of accountancy administrator, print works

Prudence Brown, 11 Downing St., London

Tel no: 0207-454545

Mobile no: 0111-2345 857

Email: Prudence@thebrowns

### Personal profile

Highly numerate and confident accountancy professional with willingness to learn and update skills and determination to succeed in professional qualifications.

### Qualifications

- Scholar Templar School, 1993–2000
- 8 GCSEs in Maths, English, Geography, Chemistry, Physics, Biology, French, Drama
- 5 AO levels in Maths, English, Chemistry, Business Studies, French
- 2 A levels in Business Studies and French

- Part-qualified Chartered Institute of Management Accountants (CIMA): completed and passed all foundation units and Intermediate IFIN course.
- Driving licence since 2000

**Work experience**
- 2000–2003: accountancy trainee, Tosh Products and Printers

**Other interests**
- French conversation
- Hill-walking
- Cookery
- Skydiving

Australian research suggests that the inclusion of competency statements (such as Prudence's in Box 4.1), can in fact play an important role in improving applicants' success in the job-search process (Bright and Hutton, 2000). Incorporating these statements increases the probability of being asked to attend later selection processes, such as an interview (Earl *et al.*, 1998) and improves the ratings candidates receive from selectors (Bright and Hutton, 2000). Exploring the effect in more detail, Bright and Hutton (2000) identified that the use of competency statements have a non-specific positive impact on recruiters' perceptions of the applicant and that there is no added advantage from inserting more than one statement. In their study, they found that there was no difference in ratings given by managers between the inclusion of verifiable statements, such as, 'I have won numerous prizes in my career', and more vague generalizations, such as 'I have developed excellent organizational skills'. More interestingly, their findings also reveal that there is no need for competency statements to address the specific job role. This suggests that selection decisions are not necessarily based on the fit between the applicant and the job role and therefore adds weight to the argument that competency statements have an impression-management role in the selection process.

Another study of impression management is that by Watkins and Johnson (2000). They looked at the role of attractiveness in the selection decision and assessed the impact of including a photograph with CVs. They found that adding a photograph had a limited impact on the probability of being short-listed for candidates who already had good CVs. These candidates already received higher evaluations, more invitations to attend interviews and were awarded higher starting salaries. However, for those with average CVs, adding an attractive picture offered a similar boost to the evaluations. They received more offers of an interview. The results of this study differ from Bright and Hutton's and are open to question as student raters were used as opposed to those with more experience. It does, however, offer some insight into the complex, but consistent patterns involved in decision-making. There is a paucity of research into CVs despite their importance in the recruitment and selection process.

# 4   Starting the application process: application forms

Instead of asking for a CV, some organizations request applicants to complete a specific application form, which allows information to be gathered in a standardized way. Application forms are very popular in the UK and are used by 93 per cent of organizations (Shackleton and Newell, 1991). Their content is usually derived from a study of the biographical data important for successful performance in the advertised role. Far more research has been done on this topic than that of CVs *per se*. Let us now examine the development of the application form in more detail.

It is worth pointing out that with the growth of the World Wide Web, such forms are being used more frequently – especially for jobs that receive high volumes of applicants. In fact, many organizations now use online applications as the sole means by which candidates can apply for a job. A recent UK study revealed the growth in preference for online applications among organizations recruiting graduates – from 44 per cent in 1998 (Park, 1999) to 78 per cent in 2001 (Reed, 2002). In response to the increased use of online applications, Price and Patterson (2003) highlight the need for more attention from the candidate perspective of these new online processes. In the past researchers have tended to focus on one specific type of application form: biographical data (biodata). I will devote most of this chapter to the topic as this is where much of the research is focused. I will then explore the use of online applications and explore the different types of data these collect and their effectiveness.

## 4.1 Biographical data collection (biodata)

Biodata forms are designed to assess an individual based on descriptions of their life histories collected through retrospective, quasi-longitudinal, self-reports. In addition to gathering standard personal information such as contact details and qualifications, they also provide information about applicants' experiences, for example as a leader, or in working in a team. Owen (1976, p.53) defines biodata as:

> autobiographical data which are objectively or scoreable items of information provided by the individual about previous experiences (demographic, experiential or attitudinal) which can be presumed or demonstrated to be related to personality structure, personal adjustment, or success in social, educational or occupational pursuits.

I shall begin this section by looking at some examples of this tool, and then move on to examine its historical roots and range of applications. I will then examine the developmental process, including some of the typical response formats that are used and discuss how biodata differs from other selection tools. Finally, I will indicate the strengths and problems this tool presents to organizations and applicants.

The high concentration of research into biodata is in contrast to the limited use in practice (see Figure 1.4). The appeal of biodata for researchers lies in the development of a biographically based psychometric tool that enables the collection and measurement of psychological factors.

What emerges, however, is a key difficulty regarding how these 'psychological factors' are identified and what their relationship is to job performance. Boxes 4.2 and 4.3 contain examples of common questions gathered from graduate application forms. Alternatively, if you log on to the website of any large organization and access their application processes, you will find examples of biodata questions.

---

### Box 4.2 Examples of biodata short-answer format for leadership, teamwork, or organization from graduate entry forms

Please describe a time when you were the leader of a group. What was the situation? How did you keep the group on track? Did you achieve your objective? (Please respond using no more than 150 words.)

Please describe a time when you worked as part of a team. What was the situation? How did you use your personal qualities to help the team work effectively. (Please respond using no more than 150 words.)

Please describe a task or project which you had to complete within a fixed deadline. What was the task/project, how did you go about completing it and what was the final outcome? (Please respond using no more than 150 words.)

---

Unlike most other selection tools used to identify and differentiate between applicants, traditionally biodata has been developed using an empirical rather than a theoretical approach. Questions are derived from the identification of a statistical relationship between job performance and particular biographical characteristics. In the creation of questions, such as those found in Box 4.2, a correlation between the biographical information (such as previous level of leadership position) and measurable job success would have been identified.

## 4.2  Background and applications of the tool

Although not a widely used selection tool, biodata has been applied in a range of occupations, including accountancy, clerical roles, civil service, hotel employees, managers, mechanical equipment distributors, consultants and naval recruits. It has been used to select service workers, for example identifying those who can deal with people from a range of different ethnic backgrounds (Douthitt et al., 1999). The volume of evidence has led some researchers to argue that the biodata tool provides some of the most effective predictors of job performance (Brown and Campion, 1994).

The first recorded application of biodata used for selection purposes was in 1894 in Chicago, where it was used to identify life assurance agents for the insurance industry. Two later classic studies were undertaken focusing on predicting success in sales roles, with Goldsmith's (1922) research into insurance sales staff and Mosel's (1952) departmental sales assistant studies.

**Box 4.3 Examples of biodata tick box questions on leadership, achievement and teamwork commonly found in graduate entry application forms**

| Please indicate any position of responsibility you have held in the last three years: | Tick | Please indicate which of the following certificates of achievement you have obtained: | Tick | I was/am an active member of a: (tick all that apply) | Tick |
|---|---|---|---|---|---|
| President of a University Student Union | ☐ | Duke of Edinburgh Award | ☐ | Community/University society/group | ☐ |
| Student Union officer | ☐ | St John's Ambulance | ☐ | Debating society | ☐ |
| Chairman/Deputy of a University/Community Society | ☐ | Instructor/Coach for an activity | ☐ | University Staff–Student Committee/Student Rep. | ☐ |
| Treasurer/Secretary of a University/Community Society | ☐ | Certificate in Engineering Education Scheme | ☐ | Community/University sports team | ☐ |
| Elected student society representative | ☐ | Young Enterprise | ☐ | | |
| Course/faculty representative | ☐ | 6 Sigma certified | ☐ | Voluntary and charity work, e.g. Niteline | ☐ |
| Major student event organizer | ☐ | | | Religious group | ☐ |
| Running your own business | ☐ | | | Committee/Board | ☐ |
| University/Community Sports captain | ☐ | | | Parent Teacher Association | ☐ |
| Head girl/boy | ☐ | | | Territorial Army | ☐ |
| Prefect/house captain | ☐ | | | Other (please specify) | ☐ |
| Councillor (politics) | ☐ | | | I have not been an active member of a group/society | ☐ |
| Justice of Peace | ☐ | | | | |
| Governor | ☐ | | | | |

**Technical skills**

I have developed my own website        No/Yes

If yes, please provide the URL

The central premise behind biodata is the classical predictor model of selection – namely, that past behaviour is the best predictor of how people will behave in the future. The technique is based on empirically identifying which biographical information is predictive of success for a specific occupation. In fact, the criteria that are pinpointed as important can be very specific – for instance, during the Second World War the US Air Force found that the best fighter pilots were recruits who, as children, had built a model aeroplane that had flown. This one item was more predictive of their success as a fighter pilot than any other in the entire US Air Force test battery. The test item was not based on any theoretical prediction, but on a proven predictive success. This is an example of the empirical rather than theoretical basis that underlies biodata instruments.

Similarly, Mosel's 1952 study of department store staff found a whole range of very specific biographical criteria emerging as important. He identified that successful sales staff shared some very particular characteristics: they were widowed, female, 35–54 year olds, who were between 4 feet 11 inches and 5 feet 2 inches tall. Further, they weighed at least 160 pounds, had dependants, lived in a boarding house, had achieved a high-school education, had at least five years' sales experience, but had been in their last role for less than five years with no time off for illness.

Mosel's work profile highlights how time- and place-specific these empirical findings may be. It also demonstrates a weakness when transported to a different context. The issue of transportability will be discussed in more detail in section 4.6.1. A more recent example of the technique can be found in the selection of airline cabin crew, which identified a performance link between staff who had lived abroad before the age of twelve and had separated parents. Thus, surprising correlations emerge. For example, looking at application form details of those convicted of theft reveal that they are unlikely to supply details of relatives who can be contacted in an emergency, nor do they indicate their middle name (Drakeley, 1989). This marginal and empirically derived view of individual difference will be discussed in Chapter 6, but it is worth noting now that such biodata questions implicitly raise the issue of privacy and ethics. Is it ethical for an employer to ask such questions about your personal circumstances? Further, how these biographical details relate to job performance is not explored in any depth by researchers. It is perhaps this unexplored link which is the more fundamental issue and without it the justification for including questions that have limited face validity in the application process remains weak.

There is a very broad variety of ways in which biodata instruments can be utilized. They have been used more widely in distinguishing vocational interest (Wilkinson, 1997), in assessing training outcomes (Drakley *et al.*,

1988), and determining factors associated with organizational turnover (Reilly and Chao, 1982). This latter study suggests an underlying link between organizational fit and tenure, but biodata focuses on the empirical relationship rather than exploring any more fundamental issues relating to causality. Biodata can be used to assess different aspects of job performance, such as candidates' emotional stability, financial management and 'do-it-yourself' skills. It has also been used to distinguish between family and social orientations towards work and careers. This can be very helpful when selecting staff for overseas assignments to see how well they might adjust to living and working in a different culture.

## 4.3 Developing a biodata tool

Biodata application forms ask for simple biographical information, such as age, sex, address, through to more intricate details of personal life history and other experiences, such as early and later personal relationships, personal habits and attitudes, recreational interests, self-impressions or opinions. How the data are collected ranges from simple multiple-choice questions to short question formats or 'life essays'.

The common basis for every biodata test is that some specific aspects of these life experiences are predictive of future success in that job. The purpose of collecting biodata does not attempt to ascertain and understand the underlying reason or basis for these connections and relationships, merely that they exist.

### 4.3.1 Development process

There are two distinct, but related, stages in the development of a biodata questionnaire: the generation of items and their scoring. In developing the instrument, two distinct approaches are typically used. The first approach, the more traditional one, is purely empirical and the second is informed and rational. Because each is based on a different paradigm, this has implications for the processes used to generate items and in developing scoring keys. However, the secret to an effective biodata application instrument, as with any selection tool, is a thorough job analysis.

**Point-to-point correspondence** lies at the heart of biodata development. It is produced by empirical means and starts with a thorough job analysis, from which a number of criteria emerge for successful performance – for instance, organizational commitment. Life histories of the current job incumbents are then taken, and these are used to indicate the basis of hypothesized biographical aspects, such as childhood experiences, or having a large mortgage. Empirical analysis is then undertaken to indicate *post hoc* relationships between performance criteria and biographical aspects of the role-holders. Once these relationships have been identified, a series of questions is produced and a pool from which items can be selected and tested for their validity. Job experts may be used to help devise items. An example of an item might be: 'do you own your own property?', 'do you have an outstanding mortgage on your property?', 'is your mortgage large, that is more than three times your present salary?'

For the second, or the 'rational', method (Karas and West, 1999), instead of using objective empirically-derived evidence, job experts are used to generate criteria which they believe to be of importance to the job role. This involves making theoretical, rather than empirical, judgements about the relationship between performance and personal history. For example, in looking at team-leader selection, experts might note the success of previous trade-union shop stewards in this role. Because the rational approach does not rely on existing job incumbents, it can be particularly useful when considering the criteria for *new* roles, or where long-standing selection patterns have emerged as discriminatory, necessitating the job criteria to be looked at afresh. This approach can be supplemented by a survey of the literature to identify probable relationships between biographical aspects and performance. Through these theoretical and pseudo-theoretical judgements, an *a priori* relationship between the items and the criteria is identified.

A central test for any biographical item is that it can be validated objectively. For example, some of the items suggested by the questions above could be checked by accessing land registry records, or credit-rating databases. Increasingly, some organizations, for example those recruiting for financial services, are using third-party firms to check the accuracy of these details applicants provide (Adams, 2002). This again raises the question of ethics. Although firms have to protect themselves from the minority of applicants who aim to defraud or subvert the organization, these intrusive practices are applied to all applicants. I shall return to these important issues in sections 5 and 6 below.

Biodata questions are scored using a system called 'item responses level keying' (Karas and West, 1999, p.86). As with their construction, scoring can be developed using two distinct routes. The first is based on empirical data and examines the proportion of variance accounted for between the item and the outcome criterion (Lecznar and Dailey, 1950): the higher the variance the larger the weighting given to the question. So, in our example, the question 'do you own your own property?' might receive a lower weighting than the question 'is your mortgage more than three times your present salary?'

The 'rational method' involves job experts devising weightings based on the theoretical *a priori* links. So more weight might be given, for instance, to leadership positions that have occurred in that work context, such as being a trade-union shop steward than for leadership roles outside work.

### 4.3.2 Verifying biodata

To verify biodata, a draft questionnaire is produced for each of the hypothesized scales and, using a large sample of items (450 items are recommended for reliability by Robertson and Smith, 2001), each question is tested and the results factor analysed. This process examines the clustering of items to reveal which should be selected. Items that do not show satisfactory clustering are then discarded (Chapter 6 deals with factor analysis in more detail). Although this process ensures the generation of unidimensional scales, it may result in the discarding of items that – although important – are not part of the supposed job characteristics. The ideal approach would be to factor-analyse all of the traits in one questionnaire, rather than by each scale separately. Typical biodata questionnaires comprise approximately 150 items.

There is some debate as to whether it is better to score the items at an individual item level, or by putting together scales of a number of items. Studies have examined the cross-validity of each of these different systems. Karas and West (1999), in their research into biodata for selection in the Australian public service, revealed that empirically derived items scored at the item level showed higher validities than those marked at the scale level. They also offered more support for those devised using the empirical rather than the relational approach. In contrast, when Stokes and Searcy (1999) examined the selection of mechanical equipment distributors, they compared all methods of scale development and then tested their accuracy. They found that scales developed through the more rational approach were as accurate as those derived through empirical means.

### 4.3.3 Types of responses

Typically, biodata questions can be divided into two distinct categories (as you will see in Box 4.4). The first, **'hard' items** consist of easily verifiable historical facts. However, these are often intrusive in nature and raise ethical and privacy issues, which I will discuss in sections 4.5 and 4.6. An example would be a question such as: 'what age did your parents divorce?' The second group, which Owen (1976) identified as very useful **'soft' items**, are less offensive and often more abstract in their content. These items tend to focus on candidates' value judgements, aspirations, motivations, attitudes and expectations. Although offering higher acceptability, they are far less easy to verify, an example being: 'would you describe yourself as more creative than most other people?'

---

## Box 4.4 Examples of soft and hard biodata items

### Examples of soft biodata items

- When you were at school and people were picked for team games, when were you usually picked?
- Whilst at senior school, how often did you go out on dates?
- In your first full-time job, how often did you initiate conversation with your immediate supervisor?

### Examples of hard biodata items

- During your time at senior school, what grades did you get for chemistry?
- By the time you were 25 which of the following had you done?

Owned your own home

Set up your own company

---

Drakeley (1989) developed a taxonomy to describe three elements of biodata that are usually collected. These include background information, parents' social class and the candidate's educational history. Second are those concerned with examining an applicant's commitment: these include questions about leisure pursuits and hobbies. Third are elements that explore achievements in terms of education or work performance. A central dilemma for those constructing biographical items is to find aspects that are both historical and easily verifiable. It is clear from looking at items that they frequently reflect the wider societal context, in which, for example, experience of divorce might be common. This raises important issues regarding their transportability across different cultural contexts which I will discuss more fully in section 4.6.1.

## 4.4  Differentiation from other selection tools

Biodata instruments allow the collation of data similar to that collected in an interview. The collection method, however, enables information to be captured more economically but does not allow for any further exploration into what lies *behind* the responses. It precludes the recruiter from exploring the motivation behind behaviour choices.

Biodata is not another form of personality test. Drakeley (1989) suggests the tool differs markedly from personality questionnaires in a number of ways. First, biodata has a far broader content than personality tools and includes a wider array of activities. The responses sought from biodata are *definite*, *specific* and *unique*. They aim to capture both the behavioural choices and reactions to a variety of situations. The presentation and type of items used differ. Biographical questions are often far clumsier in their construction. For example, a personality item might ask: 'I am happy with the way I look – True/False'. In contrast, a biographical item might say 'Most of my friends look better/equal/I don't feel strongly'. It could be argued, however, that on seeing both types of item, many people might find it very difficult to differentiate between the two.

Second, biodata has the advantage that it can be re-scored for a number of different roles simply by changing the required response. For example, an affirmative response to a question about previous trade-union posts might be desirable in a team-leader role, but not in a team-member role, so the item scoring is changed rather than the entire question.

Third, the biodata questionnaire is a selection instrument that could be completed, in the most part, either by the applicant themselves or someone who knows them well, whereas a personality test contains information that is less factually based and more about internal processes. (Although as you will see in Chapter 8 there is some debate on the veracity of this distinction.) Finally, research has indicated that biodata can achieve a higher validity coefficient than personality tests (Robertson and Smith, 2001; Schmidt *et al.*, 1984; Thayer 1977).

## 4.5 Strengths of biodata

### 4.5.1 Invisibility

A key strength of biodata is that the purpose behind an item is often 'invisible' to the candidate, who probably sees the request for information as routine, rather than regarding it as particularly significant or important for the job. For example, few applying for a job of pea-canners would see data such as having a telephone and living locally as important criteria. Frequently, such details can be easily collected from a standard application form, or CV. There may be occasions when candidates question this opacity as they fail to see the link between the question and the job for which they are applying, or where they find the question intrusive.

### 4.5.2 Verifiable data

The information collected through biodata forms is independently verifiable, and thus can be difficult for candidates to fake. One way of further reducing the likelihood of falsehoods is to inform applicants that the data will be checked. As I noted above, this is an increasingly common practice in some organizations, such as financial services, where identifying those with previous fraud and other convictions is vital. Studies have indicated that there are some items of information which applicants are more likely to lie about. These include overestimating their length of employment and salary level, or stating they have been working full-time instead of part-time. Drakeley (1989) found that over 25 per cent of applicants give a different reason for leaving their previous employment than their employers do. More surprising, in 17 per cent of cases this same employer had never heard of the applicant.

Some firms now offer bespoke services 'to confirm applicants' standing and probity', verifying details such as addresses, qualifications, credit checks and judicial details (Adams, 2002). These firms are working with existing personal data but using it in a novel and potentially intrusive fashion. Whilst the applicant has to give permission for this process to commence, many will be reluctant to withhold it in a high-stakes environment where any hint of non-co-operation is more likely to be viewed as a tacit admission of guilt, rather than a protest against the morality of vetting. There are also concerns about the accuracy of the data such checks may be based upon (Evans, 2002). For instance, credit checks are frequently based on candidates' addresses and as a result even if the candidate has not committed an offence personally, if they have shared an address with someone who has, this would result in a blemished record. Privacy for the applicant is not a consideration in this process.

### 4.5.3 Data-processing and management

Undoubtedly, one of the most significant considerations for users of this instrument is the speed with which large numbers of applicants can be screened. Biodata responses can be reduced to multiple-choice formats that focus exclusively on the specific job. This can hugely ease the burden for HR professionals who undertake the first sifting of applications. The costs of selection can also be reduced by using biodata screening in either an automated process, or using lower grade administrators to check for relevant details, thus freeing up more qualified professionals to undertake other duties. Harvey-Cook and Taffler (2000) showed biodata's predictive power in assisting accountancy firms to predict exam success, thereby saving not only the firm's resources, but also the individual candidates' effort and the potentially negative impact of having to re-take exams or drop out of the profession early. However, it does prevent candidates who, for different reasons, have not achieved their potential from gaining access to their chosen field.

### 4.5.4 Fairness and equal opportunity monitoring

Using biodata means that all candidates are screened on the basis of a structured data-collection tool. The same questions are given to everybody and selection decisions are made on the basis of predetermined responses without assessors' value judgements contaminating the process. Kluger and Rothstein (1993) found that business students preferred being selected on the basis of biodata measures to other tests such as cognitive ability. They saw biodata instruments as more fair, reporting that biodata gave them more opportunity to express 'who they were' and therefore, for them, had higher face validity.

Through the biodata approach, more diligent monitoring of equal opportunities can be undertaken. Reilly and Chao (1982) argued that biodata was distinct from other selection tools by showing no discrimination against minority ethnic groups. They suggested that as it is derived from an empirical assessment of the performance difference, it is therefore not subject to the same biases as other selection processes which may reflect the underlying personal prejudice of assessors. Items can be rigorously checked for underlying discrimination and removed. Indeed, biodata can be used as a means of revealing false 'racial' and other discriminatory practices in organizations; for example, by showing a bias towards Oxbridge candidates in the legal profession. In support of this, evidence has shown that the validity of biodata in predicting job success is higher for female candidates (0.51) than male (0.27).

A recent US study of biodata and equal opportunities explored the discrimination of a frequently used item – average college grade attainment ('**grade point average**' or **GPA**) (Roth and Bobko, 2000). This is used as a surrogate for assessing general mental ability. Roth and Bobko's study indicated considerable variations between candidates from different ethnic groups and there is evidence from universities of inconsistent awarding of grades depending on students' ethnic background. The research concluded that the deployment of GPAs as an item in a selection test merely compounded ethnic discrimination, rather than revealing actual performance distinctions.

### 4.5.5 High validity

Research evidence indicates that biodata has substantial and generalizable validity. This means that it measures what it claims to measure and is therefore a good predictor of performance (Salgado, 1999). In his meta-analytic study, Bliesener (1996) found that the validity of biodata scales was 0.30. This suggests that the criteria by which performance is assessed may have a significant influence on results (Robertson and Smith, 2001). Those using training criteria found a validity of 0.36, whilst those using job-performance criteria showed an increase to 0.53. Research has indicated that biodata generated on an empirical basis has higher validity than a combination of general ability and personality tests (Mount *et al.*, 2000) or cognitive ability tests (Karas and West, 1999).

## 4.6 Weaknesses of biodata

### 4.6.1 Atheoretical

The central problem behind biodata lies in its lack of underlying theory. Owen (1976) argues that the measured behaviours that predict job performance are presumably related to personality structure, or adjustment, but the bases for these tools are often purely empirical. The development of this autobiographical tool for selection stems from the statistical relationship between past experiences and current performance. A 'black box' approach is adopted where interest is focused only on what comes out, and not on trying to understand how, or why, those behaviours follow from these personal experiences. Brown and Campion (1994) lament that there are limited insights offered into the meaning behind biodata. Stevens (1951) would regard this as evidence of the unchallenged expansion of psychometric processes.

Owen (1976) argues in his developmental/integrative model that people are influenced by their experiences. These experiences include cultural, social class, family and genetic aspects. As a result of their past experiences they seek out (or avoid) new encounters based on whether they are compatible with their self-perception. While psychotherapists might have more interesting insights into why this might be the case, Owen offers no further arguments as to how these developmental experiences influence behaviour. Typical criticisms of some biodata questions are that they are psychologically meaningless, or have no apparent relevance to the occupation they are supposed to be selecting for (Stokes and Reddy, 1992).

For example, how does an item exploring between-parental relationships influence performance in many roles?

Some studies have found that the same items predict different occupational behaviour in different time periods. For example, studies of one-parent families have suggested either very low or very good educational success: this renders their use in this item as questionable at best. This illustrates the potential problems related to the atheoretical nature of this type of tool. It does not enable us to answer why something might be so. Although there may, in some cases, be ethical concerns that would be raised by more detailed investigation, biodata is merely concerned with the correlation between an aspect of personal history and job performance, and not the underlying issue. This means that it can present a marginal and curtailed view of individual differences by failing to see that such statistical relationships may reflect wider temporal, cultural and societal issues rather than be significant in themselves. For example, a firm that had previously employed white males for a job would have no empirical means of assessing the performance of women or members of minority ethnic groups in the role, but could use it as justification that their selection process was effective.

There are times, however, when the starkness of biodata relationships are revealed, and where the ethics behind such limited analysis must be challenged. Only part of the story is being revealed in a high-stakes situation; as a result, an applicant may find it difficult to object to a question without being seen as someone with something to hide rather than merely protecting their privacy when refusing to answer a question about their parent's relationship. Organizations cannot hide behind the empirical basis for their questions when ethics are challenged.

Recent research suggests that greater attention is being paid to attempting to incorporate more theory into the development of biodata items. These include the rational approach, which involves the generation of specific hypotheses about relationships between past historical experiences and performance criteria by experts (Mumford and Owens, 1987), or from a social-ecology perspective (Mael, 1991). Allworth and Hesketh (1999) highlight the strengths of using both experts on the organizational context and evidence from research as the basis for item generation. This enables the creation of more context sensitivity and therefore potential **transportability** for this tool. The deployment of further theoretical work will in the longer term enable more understanding of why these relationships between past experiences and current job performance occur.

### 4.6.2 Diversity reduction

It is likely that over time the empirical development of biodata instruments could result in more homogeneous patterns of selection and recruitment within a firm. Biodata tends to promote the *status quo* by reflecting previous policies and practices and this can restrict the sample range and the performance data used. For example, a white, male, Anglo-Saxon-dominated organization will not have the data available to compare how roles would be performed by females or Asians. Using this empirical technique, performance can only be measured against current organizational norms. As a result, over time, the adherence to biodata criteria could result in stagnation as successful selection patterns identified in a previous context are repeated in a new context that may be different.

Evidence shows that reductions in the diversity of an organization have a significant impact on creativity and innovation (Ancona and Caldwell, 1992), problem-solving and breadth of market-place (Kandola, 1995). At worst, these replicated patterns may be inaccurate and fail to take into consideration the impact of recent demographic and other changes, for example, growth in minority ethnic groups, one-parent families or ageing populations. If, for instance, in the future, university fees are increased, there might be a dearth of graduates from lower socio-economic groups, and so selecting on the basis of having a degree would also involve only those from a higher socio-economic group. It is therefore important that biodata instruments are monitored regularly to assess their current reliability and validity.

### 4.6.3 Fakeability

What about faking when candidates are completing biodata forms? Faking can occur for three reasons. First, the candidate may have the desire to deliberately sabotage the selection process, such as the 'parachutists' who in the 1970s deliberately tried to falsify their qualifications to enter large organizations like the car industry with the sole purpose of disrupting production.

Second, the issue of '**faking good**' arises: this is when candidates distort their responses in order to appear better than they otherwise would. Research indicates that applicants are consistent in their faking and tend to concentrate disproportionately on altering information that they perceive as negative. They also tend to focus on a limited number of areas. These include over-estimating their tenure with previous employers, increasing the final salary from their last position and altering their reason for leaving a previous employer. It must be noted that there may be a cultural dimension to this faking behaviour, which will be discussed in more detail in Chapter 8. Although it is possible to check information provided by applicants, it would involve considerable time and expense. Candidates are aware that there is a small risk of being found out. As I pointed out earlier, research does suggest, however, that informing applicants that the information they provide will be checked does reduce the likelihood of faking (Robertson and Smith, 2001).

Then there is the issue of 'keen' applicants – candidates who may have been rejected earlier and who, over time, will re-apply for a position and develop their own hypothesis about the 'right' answers. As a result, those who have been rejected earlier, but are still intent on securing a position, are more likely to fake their responses. Biodata can be used to alert organizations to repeat applicants with computer-scored questionnaires offering easier opportunities for storage and searching. It is also possible to retain data from previous applications and so repeat candidates can be identified, but it must be noted that, in the UK at least, this is in violation of the Data Protection Act. This raises the issue of privacy, which is only now being commented upon by researchers (Searle, 2003).

Finally, faking is found when individuals have limited self-insight and are therefore unable accurately to self-report their experiences. This problem will occur for any instrument in which self-report is required. The implicit expectation for those developing such tools is that applicants are articulate and literate about their feelings, motives and values. This may not always be the case. In order to increase the reliability of responses, information should be verified by collecting it from multiple sources. This type of triangulation technique is the basis for an 'assessment centre' approach, which will be discussed in Chapter 9. In the 'assessment centre' approach, data on each of the selection criteria are gathered from multiple exercises by a variety of assessors.

Cascio (1976) found that the problems of faking can be reduced by ensuring that candidates are aware of the penalties. They can also be diminished through developing scoring norms based on the applicants, rather than the current employees. In this way, he suggests, faking can be spotted more easily. This latter point, however, challenges the validity of the tool as a means of assessment of potential job performance. In a faking study, students who were instructed deliberately to fake and create more positive responses were found to produce a more marked distortion than that produced by legitimate applicants (Becker and Colquitt, 1992). This suggests that faking with careful questionnaire construction may more easily be identified than previously thought.

### 4.6.4 Legislation

De-selecting candidates on the basis of their sex, age and race is illegal. Therefore, in developing biodata tools it is important that legislation is taken into account: the criteria identified for success in the job must not be inherently discriminatory. Care must be taken to ensure that any item selected which offers some differentiation between low- and high-calibre performance does not unfairly discriminate. Increasingly, biased selection is being challenged successfully in the law courts. Concern has also been expressed by HR managers about the potentially intrusive nature of biodata questions. There must also be sensitivity to the applicants' increasing awareness of their personal rights (Hammer and Kleinman, 1988). As noted earlier, privacy and ethical concerns are under-explored within this field.

### 4.6.5 Limited application and temporal issues

Biodata items are developed and scored for a particular job, context and time-frame. The criteria identified as important for success do not necessarily have the same predictability for similar jobs in different organizations, nor for other jobs within the same organization. The development of biodata scales, and their testing to ensure validity in different contexts, are tedious and expensive. Initial concern suggested that the validity of adopting the same criteria in a different context is at best limited, at worst non-existent (Dreher and Sackett, 1983). A given biodata tool has a limited application period and must be kept up to date. However, a more recent study (Rothstein *et al.*, 1990) has suggested that biodata may have wider generalizability. It found validity levels of 0.32. A second study used the same instrument to assess 7,334 supervisors in 24 different organizations (Carlson *et al.*, 1999). It found predictive validity of 0.53 for promotional progress, indicating that biodata scored for one context may in fact be successfully transported to another. Care must be taken, however, to assess the generalizability within any new context.

The performance factors for different roles may change over time. As we saw in Chapter 3, these reductions in validity are termed 'shrinkage'. The underlying paradigm behind biodata is based on what has been successful in the *past*. As long as the conditions for successful performance remain the same, then the criteria will remain useful. An analogy for this is driving along the road using only the rear-view mirror: as long as the road is the same as it was in the recent past, you can drive quite comfortably, but if the road changes you will probably crash. Similarly, biodata enables you to see what type of employee has been successful in that job in the past. The rational approach does not focus so strongly on these empirical relationships, but nevertheless it will be based intuitively on expertise and experience gained from the past relating to job performance.

Evidence indicates that biodata scales show different levels of shrinkage depending on the development approach used. Empirically derived biodata show more propensity for validity reduction than rationally identified items (Mitchell and Klimoski, 1982). Overall, the validity of biodata reduces over time and therefore the typical durability of any such instrument is limited to between three and five years. As a result, existing questionnaires must be re-validated and re-weighted on a regular basis.

Regardless of their size, organizations have seen an extraordinary volume and variety of transitions as a consequence of influences such as globalization, e-business and technology developments, which are only just beginning to be assessed. Given the enormous variety and speed of change that development organizations have experienced since the 1990s, care must be taken to ensure the durability of biodata instruments in a very changed business context.

### 4.6.6 Development and re-validation costs

Clearly, the development of biodata tools can be a tedious and time-consuming exercise. Performance data from which the job performance success criteria are identified will take at least twelve months to collect for new employees. This is an important consideration when determining which jobs biodata would be useful for. Biodata requires both sufficient performance data and numbers of applicants before there are adequate data to carry out the necessary empirical analysis. In considering how biodata might be used productively, a simple cost–benefit analysis will reveal which jobs have a high number of applicants and where job success can be easily measured and assessed. The expenses of re-validating the tool must also be taken into consideration in identifying the true costs.

### 4.6.7 *Cross-cultural application*

It should also be noted that many global firms are switching their application process to the web as a means of enabling them to manage the growing number of candidates. This has resulted in an increase in the deployment of biodata items to assist these multinationals in managing the growing cross-cultural diversity of their applicant pool. Whilst the broadening of selection programmes by these trans-continental firms is to be applauded, few studies have examined the impact of culture on biodata response patterns. Research exploring response patterns in the related area of personality testing suggests that propensity to 'fake good' may differ amongst cultures. So as we shall see in Chapter 8, Italian and Japanese candidates show high levels of this impression management behaviour. How far can we assume that this same behaviour is found in the completion of initial applications? Given the high stakes involved and the kudos of working for some firms, more attention needs to be paid to the reliability of these tools within a cross-cultural context.

## 4.7 Other types of application form items

I end this section on application forms by noting the increasing use of hypothetical response items. These questions are not based on eliciting the past behaviours of applicants *per se*. Rather, their focus is on how candidates would respond to work-based situations they may find themselves in. An example from an accountancy firm's online application form is shown in Box 4.5.

These questions indicate a shift from the collection of verifiable data towards the application of situational response approaches. This type of response format is more akin to that found in situational interviews (see Chapter 5). These types of questions have two purposes. First, they enable the organization to gather more systematically applicants' responses to situations that prior critical incident techniques have indicated are important for the job. The questions are delivered as an **online multiple-choice test** rather than verbally during an interview where the candidates' response might be more restrained. From a practitioners' perspective, the inclusion of these hypothetical response items can assist organizations in their short-listing, removing candidates who reveal limited sensitivity to behaviour important within this specific context. As indicated earlier, more research is required into the reliability and validity of these questions across cultures. How far do the critical incidents themselves from which these items are produced reflect a particular cultural paradigm? How far do the responses vary with culture? These are questions yet to be adequately evaluated by those involved in global-selection programmes.

## Box 4.5 Example of a hypothetical question

One of the senior project managers has asked you to obtain urgently some critical information about a client whom you have just started working with. Place a tick in the column you consider appropriate and then in the most appropriate and least appropriate response.

| Rate the appropriateness of the following actions | Inappropriate | Fairly Inappropriate | Neither Appropriate or Inappropriate | Fairly Appropriate | Appropriate | Least Appropriate | Most Appropriate |
|---|---|---|---|---|---|---|---|
| Check with the project team to find out whether anyone is in possession of this information | | | | | | | |
| Check with another colleague to find out whom should be contacted about this | | | | | | | |
| Ask a colleague who will be meeting the client tomorrow afternoon to collect the information on your behalf | | | | | | | |
| Call the client on their mobile to obtain the information yourself | | | | | | | |

Alternatively, some organizations – most notably financial institutions – use a web-based system to deliver unsupervised cognitive ability test items to applicants (Baron and Miles, 2002). This process does enhance the short-listing process for organizations, but presents further problems of candidate verification. (This will be discussed in more detail in Chapter 7.) The inclusion of such items is important as it shows the transition and broadening of application-process practices to include the collection of biographical, hypothetical behavioural responses and ability data.

The second advantage of these questions is for the applicant, as they can act as a job preview, presenting typical work scenarios and enabling them to think not only how they would respond, but whether they want to work in a context in which such events might occur. The inclusion of these hypothetical items may be used to measure organizational 'fit' and help to dissuade some applicants from taking their application further, or remove those with low levels of organizational synergy. This assumes a benign approach from applicants. What if these questions assisted applicants to tailor their responses? Again, limited research has been undertaken to assess their impact. The effects of faking on selection are increasingly being re-evaluated. Maybe this tailoring of responses is a successful strategy that indicates the applicant's sensitivity to organizational culture rather than necessarily being seen as nefarious. More systematic study is required to see how these items actually work and to reveal their reliability across culturally diverse samples.

Overall, there has been limited research undertaken to examine the impact of applications across different cultures. Nor has there been sufficient research examining the changes to this tool as it moves from a paper-and-pencil-based instrument to an online web-based medium. Organizations will certainly reduce administration costs and ease the gathering, storage and transfer of applicant details. However, this assemblage of data creates privacy problems that have yet to be explored adequately by those interested in HR.

It is also suggested that this change of medium may increase the participation in recruitment and selection of applicants from previous disadvantaged socio-economic cultures (Baron and Austin, 2000). But how far is this actually the case? Evidence from assessing the use of web-based instruments suggests that there are gender and ethnic differences in the anxiety of applicants (Badagliacco, 1990). This research has indicated that younger, more affluent, white males have a higher familiarity and lower anxiety when using computers compared to women and older workers (Czaja and Sharit, 1998). Research in the past has clearly indicated the depressing role of anxiety in performance (Kline, 1993). Studies have also found that female and older applicants are more concerned with protecting their privacy and thus more reluctant to enter personal details on to computers (Weiss and Barbeite, 2001). In addition, Sharf (2000) indicated an inequity of access to computers on 'racial', disability and economic grounds. Therefore, although practice is moving further ahead in the deployment of the web in selection processes, more critical evaluation is required to ensure that it is not the instrument *per se*, but this new medium that is inadvertently perpetuating – or even creating – new discriminatory practices.

# 5   References

References, like CVs, are one of the most common tools deployed to assist selection decision-makers, and are used in 96 per cent of cases in the UK (Anderson and Shackleton, 1993). Research indicates that they are used between 67 per cent and 100 per cent of the time globally (Shackleton and Newell, 1997). Milkowich and Bourdreau (1994) go further to suggest that virtually every organization uses some form of reference check before accepting an applicant for a job.

The use of references as a selection tool differs from the other selection tools that we have looked at in this chapter in a number of ways. First, the information is provided by a third party, who comments on the applicant's skills and abilities. The candidate chooses these third parties and so they are not necessarily impartial or objective reviewers of the applicant. Like CVs, the choice of referees can offer an opportunity for impression management by applicants. If given a choice, candidates are not going to select someone with something negative to say about them. In some cases, selectors try to work around this by asking for a referee from the applicant's previous organization. Nonetheless, it is worth considering what the motivation of a referee may be for writing a positive reference. It could be they want to assist the applicant into a new role, or it could be to get rid of a troublesome employee and not incur redundancy and other costs themselves.

As a result of all of these potential biases and contaminants, it is not surprising that studies indicate that a reference is not a particularly robust tool (Hunter and Hunter, 1984; Reilly and Chao, 1982). In fact, in looking at the overall performance both in job and training criteria, validity measures place references amongst the lowest of any selection tool (between 0.14 and 0.26) (Robertson and Smith, 2001). They are only higher than **graphology** or **astrology** (0.02). There are, therefore, a number of potential problems associated with this tool that we will now explore in more detail.

Referees are usually asked to comment on *two* elements of the candidate's past: their work performance and their personal character. The information may be elicited in three ways. References may consist of a completely unstructured letter of recommendation. Or they can be semi-structured responses to standardized criteria – such as organizational abilities and planning skills. At the other extreme, referees may be asked to complete rating scales of standardized competencies. The added rigour of these latter rating systems enables the data to be considered in a similar way to that of job-performance ratings. This should result in similar reliability to that of typical job performance. There is, however, very little research that looks directly at the predictive validity of references.

Mount *et al.* (1994) undertook a study that involved supervisors rating applicants they knew using adjectives derived from the big five personality dimensions (see Chapter 8). The results indicated raised validity coefficients of between 0.23 for 'emotional stability' up to 0.64 for 'conscientiousness'. Salgado (1999) argues that, if properly constructed, references can produce higher validity than applicants' self-reported personality results. Properly constructed, references are a far more useful tool to selectors than their current application suggests.

References, like CVs, may often be used as an impression-management opportunity and because of this the result must be treated with some caution. They can, however, be improved to gather information in a standardized format that enables them to be used as a comparative tool.

## 6   Summary

Chapter 4 has examined three tools that focus explicitly on the historical behaviour of applicants. All three are amongst the most widely deployed, but it has been shown that their validity can vary. Despite their widespread application, limited interest has been forthcoming from academic research regarding CVs or references. Instead, most attention has focused on a specific type of application form – biodata – which has attracted less interest, until now, from practitioners. Research evidence suggests that of all the three instruments, biodata is the one with potentially greater utility for HR departments.

The topic of self-presentation was explored and it was shown that CVs offered applicants the most opportunity for image management. This re-emphasizes the two-way dynamic in selection systems, which can often be overlooked. Although application forms and references do provide some, albeit restricted, opportunities for self-presentation, there has been very little research on faking behaviour in these areas. This neglect may be short-sighted given the global selection processes now practised by some firms and the potential for cross-cultural differences to emerge.

Biodata-based forms emerged as offering organizations who receive thousands of applications a cost-effective means of managing their initial screening decisions. Care is required to select a suitable job as they are expensive to produce and maintain, but their popularity is increasing. The technique has received a wealth of attention from researchers proposing its high validity. In addition, some work has indicated candidates perceive biodata more favourably than other psychometric tools. Further, biodata may assist firms to reduce initial discrimination. The tool is not, however, without its problems – most notably its atheoretical foundations, ethical and privacy concerns, propensity for shrinkage and context, temporal, cultural and role specificity. It is important that validity of scales is re-established for older instruments or those transferred into a different context. More attention is required regarding these concerns if we are to effectively deploy this tool in selection.

This area of selection and recruitment practice is currently undergoing rapid change with the advent of novel web-based applications. Practice is ahead of research, so although claims are made about the increased access to jobs, the new internet medium may be over-rated; we await the results. Certainly, this new medium does enable a more cost-effective short-listing process, but how far this is free from discrimination remains to be seen. The type of question application forms use appears to be in transition, with combinations of hypothetical situational items and ability testing items being introduced alongside more standard biodata items. They may have an additional role for recruiters in presenting job previews and organizational-fit questionnaires, creating more conducive ways of de-selecting candidates whist retaining a positive organizational image.

In many cases, it has been argued that these commonly used tools, such as references, are being under-utilized in the process of gathering information about candidates. Suggestions were made about how these tools' reliability and validity could be enhanced by turning them into more structured instruments. This reveals a new application of pseudo-psychometric techniques into the reference field.

## Exercise: application forms

Visit your careers library and collect four applications for four job roles. Make sure you select one civil service, two large international organizations and one other of your choice. Examine the application forms and consider the following questions:

How many are biodata forms?

How many state this explicitly?

How many include biodata-style questions?

For each application form, identify and then compare and contrast themes in the questions they ask.

# CHAPTER 5

# Selection tools 2: interviews

## 1   Overview

Interviews are one of the oldest – and by far the most popular – tools used in selection. They consist of a 'conversation with a purpose'. Interviews enable several important assessments to be made, and evidence indicates that they have high predictive validity regarding future job and training performance (Robertson and Smith, 2001). They can present an important information-gathering opportunity for both organization and applicant.

There are two central theoretical perspectives that are taken regarding an interview: the objectivist psychometric perspective and the subjectivist social-interactionist perspective. Each reveals important but different facets concerning the role of the different parties. Each considers the expectations and processes that comprise the interview in distinct ways.

The first perspective we will examine is the objectivist psychometric one, which focuses on issues such as structure, reliability and validity. It asks: what qualities can an interview assess? How should the content and format of an interview be structured? What role do reliability, validity and decision-making play in the interview format? In line with this view, two distinct interview structures are compared and contrasted: the experiential and hypothetical interview formats.

Recent evidence suggests interviews are important because they begin the socialization process for successful candidates and enhance the positive image of the firm. The second perspective we shall explore stems from the social perspective. This highlights the uniqueness of the exchange: it emphasizes the *process* of the interview and the patterns of the exchange. It places particular attention on the issue of impression management, and asks questions about the power dynamics that take place during an interview. It looks at process patterns, attribution formation and the role of context and the applicant in shaping the interview. In examining the processes and patterns of interaction in the interview itself, it raises questions about perception formations and impressions, which lead to challenges about fairness.

Increasingly, employers are using new technology to facilitate the interview process and this has enhanced our understanding of perception formation and the decision-making process of recruiters. The advantages and difficulties of such new practices will be discussed. This chapter highlights new developments such as the use of new technology as a novel medium for interviews and an examination of the role training for both interviewers and interviewees can play in the process. The chapter concludes with a summary.

## 2 Introduction

The interview is a unique behavioural sampling tool for selection: it offers an opportunity for a direct experience of a candidate's behaviour coupled with the potential to ask more probing questions regarding underlying cognitive, motivational and emotional issues. The candidate is also gathering information about the organization and can use the process to raise issues pertaining to the organization's values, goals and 'fit'. With skilful planning, the interview can be used to supplement other parts of the selection process, and allow recruiters to explore issues or discrepancies that have emerged from other tools or sources. For example, a question might be added to the interview schedule that enables the recruiter to ask why a candidate reports themselves as high on a personality dimension such as conscientiousness, when their previous employer's reference indicates they do not complete tasks.

### 2.1 Objectivist psychometric perspective

The objectivist psychometric perspective places the interview at one extreme. It considers the interview an objective and accurate means of assessing an applicant's suitability for a job. Schmidt and Rader (1999, p.445) describe it as 'a measurement procedure, as are paper and pencil tests of ability or aptitude'. From this perspective, the process places the interviewee as a passive participant who provides relevant information about their experiences and capabilities. First, the interviewer is regarded as a rational decision-maker, who is capable of collecting – in an impartial manner – information on a number of relevant selection criteria. Implicit in such a process is the interviewer's ability to obtain relevant data accurately. Second, it is assumed that they have the skills to be able accurately to interpret the information, relate it impartially to the criteria and assess the candidate's suitability based on the sample of behaviour provided. Thus, this perspective reduces the interview to a verbally administered psychometric test with concerns of structure, reliability and validity predominating.

The objectivist psychometric perspective tends to dominate the field. Researchers here are concerned with the means of controlling the conditions to ensure that identical stimuli are being presented to all applicants. Much of the research has examined how the validity and reliability of the process can be maintained. Inevitably, the focus rests on the interviewer as a potential corrupter of an otherwise objective tool. The interviewer is supposed to preside in a controlled and calm manner through a series of virtually identical processes, gathering and assessing data applicants provide. The interviewer's role in producing and perpetuating bias has been the main area of interest, and there has been limited effort until more recently into questioning the candidate's motivation to present the correct information, or in contaminating the interview.

## 2.2 Subjectivist social-interactionist perspective

The alternative perspective, and one that has received much more limited attention, places the interview at the other extreme: it considers the process to be a social interaction in which a subjective, socially based negotiation occurs. In this perspective, a far more evenly balanced dynamic emerges between each party, with both the applicant and the interviewer having some power in the situation. The parties are considered to become participant observers in the process. The interview thus emerges as a complex and unique event. In the selection context, those involved are engaged in creating a variable psychological contract regarding their mutual expectations of future working relationships.

The importance of the psychological contract at the onset and its maintenance throughout the employment relationship cannot be overstated (Rousseau, 2001). Herriot (1987) argued that this interactive and social perspective is important, because it places the applicant as a far more active player in the negotiation process. This concept is particularly valid in a job market in which the applicant's skills and experience are in short supply, or important to the organization. Under these conditions, the applicant plays a key role in dictating the terms and conditions under which they will be employed.

From this perspective, each interview is potentially unique because of the players involved, with the parties creating a particular process that emerges from their current context. Each party is previewing and assessing their ability to work together in the future. But what happens where the recruiter is not involved in any future work relationship? The key research issues of this perspective are concerned with the type of psychological contract reached, processes of perception formation, bias and fairness. Like the objectivist psychometric research perspective, this approach is also concerned with the future, but not regarding job performance *per se*, instead a focus might explore what happens if the contract being negotiated is violated.

Each of the aforementioned perspectives enables a different facet of interviewing to be examined. It provides a means of examining the application and the process of interviewing in more detail. I shall now look at the issues raised by the objectivist psychometric approach, before turning my attention to the subjectivist social-interactionist perspective.

## 3    Objectivist psychometric perspective

### 3.1 What can an interview measure?

A key concern for those adopting the objectivist psychometric view of selection tools is what interviews actually measure. This is a fundamental question if we are to understand the interview's role in the selection process and ascertain whether it enhances or merely duplicates other tools. Research into this issue has suggested that interviews could be measuring four distinct dimensions. The most long-standing evidence suggests that interviews are simply measuring cognitive ability (Huffcutt *et al.*, 1966; Hunter and Hirsh, 1987). Correlations have been found between interview performance and aspects of cognitive ability, including mathematical and mechanical ability, reading and oral instruction (Campion *et al.*, 1988). The second area of measurement is job knowledge or tacit knowledge, which you will see shortly is clearly the case in situational interviews (Harris, 1998; Salgado and Moscoso, 2000).

A third aspect that it is claimed interviews measure is social skills. There is evidence of a relationship between more behavioural interview ratings and those found in personality dimensions: for example, conscientiousness, extraversion, emotional stability, agreeableness, openness to experience, locus of control and achievement motivation (Cook *et al.*, 1998; Salgado and Moscoso, 2000; Schmidt and Hunter, 1998; Schmidt and Rader, 1999). More recently, there has been a renewed concern that interviews cannot measure assessment-centre constructs, such as conscientiousness, but instead assess a general homogeneous factor related to the applicant's social competence (Huffcutt *et al.*, 2001).

Finally, research through the mid-1990s and beyond argues that interviews can measure person–organization fit (Harris, 1999; Judge, 2000; Kristof, 1996). It is worth noting that the alternative subjectivist social-interactionist perspective emphasizes the *two-way* nature of this fit assessment, but most work in this area has merely focused on the applicant's fit into the firm (see Figure 5.1).

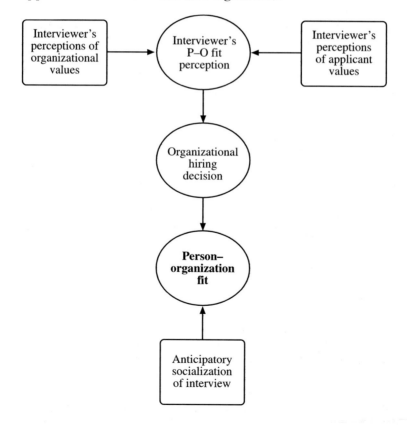

*Figure 5.1   Person–organization fit*

Parsons *et al.* (1999) argue that assessments of organizational fit are fraught with difficulties. In the first place, interviewers may compare the applicant against some imagined applicant who represents a generic ideal suitable for any organization, rather than fitting that specific context. These global, positive attributes merely reflect candidates' general employability and therefore have limited congruence with the specific values of the organization. Alternatively, the assessment the interviewer uses of person–organization fit may be based on their personal – and thus idiosyncratic – judgement of the organization's culture. At worst, this results in an incorrect image of the organization. What is of more concern, however, is that it may depict an ideal template of the organization's members that in fact reflects the assessors' perceptions of their own personal qualities (Ferris and Judge, 1991) – after all they are an example of a successful organization member. Related to this idiosyncratic view, the interview can in fact present a chance to pinpoint candidates the assessor regards as most like themselves and use the interview to their advantage as a means of increasing their organizational power by building coalitions with like-minded people (Gilmore and Ferris, 1989).

It is clear that there is no consistent view of what interviews measure. When reflecting on the numerous studies which seek to address this very question, exercise caution for four reasons. First, as I will demonstrate shortly, there is no such thing as a generic interview; instead, there are many different types of interview in terms of type of content and the level of structure. It is therefore difficult at times to ensure that, in these studies, like is being compared with like. Second, in many cases, the samples involved in the aforementioned studies were small and so results may be mixed. Meta-analysis has gone someway to providing a means of aggregating these smaller studies to identify an overarching theme. As noted in Chapter 3, in any practice that aggregates different studies, care must be taken to ensure that they are directly comparable.

Third, studies in selection are plagued with restrictions-of-range issues because the very process of recruiting necessitates de-selecting some of the data set, so information on the outcomes for unsuccessful candidates are nearly always removed. Although statistical techniques do exist to correct for restriction-of-data range, as I have raised in Chapter 3, such corrections may obscure the more interesting findings. Finally, although interviews may measure a mixture of constructs, it is not possible to conduct separate meta-analysis for each because of a lack of replication between studies. They reflect different organizational needs rather than being undertaken for pure research purposes.

Thus, there is no definitive response to the simple question of what interviews actually measure. Instead, it raises some interesting questions about the different types of processes that can be used and how far it is meaningful to use the interview as a psychometric tool as opposed to a social interaction.

Interviews can vary on four broad categories. These are the level of structure, type of content, type of format and the number of interviews held. Arguably, the most important research regarding the significance of the interview in the selection process concerns their structure and content.

We shall examine these issues first. We shall then move on to look at research concerning the number of interviews needed and questions regarding reliability and validity, and error and bias.

## 3.2 The structure of the interview

The single issue that has received most attention in research on the interview is the amount of structure in an interview. This can be conceived of as a continuum (as in Figure 5.2) – ranging from structured through to unstructured.

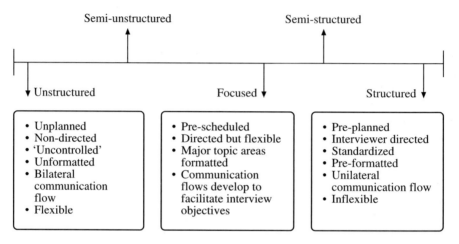

*Figure 5.2   Structure of an interview*

(Anderson and Shackleton, 1993, p.71)

### 3.2.1 Unstructured interviews

Traditionally, interviews consisted of an unstructured discussion between the applicant and a recruiter with no pre-set topics. As such, the interview can quickly degenerate into an uncontrolled, non-directive, often disordered process. At its best, this form of interviewing provides a surrogate measurement of the candidate's social skills; more commonly, it is a waste of time and effort by all the parties involved and enables no consistent means of comparing the different candidates.

In contrast, it takes far more skill and time to conduct this type of unstructured interview. For example, in psychotherapy a therapist uses such an unstructured interview technique in working with clients. This type of technique requires a great deal of training, energy and skill for the interviewer to be able to follow-up interesting leads that the client reveals effectively and to concentrate on significant details as they arise.

### 3.2.2 Structured interviews

The term 'structured' interview can cover a wide range of processes. Some structure is found in 'focused' interviews where the topics for discussion are set, but not the specific questions, whilst in the semi-structured interview both topics and the questions are prepared in advance. In fully structured interviews a 'closed question structure' is adopted in which the topics, questions and potential answers are all pre-set. This structure is typical of those found in market-research questionnaires.

According to the objectivist psychometric perspective, the structured interview process focuses on the interviewer asking a pre-set sequence of questions aimed at eliciting information relating to pre-determined criteria. The purpose of the structure is to close the process to any extraneous influences, so that even when different interviewers are involved, the same data are being gathered, thereby providing a means of comparing the candidates. As a result, the process of delivering the questions is standardized. This perspective treats the interview as a verbally delivered psychometric instrument in which the more structure is involved, the more fair and consistent the conditions are under which the information is gathered and therefore the more reliable the process becomes.

The assumption behind this perspective is that extraneous contaminators will be minimized through structuring. There is some debate about the extent to which objective assessments can be made about such interview data due to the biases and contaminants that enter the process from a number of places (this will be discussed in section 3.8).

### 3.2.3 *The development process behind the interview*

The process of structuring an interview begins with a job analysis, which is used to identify the key knowledge, competencies and experiences necessary for the job. Two common versions of structured interviews are used: situational and behavioural. In structured interviews, critical incident technique (as we discussed in Chapter 2, section 7.7; Flannagan, 1954) is commonly used as a means of providing information relating to good and poor behaviour in carrying out the role. The outcome of this technique can then be easily translated into both the interview questions and the different categories of responses.

Alternatively, questions and scoring systems for structured interviews can be derived from a more empirical basis that is akin to the development of a psychometric test. Schmidt and Rader (1999) indicate four main development stages. First, following a job analysis for the role, in-depth observations are undertaken of an incumbent carrying out the role. Second, outstanding performers are interviewed to identify the important functions and responsibilities of the job. In addition, behaviour traits which are common to this elite group are clarified. Schmidt and Rader argue that typically 10 to 15 such traits emerge. Once this process has occurred, questions are developed that focus on more broad situational or behavioural aspects, typically around 120. Third, groups of good and poor performing job-holders are identified and the questions put to them. The interviews are recorded and transcribed. Using these data, about half the questions are discarded through a statistical assessment of the differentiation in the responses between these two distinct groups. Finally, a scoring guide is developed based on the previous stage. Schmidt and Rader (1999) argue that 'it is not an objective scoring key' but suggest that such interviews should be administered (that is literally read aloud) and a separate group of assessors should analyse the results.

The alternative verbal-test process outlined above is very lengthy and it is therefore expensive to produce. Further, it almost ignores the initial job analysis. The interview schedule produced is very focused on the role and on differentiating between performance levels. Such a thorough, organizational and job-specific process has high context validity, but offers little gain in estimated mean true validity; 0.40 compared to 0.44 for the traditional structured interview (Robertson and Smith, 2001). However, what is perhaps more important is that this process removes any of the interviewers' social or negotiating role. And whilst it may satisfy the requirements of the organization, it does not attend to candidates' concerns and therefore may result in negative perceptions of the process.

The systematic application of techniques for generating an interview may be laudable for creating a well-researched tool, but it places the process firmly at one extreme of the objectivist-psychometric perspective. More research will be needed before the impact of such a process on not only the organization but also the applicant can be identified. However, I will speculate that this type of process can have three major impacts. First, it will alienate interviewers as it significantly downgrades their role and skills to merely verbally administrating the interview-cum-test. Second, it creates a selection decision-making élite who may not work with successful applicants on a day-to-day basis and therefore have limited accountability in the process. Indeed, some of the analysis in this research was undertaken by those external to the organization which further removes them from the impact of their decisions. Finally, limited attention has been paid to the perceptions of candidates about the organization as a result of going through this procedure. Although this group is frequently overlooked in selection research generally, they can play a huge role in influencing others either to (or more likely not to) apply to the organization. Candidates' views about the fairness of this system may prove critical to its success.

## 3.3 Content

The second important issue that differentiates interviews is content. A number of researchers have generated different typologies of interviews. The most common distinctions are between four types of interviews: situational, job-related, psychological or competency interviews (McDaniel et al., 1994). Situational interviews contain situation-specific questions based on the job and examine the candidate's hypothetical performance. They are typically conducted by either specialists such as work/organizational psychologists or specially trained employees. Job-related interviews concern questions pertaining to past behaviour in the job. They are usually conducted by HR professionals or others responsible for hiring. The third type, psychological interviews, are based on assessing personality traits and are conducted by work/organizational psychologists. Finally, a variation of this latter type, competency interviews (Wood and Payne, 1998) widen the psychological interview from just personality to include interpersonal skills, motivation and leadership, and other competencies identified as important for success in the job. A competency interview is typically conducted by a specialist work psychologist.

These typologies often distinguish between psychologists and others who are responsible for conducting the interview. This tends to make a false dichotomy. A more useful distinction can be made between looking at the interview questions in terms of whether they are based on hypothetical situations or actual past behaviours. I shall now compare two distinct types of interview content based on this distinction: behavioural patterned versus situational interviews. These characteristics underpin the differences in terms of their question development, scoring processes and, more importantly, validity.

### 3.3.1 *Behavioural patterned description interviews (BPDIs)*

Behavioural patterned description interviews (BPDIs) were developed by Janz (1982, 1986) in Canada, whose central premise was that past behaviour is the best predictor of future behaviour (Janz, 1989). The focus in a BPDI is on a candidate's actual behaviour, which is not necessarily job-related. The type of questions asked often provide rich detail not just about what was done, but the underlying motivation behind the answer to the questions – asking how and why this response was chosen in preference to others. The technique considers that the more frequently a behaviour is chosen, the more likely it is to predict future job behaviour. Candidates are assumed to have mastery of their behaviour and to have some self-insight as to why they consciously chose a response, rather than it stemming from an habitual or unthinking act. Thus, if someone is revealed as losing their temper, it is then assumed that they readily show their anger, rather than that the context they found themselves in caused such frustration as to provoke an extreme reaction.

BPDIs are devised through the use of job analysis, with the critical incidents of a role distinguishing between effective and ineffective performance. From these incidents a range of so-called '**performance dimensions**' are devised which indicate critical categories of behaviour that underpin effective job performance (see Box 5.1). Usually, between five and ten dimensions are produced for a role. Each of the dimensions is checked by a job expert – most commonly the job supervisor – to ensure their accuracy. These then provide the basis for detailed question themes. The interviewer, when recording the candidate's responses to the interview questions, pays particular attention to information about past behaviours in situations similar to those found in the critical incidents. Interviewers also probe the underlying motivation behind the candidate's behaviour.

## Box 5.1 Example of BPDI critical incident

Job role: Computer-controlled machine tool operator

**Effective performance:**

Frequently monitors component load-bearing gauge.

Regulates the pressure when load read-out falls below minimum.

**Ineffective performance:**

Omits to monitor gauge at regular intervals.

Fails to regulate pressure when falls below minimum requirements.

**Underlying behaviour:**

Alertness to environment and machinery.

Regular monitoring and checking against standard.

A number of related versions of this type of interview have been developed, including 'behavioural event interviews' and 'criterion referenced interviews'. The technique has been used in a wide variety of different roles at both high and lower levels. Anderson and Shackleton (1993) report the comparatively high predictive reliability and validity of this type of interviewing process, and it has been found to correlate highly with assessments of cognitive ability (Hunter and Hirsch, 1987; Schmidt, 1988) and also the personality dimension 'extroversion' (Huffcutt *et al.*, 2001). Janz *et al.* (1986) argue that the method is useful in measuring decision-making judgement ability, attitudes towards quality, interpersonal skills and negotiation tactics.

The relationship between past and future behaviour is at the heart of this technique: this raises a number of issues. First, the process relies on the *truthfulness* of the candidates' responses. Limited attention has been given to applicants' motivation to provide answers that create the best impression (Baron, 1989) or to downplay any weaknesses. Whilst it is clear that fabrications take time to devise, research attention has tended to be diverted onto the skills of the interviewer to probe effectively and identify where such discrepancies, omissions or embellishments may occur (Motowidlo, 1999).

Second, as I noted in Chapter 2, a problem emerges regarding the stability of these behaviours for organizations experiencing turbulence. This type of question relies on the carry-over of behaviours from one situation to another, which may simply not be possible, or desirable. For example, research suggests that leadership skills should change as the organization's hierarchy is scaled, altering from a transactional to transformational approach (Alimo-Metcalfe and Alban-Metcalfe, 2003). This type of interview does not take into account the possibility of any individual development or changes in behaviour. As a consequence, this places it at odds with training and development literature that considers that individual change is possible.

Finally, findings from this approach assume that the behaviour elicited is directly under the individual's control. Those new to a job may have limited opportunity, certainly at the onset, to behave as they might wish. If we are to assume a valid link between intent and behaviour, attention must be paid to identifying which aspects of behaviour the applicant perceived as under their control and which were regimented by the context in which they were working. This may, however, prove difficult to tease out.

### 3.3.2 Situational interview

The situational interview method – also Canadian in origin – was developed by Latham *et al.* (1980) and is based on his goal-setting theory, which regards an individual's intentions as an immediate precursor for their action. It too uses critical incident technique to identify crucial facets of the job. The main difference between this technique and BPDI is that, instead of being interested in *past* behaviour, this type of interview focuses on hypothetical situations and explores candidate's potential, or *future* behaviour (see Box 5.2 for an example of a situational interview format).

---

#### Box 5.2 Example of situational interview question for the motor industry

You are the new personnel officer in the manufacturing plant and the boiler is not working properly. The temperature has dropped below the legal minimum and the shop-floor workers are threatening to walk out. Production is already way behind schedule for the week. What would you do?

---

Through the critical incidence technique questions, job experts devise a rating scale of behaviours which indicates a hierarchy of potential behavioural responses from poor, through average to outstanding (see Box 5.3). These descriptions are termed '**behavioural anchored rating scales**' (BARS).

---

#### Box 5.3 Example of situational interview question and BARS

A female customer is choosing a lipstick to wear to an important dinner and to match an outfit. She is undecided which to choose and asks your advice. How do you respond? Please tick appropriate response.

1   Ask her what she would wear it with and try to find suitable item to compare colour against

2   Suggest she looks in clothes section for something similar and come back

3   Ask the colour of the outfit and advise accordingly

4   Say it is a matter of personal taste and that she should choose

5   Choose the lipstick that you like most

Latham and Saari (1984) used this technique in creating a structured interview for a saw mill. They found reliabilities of 0.76 for workers, rising to 0.79 for overseers. The success of this approach was attributed to the identification of specific and critical job behaviours. Other researchers have used the approach for the selection of clerical personnel (Latham and Saari, 1984), correction officers (Stohr-Gilmore et al., 1990) and retail jewellery sales assistants (Weekley and Gier, 1987).

Evidence indicates that a particular strength of this type of approach is the reduction in discrimination it offers compared with panel ratings. Lin et al. (1992) found that same-race bias for White and Hispanic applicants was reduced by this approach. They identified that Black candidates were more favourably evaluated by Black interviewers regardless of the method, but that situational interviews reduced the discrimination of this group by White and Hispanic assessors. The technique has also been shown to reduce gender bias, especially in hiring for stereotypically male occupations (Campion et al., 1988; Maurer and Lee, 1994).

Research on students that examined candidates' perceptions reveals that they too favour this approach (Latham and Finnegan, 1993). They perceived that the technique was administered more consistently, that there was higher inter-assessor agreement and that it provided a more objective basis for selection. However, the students involved in this survey felt that it limited their ability to take control of the interview process and restricted their opportunities to create more positive impressions. In contrast, Robertson et al. (1991), in their study of a UK banking organization, found that those who were not successful in gaining promotion perceived it less favourably than other interview formats.

Given the strengths of the technique, a critical factor that limits its more widespread application is the cost of development. Green et al. (1993) calculated that it cost on average $1,000 per question to devise such a tool, placing typical development costs of $20,000–30,000 outside the reach of many organizations. In its defence, Campion et al. (1988) argued that these costs would be more than matched by the salary savings that could be made by employing the superior candidates the system identified.

Finally a new variant of the situational interview, the 'multi-modal' form, has been developed (Schuler, 1989). It has four parts: self-presentation, vocabulary assessment, biographical questions and situational issues. It comprises both situation aspects, biographical issues more akin to those found in biodata forms (see Chapter 4), and ability psychometric tests, which we will explore in more detail in Chapter 7. There are limited studies using multi-modal forms.

## 3.4 Delivery formats

How important is the delivery of the interview itself? A central distinction can be made regarding *how many* assessors are involved in the interview. This can range from one person through to a panel of different people. Panel, or board interviews, involve more than one assessor per candidate and can therefore be difficult to coordinate and expensive to hold. They do have the advantage, however, that all of the important stakeholders for a particular role can be involved in the hiring decision. There is also evidence to suggest that they are more valid than the use of individual assessors (Avery and Campion, 1982; Purcell *et al.*, 1980; Wiesner and Cronshaw, 1988) (see Figure 5.3). However, on closer examination, these studies reveal many were compounding issues of structure and format. Evidence indicates that unstructured panel interviews are more valid than unstructured single interviewers, with validity coefficients of 0.21 and 0.11, respectively. The validity of structured individual assessor interviews suggests that they are more effective than using a panel (validity coefficients of 0.43 and 0.32, respectively) (McDaniel *et al.*, 1994). Overall, this evidence indicates that the structured one-to-one interview appears to be more valid.

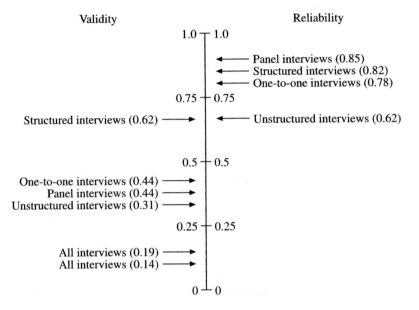

*Figure 5.3   Validity and reliability based on structure*

(Anderson and Shackleton, 1993, p.51)

## 3.5 Number

There is very little research examining the impact of the number of interviews on their effectiveness as a selection tool. Nonetheless, I have included this issue as it reveals an important cultural difference in the format of the interview in different countries. For example, in France applicants are typically interviewed on a one-to-one basis by everybody with whom they would be working, which means that they may go through a number of different interviews with a number of different people. In the UK, however, it is more common to have fewer interviews. Typically, UK graduate applicants take a first interview as part of the university-based 'milk round' where the interviews are conducted at their place of study, and a second as part of an assessment centre. There are political advantages to the French system because it ensures that all employees with whom the new job-holder will interact significantly are involved in the decision-making process. There are limited insights into the structure of these interviews and so it is not possible to evaluate whether each interview is in fact assessing a different aspect of the role, or merely assessing whether the candidate, at the simplest level, is liked.

## 3.6 Reliability and validity

A key issue that concerns the objectivist psychometric perspective is the selection interview's reliability and validity as a selection tool (see Figure 5.3). Attention has focused on distinct parts of the measurement and assessment process in order to identify the value of different approaches. Evidence regarding the predictive validity for both job performance and training outcomes indicates that the interview can make a valuable contribution to the selection process. In interviews, criterion validities of 0.51 are common in predicting future job performance and this can rise to 0.63 when used in conjunction with cognitive ability tests (Robertson and Smith, 2001). McDaniel *et al.* (1994), in their large and most widely cited meta-analysis of the interview ($n$ = 25,444), identified some key factors that affected their validity, including differences in structure and the outcome criterion used.

In terms of the content of interviews, three types were evaluated: situational, job-related and psychological. The observed validities were highest for situational interviews (0.27), then job-related interviews (0.21) and, finally, psychological interviews (0.15). These validities rose to 0.50, 0.39 and 0.29, respectively, once corrections had been made for restrictions of range. They found that the type of performance outcome used was also an important factor. The validity for job performance and training outcomes were similar (0.37 and 0.36 respectively), whilst that for tenure were much lower (0.20). In addition, there is evidence suggesting that the validity of an interview correlates with a number of other characteristics. Most notably, in addition to structure: the number of assessors, the length of an interview ($r$ = −0.29) and the gender mix between assessor and applicant ($r$ = −0.27) (Marchese and Muchinsky, 1993). I will discuss the impact of gender in the next section.

Researchers have conducted a broad range of studies to identify the effectiveness of the two main types of structure – situational or behavioural – and evidence suggests corrected validities of 0.46 and 0.57 for each, respectively (Taylor and Small, 2000). A central issue is the differences of focus between actual past behaviour compared to potential future behaviour. The results favour past experience as a more valid predictor of future job performance (0.50 and 0.39, respectively) (Salgado, 1999).

Some evidence suggests these two types of interview may be measuring different dimensions. Harris (1999) argues that situational interviews are more amenable to collecting data on candidates' job knowledge and cognitive ability, while behavioural questions are better at eliciting interpersonal data. Correlations between ability scores bear this out, with 0.32 for situational interviews and 0.18 for behaviourally based formats (Huffcutt *et al.*, 1996). It appears that situational questions can provide bright applicants with the opportunity to articulate the right answer, while the emphasis that behavioural interviews place on actual behaviour reduces the role of cognitive skills.

Attention has focused on the effectiveness of these different approaches to different levels of job, with studies producing a taxonomy of job complexity from low-complexity unskilled jobs, to skilled medium complexity roles and highly complex managerial jobs (Hunter *et al.*, 1990). In reviewing the application of different interview techniques, it is clear that studies of situational interviews have predominantly been used for low-complexity roles.

In order to examine more accurately the effectiveness of the different approaches to interviews, a study was set up directly comparing their merits in the recruitment of federal investigative agents (Pulakos and Schmitt, 1995). Huffcutt *et al.* (2001) replicated this work for two other high-complexity roles: military officer and district manager. Their findings concurred with the previous study and identified that situational interviews were less good at predicting success in higher level jobs than BPDI formats. In their detailed study they found limited correspondence between questions from each type of interview that were aimed to test the same facet of behaviour. They argued that situational interviews may be too simplistic and are therefore less able to pick up and differentiate the subtle details underlying complex situations. Moreover, they suggested that behaviour-based questions allowed candidates to bring in a wider arena of experiences from both work and home environments. They question how far these different types of interview are actually measuring different job constructs, with behavioural-based questions more suitable for higher level roles. More problematically, they conclude that such techniques may actually be effective in measuring only one homogeneous construct – such as job-related social skills. This challenges directly the adequacy of interviews in measuring distinct multiple constructs, which is an issue I will return to in the next section. Finally, behavioural-based questions enable a more thorough probe of issues pertaining to how or why such actions were taken. In particular for higher level jobs, although the same action may be chosen, the reasons behind this choice may be just as important as the action itself.

For some researchers, the structured interview is being reduced to a work-sample test. Schmidt and Rader (1999) argue that the strength of the interview lies as a verbally administered psychometric test. They argue that it is important to collect first responses to the questions as these first reactions are more valid that those that emerge later, which are more likely to be the hypothesized 'correct' responses. (This issue will be considered in more detail in Chapter 8 when looking at personality-type questionnaires and response sets.) Second, they argued that many international interviewees may lack the requisite English writing skills, but have better verbal skills. This latter point is somewhat contentious as most employers regard it as imperative that their employees can read and write in order to enable the wide and rapid dissemination of organizational communications and to assist with their training and ability to understand standardized operations, practices and procedures.

## 3.7 Errors and bias in the interviewers' decision-making process

Consistent with the premise of objective assessment, in the objectivist psychometric perspective, a reduction in validity is understood to indicate sources of bias and error. A number of studies have tried to examine such contamination. In the main, the research has been concerned with errors introduced by the *interviewer.* The focus on the interviewer as the source of bias emphasizes the view that they are the more active and thus influential party in the process, delivering the assessment and evaluating the results. In contrast, far more limited attention has focused on the *applicants* as a source of bias. I will return to the question of the role the candidate might play in shaping the interview and the role of perceptual differences in the next section when I explore the subjectivist social-interactionist approach. For now, it is important to note that central to ideas of contamination, bias and distortion is the assumption that there is a value-neutral (objective) position which the subjectivist social-interactionist perspective challenges. I will return to why this perspective questions whether such objectivity is possible later.

In reviewing studies of errors, a range of potential contaminants emerges. Avery and Campion (1982) undertook a large study that revealed that a range of biases against applicants was made on the basis of 'race', gender, appearance, age, attitude, non-verbal behaviour, physical setting and job-market situations. Many authors suggest that these biases can be reduced through training; however, Aiken (1987) questions how far the influence of such prejudices can be truly eradicated. I will return to this question in more detail later when exploring the topic of training in section 5.2.

In terms of 'race', many studies have shown that applicants with foreign accents can be discriminated against. However, the level of job can mitigate this effect, increasing the ratings of those with foreign accents applying for lower level jobs, but lowering those of applicants in higher ranked roles (Kalin and Rayko, 1978).

Gender emerges as a contaminant of selection decisions both in terms of the sex of those involved and also the perceived sex role of the job (Arvey, 1979). Research has suggested that for many jobs there is clear evidence of unfair discrimination against women, who have been found to receive lower evaluations than men regardless of their similar, or identical, qualifications when applying for 'masculine' roles. Forsyth *et al.* (1985) found that female applicants for such roles could boost their evaluations by wearing more masculine clothes, such as suits. The impact of clothes is limited by the gender-context stereotype of the role, so wearing a masculine-style suit for a 'feminine' occupation would not help. Context stereotyping varies with the type of job (Van Vianen and Willemsen, 1992). For example, consider how a female plumber is received, or in the past a woman chef. A good example of spurious stereotyping emerges when examining more closely the case of the Vienna Philharmonic Orchestra, which has recently employed its first female musician. In the past, it was argued women were not employed as they would distract their male colleagues and, more importantly, did not have the physical strength required in their playing. This latter point is somewhat questionable given that this orchestra is world renowned for its lightness and what could be seen as a 'feminine' tone.

Several explanations have been proposed as to why such errors and biases are made, with much attention paid to the process of data evaluation and judgements by interviewers. First, interviewers have been found to make different attributional judgements about candidates. An attribution is a sense-making cognitive process that is used to explain or justify the past actions of ourselves or others. Miller and Ross (1975) found that success becomes attributed to dispositional causes (a person's own personality and character), while negative outcomes are externally attributed to the situation or circumstances. There is clear evidence that shows that sex differences play a role in the type of attributions candidates make. Both male candidates and interviewers attribute successful performance to internal stable attributes, such as intelligence and ability, whilst women regard similar performance as the result of external and unstable attributes, such as luck or 'being in the right place at the right time'. This shows that even with a structured interview process the analysis of the collected data can become distorted.

Research has revealed that contamination emerges during the assessment and rating of information, with assessors tending to rate information concerning aspects of their own behaviour more positively. This is termed 'similar to me' effect. Evidence indicates that interviewers enhance the rating of those who look like themselves, respond in a similar way, or appear to have had equivalent experiences. Through this process, assessors are not actually assessing the candidate, but instead validating themselves and their own decision-making, and as a result they fail to analyse the applicant's behaviour against the agreed criteria. In subsequent studies, research has suggested there may be a further gender factor to this distortion, with female recruiters perceiving female applicants as more similar to themselves, whilst male recruiters did not appear to be prone to the same-sex bias (Herriot, 1989).

A number of similar errors which distort assessors' judgements have been found. Two are particularly common: the '**halo effect**', which emerges when one aspect of the candidate's qualities – most commonly physical attractiveness – influences all other aspects and thereby boosts their entire assessment. Likewise, the '**horns effect**' reduces a candidate's ratings due to over-attention to some negative aspect. It appears that physical characteristics of candidates can play a role in their success in gaining a job, with, for example, 'ugly' but capable applicants being marked down. Indeed, some work suggests a gender link, with attractive female applicants receiving lower ratings for managerial jobs than clerical ones (Heilman and Saruwatari, 1979). Studies suggest that a key horn effect is candidate's weight. Pingitore et al. (1994) conducted a study using candidates who were average weight and those who were at least 20 per cent above average. They found their student raters were biased against overweight applicants, particularly those who were female. Kleges et al. (1989) also explored this bias and revealed the negative attributions this group of raters made of overweight applicants. They were seen as having lower qualifications, poorer work habits, higher absence rates, reduced self-control, and not being able to get along with others.

Physical disabilities also can have an impact on the assessment made about applicants, even by experienced interviewers, as Christmas and Branson (1990) demonstrated by contrasting the higher assessments made for able-bodied people when compared to wheelchair or crutches users.

A further source of error lies in the way evidence is weighted, with studies showing that positive information is regarded as superior to negative data; preference is given to positive confirmatory information, whilst negative information is regarded as more damaging and appears to take more time to process than confirmatory data (Wason, 1966). Once a negative impression has been made, it takes on average 8.8 pieces of positive data to reverse it in comparison to 3.8 required to change positive perceptions to negative (Bolster and Sprinbett, 1961). However, this is only part of the picture. It appears that negative data may be discounted if it is in an area that is not seen as critical to the job (Hakel *et al.*, 1970), or if it does not emerge at the start of the interview (Peters and Terbury, 1975). Thus, the issue of data-weighting emerges as more complex than initially thought.

Seemingly trivial aspects such as the ordering of candidates can cause errors by distorting the attention of interviewers. Those who are seen first and last are more readily remembered. These are termed 'primacy' and 'recency' effects. As a result, candidates who are seen at some point in the middle of a series of interview sessions can be more easily forgotten. In a similar way, 'contrast errors' can occur when the assessor makes a comparison between the current candidate and the one seen earlier, instead of against the specific selection criteria. Research has shown that as a result average candidates can be adversely rated particularly if they follow an applicant who was superior to them. Conversely, ratings can be boosted if they follow a poor applicant (Anderson and Shackleton, 1993).

A common problem for interviewers arises when they try and make their decisions too quickly by giving an inappropriate weight to first impressions, which emerge as difficult to disconfirm and change. This problem is created when interviewers try to read too much into the candidate's behaviour. This is termed 'temporal extension' and occurs where an interviewer incorrectly draws conclusions about the candidate's affective state based on their interview behaviour (Anderson and Shackleton, 1993). For example, if a candidate is very nervous, they can be perceived as being over-emotional, or highly strung. Through this error, the interviewer extrapolates a more broad-ranging mood/emotion state, or a more long-term dispositional personality trait of the candidate based on a very small sample of behaviour.

Finally, errors are found where interviewers are simply given too many criteria to attend to. As a result of this cognitive overload, recruiters may condense or cluster criteria together. (I shall consider this issue of criteria overload in more detail in Chapter 9.) This problem may underlie claims that only generic social competence can be effectively measured through this interview process (Huffcutt *et al.*, 2001).

# 4   Subjectivist social-interactionist perspective

The subjectivist social-interactionist perspective contrasts with the objectivist psychometric position because it regards the interview as a two-way process in which the actions of each party inform and shape the actions of the other. It does not regard this process as necessarily objective, and instead focuses on the processes of subjectivity. From this perspective, attention shifts towards understanding the very processes of the interview, which emerges as an ongoing exchange, informed and transformed by those involved. This illuminates the role of all of those involved. In this perspective, however, the role of the interviewee *per se* may also change. The function of the interview emerges as not concerned with the verbal delivery of a test to gather data from one party and to assess it against some specific criteria. Instead, the interview process becomes an important preview for both the organization and the applicant (Herriot, 1989).

Rousseau (2001) highlights the importance of the formation of the psychological contract in shaping future expectations of both parties about their employment relationship. This tool is a key part in the development of such understandings. It therefore raises an important question about who should be involved: any member of the organization or the direct supervisor? The social-interactionist perspective is critical to our understanding of the impact of the interview, as it illuminates issues of power, processes and perception formation, which will now be discussed.

## 4.1  Redressing the power balance

Typically, the interview is the first time the interviewer has met the applicant. It is perhaps more importantly the first time that the applicant has met a representative of the organization. This point is often forgotten by recruiters who through their words and actions in the interview process are presenting an image of the organization in terms of its standards, values, expectations, ambitions and goals. The interview is therefore a public information exercise providing candidates with valuable data that will assist them in deciding whether to accept the job or not if offered it. It is vital to see the two-way role the interview plays in decision-making for both parties: both use it to gain first-hand information about each other. This is potentially why, despite its limited predictive validity, the interview continues to dominate the selection process: each wants to meet the other in person.

## 4.2  The interview as a process

The subjectivist social-interactionist approach considers the interview to be a social process. Interest has focused on trying to examine the different processes that candidates experience as a means of examining the fairness of the decisions recruiters reach. Studies that have examined the interview process have found that interviewers vary in their communication competence, in their following-up of topics, their rapport-building and their adherence to the formal structures imposed upon them.

Jablin *et al.* (1984, 1999) have lamented the dearth of attention paid to the interaction processes that characterize highly structured versus moderately structured interviews. They found that the experiences of those who were not successful were very different from those who were. In examining the interaction that occurred in detail through video and audio tapes they showed that, paradoxically, successful candidates spent less time in the interview responding to the questions asked of them and more time talking outside of the pre-set questions. If recruitment decisions are in fact being based on extraneous information rather than criteria-related data, then the notion of an objective process may be flawed.

Those exploring the type of interaction have found differences in the patterns of successful versus unsuccessful candidates in terms of interruption rates and question-and-answer response latency (the gap between responses and the next question) (McComb and Jablin, 1984). In following up on the interaction sequence, Axtmann and Jablin (1986) identified that successful candidates experienced fewer interrogative interaction sequences, and more conversational sequences. In this way, the experiences of applicants vary significantly.

Studies of the interaction have focused on different points, but a key to the creation of these sequences is the initial openings, with evidence revealing the impact of the first four to seven minutes in determining the subsequent sequence (Springbett, 1958). This opening section emerges as important for shaping the power dynamics of the interaction created through the use of opening statements which serve to either reinforce, or minimize, status differences between the candidates and the interviewer (Cheepan, 1988). It also emerged as creating the format for the rest of the process, with interviewers who had a more positive initial impression asking fewer closed or probing questions (Dougherty *et al.*, 1994). Some have gone further to discuss how 'scripts' emerge to govern the interaction between the two parties (Eder and Harris, 1999).

The processes experienced by successful applicants were characterized as more balanced in terms of 'push–pull' behaviours, with turn-taking, whereas unsuccessful candidates were more likely to show extreme push or pull behaviours (Engler-Parish and Millan, 1989). This idea of a reciprocating interaction pattern is important, with Tullar (1989), for instance, indicating how, in successful candidate exchanges, dominance from one party is followed by submission from the other. In contrast, a clash of styles was evident for those who had a less positive outcome; here, dominance in one party's behaviour was matched by the other. In a laboratory-based study, Liden *et al.* (1993) focused more on the type of nonverbal behaviour that characterized these dominance clashes. They identified that a hostile environment was characterized by lack of eye contact between the parties, leaning away from the other party, limited smiling and failing to face each other.

A recent review identified the role gender and 'race' might play in setting up such interaction patterns (Prewett-Livingstone and Field, 1999). Although traditional statistics reveal insignificant effects, qualitative analysis paints a very different picture. In studies exploring interview processes involving candidates from minority ethnic groups, the aforementioned clashing of dominance behaviour was a more common experience in interactions involving a minority group and female interviewers (Kacmar and Hockwanter, 1995). 'Race' differences appear to be important in terms of limiting the quantity of information, with research indicating that Black interviewers gained more responses from Black applicants than their White counterparts (Ledvinka, 1971). These studies point to the complexities underlying the formation of passive, or active, roles during the interview process and how far initial stages can influence the subsequent interview experience.

## 4.3  Attributions and process

The subjectivist social-interactionist perspective has also examined the transfer of symbolic information during the interview process. Cahn (1976) proposed the self-validation model as a means of showing how perception formation occurs. This model suggests that two important processes are at work. The first, 'self-concept formation', shapes how the individual perceives themselves in relation to the external world of objects, places and others, while the second, 'meta-self-concept' formation, is concerned with how we think others see us. Through this model, it is easy to see how misunderstandings can be created.

In-depth explorations of the type of attributions interviewers and candidates make has been conducted by Silvester (1997, 2002). She has revealed the different attributional explanations that arise in the interview and how these affect the final ratings candidates receive. In her research, she found that those who made internal-controllable explanations for events, for example responses such as 'I did not do well in the exam as I did not prepare properly', conveyed a more positive impression than those who used internal-uncontrollable attributions (being ill), or external-uncontrollable attributions (poor exam supervision). This work is important as it shows how both candidates and interviewers shape their understandings of the world. It also suggests a personality dimension underlying the type of attributions individuals make.

Further work on the process by which such misunderstandings are created has revealed the importance of the candidate's perceptions of *tacit* interview rules. Research suggests that applicants have implicit assumptions of how an interview should work (Shaw, 1983). Early misunderstandings can emerge where interviewers are not perceived to have paid due attention and interest to the candidate's qualifications. As a result of this perceived violation, candidates often respond by withdrawing from the process, becoming more reserved and reticent in their responses to questions. This study also revealed the pressure applicants felt to avoid pauses during the interview process. Paradoxically, through these tacit assumptions about the interview's negative perceptions of silences, candidates failed to give themselves sufficient time to consider their answers. More interestingly, based on an analysis of the content of this spontaneous fill-in talk, applicants were revealed as spending less time talking about themselves.

## 4.4 Illuminating the applicant in the interview

The subjectivist social-interactionist perspective focuses on the applicant as much as the assessor in shaping the interview process. Recent evidence challenges the concept of the applicant as passive, instead showing the applicant as a proactive seeker of information during the interview (Parson *et al.*, 1999).

The 'similar to me' effect has been shown to be equally important in the candidate's decision-making, with Graves and Powel (1995) indicating how candidate's expectations were affected by how much they were attracted to, or liked, their assessor. This was revealed as a cause of potential problems later when the interview experience was found to have shaped expectations concerning the quality of the relationship they expected with their supervisor.

Other research focused on the applicant has suggested an important dynamic between the two parties with different behaviour emerging as important during distinct stages of the interview interaction (Berkson *et al.*, 1999). Studies examining the effectiveness of organizational perception influence have shown that more experienced applicants are less susceptible to an organization's attempts at positive influence (Barber, 1998).

The interview process can have a significant impact on the fairness perceptions of the applicants. Gilliland (1993) revealed how fairness was reduced if candidates perceived that the interviewer had not treated them well at an interpersonal level, given them limited opportunity for a two-way dialogue and failed to provide an opportunity to perform well. Similarly, researchers looking at the quantity of conversation found that applicants developed negative perceptions of their interviewers if the interviewer talked more than they did themselves (Fletcher, 1981). In contrast, their interviewers perceived these exchanges as more positive experiences. This boost to the candidate's ratings may indicate an affirmative assessment by the interviewer of their own, and not the candidate's, skills.

## 4.5 The role of context

The context of the interview may also shape the assessment more than initially expected, but this research theme has received limited attention from work/organizational psychologists. In his review, Eder (1999) identified how the process is affected by the interviewer's perceptions of the clarity of the task and their role. For example, those who are given more complete job information were found to have higher interrater reliabilities (Langdale and Weitz, 1973). Their engagement in the role was improved if they perceived their task to have consequences and that they were accountable. This links into the issue of assessor training which will be raised in section 5.2.1. Dipboye (1994) clearly showed how political forces were involved in shaping the interview process. The decision who to involve as an interviewer, which jobs to recruit for and who to select can all be seen in a political light.

## 4.6 Impression management (IM)

The selection process is a high-stakes one for the candidate and one where the candidate is likely to be highly motivated to impress the assessors. As a result, attention has turned in recent studies to look at the issue of impression management (IM), particularly during the interview. Two different perspectives have been suggested. In the first, 'symbolic interactionist' view, IM is regarded as a conscious behaviour, and so the question of deliberate distortion emerges, whilst the 'adaptive interpretivist' approach argues that such behaviour may not necessarily be either conscious or deliberate. This creates an interesting quandary and highlights the issue of self-insight. This second view is more sympathetic to Goffman's (1959) view that all behaviour may have IM value and that the audience may include the self, as well as others. Recent evidence does suggest individual differences regarding the propensity to use this type of behaviour (Gilmore *et al.*, 1999).

It is clear that the interview, as in any selection process, includes the presence of an evaluating external audience. Given the high-task forced behaviour and the normative ritualized processes that dominate, there is an increased likelihood of IM. In researching the typical forms of IM, Jones and Pittman (1982) revealed three distinct facets. Ingratiating behaviour, such as agreeing with the other's opinion, faltering and complementing them, or offering to do them a favour were common where candidates were trying to enhance their likeability. In contrast, when a candidate was trying to boost their competency ratings, self-promotion was more evident. Finally, where attempts were being made to show fearlessness, displays of anger and intimidation emerged. Thus, the normative ritualized patterns of how to influence become illuminated. It could be argued that this research reduces the influencing process to a somewhat simplistic and crude number of behaviours.

Other research suggests that individual difference factors, such as gender and age, affect candidates' propensities to manage their self-presentation. Fletcher and Spencer (1984) found that female applicants showed more openness, whilst older and more experienced candidates maintained more eye contact, projected a more positive image and asked more questions (Fletcher, 1990). The behaviours can boost candidate's evaluations compared to those obtained from reading and rating CVs (Gilmore and Ferris, 1989). Other styles of IM behaviour also varied with age: older candidates were shown to reduce the number of **entitlement statements** they used, and increase their use of self-enhancement and self-promotion statements (Delery and Kacmar, 1995). Of all these behaviours, self-promotion has been found to have the most enhancing impact (Kacmar *et al.*, 1992).

Studies have shown that job context can mediate IM behaviour. Those jobs with more role ambiguity have been found to raise IM activity (Ferris and Jones, 1991), whereas aggression was more commonly found in candidates pursuing supervision roles than editorial roles (Dipboye and Wiley, 1978). The success of these strategies may vary, with Gilmore *et al.* (1999) suggesting a better outcome for those who display dominant rather than non-competitive behaviours.

IM behaviour is also used by interviewers and can have a critical impact on candidates' decisions to accept a job offer. In their study, Stevens *et al.*

(1990) found that interviewers who used self-enhancing statements received lower ratings from candidates and reduced the likelihood of encouraging them to accept any job offer.

A word of warning emerges from Baron (1989), however, whose study examined the impact of three different image-enhancing tactics – professional dress, friendly non-verbal behaviour and scent. He found that 'too much of a good thing' could backfire and argues that it is better to use these tactics separately rather than all at once.

Anderson and Shackleton (1993) present a useful model that shows various social and cognitive factors and the combination of initial expectation, interview process and perception formation that shapes the interviewer decision-making. It suggests a range of different influences, but does not include the interviewer as a factor in the candidate's behaviour. I have modified their original model to try and incorporate more of the dynamic interaction between candidate and interviewer.

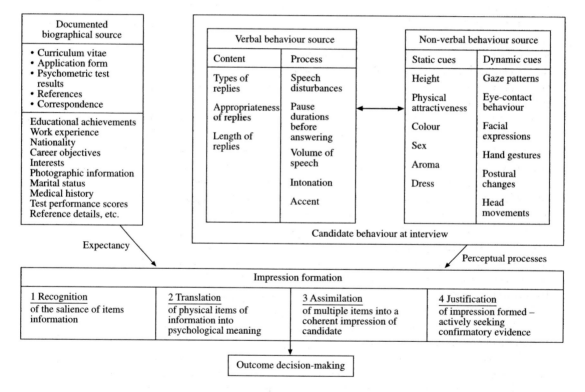

Figure 5.4   Factors shaping interview decision-making

(Anderson and Shackleton, 1993)

# 5 New developments

In turning our attention towards new developments, two distinct aspects emerge. The first involves research that examines the applications of novel media, such as the telephone, or video link for conducting interviews. The second assesses the impact of training, particularly the emergence of applicant-training programmes.

## 5.1 Media

Increasingly, the media used for conducting an interview is changing. Developments in technology and the rise of global market-places for applications have resulted in more use being made of different media – such as the telephone, or video link – as a partial or sole means of conducting an interview. Both technologies offer advantages by reducing the cost and time of travel for both applicants and organizations. Furthermore, new media can increase the diversity of organizational membership by expanding the geographical area from which potential candidates are drawn (Kandola and Fullerton, 1994). For some jobs, a second face-to-face interview follows an initial telephone-interview screening (Silvester et al., 2000, 2002). There has, however, been very little work assessing the equivalence of telephone and face-to-face modes of interviewing (Schmidt and Rader, 1999).

Silvester et al. (2000), in their study of the selection of applicants to an oil company, explored this issue of equivalence in more detail. They identified that the mode of an interview did affect the ratings interviewees received. In telephone interviews, assessors focused more on the verbal content of the replies, for which candidates received lower ratings. On the other hand, the ratings of face-to-face interviews rose because aspects such as non-verbal communication could be assessed. They found that candidates who were interviewed first by telephone and then face-to-face improved their ratings compared to those who were interviewed face-to-face first. In contrast, Chapman and Rowe (2001) found a bias towards those interviewed by video when compared to candidates assessed in a traditional face-to-face format.

Whilst the telephone reduces attention to the candidate's physical attractiveness, it makes some important changes to the nature of the interaction (Schmidt and Rader, 1999). Telephone interviews can produce a psychological distance between the interviewer and the candidate (Anderson et al., 1999). Because of cue deprivation, the absence of non-verbal behaviour can create and exacerbate misinterpretations and misunderstandings of both questions and responses. In addition, the candidate is disadvantaged by not being given the opportunity to preview face-to-face the organization and its members. While this may be unimportant in an initial screening process, it may affect negatively candidates' final decisions concerning joining an organization they have never actually met. More research is required to examine how far video-phone will alleviate these concerns.

Another key issue regarding the more widespread application of new media is how to control cheating. In meeting the candidate face-to-face, a memory or a more formal record (even a photograph) is often made. In a telephone interview, the opportunity for substitution is far greater. Schmidt and Rader (1999) argue that the type of detailed responses required from a well-structured interview would make it very difficult for a deception to occur. Nonetheless, this overlooks the potential gains of such faking for individuals who might benefit greatly from new roles. In high-stakes jobs the benefits may outweigh the dangers of being caught. There may be some cultural differences in the acceptability of more nefarious behaviour, but more work needs to be directed into examining the equivalence of using technology in the interview.

A final concern arises regarding the differential adoption rates of new media. There appears to be differences in the type of organizations that are using these approaches, with telecommunications and large blue-chip firms leading the way (Chapman and Rowe, 2001). More attention needs to be given to how far these approaches offer more rigorous processes, or merely replicate previous discriminatory practices (Searle, 2003).

## 5.2 Interview training

Recent research has explored the impact of interview-skills training on the interview process – both for the interviewer and the interviewee. We will look first at the evidence supporting its impact on the skills of interviewers.

### 5.2.1 Interviewer training

It should be noted from the outset that there has been very little research on the issue of interviewer selection. Allport (1937) identified six key attributes of good interviewers. They should have a breadth of experience, and come from diverse backgrounds. They should be of above-average intelligence and have some self-insight and understanding into others. It is also important that they are emotionally stable, well-adjusted individuals who have good social skills. Further, a degree of detachment is necessary. Finally, he argued that assessments are most accurate if the candidate is similar to the interviewer, and it is important to choose assessors who have some expertise in a role.

Training programmes may be the first opportunity staff have to learn effective listening (clearly an important social skill for any interviewer) and can offer an insight into a complex array of interpersonal skills. An important part of training revolves around the selection criteria and how the interview fits into the overall recruitment process. The purpose of training is to develop skills of assessment so that the interviewer is able to effectively and accurately use the identified selection criteria. Through this process, they become more aware of the job requirements and the precise organizational characteristics, such as citizenship behaviour, which may have been identified as important for the job. The aim of such training is to ensure a standardized approach is taken between different assessors for the same job. Assessors also learn how to use the structured interview questions as a selection tool, in order to gather information about the criteria that have been identified, and to avoid irrelevant issues.

An important part of any training is developing objective rating skills. During any training, interviewers learn with the other assessors how to assess the data they have collected, systematically rating information using the criteria. This plays an important role in increasing their accountability and knowledge of the role, which was earlier shown as important in improving the assessor ratings.

A key issue indicated in the preceding section was fairness. Awareness of the need for equal opportunity plays a role in any training programme, revealing the underlying prejudices and stereotypes that an assessor may hold and how changes to the standard process can creep in. Few can dispute the need for such training and this is evident when reviewing the popularity of such training within organizations. However, there has been limited attention on the impact of this training in raising the quality of the interview. Some evidence indicates that interview judgements improve following intensive training, including training in job-related questions, rating scales and interview practice (Dougherty *et al.*, 1986), but many other results have been ambiguous. Palmer *et al.* (1999) lament the lack of attention paid to studies that have evaluated the changes in interviewer behaviour following training in rapport-building and other issues focused on the assessor's role in shaping the process.

### 5.2.2  Applicant training

Although candidates are increasingly receiving training, there is a similar lack of evaluation about its effects; there is also some debate concerning its impact. A recent study of a coaching session for promotion applicants in fire and police service jobs identified a number of benefits (Maurer *et al.*, 2001). The study suggested that voluntary attendance at such sessions was positively related to interview success, and that this type of training gives candidates important insights into preparation, presentation and persistence. Training courses can also emphasize to candidates the importance of researching the organization to which they have applied. They also provide a chance for reflection, giving the candidate the opportunity to consider how they might present their experiences in answering questions.

Training for interviewees also gives an insight into the candidate's presentation at interview. Through mock interviews, there is an opportunity for rehearsal and feedback on their performance. This will often be the first time candidates have been given information about their non-verbal behaviour, in particular how they show and cope with their anxiety. They may also be coached in how to answer difficult questions, and also which questions from an equal opportunity perspective they should *not* be asked. Maurer *et al.* (2001) found that as a result of such training candidates provided more organized answers to questions.

Finally, training can offer candidates information about their motivation for the role and encourage them to gain feedback about their actual performance and how they could improve. These courses may also help candidates to manage the impression they give, for example by giving them information about dress and image codes of their preferred organization. For example, a man could find out about an organization's views on beards, or a woman its views on trouser suits. (One US-based IT firm frowns on both.) Nonetheless, there has been little research on how far such training increases the candidates' impression management behaviour.

# 6   Summary

Evidence suggests that the interview can become a robust tool – provided it is based on a valid job description and involves structured questions based on candidates' actual past behaviour. This is the tool that fits both the organizations' and the candidate's expectations. It can offer a means of assessing social skills, cognitive ability and establishing a candidate's organizational fit. However, the interview is a two-way process in which the candidate is evaluating the type of organization, its goals and culture. Increasingly, work looking at the processes of social interaction involved in the interview is challenging the view of the interview as a fair and standardized process. This casts doubt on the claims of its objectivist psychometric properties. The shift of attention towards the interviewer as a dynamic player in the process and the candidate as an active and involved part of the interview is significant as it can begin to enhance our understanding of this complex undertaking. Reducing it to a verbally-administered assessment system belittles the multifaceted streams of activity and re-activity that are occurring.

Although it clearly has an important role to play, I feel we must also look again at the interview process if we are to ensure that new media will not compound discrimination. It is evident that although much research has been undertaken in this field, it has illuminated a very narrow range of issues and reduced the complexity of the process of the interview. Limited attention has been paid by work and organizational psychologists to using alternative approaches to analysing this selection tool. The dominance of positivist approaches does not necessarily increase our understanding of the complex dynamic that is created by this process. Finally, the studies reported here suggest some good practice, but I wonder how far they reflect what is occurring in organizations, who frequently rely on 'likeability' as their overarching selection criterion.

---

## *Exercise*

Computers and decision support – what products are on the market to assist you in interviewing? How do they work? Outline the advantages and disadvantages of them.

Develop an interview schedule for a job that you know well. Devise both hypothetical and actual behaviour questions and use them in a mock interview. Compare and contrast your findings on the benefits and drawbacks of each.

In the light of research evidence, consider what role, if any, the interview has in selection.

---

# CHAPTER 6

# Selection tools 3: psychometric testing

## 1 Overview

Psychometric tests play an important role in selection practice: 70 per cent of firms use them (Shackleton and Newell, 1991). They offer organizations a means of discriminating between large numbers of applicants in a rapid and often cost-effective manner. Moreover, their power in predicting successful subsequent job performance is – especially for cognitive tests – amongst the highest of any selection tool (Robertson and Smith, 2001). Through the growth of instruments such as organizational-fit questionnaires, different attitudinal and trait assessment measures and novel ability tools, the range of psychometric tools available to organizations is increasing.

In Chapter 6, I explore the history behind the development of individual difference assessment in order to reveal the tacit assumptions that underlie the creation, interpretation and application of such instruments. As you will see, this raises important questions about the role of these assessment tools in selection and recruitment decision-making. Although at least half of the variation in job and human performance cannot be accounted for by psychometrics, it could be argued that their validity as a selection method is assured – provided strict guidelines are adhered to. I explore beyond the guidelines to assess how these tools can best be used.

I review the role of psychometrics in selection and examine different approaches to psychometric test construction. A distinction is made between tests of typical and maximal performance and I discuss their different roles in organizations. The emphasis within a selection context tends to focus on maximal performance, but assessment of typical performance is also important. I also examine classical and new approaches to developing these measures.

I discuss the concept of error for these different approaches and look at how test results can be interpreted in a meaningful way. The different factors that affect test performance are raised, including the impact of new media, time deadlines and experience levels. Challenges to this psychometric approach to assessment are raised – notably concerning their stability, inherent biases and ethics. Throughout Chapter 6, the problems of creating a universal test are considered as well as the wider ethical issues concerning the application of these tools for selection and recruitment. In the final section I highlight a number of implicit assumptions that underpin psychometrics. I will return to the issue of psychometric testing in a more fundamental way later in Chapter 10.

The tools have also benefited from the advent of computer delivery systems. There are concerns, nonetheless, regarding the potential adverse discriminating impact of some tools – particularly for test-takers from minority ethnic groups; indeed, the advent of new technology may merely exacerbate this issue, as I shall reveal later.

## 2   Introduction

Although there is an increasing use of psychometric tools in HR selection and recruitment decision-making, the method is not uncontentious. For instance, in cultures that rely on these tools, there is an increasing disparity in the distribution of wealth (Fischer *et al.*, 1996) and there are concerns in the USA, for example, regarding the relationship between low psychometric scores and those who experience social sanctions, such as custodial sentences, or who receive welfare benefit (Herrnstein and Murray, 1994). Perhaps more importantly, ethnic group differences in intelligence test results reflect the ethnic divide that exists in the distribution of rewards and sanctions in our wider society (Gordon, 1997). This is becoming an increasingly explosive issue in many societies. Some argue that high intelligence quotient (IQ) scores are not important; rather, what is significant is the identification and means of assessing specific cognitive skills that are linked to job performance (Hunt, 1999). This latter group of more focused cognitive assessment tools can have a significant impact in organizations, revealing how close an applicant is to the requisite skills level and estimating how much training an applicant needs to reach an acceptable standard. This is important information as it indicates the cost implications behind each decision to hire.

A critical and often overlooked issue in the use of tests is the prevailing employment climate. Psychometric tests can provide an indication of the expected or potential performance of a workforce that has been selected on the basis of some criterion score. The test cut-off score represents the proportion of those accepted. Tests with a high cut-off have few successful applicants. Some suggest that the application of these tools is counter-cyclical to the prevailing employment climate: during a recession many more applicants apply for each vacancy and so these instruments come into their own. However, there are some jobs, such as management roles, which always attract a plethora of candidates. In these situations, psychometrics are a significant decision-making aid, helping to manage the high volume of applications. Test scores can also provide a useful insight into post-hire training costs, on-the-job experience requirements and for revealing who has the relevant aptitude and attitude for a *particular* role within a *particular* organization. Figure 6.1 indicates the potential relationship between test results, experience levels and category of score within a military context. These data cover a variety of military occupations. There are clearly different attenuation rates for these tests. (This attenuation issue for work-sample tests will be discussed in more detail in Chapter 9.)

Cognitive competence is an important element in workplace performance. Some argue in fact that it is the single most predictive factor (Robertson and Smith, 2001). However, studies still reveal that at least half of the variance in performance remains unexplained by test results alone (Schmidt and Hunter, 1999). More work is needed to enable us to understand the connection between cognitive skills and work performance. Organizational psychologists and HR professionals need to expand the current narrow focus of these assessment processes to include personal, motivational, social, situational and cultural variables in order to gain a

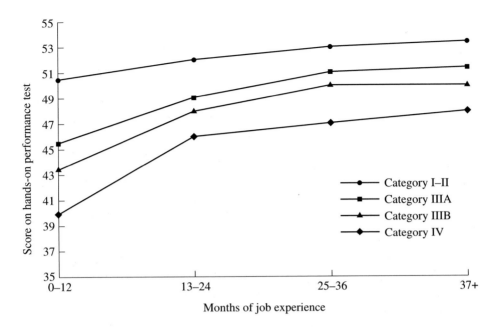

*Figure 6.1  Relationship between test scores and experience for the US armed services vocational aptitude battery*

(Hunt, 1999, p.22)

better understanding of the link between organizational performance and psychometric tests. It could be argued that without this new insight, discrimination and the disenfranchisement of complete groups within our society will be perpetuated. At a social level, the possibility of wealth creation is diminished for these groups. At an individual level, their mental health and well-being is affected as they continue to be de-selected.

## 3  Historical dimension

Humankind has always sought ways to identify and categorize the world around them. Around 500 BC Hippocrates created the first known tool to differentiate individuals based on their personality. He identified four temperament types, who were characterized in terms of their bodily fluids or excretions: sanguine, choleric, phlegmatic and melancholic. His typology had a widespread and enduring appeal (for example the Swedish Royal Ship, *Vasa*, which sank on her maiden voyage in 1663, was decorated with symbols of each).

The acknowledged initiator of psychometric ability testing was Darwin's cousin Francis Galton in the 1860s. However, we can find the earliest record of using ability assessment to distinguish between job applicants in China around 200 BC where it was used for selecting civil servants (duBois, 1970, 1972). Its application in Europe is recorded in Samuel Pepys' diaries during the 1600s: in his role as Clerk of the Acts of the King's ships, he tried to thwart the long-standing practice of purchasing offices by introducing ability assessment for the rank of lieutenant. He hoped that introducing this assessment would mean that rich and unmotivated

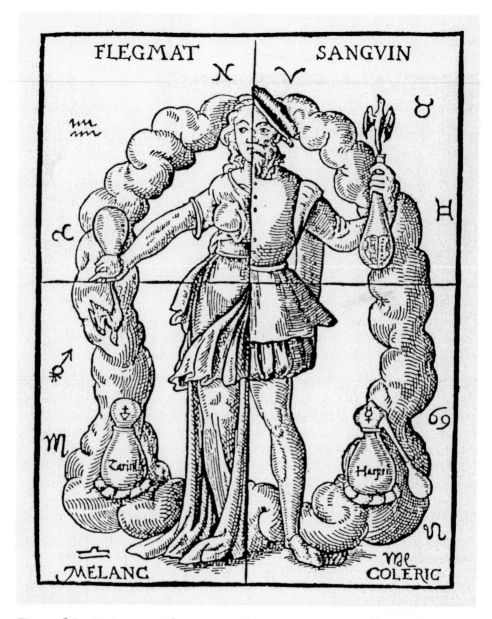

*Figure 6.2a Hippocrates' four personality types: sanguine, choleric, phlegmatic and melancholic*

applicants would fail. In 1832, the East Indian Company adopted new systems for selecting overseas staff; and the UK first civil servant selection assessment was introduced from 1855. More widespread interest in differentiating between individuals came to the fore in the late eighteenth and the early nineteenth centuries and resulted in the developments which inform much of today's practice.

The capacity to identify individual differences in any systematic manner was developed by medical doctors, the Frenchmen Esuirol (1838) and

Seguin (1866), who were looking after the insane. They developed phrenology and other physiologically based systems as a means of distinguishing those who deviated from the rest of society.

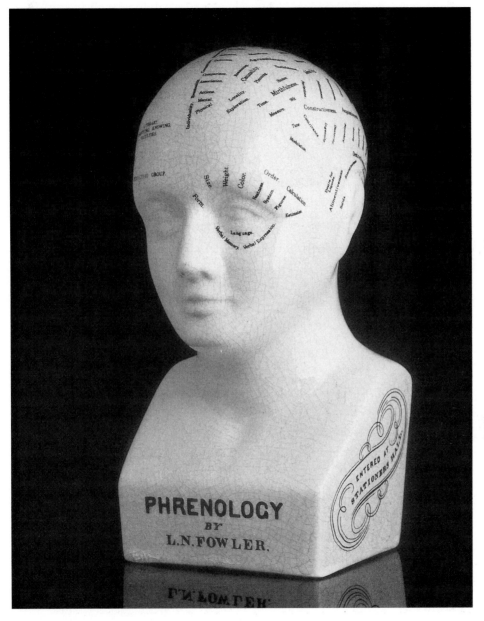

*Figure 6.2b Example of a phrenology head*

Esuirol and Seguin worked with groups that included the insane, the criminal and the feeble-minded (Rose, 1989) and claimed to have developed taxonomies for criminal anthropology and phrenology that enabled the trained eye to identify those who would put society at risk. Thus, they argued that 'deviants' could be recognized by facial and other physical attributes.

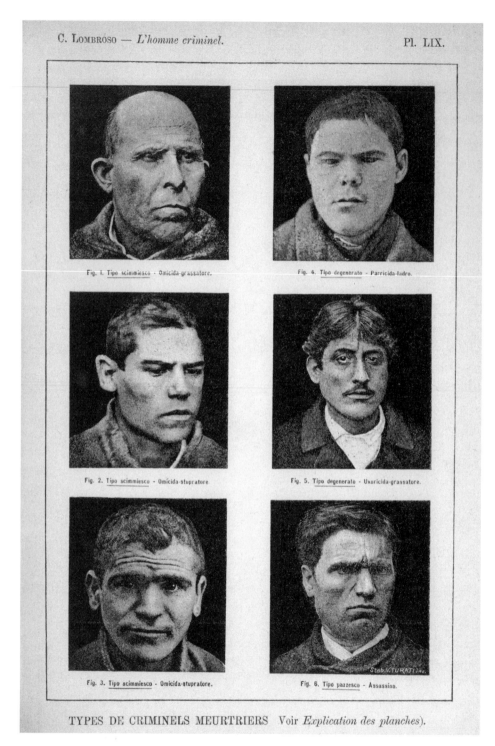

*Figure 6.2c Early photography of criminals used by Lombroso to develop this diagnostic system*

The impact of these new techniques was limited, not because of obvious internal inconsistency or theoretical problems, but more simply because they could not match the level of demand placed on them (Rose, 1989). This demand arose from the increasing regulation and bureaucratization of society created by burgeoning new penal, industrial, educational and military systems. Alongside these increased demands for categorization and the identification of human differences, the eugenics movement emerged. This was founded on the belief that the feeble-mindedness was hereditary and would cause the degeneration and deterioration of society unless it was controlled. Of course, there had to be authoritative techniques for identifying such people and psychometrics appeared to be the answer – endowed as it appeared to be with the authority of science.

The solution to this pressing need to assess individual differences emerged through two concurrent developments. The first, in the fields of biology and psychology, was Francis Galton's (1869) work on the role of heredity in intelligence. The second was the development and application of new mathematical and statistical procedures, such as the normal distribution curve and factor analysis, notably Fisher's (1925) difference testing and the introduction of the **null hypothesis**. These new techniques greatly facilitated the emergence of a new field that came to be called 'individual differences'. Given that statistical techniques allowed large numbers of individuals to be measured, and given that people were categorized into groups as a result, 'group differences' may have been more appropriate.

The new science of individual differences was used to further the eugenicists' aspirations. All of the early developers – Galton, Cattell, Pearson and Spearman – explored individuals' social worth by linking genetic heredity to variable mental characteristics and behaviours. As a result, mental assessment was imbued with moral and social values. It is important to identify these issues as they reveal many of the tacit assumptions that underpin and guide current psychometric practice. I will discuss these implicit aspects in more detail later.

Early applications of mental testing were used as a means of separating and segregating people classed as 'inferior'. The first attempt to measure mental ability systematically in the UK was developed by Cattell in the late 1880s based on Galton's work. He devised a battery of mental tests and measurement to 'assist in training, mode of life or the indication of disease'. Concurrently in 1904 in Europe, the Frenchman Alfred Binet devised a test to identify feeble-minded schoolchildren to enable their removal from the mainstream education system into special schools (Wolf, 1973). This test for children was subsequently introduced into the USA by Goddard, and developed into the well-known and still used Stanford–Binet test.

These new techniques of intelligence testing quickly found application in Europe and America. In the USA, mental ability testing was adopted at Ellis Island in 1892 as part of an immigrant-assessment programme forming a much wider social-engineering project to build a new society by assisting the authorities to identify and reject 'enfeebled' immigrants. With hindsight, it is clear that its underlying purpose for the political elite, who comprised earlier northern and western European settlers, was to legitimize their rejection of immigrants from southern and eastern Europe. Terman (1916, p.22), in his introduction to the US manual of the Binet test, echoes these views. He sought to identify 'high-grade defectives' in order to place them under the 'surveillance and protection of society ... resulting in the curtailment of the reproduction of feeble-mindedness and in the elimination of enormous amounts of crime, pauperism and industrial inefficiency'. The fears of these elite groups are by no means new, or radical: such anxieties had underpinned the English Poor Laws since the 1530s. Terman and others saw a value to society in intelligence, claiming that bright children had 'no serious faults', that they were 'socially adaptable', 'leaders', sociable, and 'not withstanding their many superior qualities they are seldom vain or spoiled'.

Significant modifications were made in the USA to Binet's original work that altered his original conception of mental ability. First, US scholars mistranslated his central concept of 'mental level' as 'mental age'. In doing so they created a scientific means of benchmarking mental development. Second, Goddard devised a new set of pejorative terms as descriptions for specific test scores. These included 'idiot', 'moron' and 'imbecile' for those of lower IQ. Finally, a new claim emerged (conveniently for those in authority) that intelligence was inherited and therefore that mental scores were unchangeable. This view is still being debated today (Hunt, 1999) and finds new outlets through evolutionary psychology.

The application of ability testing within an occupational setting emerged from Taylor's (1911) scientific management approach to work, which focused on maximal performance. The first documented use of these systems was at the Western Electric Company (Rose, 1989, p.92), but it was the entry of the USA into the First World War in 1917 that heralded their mass application. Testing was used to match men to specific roles and functions (Hollway, 1991, p.55). Based on the success of this military programme, Scott set up the first selection-testing company, which was quickly followed by Cattell who founded the Psychological Corporation in 1921 (Rose, 1989, p.93). Psychologists were not alone in the field of selection; there was a parallel industry of phrenologists, palmists, graphologists and other 'character analysts'. The early use of tests was not particularly auspicious as they frequently fell short of industry's expectations. Their credibility was only improved when European immigrant Mayo arrived in the USA in 1922. He applied the tools in a steel mill and they had a spectacular impact on reducing labour turnover (Rose, 1989). In 1921, building on the strength of earlier psychometric work by Burt in the education field, the British government supported the foundation of the National Institute for Industrial Psychology (NIIP) and the application of these instruments increased for UK firms.

## 4   Individual differences?

At the heart of psychometrics lies the assumption that people differ from one another, for instance in terms of their friendliness, their ability to use mathematical concepts, or their drive and determination to succeed, and that these differences *can be measured*. It is assumed when measuring these different aspects that they relate to actual behaviour – that is, they relate an external event (a behaviour) to an internal cause (the trait). A definition offered for a psychometric test is 'an objective and standardized measure of a sample of behaviour' (Anastasi, 1990, p.23). From this perspective, an individual who reports themselves, for example, as having high 'friendliness' could, it is assumed, be seen chatting with newcomers and mixing with other people in most social situations. These traits are inferred generalizations that rely on personal insight. Traits are assumed to have a quantitative structure so that they can be quantified and measured and allow individuals to be compared more easily. As with any quantification process, there is an assumed stability to the measure, and so it is accepted that a person who has this high 'friendliness' trait does not only engage with others just on Wednesdays and Saturdays, but most of the time.

Psychometrics tests aim to quantify three key aspects of individual differences: ability, personality and motivation. In the forthcoming chapters I will look in more detail at the development of different models and measurement tools for ability and personality and related work, and suggest a relationship between these two and motivation. In Chapter 6, my focus is the process of developing psychometric tools. It will become clear in Chapters 7 and 8 that there is some debate about the notion of a quantitative structure underlying these traits. Kline (1998, p.42) raises concerns that 'no evidence is usually presented' for this underlying quantitative structure. A continuum is devised that imposes a scale ranging from less to more with numerical values assigned on an arguably arbitrary basis. Failure to examine the quantitative nature of these variables is seen by some as a central issue in differentiating psychology from all other natural sciences and weakens its claim to be a science (Michell, 1997). Although these wider philosophical concerns exist, I will focus on the problems that arise from the attempts to develop and apply such measurement tools. [However, if you are interested in looking at this debate in more detail you might find Kline (1998) interesting.]

## 5   Occupational testing

Occupational tests are measurement tools used in the world of work. They can be applied to other settings also, but in Chapter 6 the focus will be on their applications in this context. Many attempts have been made to define precisely what such tests should measure. Occupational tests involve looking at a standard sample of behaviour that can be expressed as either a numerical scale or a category system (Cronbach, 1984). Test items are chosen specifically for their relevance to the domain of interest; for example, a percentage computation, or word recognition. There is also an effort to standardize the *delivery* of the tools: the aim of standardizing in this way is to ensure that candidates have the same test experience so that the only variable is their mental process. As part of this standardization process, the content of the initial instructions is fixed and, as in an examination, an attempt is made to control the candidate's local environment by minimizing noise and other potential distractions. Time parameters are also regulated and test administrators are given special training in how to score and interpret the results. In section 7, we shall look in more detail at these aspects. Tests used in an occupational context can be divided into two distinct groups: typical and maximal. These are based on the type of behaviour they are designed to measure (see Figure 6.3).

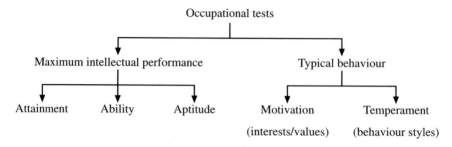

*Figure 6.3   Taxonomy of psychometric tests*

## 5.1 Typical behaviour tests

The purpose of **typical tests** is to identify the direction of a person's interests and suggest types of jobs associated with these areas (as in Figure 6.4). Personality and interest-assessment tests used in career guidance are examples of typical behaviour instruments. However, it should be noted that they do not measure the level of skill that might be associated with this vocational choice. So, while a test might show that a test-taker is interested in working with animals, it will not show whether they have the skills to be a veterinary surgeon or those skills required for a kennel worker.

| | |
|---|---|
| Working with people | Teaching, training, social work, hospitality industry |
| Working with data | Accountancy, financial services, administration, information analysis, systems analysts |
| Working with animals | Small animal care assistant, kennel maid/stable maid, veterinary surgeon, farmer, jockey |
| Being an entrepreneur | Starting new ventures, sales and marketing |

*Figure 6.4   Areas of work and occupation that an interest inventory might include*

   Typical behaviour tests are divided into two groups: motivation and temperament assessment and focus on 'typical' behaviour and on identifying how – most of the time – a person acts. Interests and values are seen as providing an insight into the volition underlying behaviour. So, while it is acknowledged that motivation is not behaviour *per se*, it is regarded as a precursor to behaviour.

## 5.2  Maximal performance tests

Maximal performance tests are designed to assess 'maximal' behaviour. These are not concerned with typical performance; rather, they aim to find out what is the *best* the test-taker can do (Cronbach, 1949; Fiske and Butler, 1963; Kline, 1998). Nonetheless, it has been argued that it is naïve to make such a simplistic distinction between maximal and typical performance, as it artificially separates the measurement of affect and intellect and their combined relationship to performance (Goff and Ackerman, 1992). Increasingly, researchers are identifying a relationship between ability, motivation and performance. I will return to this interrelationship in Chapter 7 when I examine different models of intelligence.

Measures concerned with maximal performance can be subdivided into three distinct types: attainment, aptitude and general intelligence ('***g***'). What becomes evident when we explore these subcategories is that a range of different applications and contexts emerge. (You will find a summary in Table 6.1.)

### 5.2.1   Attainment tests

All statutory examinations – GCSEs, A levels, university degrees, driving tests, National Vocational Qualifications (NVQs) and so on – are examples of **attainment tests** (or 'achievement tests' as they are sometimes called). These are tests designed to evaluate the performance level that has been achieved following a known, or controlled, set of experiences (Kaplan and Saccuzzo, 2001, p.343); they concentrate on measuring the current level that the test-taker has reached. They assess what has been learnt from this set period of experience or training. This might be a formal education experience, or an occupational training programme to learn a specific skill. Alternatively, they are used to ensure that a requisite standard has been reached. For example, electrical regulations tests ensure that electricians know the latest safety and technical practices. The successful award of these qualifications can be used to indicate current suitability for a particular job.

This type of testing is, however, not without its problems. There may be concerns about the validity and reliability of the test itself. One instance is the regular debate most summers in the UK regarding the standards of A-level awards. Two central concerns are their *breadth* and *durability*. For example, many consider that the standard UK driving test syllabus omits key areas, and so does not adequately reflect the whole domain of driving skill. It has been said that people only really learn to drive after passing the test and gaining experience of driving alone. Others claim that the test can only measure the individual's knowledge on that particular day and at that point in time. As a result, it could be argued that passing the test today does not necessarily mean the successful application of those skills in the future. These concerns focus on two aspects of validity: content, that is, the adequacy of what is included in the assessment, and predictive, that is, how someone will behave in the future (you will recall our discussion on these factors in Chapter 3).

### 5.2.2 Aptitude tests

**Aptitude tests** are designed to measure a person's ability level regardless of previous experience. There can be confusion regarding the distinction between 'aptitude' and 'ability': *ability* tests measure an individual's *current* skill level. An example might be a person's knowledge of, and ability to apply long division. *Aptitude* testing, on the other hand, assesses 'an individual's capacity of acquiring some skills, or ability' (Statt, 1981, p.9). Some researchers have argued that these measures are in fact measuring an underlying level of intelligence (Kline, 1993, p.201). Others argue that they reflect the underlying potential for learning (Kaplan and Saccuzzo, 2001). Reflecting this emphasis, these tools are sometimes termed 'trainability' tests.

What is important to note is that the focus is on measuring a criterion related to *future* performance. The tools are designed to differentiate between test-takers with widely varying sets of experiences (Kaplan and Saccuzzo, 2001, p.343). Their aim is to measure how well the person can adapt and learn a new skill. The developer of such instruments therefore needs to establish a relationship between the items that comprise the tool and a future performance level. It is important that they do not reflect current skills and experience but tap into an underlying potential – hence, the surmised relationship with intelligence.

Aptitude instruments are used to identify those who show more potential in a particular occupational area and so are often developed to focus on a specific performance domain. For example, technical aptitude might be useful for selecting engineers. Aptitude is important in occupations which require high numbers of applicants, such as financial services, or when long and expensive training is required – for instance, in accountancy.

Diagram

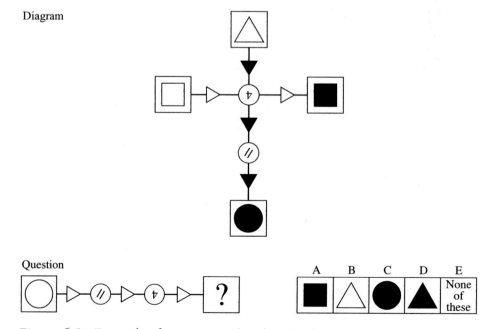

Question

*Figure 6.5   Example of a contextualized aptitude test*

Aptitude instruments can be divided into two distinct groups: those assessing more specific ability levels and those assessing a collection of traits, such as clerical or technical skills. Psychometrically, it is important to distinguish between the two. For instance, a test of verbal aptitude may comprise a primary factor, while a test of clerical aptitude comprises a collection of traits, such as verbal reasoning, clerical speed, spelling and grammar. The test battery may include items placed together for convenience, rather than based on an underlying rational (Kline, 1993, p.202). It is important when choosing a test to look at the development of the distinct parts and the context in which it was developed. Tests of this type have an appeal in a selection context due to their high face validity (see Chapter 3).

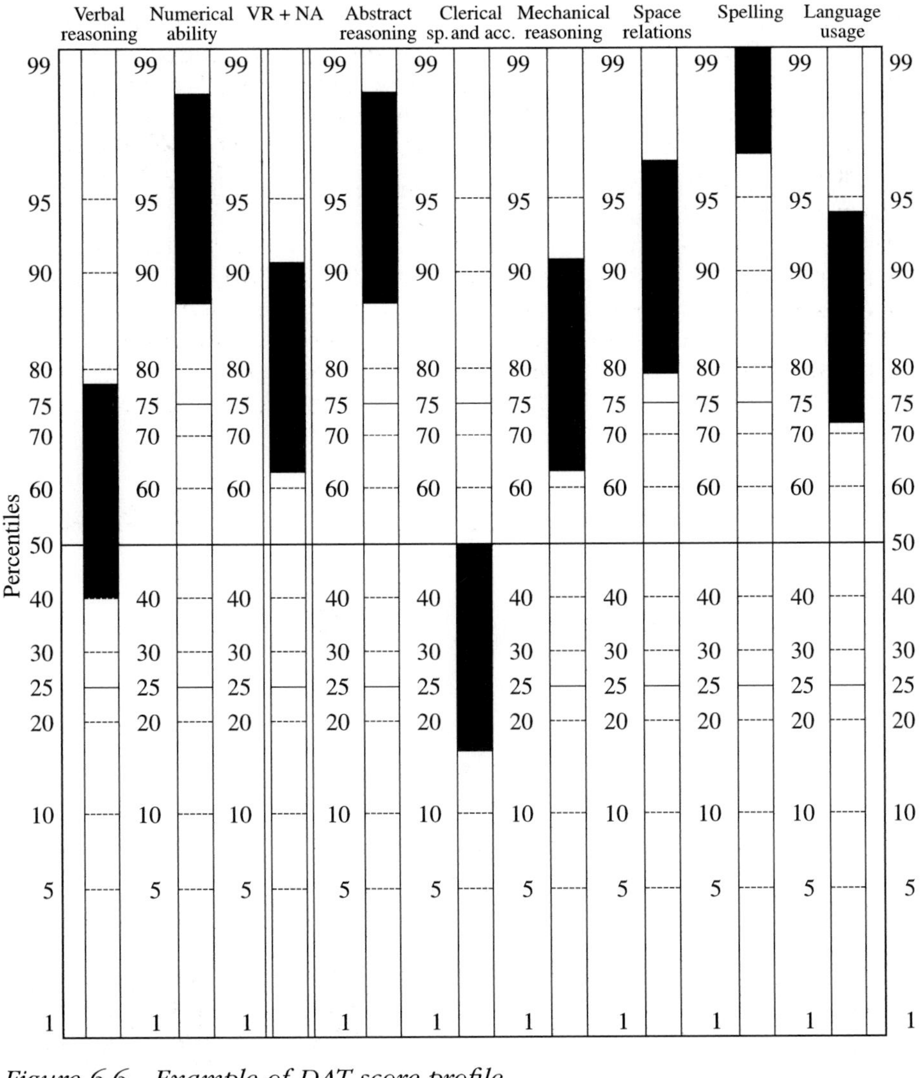

| Verbal reasoning | Numerical ability | VR + NA | Abstract reasoning | Clerical sp. and acc. | Mechanical reasoning | Space relations | Spelling | Language usage |
|---|---|---|---|---|---|---|---|---|

*Figure 6.6   Example of DAT score profile*

(Anastasi, 1990, p.136)

There are also more general collections of aptitude tests such as the Differential Aptitude Test (DAT) (Bennet *et al.*, 1962). These are designed for use in career guidance to identify areas where the candidate may have more aptitude (see Figure 6.6).

Evidence suggests that there may be limited differences in the outcomes of these tests for different occupational groups. For example, engineers performed better on all of the tests, rather than just on those assessing mechanical aptitude, than clerical workers (Kline, 1993). This indicates that although the tests may claim to be useful for guidance they do not necessarily differentiate sufficiently between occupational groups to provide useful vocational insight. Indeed, the manuals for aptitude tests often reveal very high correlations between these tools and other general intelligence measures. Evidence from the DAT suggests that the best predictor of job success is the sum of scores across the instrument as a whole. This suggests that they may be a surrogate general ability measure: 'g' (*ibid.*). There is limited corroboration for a specific aptitude test being more effective than a general cognitive intelligence test in predicting occupational performance (see Table 6.1).

**Table 6.1 Observed validities of occupation aptitude and personality tests for different occupational groups**

| Type of job | Type of predictor | | | | |
| --- | --- | --- | --- | --- | --- |
| | Intellectual abilities | Spatial and mechanical | Perceptual accuracy | Personality[1] | Interest |
| Executives | 0.29 | 0.18 | 0.24 | 0.27 | 0.31 |
| Foremen | 0.24 | 0.23 | 0.14 | 0.15 | 0.15 |
| Clerks | 0.27 | 0.20 | 0.27 | 0.24 | 0.12 |
| Sales clerks | −0.10 | — | −0.05 | 0.35 | 0.23 |
| Commission sales | 0.31 | 0.07 | 0.21 | 0.24 | 0.31 |
| Protective services | 0.23 | 0.16 | 0.17 | 0.24 | −0.01 |
| Personal services | 0.03 | — | −0.10 | 0.16 | — |
| Vehicle operators | 0.14 | 0.20 | 0.36 | — | 0.26 |
| Trades and crafts | 0.19 | 0.23 | 0.22 | 0.29 | −0.13 |
| Industrial occupations | 0.16 | 0.16 | 0.18 | 0.50 | 0.14 |
| Median validity | 0.21 | 0.19 | 0.20 | 0.24 | 0.15 |

[1]  Only those results where the traits seemed pertinent to the job in question were included in this summary (Ghiselli, 1966, p.21)

(Adapted from Furnham and Heaven, 1999, p.187)

Limited attention has been paid to the effects of culture on performance in aptitude tests. Because the skills that these tests are developed to measure are considered important within a particular context, there is a cultural dimension to the valuing of these abilities, so that the type of ability esteemed in one context may be seen very differently in another. For example, involving others in decisions might be seen as a weakness in some contexts and a strength in another. This is an important consideration if you are seeking to devise and use tests in different countries and across different cultures.

### 5.2.3   *General intelligence testing*

Measurement of general intelligence is inextricably linked to cognitive science. This is not in order to produce better tests: it reflects the reductionist goals of attributing psychometric outcomes to biological factors and thereby offering some explanation of why occupational and educational assessment tests work in the way they do. Evidence from a number of studies indicates that there is a link between genetics and intelligence, with heredity accounting for between 0.4 and 0.7 of the variation in intelligence (Hunt, 1999). This is an unpalatable finding for many. Some dispute it and argue that no mechanism has been found for it (Jencks, 1992).

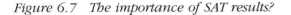

*"You're kidding! You count S.A.T.s?"*

*Figure 6.7   The importance of SAT results?*

Cognitive studies focus on two distinct sub-disciplines: they study human information-processing and the organization of knowledge. The latter emerges as important when considering the uses of intelligence, while the former is concerned with the performance of components such as working and long-term memory. I will return in Chapter 7 to highlight how our improved understanding of human information-processing is changing psychometric assessment.

Although general intelligence measurement suggests an overarching assessment tool, closer examination reveals that most of these tests are in fact batteries of sub-tests. These sub-tests evaluate a narrow range of cognitive skills, such as arithmetic reasoning, verbal intelligence and digital symbol tests, with the results of each component test aggregated to provide an overall intelligence measure. The Wechsler test (WAIS) or the Scholastic Attainment Test (SAT) are examples.

One long-standing debate concerns general intelligence versus multiple dimensions of intelligence. Different models of intelligence will be examined in Chapter 7, but here I want to focus on the assessment of general intelligence, or Spearman's (1904) '*g*'. Instruments designed to measure a single factor called 'intelligence' are more commonly found in a developmental or clinical context, such as identifying special needs in children or in assessing head-injury patients. I will not comment at this point on the merits of such tools; instead, let us assume that intelligence in this context concerns general reasoning skills which can be applied in any situation. Interestingly, some occupational psychologists use them in selection: their strength lies in being able to compare the measure obtained to some benchmark. They are expressed in terms of an age-related measure called **'intelligence quotient' (IQ)** (see Figure 6.8 for an example).

*Figure 6.8   Examples of IQ test items*

A is to H as G is to:

i. O   ii. M   iii. E   iv. N

Intelligence tests measure two distinct aspects: **fluid** and **crystallized** ability. We will return to these dimensions in Chapter 7, but note for now that *fluid* intelligence is concerned with applying reasoning skills to novel situations, while *crystallized* intelligence reflects reasoning that involves a culturally specific component. Intelligence tests usually combine assessment of both and, as a result (like aptitude testing), intelligence measurement is culturally bounded. There are, nonetheless, increasing examples of tests designed to measure just fluid intelligence. Care must be exercised when transplanting items into a different context. To assist test-users, many manuals contain norms on a country basis to try and control for cultural difference. (Figure 6.9 gives an example of the changes in IQ for different nations over time. Each nation completed a culture-free test and was assessed against its own set of norms; thus, it is not possible to say whether one nation has a higher IQ than another, merely that the rate of change in IQ varies.)

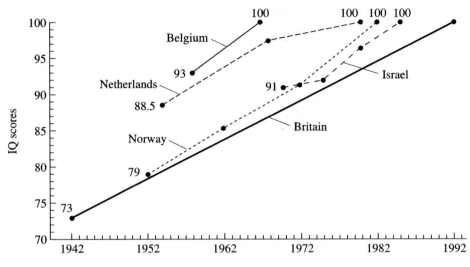

*Figure 6.9   Gains in average IQ over time for five countries*
(Kaplan and Saccuzzo, 2001, p.532)

Studies of intelligence reveal a developmental component: the hallmarks of intelligence in an infant are very different from those found in an older child, or an adult. There is also increasing interest in the impact of ageing on cognitive performance. Over a life span, research suggests that the ability to represent and reason about novel problems (fluid intelligence) reduces, whilst skills in applying culturally specific problem-solving increase (crystallized intelligence) (Horn and Noll, 1994). Age, therefore, is an independent variable that has different effects in these two broad categories of cognitive skills. This finding is important when considering not what *causes intelligence* but what *intelligence causes*. In order to take into account age-based difference, item content and difficulty levels are varied. For example, child and adult versions are found for the Wechsler tests which can be used to test intelligence from 4 to 70 years, whereas the Stanford–Binet's test (1960) can only be used for those aged from 2 and a half to 17 years.

It is important to note that, despite claims to the contrary, intelligence is not normally distributed. Instead we find that at the bottom end of the distribution of cognitive tests, scores are tightly grouped, which suggests a strong general factor. In contrast, at the upper end, scores indicate more independence between the sub-tests. This suggests the emergence of specific intelligences (Detterman and Daniels, 1989). Hunt (1999) contends that whilst having a good brain permits intelligence performance, it does not dictate it. Instead, what is important is the effective application of these skills. What emerges is a complex situation that suggests there are few generally intelligent people but some generally unintelligent individuals. Table 6.2 shows the difference between these three types of maximal performance measures.

**Table 6.2  Summary of three types of test**

| Type of test | Temporal focus | A measure-ment of | Breadth | Main type of validity | Restrictions |
|---|---|---|---|---|---|
| Attainment | Current | Known and controlled experience | Specific domain | Content-related | Context-related |
| Aptitude | Future potential | Unknown and variable experiences | Narrow specific skills | Predictive and criterion-based assessment | Culture-related |
| Intelligence | Current | Underlying reasoning ability | Broad cognitive skills | Construct-related | Culture-related |

We shall now move on to examine test construction and results interpretation in more detail. In the main, these issues are generic to psychometric tests and therefore can apply to the development of both personality and ability instruments.

## 6   Test construction

Psychometric tests are constructed from individual items. Traditionally, tests are developed through the generation of a large number of sample items: these are then given to a group of test-takers to respond to. Only those items that discriminate between test-takers are retained (see Figure 6.10). Therefore, items that everyone gets right, or wrong, are discarded. There are differences, however, between how maximal and typical performance instruments are devised.

Maximal performance tests are formed from items that relate to a piece of knowledge or information. These items are selected based on their relationship to the domain of interest so that verbal ability tests might contain items to do with understanding words and ideas, such as vocabulary, synonyms or analogies (see Figure 6.10). The items retained in maximal performance tests identify what the test-taker does and does not know. The scoring systems therefore reflect this: an answer is either wrong or right. Responses can be recorded by the test-taker completing an open space such as in attainment tests, or more commonly, through multiple choice with alternatives being supplied, some of which are plausible, but with only one correct answer.

In contrast, items in typical performance tests are based on aspects of the person: their mood, attitude, personality, or temperament. Since holding one attitude does not necessarily preclude the holding of another, this type

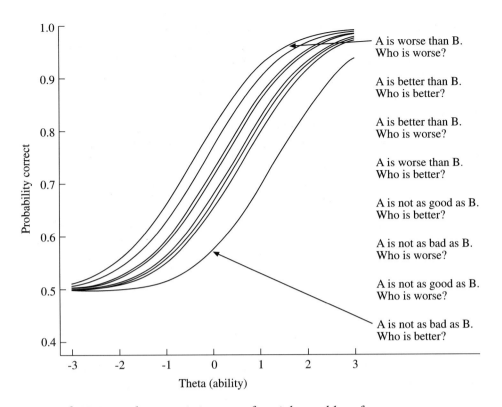

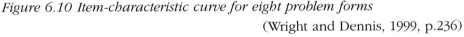

*Figure 6.10 Item-characteristic curve for eight problem forms*

(Wright and Dennis, 1999, p.236)

of test is not constructed in the same way as ability tests. In personality test construction, scoring is not related to some external universal criterion regarding the 'correctness' of the responses. As a result, there are no right or wrong responses for most items. However, the comparison groups used to interpret the results will reflect some notion of how 'typical' population groups respond.

In some cases, questions are included that assess the social desirability of the answers (I will discuss this in more detail in Chapter 8). These items alone contain a notion of cultural convention, or 'correctness', so are strongly related to a particular context. One question a test-developer might expect everyone from a Western culture to respond to affirmatively is 'I like to gossip at times'.

Both ability and personality tests can be constructed using five main methods: (1) **criterion-keyed**, (2) **factor analytic**, (3) **item analytic**, (4) **Thurstone scales** and (5) **Guttman scales**. Each method typically involves writing many more items than those eventually selected for the final test. I will briefly highlight the main advantages and disadvantages of each method. I will then contrast these approaches with those found for tests developed using IRT. This is an increasingly popular way of devising tests, but is different in many ways to the traditional approach adopted.

## 6.1  Criterion-keyed method

The criterion-keyed method focuses on an external domain or criterion. For example, if a test-developer is developing an interest inventory, the criteria are interests that are related to a specific occupational group. For instance, a selection test for a manager would identify skills such as those involving the analysis and interpretation of numerical data. Items are developed and then selected on the basis of whether they can discriminate between those in the criterion group and other control groups. The most famous example of a test based on this technique is the clinical Minnesota Multiphasic Personality Inventory (MMPI) developed by Hathaway and McKinley (1951). It was devised with items derived from the symptoms of a criterion group of patients seeking psychiatric help.

This method of test development could be used by organizations undergoing continual change (the criterion) to devise a screening selection test in order to identify and remove those who do not show flexibility or any propensity to change.

The criterion-keyed method is not without its drawbacks. A central criticism is its atheoretical basis: the decision whether to select and include an item is based purely on empirical data relating to its discrimination level, and not on any intuitive or theoretical rationale (Kline, 1993). Thus, tests of this type merely assess similarities and differences between particular groups and do not address the often more important underlying question as to why this might be the case. (You will recall a similar concern arose earlier for biodata in Chapter 4.)

The basis for the development of such tests involves using an external criterion, so it is important that we are clear how membership of this criterion group is established. A central problem of assessing against some particular work performance criterion is that performance can rarely be categorized as 'acceptable' or 'unacceptable'. It can be difficult to discern membership of one group in preference to another. For example, how distinct are the interests of managers in comparison to other professional occupations? If we wanted to make a test to identify 'managers', do we assume they are a group with any unifying characteristics? Or does the type of manager vary according to seniority, responsibility, budget, staffing resources, or the context in which they work? The less clear the external criterion used, the more we need to examine it. (You will recall that this issue was explored in more detail in Chapter 3.)

Related to this is the question how psychologically meaningful is the domain of the test. Kline (1993, p.128) found that, in the MMPI, mania was diagnosed based on only one criterion scale, when it might be better described by a collection of variables. This is important because, over time, scales which are not meaningful do not further our understanding or knowledge concerning the domain of the test. Indeed, they are likely to restrict it.

Finally, the more specific a measure, the more limited its generalizability. Like biodata measures, these instruments can have problems when moved from one context to another, because the domain changes may render the measure meaningless. For example, it would be difficult to transport an organizational-fit questionnaire to a different context. This can be a particular problem where attitudes or abilities are valued in different ways across different cultures. Items assessing crystallized intelligence are particularly susceptible to this type of problem. For example, a tool measuring 'good leaders' might not travel well if it was based on those aspects valued in a paternalistic culture and used in an achievement-based individualistic context. Behaviours seen as important in Asia or Africa may have a different meaning in Europe, or the USA.

## 6.2 Factor-analytic method

The factor-analytic method involves identifying items that load on to one factor only and not on to others. The advantage of this uni-factorial approach is that scores always have the same meaning. However, if the test measures two factors, the meaning might change. For example, with a uni-factorial test a score of '8' is always '8', but on a multi-factorial test a score could comprise of '3' and '5' or '4' and '4', and so on. The problem for test-developers is that it is not always simple to develop a test that meaningfully measures anything of importance through just one factor.

Items for factor-analytic tests are developed on the basis that they are believed to relate to only one factor. A test is devised of these items and is given to a group of test-takers. The developers are interested in the correlation between items and their loading on to the factor. Items that load onto more than one factor are problematic and are often discarded. In developing a test, a number of different or related factors may emerge. These can be clearly seen in Figure 6.11, which shows the number of potential factors for a specific questionnaire.

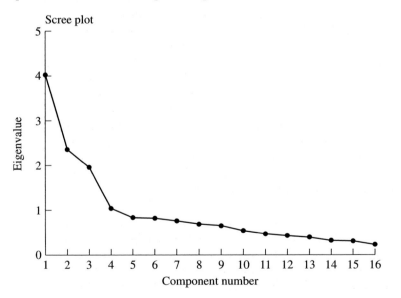

*Figure 6.11 Scree plot showing item loading onto the factors*

The most famous example of a test developed using this technique is Cattell's 16 Personality Factors test (16PF™). Building on earlier work from the 1930s, Cattell began to develop the items by assembling all of the names given to personality traits that he found in the dictionary and in the psychiatric and psychological literature. After removing obvious synonyms, he had a list of 171 trait terms. He gave these items to a heterogeneous group of 100 adults to rate and examined the intercorrelations and factor structure of the data that emerged. Following this, he reduced the items and gave the second draft to a group of 208 men. Cattell used factor analysis not as a means of data reduction, but as a way of helping him develop his theory of the structure and underlying interrelationships between personality factors. Based on his findings, he went on with colleagues to develop what we now know as the 16PF™ model of personality. Validation data for this questionnaire has assessed the relationship between personality factors of over 50 different occupations and a similar number of individuals with psychiatric problems.

A critical issue in the development of a test using this approach is the size and representativeness of the sample group used in comparison to the wider population. The larger the group's size, the lower the standard error of the correlations: therefore, a minimum ratio of two sample test-takers per item is required. For example, if a test with five scales, each consisting of twenty items, is being developed, then more than 200 items would be required and a sample of at least 400 test-takers.

In adopting this method, test-developers take a lot of care to ensure that differences between test-takers are a function of the items, and not the sample. Therefore, items are chosen based on the similar performance, for example, between the sexes or different ethnic groups in order to ensure that gender and ethnicity differences in the test are controlled for. There may, however, be theoretical or empirical grounds for such differences to exist: for instance, women generally perform better at verbal items than men. In these cases, further research is required in order to establish how far this reflects a 'true' difference and how far it is the product of the items. Techniques such as Item Response Theory (IRT) have been devised to assist test-developers in assessing the nature of these differences. There are also considerations relating to the application of factor analysis technique *per se*, involving the level and type of loading that is adopted (Kline, 1993, p.143). I will not expand these here other than to say there are a number of books written on the subject of factor analysis.

## 6.3  Item-analytic method

The third approach to test construction is the item-analytic method. This is remarkably simple and, as its name implies, it focuses on the items. In item analysis, the correlation between each item and the overall test is assessed. This technique can be a simple and expedient way of eliminating unsatisfactory items prior to using factor analysis (Nunnally and Bernstein, 1994) and as a result is often used in conjunction with factor-analytic methods.

The approach allows homogeneous and uni-factorial tests to be developed and can provide a useful way of developing ability tests where the domain of interest can be distinguished easily. It can be used to boost the reliability and validity of longer tests by helping to identify poor items. However, this is where a potentially terminal problem can be found (Kline,

1993, p.145). If the domain of interest is inadequately defined, then the item-analytic method merely compounds this error by creating a tautologous basis for any argument. For example, it would be unwise to have a test examining trust that asked if a test-taker trusted someone, rather than examining aspects of trust-related behaviour. It is important to consider how far a homogeneous measure is necessarily a meaningful measure. In some cases, scales are developed which initially show high reliability, but on closer inspection are actually found to be a repetition of the same item. This is termed a '**bloated specific**'.

The item-analytic method of test construction can be very useful for test-developers devising a test for a very specific group in a very specific context. It does not require such a large initial sample as the factor-analytic approach. However, the definition of the domain is critical, because without it, the whole basis of the test is questionable. In this approach items which load on to two factors would simply be excluded, whilst in practice, as Cattell *et al.* (1970) found in his model of 16 personality factors, the inter-relationships between items and factors can play an important role in helping develop new theories. Kline (1998, p.72) cautions against this method being used as the sole construction technique for a test.

Concerns also emerge regarding the *transportability* of tests developed from this approach: they are implicitly based on social and other domain-related values that might be particular to that context and therefore do not necessarily transfer into another culture or context.

## 6.4 Thurstone scales method

In contrast with the last approach the Thurstone scales are used widely, particularly in the assessment of attitudes. This method involves identifying potential statements concerning an attitude and assessing their relevance by a panel of judges. Items are chosen on the basis of their standard deviation of the rating the experts give them; only those items with small deviations are included in the final test, because this indicates high agreement between the expert judges. Care must be taken to ensure that the statements included in the scales cover the whole range of potential attitudes. Edwards (1957) argues that this method can be significantly affected by social desirability to such a degree that attempts to counter it render it impractical, as upwards of 100 judges would be required. Nunnally (1978) found that scaling models may not fit into the real world of attitudes. For example, an item 'racism is unfair' might be endorsed by those at the midpoint of a racism attitude scale, but would also be endorsed by those at the extreme. By their very nature these scales are imbued with implicit values which may or may not be appropriate to the context. Their transportability is an important issue.

## 6.5 Guttman scales method

Although less widely used, the Guttman scales do have an intuitive appeal. The technique is based on the cumulative and hierarchical aspects of ability. The process aims to provide a sorting process so that each item is graduated in terms of its difficulty or intensity. An incorrect response to an earlier question would *ipso facto* imply failure later in the test. For example, the use of attitude surveys to determine an individual's most extreme response according to this model would enable the determination of all of his or her other responses. In principle, this sounds sensible. The Guttman scales' appeal lies in the additional information it provides so that a result informs the test administrator not only about what the test-taker knows, or has ability in, but also what she or he does not know and needs more training in. Problems arise in the practice of developing the scales. In order to achieve this graduation, every item must be perfectly correlated with the total score. The complexities of achieving this require both large numbers of potential items and large samples.

The underlying model implies that the trait or ability being measured is constructed hierarchically. This can prove problematic with no theoretical or empirical justification of this structure being proposed. There are also difficulties associated with developing a uni-dimensional scale, which disappointingly can render them of very little practical value (Kline, 1998, p.75).

## 6.6  Item Response Theory (IRT)

In traditional test development a test contains items selected on the basis of their content, difficulty level and discriminating characteristics. Those items showing high discrimination between good and poor candidates are the most desirable. The level of difficulty of each test is based on its purpose and the anticipated distribution of the ability levels of the test-takers. It is the similarities between intended and actual test-takers that are important. In many actual situations, the intended group and the group who finally take the test may be quite different. As a result, an imprecise test – and therefore an imprecise result – are achieved. In response to this situation, item response theory (IRT) was developed. This offers a different approach to test construction. IRT enables the difficulty of an item and the ability of the test-taker to be measured on the same scale. Using this approach, it is possible to construct a test that would differentiate between novices and experts in a particular field based on the questions they responded to – the novice would get different ones correct.

IRT rests on the assumption that an individual's performance on a test item can be predicted by a set of factors or abilities (Hambleton *et al.*, 1991, p.7). However, this is based not on performance in the entire test, but on how each individual item is completed. Tests developed using this model assume that the probability of a correct response is dependent on the test-taker's ability and the characteristics of the item. Central to this is the uni-dimensionality of each item. This can be problematic to achieve as other factors, such as other cognitive skills, personality and motivational dimensions, test anxiety and other conditions, may affect the response to an item.

Each test is comprised of items which have a characteristic curve and relate to the probability of gaining a correct response. In Figure 6.12 item 'C' can be clearly seen as the best item, showing its superior differentiation between differing ability levels. It is important to note that in many of the items the flattening of the curves at the 20 per cent level implies that there is a 20 per cent probability of achieving a correct response through chance.

Note also that item 'F' is a reverse scored item as the curve lies the opposite way.

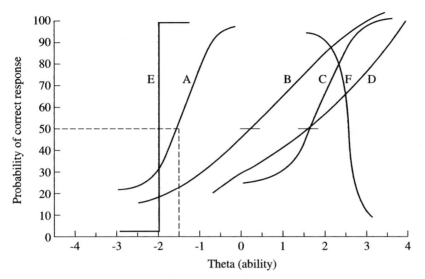

*Figure 6.12 A range of item characteristic curves*

(Hogan, 2003, pp.252, 254)

Like the Guttman scales, items used in this method are chosen on a hierarchical and cumulative basis. For example, in Figure 6.13 both applicants were given item 6, which was at the midpoint of the scale in terms of item difficulty. Following this initial response by the applicants (Candidate 2 got it wrong, but Candidate 1 got it right), different items were then selected that enabled a final assessment of their ability level to be made. The quality of each test relies on the relation between the underlying response model and the test data.

Item no.

| 1 | 2 | 3 | 4 | 5 | 6 | 7 | 8 | 9 | 10 | 11 | 12 |
|---|---|---|---|---|---|---|---|---|----|----|----|

Item difficulty

    Easy                    Moderate                    Difficult

Candidate 1

                        ✓1    ✓2    ✓3    ✗4    ✓5    ✓6

Candidate 2

    ✓3    ✓4    ✓5    ✗2    ✗1    ✗6

Key   number = item order; ✓ = correct response, ✗ = incorrect response

*Figure 6.13 Item selection and numerical ability assessment using IRT*

The score obtained in an IRT test is a function of the test-taker's response and the characteristics of the item (Hogan, 2003, p.82). Thus, it is clear in Figure 6.13 that despite being given a test of the same size, Candidate 1 has responded correctly to more of the difficult items than Candidate 2.

IRT is not without its critics. First, it requires large sample sizes in order to identify item characteristic curves. Second, there is a basic assumption of the uni-dimensionality of the underlying domain being measured. This is increasingly being challenged.

# 7   Test assessment

Whenever a test is completed, a raw score is obtained. In classical tests this would be based on aggregating the correct responses, while tests using IRT involve identifying the difficulty level of correct responses. There are two important theoretical considerations that must be addressed: first, calculating error levels and second, how the results are interpreted.

## 7.1  Calculating error levels

In classical test theory, each score obtained is treated as if it contains two separate measures: a 'true' score, which is the objective level reached on the tests and an error score. Even with tests of the highest quality, there is assumed to be error. Error affects the validity of the measurement, calling into question how far it is actually measuring what it claims to. There are two distinct sources of error. The first, **'systematic' error,** is paradoxically of limited importance to psychometricians as it is assumed to affect all of the test-takers' scores equally. (Suggested means of eliminating these systematic errors will be explored later in section 8.) The second is **random error,** which is far more problematic and difficult as it impacts randomly on results, so is less easy to remove. We will examine random error in more detail now.

### 7.1.1  Random errors

'Random' errors, which have a significant affect on the accuracy of the measure itself, can enter psychometric measures in a variety of ways. First, they can be introduced by test-takers themselves, who can create a discrepancy in the test through the practices they choose to adopt. If, for example, they guess the answers, instead of carefully considering them, they create an error as they may get the right answer by chance. In addition, errors can be produced if a test-taker is feeling unwell or tired. Similarly, the test-taker's affective state can affect their performance. They may feel upset due to the test conditions, for example if the administrator reminds them of a terrible teacher they hated from their school experience, or because of some extraneous incident happening outside the immediate context, such as a bereavement. Although the control of these issues may ultimately lie outside the control of the test-user, they do affect the validity of the test.

The second source of random errors resides within the test itself and concerns two issues. First, as indicated in the section on constructing tests, the content of a test can affect performance. If the domain in question has not been defined thoroughly, or if there are insufficient items so that the domain is not fully being investigated, the test score may not reflect the candidate's true ability. In addition, how the test is explained may affect the test-taker's performance: poorly expressed instructions, lack of breadth or an unclear response format can both undermine performance (see Figure 6.14).

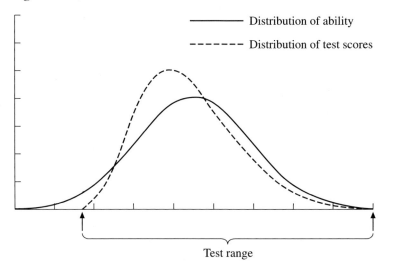

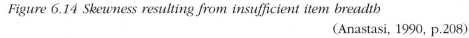

*Figure 6.14 Skewness resulting from insufficient item breadth*

(Anastasi, 1990, p.208)

Finally, the test-user can create random error initially through lack of attention to the environment, which has to be conducive to concentration (see Table 6.3, p.157). A standardized set of administration instructions is provided for each test to ensure that all test-takers have the same information and the same opportunity for questions and practice. This process guarantees that when the test session begins, the test-taker knows what they are to do and how to do it. In addition, tests are designed to be taken within a specific time frame and so any changes by the test administrator to the duration of a test will have an impact on performance. Therefore, care must be taken to manage the duration of each test – especially in a session in which multiple tests are being used.

### 7.1.2  *Errors arising from marking*

The second contamination and source of error from test-users arises through an inconsistent, or subjective, approach to marking. All tests contain standardized scoring systems so that the scores are marked in the same way. Classical test theory is concerned with measuring and controlling this form of error. It does so by measuring the amount of error through the **standard error of measurement**.

| | |
|---|---|
| $SE_{meas} = SD_t / \sqrt{(1 - r)}$ | Key $SD_t$ – standard deviation of the test. $r$ – test-re-test reliability |

### 7.1.3   Error assessment in IRT

More recently, researchers have argued that there are problems with the conception of how the standard error of measurement is devised because this equation assumes that the amount of error is the same for all test-takers (Hambleton *et al.*, 1991, p.4). Evidence indicates, however, that different groups of test-takers may find some tests more difficult than others. IRT takes a different approach to the assessment of error by differentiating between the characteristics of the tests and those of the test-takers. The advantage of this approach is that it enables test-developers to create instruments that can be used to compare very different populations. Hambleton *et al.* (1991) argue that in IRT test development the choice of items, and the reliability and validity of test scores may all vary depending on the type of test-taker. Their claims offer a fundamental challenge to how test reliability and validity are assessed. They are not concerned with reliability in terms of the correlation between scores found in parallel testing ('test–re-test', or 'split-half') (see Chapter 3). Their approach has permitted more research to be undertaken that focuses on why different groups of test-takers do better, or less well, in particular types of test.

IRT tests are more concerned with the internal consistency of items. The standard error is therefore expressed in terms of each item's relationship to the overarching domain. The standard error in IRT involves an index of measurement precision. It has a major advantage over classical test theory's standard error of measurement as it is not dependent on either the homogeneity of the test items or on the heterogeneity of the individuals taking the test.

$$SE(0) = 1/\sqrt{1(0)}$$ where $0$ = ability/trait score and $1(0)$ is the test information function = sum of item information function.

IRT is becoming increasingly popular with organizations with high numbers of applicants – such as financial services – as the items are selected from large banks of potential items. These items can be cloned to produce families of items. IRT has enabled the generation of bespoke tests, where items are chosen based on the test-takers' responses to earlier items and so each test is unique. Bespoke tests reduce the problems experienced, for example, by graduate recruiters who fear overexposure for particular traditional tests and their items.

## 7.2  Interpretation of scores

The score obtained on any test is not meaningful in itself – it is relative and it is only through a comparison with other scores that its value emerges. Test results can be interpreted using three different techniques – criterion related, domain-referenced and norm-referenced scoring.

### 7.2.1 Criterion-related scoring

The first approach, **criterion-related** scoring, interprets the raw score based on the likelihood of the applicant achieving some external criterion. This is achieved by identifying a proven statistical relationship between the obtained score and some external measure, such as the outcome of a training course. Criterion-related scoring is not without problems as Figure 6.15 shows. In Case 1 no bias is found as it is clear that while distributions in the results differ for the two groups, there is an identical regression line between test and the criterion. In Case 2, however, a lower validity co-efficient emerges for the minority group. In Cases 3 and 4, although the same test result is found, the criterion is different. These diagrams reflect the findings of a number of studies that show gender and ethnic differences in the relationship between the test score and an external criterion. I shall discuss this problem later in the chapter.

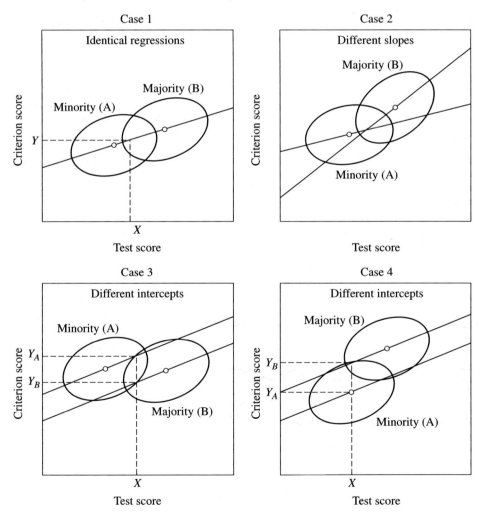

Figure 6.15 *Slope and intercept bias in predicting criterion scores*

(Anastasi, 1990, p.196)

### 7.2.2 Domain-referenced scoring

A second technique used with aptitude tests is called the **domain-referenced** scoring system. When learning to drive a car a person's skills are assessed against a standardized set of behaviours that competent drivers have. This is the domain. The skills level is not assessed against any driver, but against a competent driver, who has mastery of this domain. As we shall explore in Chapter 9, manual dexterity tests are interpreted using this approach.

### 7.2.3 Norm-referenced scoring

The third interpretation technique for ability tests is **norm-referenced** scoring. This is by far the most commonly used method and involves comparing the individual's performance on the test against a comparable group from a specific population, such as a group of employees who currently perform the role well. This can add a context element to the scoring, so for example you would not expect all managers, regardless of the organization, to achieve the same ability score. The interpreted scores are relative measures so that, as the comparison group changes, the outcome score might also change (see Figure 6.16). In IRT tests the result of each item is compared as each test is unique. The test-user decides which norms to use. Dilemma box 6.1 illustrates the problem of finding the appropriate norm group. It can easily be seen, however, how the interpretation of results can be distorted either through a lack of availability of appropriate norms, or through an inappropriate choice of norms.

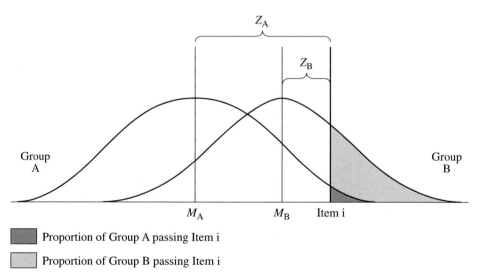

*Figure 6.16 Normal curve showing relative difficulty of the same item in Groups A and B*

(Anastasi, 1990, p.207)

## Dilemma box 6.1 Choosing the right norm group

You are asked to arrange a programme to select a marketing manager for a water utility company. Following an in-depth job analysis you decide to use a battery of cognitive ability tests that are designed for management candidates. This test battery includes verbal and numerical tests, which the job analysis indicates are particularly important in this role. In examining the norm tables in the manual you find a potential comparison group of general managers from a multinational manufacturing organization. There is also a small norm group of production managers from an electricity utility firm, but there is no ethnic diversity in the group and your application forms indicate that several of the candidates who have been short-listed for testing are from different ethnic groups. The manual contains a third norm group of marketing managers which does include ethnic diversity in the sample, but the context is different as they are from a financial services organization. Which norm group do you use?

In the next section I will highlight a range of factors that may suppress the score that test-takers achieve. I have divided these influences into two groups: those concerned with the test experience and issues concerning the test itself.

## 8   Factors affecting the test experience

As Table 6.3 shows, three distinct sets of factors can adversely affect the performance of test-takers. These relate broadly to the test, the test-taker, and the environment. The factors all relate to potential systematic errors in the test experience.

**Table 6.3 Conditions affecting test performance**

| Test | Test-taker | Testing environment |
| --- | --- | --- |
| Pre-test info | Past experience | Environment of room – light, heat, noise |
| Type of test | | |
| Language | | |
| Clarity of instructions | Confidence | Test administrator |
| Structure | Emotional state | Distractions: room |
| Delivery medium | Motivation | Distractions: other test-takers |
| Timing | Memory/recall | |
| Length of test | Culture/support towards assessment | |

## 8.1 The test

In Table 6.3 I highlight a number of concerns that affect the test. Here, I will concentrate on four that have received limited attention from researchers: the choice of language, the medium for delivery, the influence of time limits and the durability and stability of test performance.

### 8.1.1 Choice of language

A primary issue in a global business context is that of the language used for testing. It does not matter how intelligent a candidate is: they will perform badly if they do not understand what they are to do. As a result of this concern, test-developers argue that tests should be taken in the dominant language of the test-taker. However, test-users are increasingly distorting the test process by using it as a means of indirectly testing the applicant's ability to use English.

### 8.1.2 Medium of delivery

A second issue is the medium used to *deliver* the test. Computers are playing an increasing role in the test experience, replacing paper and pencil-based systems with computer-based testing and internet delivery. The computer is also assisting in test administration, scoring and interpretation. The influence of the medium can be divided into two distinct impacts: those affecting the developers and users of psychometric tests and those influencing the candidate.

Computers can assist test-users to score and analyse the raw results. They also have an important role in providing test-users with the statistical computation necessary to speed up data analysis and interpretation. Although many such packages exist, all those seeking formal test competency qualifications (for example, British Psychological Society Level A and B competencies) are required to undertake all their computations by hand in order to demonstrate their understanding of the underlying principles.

In the case of IRT-based systems, test-users may be further removed from the test itself, receiving only the final results. They may have little or no insight into either the test items candidates were presented with, or into how the difficulty gradations for each item are made. Increasingly, organizations, as the purchasers of psychometric tests, are beginning to buy a complete testing service with item delivery, scoring and interpretation of results being done by the developer. The organization receives an interpretation of the final results and remains ignorant of the process. In the past, the test-developer had limited control over their paper and pencil products, passing them over to the organization to use. Now, through the application of IRT-based tests, the test-developer's control and power has increased. IRT-based systems and the complex statistical analysis that underpins them further remove the organization from the candidate's assessment experience.

Test-users need to be reminded that the presentation media used can have an impact on the perception and interpretation of items by test-takers. This means that generalizability between test items presented through a computer medium, rather than through the traditional paper and pencil approach, is not assured. More work is being done to examine the comparability of tests presented in different ways.

Multi-media test delivery systems are enabling new criteria to be assessed, including previously inaccessible behavioural selection criteria, such as interpersonal and teamwork skills (Drasgow, 2002). Test-developers have long heralded these potential new applications, although test-users have been slow to move away from their more familiar tests, presented through a PC medium. For example, new types of tools involve presenting candidates with video scenarios and ask them to choose from a range of potential outcomes, or creating an interactive in-tray exercise (see Chapter 9). Practice is far ahead of research in this domain and we must await the outcomes of studies to reveal the added value that these systems may provide.

Through IRT models, computers offer great potential as a tool for identifying the exact level of candidates' abilities. They can create individually tailored tests that reduce the problems of item overexposure common to particular groups, such as in graduate selection. They create a different test experience, however, as each question must be answered as it is presented and applicants can no longer leave items and return to them later. More research is needed to examine the impact of this change on candidates' assessment scores.

The new delivery mechanism removes the previous security considerations of paper and pencil tests but creates new delivery and security management problems of testing across multiple sites. In particular, attention focuses on candidate verification. Given the high stakes and the reluctance to use unsupervised testing, many organizations invite candidates to take their assessment in a supervised environment with adequate computer provision. Further, through the use of personal documents, candidate verification is possible. Alternatively, more sophisticated means of controlling cheating are being tested through the collection of additional data, such as response latency (the gap between question presentation and the answer being supplied), during the test session itself. Work is being done to explore ways of reducing cheating in non-supervised assessment contexts, for example by using honesty questionnaires (Baron and Miles, 2002), biological candidate recognition systems (through iris and finger prints) or by using video technology to survey the assessment room remotely (Bartram, 2002). These new processes would have the effect of expanding the range of the applicant pool.

Electronic media can offer a dramatic reduction in administration time, aid scoring efficiency and generate test-use and test-taker reports. Care must be taken, however, to ensure that this new medium does not adversely affect the test-taker's ability to ask questions and seek clarification. Technology changes the test experience, for example with glitches in the downloading of questions via internet connections adversely affecting the smooth running of test sessions (Lievens and Harris, 2003). In some cases, test-takers can feel more comfortable answering questions from a machine rather than from a human, but this openness will obviously vary depending on the content of the questions and the purpose of the test.

While it is clear that many test-takers are becoming increasingly competent in using a computer keyboard, concerns still remain about the variability in this exposure. Some studies have raised concerns about bias by revealing that minority ethnic groups, people with disabilities and low-earning groups have less exposure to and experience of computers (Sharf, 2000). What emerges is that White males dominate in terms of their exposure and access to this medium, showing higher familiarity and lower anxiety in using computers in comparison to women and older workers (Czaja and Sharit, 1998). The link between anxiety and test performance has already been established (Kline, 1993). In addition, research suggests that increased computer experience enhances test performance. Klinch (2002) compared internet and traditional versions of tests and found that those with more experience of computers tended to perform better – regardless of the medium used. She found that high test scores were significantly correlated with computer experience. The advent of this new medium appears to be exacerbating existing adverse impacts for groups already under-represented within the workplace. The challenge for test-developers and organizations is to lower anxiety levels within these groups by increasing their exposure to new technology.

### 8.1.3  *Time limits*

A key issue in maximal testing is the effect of time limits on performance. Tests of this type are designed to measure the maximum number of correct items achieved within a given time. This creates a dilemma for candidates as they must compare the advantage of responding rapidly with the merits of taking time and responding accurately. This is termed the 'speed/accuracy trade-off'. Brand and Deary (1982) found a correlation between an accuracy measure and intelligence of 0.9, but attempts to replicate this finding have not corroborated its initial correlation size and have disputed how far it is actually a measure of perceptual speed and visualization (Kline, 1998, p.117). Intelligence is often attributed to those who possess both rapid thinking and responses, yet successful performance in the real world often depends on taking time to reflect.

Evidence suggests that the inclusion of a time limit in a test has a significant impact on the test experience, fundamentally altering the test to include an additional attention requirement. The test is not merely about assessing a particular trait or skill, but adds to the ability to manage one's time in an unfamiliar situation. Some researchers argue that the imposition of a time limit in effect introduces a surrogate flexibility measure since some applicants find it difficult to operate effectively with this added time pressure (Wright and Dennis, 1999).

Reductions in response time change the candidate's behaviour regarding the speed/accuracy dilemma, as the greater the time pressure, the more candidates rely on chance rather than accuracy in their response formats. Operating under time restrictions requires the candidate to pay attention to the passing of time, thereby distracting them from their main task of optimizing their test performance. IRT-based test formats have enabled test-developers to explore this behaviour in more detail because the pacing of items, rather than the test as a whole, can be analysed. Accuracy levels emerge as dependent on the type of item and the candidate's ability level.

One important way that test exposure can be minimized is through proper security. Tests and results should always be kept locked up and access restricted to those who have sufficient training and expertise. At times, great pressure is exerted on those who have access to these resources to assist those undertaking a test. There can also be pressure by interested parties to know the results of friends, colleagues, or family (Dilemma box 6.2 gives a typical example). In many countries there are additional data-protection requirements that must be adhered to. You can visit the British Psychological Society's website test centre domain to check the rules that apply to UK users.

### 8.1.4  *Durability and stability*

A paucity of research has examined the durability and stability of psychometric measures over time (see Dilemma box 6.2). There are two key issues here pertaining first to the test itself and second to the test-taker.

As we shall explore in Chapter 8, test-developers, through the 'test–re-test' protocol, attempt to ensure some temporary stability of the measure, but there have been few studies examining such aspects over a longer time. Chan *et al.* (1999) examined a battery used by the US army at five intervals over a 16-year period. They found that test items that were more semantically laden were more susceptible to the effects of time, compared with items measuring skills or principles. They argued that more attention needs to be paid by both developers and users of psychometric instruments to the shelf-life of the tests.

There has been increasing interest in the stability of test results over the years. There are two main concerns here. First, as our populations grow older there is interest in what happens to mental processes over time. Ackerman (1987) found considerable evidence for the durability of mental processes, thereby challenging the perception in many Western cultures that old age equals redundancy.

Second, knowledge of the physiology of mental processes has grown with improvements of our understanding of the impact of brain trauma on mental performance. The insurance industry is keen to deploy psychometric instruments as a means of identifying and quantifying the amount of mental deficit that has occurred following injury, in order to assist them in settling compensation claims. This is a novel application of the tools because attention is paid to trying to measure previous levels of mental abilities of a currently injured person instead of the usual focus on predictive validity. This new application is increasingly common in Australia, where the insurance industry is funding studies into this area.

There is a wider issue about people changing over time, as they mature. I will return to this in Chapter 8 when examining personality stability.

### Dilemma box 6.2

You have devised a recruitment programme to select a team leader, which is the first level of management in the firm. You decide to include some managerial level ability tests. A year ago you were involved in a similar exercise and rejected a number of applicants. During the feedback you offered applicants you outlined how they had not met the criteria for this particular job, but encouraged those who were unsuccessful to apply for later vacancies. Three of the previous applicants have decided to reapply for this vacancy and you are going to use the same ability tests. Do you omit them from this part of the selection process and save the firm's resources, or should you let them have another go?

## 8.2 The test-taker

There is little doubt that previous experiences of test–taking can have an impact on the current testing experience. They can affect the confidence, motivation and emotional state of the test-taker. This is where feedback can provide invaluable information for test-users.

An often overlooked factor is the increasing exposure to testing from certain populations. For example graduate trainees. As a result of the more widespread use of tests, the raw scores candidates achieved may reflect extraneous factors aside from their ability. Limited research has examined the role of repeated exposure and test performance. The consultants Kerr Brown (1992) explored this issue and found that 22.6 per cent of graduate applicants had completed the same paper and pencil test a number of times, often with short intervals between each test session. As we saw in Chapter 3, these **carry-over effects** are of concern in this situation due to the random nature of the time intervals between test sessions (Kaplan and Saccuzzo, 2001).

In examining the components of test performance, two factors affecting improvements in performance can be identified. The first, termed **alpha ability** – relates to a real improvement in the ability that the test was designed to measure. As a result of taking the test, the applicants learn new skills related to the domain the test is concerned with. As a result, their scores improve, and so which is the 'true' result: the initial score or that following exposure? The second, **beta ability**, is not specific to the individual test, but is concerned with more generic skills regarding the management of the process by the candidates. These include improved time management strategies and better allocation of resources by skipping difficult questions.

In addition, extraneous factors outside the room can reduce performance by upsetting the test-taker. In Chapter 7, I shall outline in detail the suggested relationship between motivation and intelligence that calls into question a simplistic dichotomy between tests of ability and motivation.

## 8.3 The environment

Given that multiple test sessions are often held, it is important that extraneous influences are kept to a minimum. As tests are commonly taken in a group context, the environment of the test can influence performance. Evidence from the early work of Mayo in the 1920s indicated the adverse effects that sound, light, noise and smell can have on optimum performance. Also, distractions of a strange and unfamiliar room can impact on the performance of young test-takers in particular. The test administrator has a crucial role to play in making test-takers feel comfortable, safe and able to achieve their best.

---

### Dilemma box 6.3

The niece of a senior manager is a candidate in the selection of new graduate trainees for your firm. The manager approaches you after the ability assessment has taken place and is keen to find out how her niece has got on. What do you tell her?

---

## 8.4 Implicit assumptions

Behind the development and application of psychometrics are some inherent assumptions that are easily forgotten but are important in their implications. These include four issues: the limitations to the definition of the assessment criteria; bias in the focus on individual differences; poor application of tools and ethical problems.

### 8.4.1 Adequacy of concept definitions

The most fundamental issue behind all psychometrics lies in the adequacy of the definition of the concept to be measured. Psychology began with the measurement of an abstract concept – 'intelligence'. In order to measure anything we must first define what it is, but implicit here is also the need to establish what it is *not*. Behind the operationalization of this concept are tacit views about society and the basis for individual difference. Binet's test, for example, with its eugenicist slant, was imbued with values about low intelligence as the causes of crime, poverty and sloth in society.

Behind the development of any measure is a quest to define and identify the appropriate domain. In many cases, the manuals reveal limited and insufficient exploration of the domain. You will see in the next chapter how Spearman, Thurstone and Guildford challenged each others' assumptions as to what was intelligence. Implicit in current intelligence measurement are assumptions derived from the notion of the brain as an information-processing system that works hierarchically like a computer. This places basic elements such as short-term memory, ability to recognize angles, or to recall the meaning of words as the building blocks for higher-order ability. For example, implicit in the assessment of numerical ability is effective short-term memory retrieval, so it would follow that in order to be a skilled mathematician, basic numerical recall skill is required (Rust and Golmbok,

1989). Therefore, in creating such measures does the developer look for higher or lower order functions? Is ability more reliably measured through simple components such as the number of digits we can recall, or more complex computations? In Chapter 7, I shall explore the impact of different models of intelligence on their approach to assessment.

### 8.4.2   *The bias in what constitutes an individual difference*

By their very nature, tests are designed to differentiate between individuals. However, in the interpretation of these differences, social and political values can be used to legitimize and confirm bias, rather than to show variance in actual performance. The biased interpretation of the earlier eugenics movement was replaced in the 1950s by scientific socio-biological, or socio-medical models of individual difference. These ideologies tended to focus on differences not in Mendelian terms (which emphasizes absolutes such as hair colour), but on the amount of variation between different groups. As a result of this work, the nature/nurture debate shifted back to an emphasis on the impact of genetic differences over that of environmental influences. The genome project will serve to re-emphasize these hereditary factors, despite evidence to the contrary from a number of fields. For instance, research has indicated that economically disadvantaged and Black communities in the USA are three times more likely to be given a diagnosis of schizophrenia, whilst this figure rises to 16 times for such groups in the UK (James, 2002). Diagnosis rates from comparable genetic groups in the West Indies or from twin research challenge these heredity arguments. The claim that genetic rather than social factors determine poor performance or deviant behaviour offers élites a convenient political excuse for not prioritizing policies that could enhance social equality.

There are many examples of how test results indicating particular sex or ethnic differences have been changed either to adjust the 'offending' items, or to offer a re-interpretation of the results. The effect, however, is the same. Instead of regarding their results as a legitimate scientific finding of difference, or of offering validation for the existing tool, items that unfavourably differentiate against the dominant group are changed to maintain the social order. For example, when Terman (1916) found evidence in the Stanford–Binet test of a gender difference in performance, these items were treated as biased and those items in which boys performed less well were removed. Alternatively, he could have treated his original findings of higher female ability as offering new scientific insight, or a boost to the test's validity if he had expected females to do better than males. Instead, he chose to reinforce the existing social and scientific paradigm. Similarly, scales have been changed as a result of bias against particular classes, cultures and 'race', for example in the UK with the treatment of secondary school entrance examination, termed 11+, results in the 1960s. Thus, social values are inherent in test production.

One of the biggest and most controversial studies of 'racial' differences and intelligence occurred in the 1950s in the USA with the 'Head Start' project. This programme was based upon progressive education ideologies developed by Dewey and others, who saw education as a means of stabilizing democracy and of creating new opportunities. The project aimed to ameliorate the adverse environmental factors affecting young Black Americans. Psychologists Jensen and later Eysenck studied its impact. Jensen interpreted the initially poor results of the programme as showing a hereditary and 'racial' difference in intelligence, with Black Americans being outperformed by their White counterparts. This led to further ethnic-based studies, which went on to reveal the lower levels of intelligence of other groups such as the Irish.

Unsurprisingly, a heated debate ensued with Kamin (1974) and others indicating the shortcomings of both the measure Jensen had used and also the biases in their ideology. As a result of this controversy, intelligence testing has been outlawed in many states in the USA. Yet, since the 1980s, there has been a rapid increase in the application of ability and personality testing for selection purposes with far more limited debate considering the adverse impact of the results on various minority ethnic groups. Despite findings indicating differences between the performance of Caucasians and African-Americans, limited studies have been undertaken as to why this might be the case, or to question the reliability and validity of such instruments for organizational selection (Hunter and Hunter, 1984; Schmidt *et al.*, 1996) (see Figure 6.17).

*Figure 6.17 Ethnic difference in performance on SAT maths tests*

(Hogan, 2003, p.531)

However, when results do not suit those who believe in White superiority, their interpretation is changed in order to defend that belief. For example, research has found that, of all the cultures, the Japanese obtain the highest scores in standard IQ tests. Instead of being seen as an indication of their superior mental status, it has been interpreted as indicating their lack of creativity.

Evidence does reveal that there is a link between intelligence testing and the environment of the applicants. For example, in French Canada a decision was made to change the major language of instruction from English to French. This was quickly reversed, however, when French-speaking children began to outperform their English-speaking counterparts. So the social hierarchy was reinstated. Rust and Golombok (1989) use this example to illustrate how those in power are unwilling to relinquish their privileged position.

In reviewing selection methods, Robertson and Smith (2001) argue that cognitive tests are consistently shown to be valid and fair when applied across different ethnic groups. Evidence does indicate that performance on these tools varies across different occupational groups. Although they note that 'cognitive ability testing does not provide differentially "unfair" predictions', there is evidence that members of different ethnic groups 'obtain lower scores on such tests' (2001, p.453). Schmitt and Mills (2001) provide an example of this tension: on the one hand, they say there is 'little or no evidence that these tests show any form of differential prediction or psychometric bias when they are used to predict the performance of people belonging to different demographic groups' (*ibid.*, p.451); on the other hand (in the very next sentence), they report that 'mean differences of approximately one standard deviation are frequently observed on these tests between African Americans and Caucasians.' In trying to understand more about these differences, Schmitt and Mills devised a study to assess the impact of presentation medium on test performance. They compared traditional paper and pencil tests with a telephone-based simulation designed to measure similar constructs. Their study confirmed that whilst the two tests did measure similar concepts, the telephone simulation showed a lower adverse impact on the African-American group. I will return to the importance of contextualized assessment systems of work performance in Chapter 9.

Studies of this type are important as they try to understand the role of perception in selection performance. Schmitt and Mills' research looked at how different presentation can affect performance with the more job-relevant tests (or what psychologists term higher 'face validity' tests), improving performance as we saw in Chapter 3. Research like this offers more understanding but also a means of amending selection instruments to reduce such underlying bias. Similarly, Bobko *et al.* (1999, p.561), in their review of cognitive ability, conclude that 'adverse impact continues to occur in many commonly used selection ratios'.

In their review of selection methods, Robertson and Smith (2001) place the responsibility for resolving the complex issue of adverse impact on 'people involved in the design and validation of selection procedure' (*ibid.*, p.453). This creates a narrow focus of responsibility, placing it solely with test-developers and not also with test-users. Despite the validity evidence in favour of cognitive tests, they propose that tests should not be deployed universally. I concur with them but suggest that more understanding is required about what affects performance of candidates so that we can ensure that suitable selection tools, in which unfair bias has been reduced and not perpetuated, are developed. This is particularly important given the increased influence of computerized testing, which is being adopted by organizations to help them manage high applicant volumes. The high number of applicants reflects the large remuneration levels offered to successful candidates. Failure to attend to this important issue will result in the perpetuation of bias and contribute to increasing polarity of society.

### 8.4.3   *Poor application of tools*

A further way that implicit bias enters testing is not due directly to the test-developer, but through the corrupt application of these tools by test-users. As we saw in Chapter 2, test-users often fail to ensure that the choice of psychometric instrument is based on a thorough job analysis of the role. They should be responsible for identifying the key competencies important for candidates and search for an instrument that matches those stipulated requirements.

Properly developed tests have a manual in which the test-developers identify and define the domain that their test covers. They show the parameters for that measure. However, these can differ in two important ways. First, two developers can use the same term to mean *different things*. For example, in personality assessment, 'extroversion' may mean simply sociability; in another test it indicates 'energy gained through interaction with others'. Second, the same concept can be defined at *different levels*. For instance, 'innovative behaviour' for Kirton (1967) is a simple uni-dimensional scale differentiating between adapters and innovators, whilst Patterson (2000) uses four dimensions to measure the same concept. Ultimately, test-users are responsible for ensuring the tests they select are suitable for the task and the context.

Test-users can also influence the application problems of tools through inadequate analysis and interpretation of results. Raw test scores, as I have indicated, are meaningless in themselves: their value lies in a comparison with specific populations. Through norm tables, the underlying characteristics of test-taking populations are identified. For example, if only White employees were involved when developing a test to help select retail banking assistants, the resulting test cannot legitimately be used to assess the performance of Black or Asian candidates.

The ultimate control in using tests rests with the test-user, and not with the test-developer. Therefore, users must be certain that the tool they choose differentiates between applicants in an accurate and consistent manner and shows who will perform a role well. The user must assess the relevance of the populations against which the scores have been standardized. More importantly, however, they should ensure that the norm tables reflect their own contexts. As a result, the choice of norms must reflect the sex, 'race', age, educational and experience levels of the applicant pool. Frequently, this is not the case. For example, in a recent court case a train operator was found to have unfairly rejected Afro-Caribbean applicants by using an inappropriate norm group who had higher education levels and a different ethnic composition than the applicant pool. Cases such as these underline the importance of the job analysis as a basis for selection. Equal opportunities are concerned with the appropriateness of the criteria: inappropriate criteria or inappropriately high cut-off levels discriminate unfairly against applicants who could have performed the job adequately. This case also showed insufficient care on the part of the test-developer in generating suitable norm groups for their users. It underlined the importance of ensuring that test results are interpreted appropriately.

The Sex Discrimination Act includes discrimination against people on grounds of their marital status, part-time or maternity status as well as their gender. Similarly, the definition of 'racial' discrimination is broad and includes colour, race, nationality, national or ethnic origins, where a group is distinguished from others through shared customs, beliefs, traditions and characteristics. (Codes of practice regarding selection are available from the **Equal Opportunities Commission** and the **Commission for Racial Equality**. In addition many test publishers have specific booklets on these issues as they pertain to psychometric testing.)

Job analysis can provide protection from unlawful discrimination for individuals seeking to join a firm by ensuring there is a robust basis to the selection and performance criteria that organizations apply. Such discrimination can, however, occur (and be lawful) where genuine differences in occupational qualifications can be proven – for instance, where a job requires particular physiological (excluding physical strength) or authenticity demands (such as for actors in the entertainment industry). Exclusions apply where it is necessary for decency or privacy to have a particular sex, such as in the body searches undertaken by Customs and Excise, or in care roles. In addition, the European Court of Justice has permitted the positive discrimination of females and members of minority ethnic groups for a limited period in order to redress previous imbalances (see Marshcall *v.* Land Nordrhein-Wesrfalen [1998] IRLR 39). Across Europe, there is an increasing call for the appointment of women into senior roles and some Scandinavian countries, such as Norway, are taking active steps to force organizations through legal means to appoint more women to their management boards. They are seeking about 40 per cent female composition of boards.

One way that test interpretation has been changed is to artificially extend the top or bottom levels of tests. This distortion, however, runs counter to the view that selection tools are designed for a purpose. Traditional tests with a falsely extended range have been found to discriminate against African-American and Afro-Caribbean applicants who show more variation in results. The distortion of tests' ceilings will influence the interpretation of results and in particular affect minority groups. Tests are designed to predict job performance: the more they are distorted during their development, the more likely such distortions are magnified in the interpretation stages.

Test-users must also consider how the results of testing are given to the test-taker. Psychometric tests are powerful tools that can discriminate, devalue and seriously erode the self-esteem of those who take them, particularly if the results are handled in an inappropriate manner. They can become a label from which the individual cannot escape (though probably not to the extent Figure 6.18 suggests!). The BPS has strict guidelines on this (see BPS level A and B competencies). What is often omitted from feedback is care in recognizing and identifying that the results pertain to the applicant's suitability to *this* role in *this* context. What applicants may actually hear, or sometimes incorrectly infer, from feedback is that they are not suitable for this role *per se* and therefore their career aspirations are dashed. The information that psychometric tests provide may not even be accessible to the test-taker. Test-users are therefore often in a privileged and powerful position: they should not abuse it in either the gathering of data, its use, or in the feed-back of results.

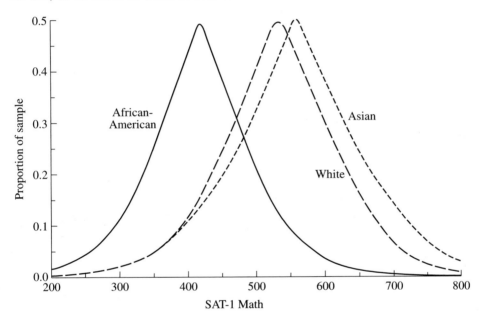

*Figure 6.18 The labelling impact of test results*

### 8.4.4 *Ethics*

Underlying each of these issues is the question of ethics. Ability and personality tests are designed to measure something. Cognitive ability has the highest correlation with performance of all selection tools. Similarly, intelligence tests have a high correlation with academic achievement. However, Rust and Golombok (1989) argue the direction of causation may be open to question, so that the core items of intelligence may be derivative and not determining.

The ultimate question for both developers and users is the ethics behind the tool and its application. Is it designed to match an individual to an environment so that attention is paid to the context of application, or is the purpose to de-select those who are unfit? Tests have a mystique surrounding them. Given their historical application to identify those who were unfit, care must be taken in their use. For example, should a test that can indicate a test-user's motivation to change be used to inform a manager's decisions about redundancy? Could a test be developed to measure integrity? Should tests be sold on the basis that they reveal the 'dark side' of human nature? Should tests such as the Myers Briggs Type Indicator⊗, conceived of as a development instrument, be used in selection practices? These are all questions that raise ethical issues and concern as to whether it is appropriate to construct tests to measure every facet of human experience. They also relate to wider issues regarding the promotion and the application of psychometric tools.

## 9   Summary

Psychometric tests will always be open to abuse as they offer a potential means of legitimizing discrimination by those in power and authority. In this chapter I have sought to examine the underlying issues of test production and make explicit some of the assumptions that underpin psychometrics, revealing how social values and prejudice can have an impact on the development, application, analysis and interpretation of results. Whilst some may feel both confident and comfortable to reduce the value of human beings to an empirical value, there are others who see humans in terms of their potential, regardless of the social context they find themselves in.

A critical issue underlying any test is the definition of the domain. Often tests are devised on an atheoretical basis, or they use the same term to mean different things. It is important that test-users require adequate conceptual rationale for a test. Concept validity is key here; nevertheless, it is often weakly developed or ignored. Without attention to this core issue, psychometrics will fail to offer any meaningful assessment and instead intelligence will be what intelligence tests measure – not what intelligence actually is.

There are fundamental differences in the assessment of typical versus maximal performance. Whilst many regard the scores obtained as set in stone, studies do indicate that they can change over time (Bayley, 1968). In the next two chapters I will reflect on the different approaches taken to measuring ability and performance and suggest that the distinction between the two may be a false dichotomy. It may be that only through increasing our understanding of the influence of personality, motivational, social, situational and cultural variables on psychometric test performance will we begin to understand the relationship between tests and job performance.

### *Exercise*

Taking a test manual look at the domain the test is designed to assess, what type of study has been undertaken to define the content of the test? What limitations might this hold for the test? Examine the composition of the norm groups. What problems might this present from selectors? What can they do to overcome these?

# CHAPTER 7

# Selection tools 4: ability tests

## 1 Overview

Ability testing is an increasingly common tool used in organizational
selection and recruitment. It has long been a factor identified as predictive
of subsequent job performance. Arguably, ability testing is the most cost-
effective selection tool; it is not without controversy, however, as a high
proportion of the variance in job performance remains unaccounted for.
Chapter 7 focuses on the current application of ability testing. I begin by
tracing the development of psychological theories of intelligence
underpinning the creation of ability tests. These include three distinct
taxonomies into which various different models of intelligence can be
placed: uni-factorial measure, multiple dimensions, or multiple-hierarchical
factors. I examine the divergence between practitioners and researchers and
contrast the application of tests of specific abilities with tests of generic
cognitive performance. The incremental validity of ability tests is raised and
some of the problems of studies in this area are considered. I will return to
a more fundamental critique of this approach to testing in Chapter 10, but
the focus in this chapter is on the current use of ability-testing tools within
an occupational setting. One interesting recent development is the
challenge to the dominance of maximal tests in this area and a call for
more measurement of typical performance. This issue identifies the
importance of motivation as a significant factor affecting ability test
performance. I also highlight the expansion of intelligence into the
measurement of practical, situational and emotional abilities. The chapter
ends by reviewing the emergence of 'culturally free' testing – tests that can
fairly assess candidates regardless of their culture and 'race'.

## 2 Introduction

From the 1900s, a key research topic of psychology was to understand
what human intelligence was and how it could be measured. A natural
development leading from this was adult-level cognitive ability testing,
which offered a means of predicting performance differences amongst job
applicants. Since the 1980s the dominant view has been that cognitive
ability tests are the single best predictor of job and training performance
across a wide variety of different occupational groups (Hunter and Hunter,
1984; Reilly and Chao, 1982; Schmidt *et al.*, 1992). This research evidence,
coupled with the administrative ease and their relatively low cost of ability
tests, has led to their increased acceptance within selection processes, yet
few would use these instruments as the sole basis for their selection
decision. In this chapter the role of cognitive testing in selection is
considered and how much incremental validity this tool offers over other
selection systems is highlighted. We begin by identifying three distinct

perspectives for the definition of intelligence, each situating intelligence in a distinct framework, and go on to discuss the chronological development of three different conceptions of ability: uni-factorial, multi-factorial and multi-hierarchical models.

## 3  What is intelligence?

At the heart of psychometrics lies the identification of differences between the mental processes – or 'intelligence' – of individuals. These in turn result in differences in job performance. The key question underpinning this measurement is: what actually is intelligence? And how can it best be assessed? Three distinct schools of thought emerge to answer what might appear to be a straightforward question. The first approach involved a one-factor model of intelligence that stemmed from a socio-biological position, and argued that intelligence was related to biological or genetic factors. From this view, it is biological differences that underlie different levels of cognitive skill; as a result, the emphasis is on trying to uncover distinct biological dimensions. This approach assumes that intelligence is independent of any social, ontological or linguistic context. Thus, a set of interesting questions arises: what value does intelligence hold? Is its value not socially constructed with different cultures valuing different abilities?

A second approach emphasizes the existence of distinct abilities and highlighted the role environmental processes play in forming intelligence. It also focuses on the link between *learning* and intelligence. From this

*Figure 7.1  The first mental testing measurement*

social-learning perspective, intelligence is not fixed; it is dynamic, and research tries to identify the optimum ways of boosting everyone's intelligence. The range of educational attainment measures, discussed in Chapter 6 (typified by the current school SAT assessment in the UK) fall into this category.

The third and more emergent conception of intelligence has widened the scope of assessment to include volition, or motivation. In this model, differences in cognitive performance cannot be explained by ability alone; instead, it is how a person *applies* these skills that makes the difference. This view is a recent one, developed in response to dissatisfaction with the results of ability- and personality-based measures alone. The focus has shifted to trying to understand the link between measured ability and observed behaviour.

If we take a chronological view of how these distinct perspectives emerged, it is possible to see how these concepts were created, critically appraised and then developed into new ideas. Different conceptions of intelligence underpin many of the developments in the psychometric field, and later in the chapter I will explore the relationship between different types of test and successful performance in an occupational setting. Now I want to turn my attention to three distinct conceptions of intelligence that underpin the development of psychometrics in the selection field.

Research into intellectual ability has broadly developed from three distinct categories that chronologically developed and built on each other, each emerging from criticisms of earlier ideas. When looking at these studies as a whole, what is important to note is that much of the initial work in this area was based on samples of Western university students while subsequent research has been dominated by selection and training performance within a *military* context. Neither students nor military trainees are typical of the general population. It is also important to note that both are located within a Western paradigm. As a result, the samples used have been biased in terms of those who have already succeeded in applying their intellect within a particular Western context.

## 3.1 Uni-factorial models of intelligence

Working in the nineteenth century, Galton proposed (but never found) a general model of intelligence. Instead, Spearman (1904, 1927) was responsible for the first model of the structure of intelligence. This was based on a factor analysis of human ability. He argued that all human abilities were linked – correlating together to form one super factor called 'general intelligence', or '*g*'. He conceptualized this in terms of a 'psycho-physiological energy'. This notion of energy was not a new concept, but a development of an earlier metaphor used to describe the halo around saint's heads. Through such a device he did not regard intelligence as some simple ability, but one imbued with higher moral and social tones. Spearman was interested in what it meant for one person to be smarter than another and conceived of cognitive differences as distinct sensory perceptions; as a result, he saw a role for both physiological and psychological aspects of intelligence.

He also regarded general intelligence as a quantitative variable. He did not question this assumption which some later theorists regard as a serious flaw in the scientific process (Kline, 1998, p.48; Michell, 1997). Nor was he interested in the specific content of the tests: he felt that ability tools could not reveal anything interesting about the nature of intelligence. Instead, he described cognitive tests as 'miners excavating forward into wonderful rich new ground, but repeatedly missing the correct direction on account of labouring in the darkness' (Spearman, 1923, p.35). Spearman conceptualized intelligence as a unitary construct with test results comprising the all important 'g'. He did, however, include an error score, a 'will' factor and an amount of 'character' as influencing the final result.

## 3.2 Multi-factoral models

Researchers took this idea and tried to study 'g'; however, they found it elusive. Thurstone (1938) looked at the correlations between results on different tests and disputed Spearman's general view. He argued that these correlations were in fact weak, and therefore took a contrary view, suggesting intelligence was comprised of distinct and largely independent factors. Thus, the first of many multiple factor models for intelligence was proposed. Thurstone's initial work, based on a sample of 240 male university students who undertook a battery of 60 tests, eventually reduced intelligence to nine primary factors (see Figure 7.2). From these abilities a series of tests was devised, each measuring a distinct aspect of cognitive ability.

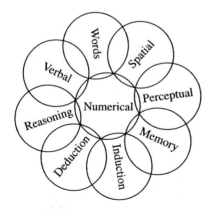

*Figure 7.2   Thurstone's primary mental abilities*

Other models of these key abilities soon emerged, such as Guildford's cube (1956, 1959) (see Figure 7.3). This model focused on three axes: contents, products and operations, with each axis containing a number of subcomponents. Guildford argued that each cell in his cube represented a unique mental ability. As a result, the model suggested that intelligence was comprised of 180 distinct cells.

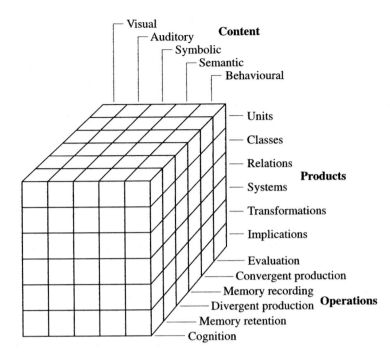

*Figure 7.3  Guildford's cube*

## 3.3  Multi-hierarchical models

In response to the concerns regarding the unwieldy nature of these multiple factor models of intelligence, a third type of model was developed. Like their predecessors these models built on the idea of distinct abilities, but placed them in a hierarchy (for example, Gustafsson, 1984). Four hierarchical models are worthy of more note as they have enabled significant developments in our understanding of intelligence.

### 3.3.1  Horn and Cattell's model

Horn and Cattell (1966) devised the most widely accepted model: theirs has five second-order factors for intelligence: (1) fluid intelligence, (2) crystallized intelligence, (3) visualization, (4) retrieval and (5) cognitive speed. Of these five components, two are regarded as most important: fluid intelligence and crystallized intelligence. Fluid intelligence ($g_f$) focuses on figural, or non-verbal, general reasoning ability. This dimension is involved in reasoning in novel situations. In contrast, crystallized intelligence ($g_c$) is more concerned with the application of verbal or conceptual knowledge, such as verbal ability, language development, reading comprehension, sequential reasoning and general information (Kline, 1998). Crystallized intelligence is regarded as different from the other factors as it is seen to cut across different cultures and is more akin to that measured by traditional intelligence tests (Kline, 1993). The visualization, or '$Pv$', factor concerns spatial orientation, whilst retrieval and cognitive speed are aspects that underpin how intelligence is applied.

Most studies have concentrated on the two higher order dimensions of intelligence: $g_f$ and $g_c$. Research evidence suggests that crystallized intelligence is the more dynamic element, and can improve through cumulative learning. It therefore has an experiential component associated with it. In contrast, it has been argued that fluid intelligence is a result of biological factors and causal learning. Although the two are related (correlations of $r = 0.4$ are common in adults), it has been contended that crystallized intelligence is more theoretically important as it indicates how a person engages with their environment (Goff and Ackerman, 1992). Therefore, a link is made between the mental process of intelligence and the more behavioural component, which concerns *what we do with it.*

### 3.3.2 Vernon's model

A second important hierarchical model was devised by Vernon from 1950 to 1961 (see Figure 7.4). Undertaking original research, he made a significant differentiation between verbally/educationally based and spatially/mechanically based intelligence. (The second form of intelligence is sometimes referred to as the 'practical factor'.) From this, a series of sub-factors emerged, which then divided further into a series of more narrow specific abilities. Wisely perhaps, Vernon did not identify precisely how many specific abilities there were, but did note some prominent ones, such as verbal and numerical abilities.

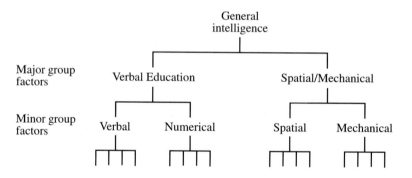

*Figure 7.4   Vernon's hierarchical model of intelligence*

### 3.3.3 Carroll's model

The third model, Carroll's (1993), was based on results obtained from psychometric testing (see Figure 7.5). His model has three stratums, with general intelligence at the top level, followed by fluid and crystallized intelligence and visual perception. The bottom strata include a range of different abilities.

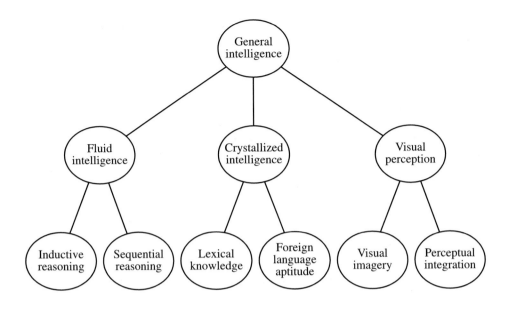

*Figure 7.5   Carroll's hierarchy of intelligence model*

### 3.3.4   Garner's model

A more idiosyncratic model of intelligence (and one that has found favour amongst educationalists) is Garner's (1983) model. This sought to widen the range of abilities included in order to include factors previously considered outside the domain. Garner identified seven distinct elements to intelligence: (1) linguistic, (2) musical, (3) logical-mathematic, (4) spatial, (5) bodily-kinaesthetic, (6) intrapersonal and (7) interpersonal. Whilst it is clear there is an overlap in some of the elements, indeed many of the factors Garner included are more commonly considered as aspects of personality or *psychomotor,* rather than cognitive ability skills *per se.*

All four hierarchical models focus on the content and organization of knowledge. Some have led directly to the development of specific tests; others have used the findings from existing instruments. An alternative starting point for researchers is to examine intelligence in terms of cognitive information processing. This perspective is not interested in the development of better psychometric tests *per se*, but instead focuses on the identification of underlying biological dimensions and in exploring why occupational tests work as they do (Hunt, 1999).

A key researcher in this area is Sternberg, who has a wide body of work exploring the whole issue of intelligence. His 1985 model proposed three basic constructs. The first, 'meta components' or 'executive functions', included planning, monitoring and evaluating of other operations. The second, 'performance' was concerned with how solutions are reached. The third is 'knowledge-acquisition', which included three elements: encoding, the combination of elements to be encoded and the comparison component, which compares the encoded elements. Sternberg's model is important as it highlights an important choice in information processes regarding whether to remain the same, or adapt and change. This aspect underlies 'tacit' intelligence (Sternberg and Wagner, 1986), which I shall discuss in section 5.1.

In a selection and recruitment context, the main type of underlying model that tends to be used for testing focuses on distinct factors. There is a limited role for measures of '$g$', but it is important to be able to measure specific types of abilities, as indicated by the job analysis. The next section reviews different factors that are commonly measured in a recruitment context, before reflecting on the values of specific versus general intelligence data. We then turn our attention towards the identification and assessment of new 'abilities', such as tacit and emotional intelligence, before addressing the more significant issue of whether it is possible to separate and measure intelligence from culture.

## 4  Choosing and using ability assessment tools

Business and military organizations have long been interested in the application of ability testing to assist with selection and recruitment. Although research suggests that general intelligence measures account for a high proportion of the variance in job performance, few recruiters would use a generic test, such as AH5. Instead, based on the findings from their job analysis, those involved in selection tend to use tests that enable them to measure distinct abilities. This is important as it increases the face and content validity of their recruitment processes. As a result of these market forces, occupational ability testing has expanded to include five key areas (see Figure 7.6). These areas are broadly related to Guildford's differential model, with each ability being regarded as independent from the others (see profile in Figure 7.7).

*Figure 7.6  List of five main occupational testing categories*

| Area | Ability tested | Example |
| --- | --- | --- |
| **Verbal** | From simple word recognition, spelling and grammar to critical verbal reasoning and comprehension | Text: 'Alison was particularly sorry not to be going to the development centres as her manager needs her to remain at her desk.'<br>Response format: True, false, can not say<br>Question: Was it Alison's decision not to attend the development centre? |
| **Numerical** | Basic numerical calculations to numerical reasoning where inferences can be drawn | Fill in the missing numbers in the series:<br>4.5, 9.5, 14.5, ?, 23.5 |

**Spatial**      Rotation of shapes in 3-d      See 7.6a

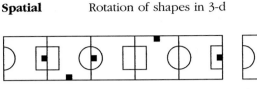
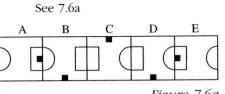

*Figure 7.6a*

**Dexterity**      Hand speed, accuracy and      See 7.6b
                   co-ordination

*Figure 7.6b*

**Sensory**      Visual acuity, sound or colour      See 7.6c: can you identify any
                   discrimination                         pattern within these dots?

```
O     O     O     O     O

O     O     ●     O     O

O     ●     O     ●     O

O     O     ●     O     O

O     ●     O     ●     O

O     O     ●     O     O

O     O     O     O     O
```

*Figure 7.6c*

---

Many of the psychometric ability tests are designed with a particular job
level in mind. For example, verbal ability tests can be used at many grades
– from clerical through to management. The complexity of the tests
increases in line with the different level of skill required.

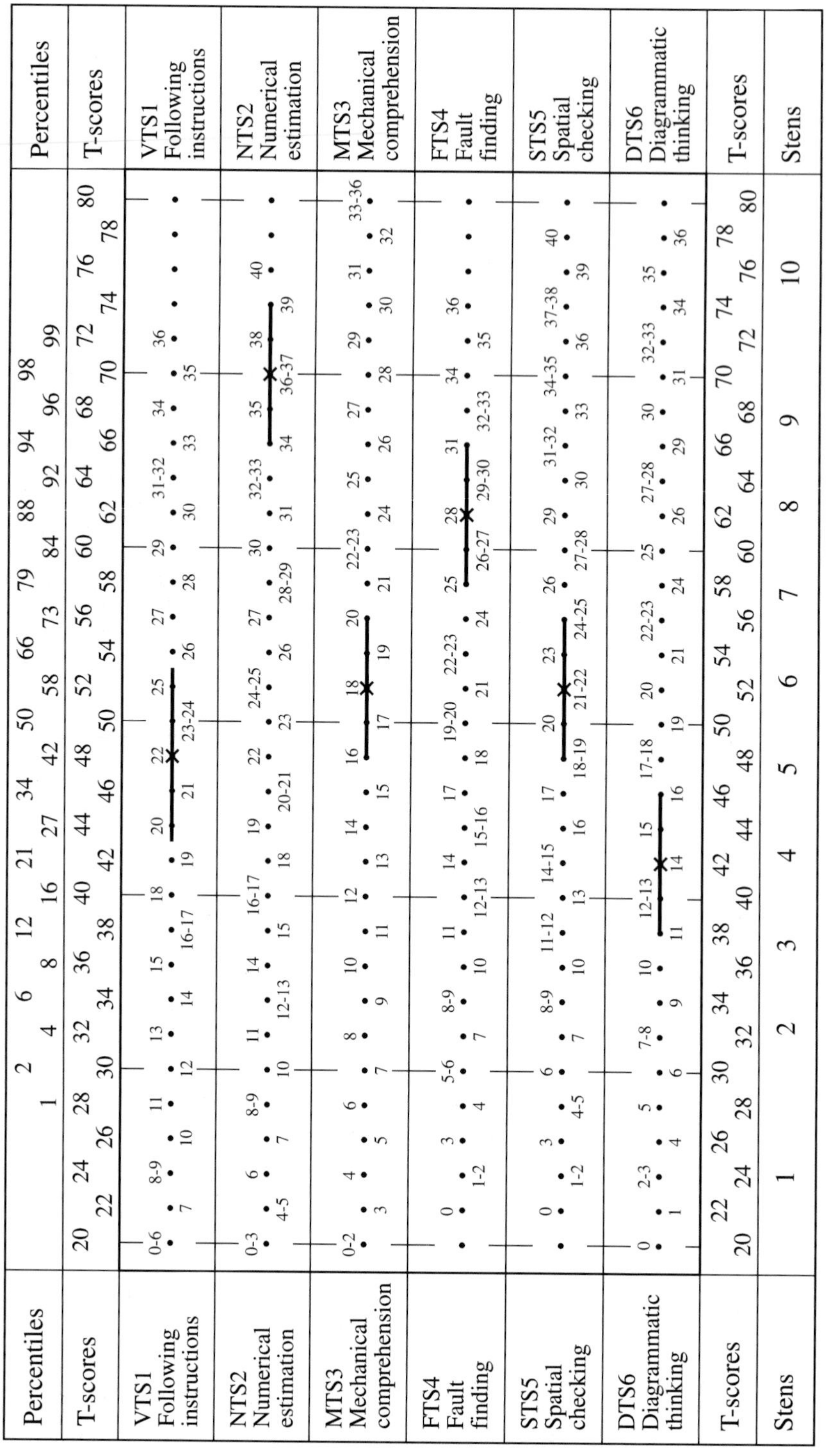

Percentiles

T-scores

VTS1 Following instructions

NTS2 Numerical estimation

MTS3 Mechanical comprehension

FTS4 Fault finding

STS5 Spatial checking

DTS6 Diagrammatic thinking

T-scores

Stens

*Figure 7.7   ATB profile chart*

Many tests have been devised with specific occupational categories in mind. In some cases, tests aimed at focusing on specific abilities have been devised. The following tests are based on different forms of spatial ability (see Table 7.1).

**Table 7.1 Variations on spatial abilities**

| | |
|---|---|
| Mechanical | Problem-solving based on understanding of mechanical and physical principles. |
| Diagrammatic | Linear reasoning based on understanding spatial relationships. |
| Clerical | Speed and accuracy measures of error checking and classification and sorting skills. |

In choosing precisely which test to use, it is important that recruiters examine the **test manual**. Manuals contain important information about the domain that is being measured, how the test has been constructed and how the results compare to other existing and standard measures of intelligence. This latter aspect provides an insight into how much incremental validity the test provides. The manual should also include all validity studies relating to the tool.

In addition, the manual will provide key comparison data. The norm tables found in each manual provide the means of comparing the raw scores obtained on the test with those of other groups. As I noted in Chapter 6, it is important that the samples included in the manual reflect the demographics of the populations being measured.

One ongoing problem for those involved in recruiting is the lack of information available regarding testing people with disabilities. Whilst many reputable test publishers and psychological organizations (for instance, the British Psychological Society) offer generic guidelines about using psychometrics with those who have disabilities, few manuals contain relevant information, such as how much more time dyslexic applicants require in taking a test. In a high-stakes environment of selection, there is an enormous pressure to hide disability and to show no complicating factors that could differentiate an applicant from others. In a high-stakes situation applicants with a minor disability might be reluctant to reveal any problems they may have, but it is clear that those applicants with dyslexia, for example, might do significantly worse in ability tests, regardless of their level of intelligence.

## Dilemma box 7.1

You are asked to test 10 applicants for an apprenticeship scheme. During the practice session you watch one of the applicants as they attempt to answer the questions. They appear to be getting very close to the paper. You approach them and ask if they are all right as you suspect they have a problem. Perhaps they have not put on their glasses. The candidate responds that they are fine. Throughout the rest of the test you notice they are still holding the paperwork very close to their eyes. When you mark the completed test you notice that this applicant has only completed about two-thirds of the questions that the others have; of these 75 per cent are correct. You suspect that there is a visual problem they do not want to admit to. The applicant has done well on their interview. What do you do?

## 4.1 Comparing general and specific ability assessment

Research evidence has suggested a strong relationship between job performance and the scores obtained from cognitive ability tests, with mean validity of 0.30 (Bobko *et al.*, 1999) to 0.45 (Hunter and Hunter, 1984; Schmidt and Hunter, 1998). Criterion-related validity studies suggest that the value of using cognitive testing generalizes across all occupational areas (Robertson and Smith, 2001). A central theme amongst researchers in this domain is a comparison of the relative values in the assessment process of each distinct selection tool, such as the cognitive test and the interview.

In Chapter 5, I reviewed evidence of the relative value of the interview, which suggested that intelligence is one of the main factors that is being assessed well. Much research has centred on the relationship between cognitive ability testing and the scores obtained from structured interviews. Some have gone so far as to argue that the interview is in fact an inferior surrogate cognitive assessment offering little incremental validity above the score obtained from ability tests (Campion *et al.*, 1988). Studies comparing the difference between interview and SAT verbal and mathematical attainment scores with acceptance decisions from universities and first-year performance results have found that the interview, although a valid tool, added nothing to ability test results (Shahani *et al.*, 1991). These findings were replicated in comparing the predictive validity of these two tools in pilot training (Walters *et al.*, 1993). However, these predictive validity findings were not replicated when the outcome dimension was changed to supervisory appraisal ratings (Campion *et al.*, 1984). Cortina *et al.* (2000) undertook a meta-analysis to examine the incremental validity of these two processes and also the 'conscientiousness' personality scale. In reviewing 30 studies, they found that the unstructured interview had a weak relationship with ability tests (Rho = 0.55), rising for more structured versions (Rho = 0.253). They argued that while unstructured interviews remain problematic, the interview can assess job knowledge and other facets more effectively and therefore has a value over and above that offered by ability tests. Few, however, would argue that interviews are merely verbally delivered cognitive tests (Harris, 1989; Huffcutt *et al.*, 1996) (see Chapter 5 for more details).

A key advantage of ability tests over face-to face approaches to assessment is that they can increase the objectivity of the assessment, particularly where gender, 'race' and ethnicity details are removed. However, as I reported in the last chapter, ability tests do not remove all discrimination. Evidence indicates that ability tests do adversely discriminate against members of minority ethnic groups, with lower scores (1 standard deviation) being common between White and Black applicants (BeVier *et al.*, 1998; Bobko *et al.*, 1999). Despite this finding, Robertson and Smith (2001) argue that there has been no evidence suggesting a comparable difference in their validity.

The search for fairer assessment processes has been an important one as it has extended and broadened previously narrow performance dimensions to include other factors, such as organizational citizenship (Smith *et al.*, 1983) and contextual performance (Borman and Motowidlo, 1993). Cognitive ability has been shown to be less predictive of these wider performance dimensions. I will return to examine the development of alternative assessment approaches that offer a fairer measure of job performance in Chapter 9.

Despite the plethora of different ability tests available, the incremental validity of such instruments above general cognitive assessment has not been established (Olea and Ree, 1994; Ree *et al.*, 1994; Schmitt *et al.*, 1984). In reviewing the meta-analytic studies in this area, problems emerge. In some cases, researchers have chosen to use a specific ability measure, such as verbal ability as a surrogate for '$g$' (Pulakos and Schmitt, 1996), whilst in others the results reported involve the aggregation of complete batteries of tests. Each study has involved different batteries with different types and numbers of sub-tests. It is therefore difficult for organizations to identify which of the available measures is the most effective.

Some specific work has been undertaken to examine the value of subcomponents above that of '$g$' in a number of military settings. A study exploring the construct and criterion validity of the Armed Services Vocational Aptitude Battery (ASVAB), examined '$g$' and three sub-factors – speed, verbal/maths and technical knowledge (Ree and Carretta, 1994). They found that 63.8 per cent of the total variance was accounted for by '$g$', but only 6.2 per cent was accounted for by speed, 2.4 per cent by verbal/maths and 7.7 per cent by technical. Olea and Ree's (1994) work on a comparable air force test showed the incremental validity of other tests to '$g$' was only 0.02 for navigator training and 0.08 for predicting pilot training success. The problem of these studies is that whilst sample sizes are relatively high, the vocational domain is narrow and the outcome relatively easy to measure. Replicating such studies in a broader work setting is more complex.

## 4.2   Maximal vs. typical intelligence testing

One of the most interesting developments in the field of cognitive testing is that devised by Ackerman and colleagues (Kanfer and Ackerman, 1989; Goff and Ackerman, 1992; Ackerman and Heggestad, 1997). Their work challenges the dominant focus on measuring of maximal performance which traditionally underlies all ability assessment. They argue that much of the variance in job performance remains unaccounted for by maximal cognitive tests; indeed correlations between ability test and job performance are around 0.5 or 0.6 (*ibid.*, 1994). As a result, Ackerman argues that it is more important to look at *typical* performance, than try to separate test performance from the usual job environment. For example, he noted that administrators are encouraged to build a rapport in a test situation in an attempt to encourage the test-takers' co-operation and motivation to succeed. This reflects an earlier distinction Terman (1924) made when he asserted that an individual's 'chronic' intelligence is far more important than their 'acute' intelligence which is elicited in a short-term effortful time frame. Ackerman suggests an alternative multiple component model of typical performance, which includes intelligence, but adds intelligence-as-process, personality and interest dimensions. The 'typical intellectual engagement' (TIP) tool was devised to assess this typical form of intelligence.

Ackerman and Kanfer (1993) examined the different performance outcomes of air traffic controllers and identified how individual ability combined with different engagement levels in goal-setting behaviours offered the best insight into predicting performance change levels. They found that individuals differed in *where* they chose to focus their attention, and also in the *effort* they expended on the task. In this way, they identified that performance is not just a product of intelligence, but also includes interest and motivational dimensions. Through this work they suggested that motivation was linked to the application of an individual's attentional resources. Thus, an individual could be very bright but score poorly in a test if they had no interest in doing well. As a result of this work they suggest that it may be more important to understand how someone typically engages at work, rather than focusing on their maximal possible behaviour.

Goff and Ackerman (1992) went on to show significant relationships between typical intellectual engagement measures and crystallized intelligence, which is a surrogate measure for learned ability, with TIP accounting for 11 per cent of the variance in $g_c$. In contrast, maximal performance is more concerned with measuring *fluid* abilities and so TIP was found to account for lower levels of fluid abilities (1 per cent of the variance).

Farrell and McDaniel (2001) have examined Ackerman's (1988) underlying skill acquisition model for the TIP tool for over 24,000 individuals within a variety of jobs within the US Employment Service. They found that cognitive ability tests were the strongest predictor of initial job performance but declined in their power as tenure increased. These results showed mixed support for Ackerman's model. We still await a study examining the TIP model in a selection context; nonetheless, it is clear that pursuit of the relationship between intelligence, personality, motivation and ability is important in trying to understand job-related behaviour.

In support of the impact of motivation on test performance, Furnham's (1992) model *below* (Figure 7.8) identifies five factors that contribute to behaviour at workplaces. Notice that he has placed personality at the centre, but also he suggests it has a reciprocal influence on the four other factors of intelligence, motivation, demographics and ability. He also indicates that each of the factors will have a distinct influence in their own right on behaviour. In addition, this model separates intelligence and ability to imply that they are different and distinct dimensions.

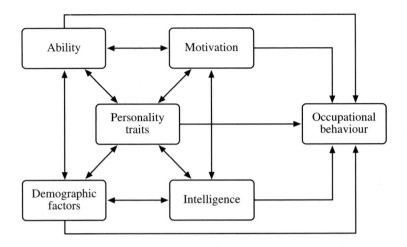

*Figure 7.8   Main factors predicting occupational behaviour*

(Furnham, 1992, p.13)

## 5   New forms of intelligence testing

Recent attention has turned towards new distinct forms of so-called 'intelligence' which differentiate between successful and more average levels of performance in the workplace. As a result, two new tests of 'intelligence' have been devised: one to measure tacit, or applied, intelligence and one purporting to measure emotional sensitivity.

### 5.1 Tacit ability

As we saw earlier, Sternberg's model of intelligence resulted in a new way of looking at intelligence that placed more emphasis on acquired knowledge. As a result, Sternberg with Wagner (1986, 1995; Sternberg, 1997) proposed a form of intelligence that is unrelated to academic success, but rather focuses on abilities developed from attaining daily goals. This measure is a significant departure from other instruments as it applies intelligence gained from experience. Although their ideas have stimulated some debate between researchers, little conclusive evidence suggests this novel form of intelligence offers anything to selection above that measured by 'g', nor has there been any significant advantage found between this form of intelligence measurement and subsequent job performance (Sue-Chan *et al.*, 1997). Studies of this instrument have been hampered by low sample sizes, restriction of range issues and other attenuation problems (McDaniel *et al.*, 2001). In addition, some would argue that such a measure may be very dependent on cultural context – however, its application into other cultures has yet to be examined in detail.

A more long-standing tacit and social ability test, termed 'situational judgement testing', has received increased attention over the same period

(Chan and Schmitt, 1997; Clevenger *et al.*, 2001; McDaniel *et al.*, 2001). Situational judgement tests are designed to assess candidates' perceptions of the *best* and *worst* actions in a work situation, and therefore these instruments reflect their experiential knowledge. A recent meta-analysis indicated correlations with general cognitive ability and corrected validity of 0.56, placing it ahead of many other selection tools (McDaniel *et al.*, 2001). Moreover, studies suggest that this type of test showed smaller differences across different 'racial' groups than other cognitive ability tests, indicating that it may reduce discrimination (Motowidlo *et al.*, 1990; Clevenger *et al.*, 2001). These tests offer organizations a boost to the face validity of their selection practices and indicate favourable support for an alternative ability assessment, which may reduce discrimination against minority groups. I will return to job-based assessment tools in more detail in Chapter 9).

## 5.2 Emotional intelligence

Another new development that has gained much interest amongst practitioners is the assessment of a concept pioneered by Goleman (1996): 'emotional intelligence'. Related to practical intelligence, emotional intelligence is concerned with measuring the individual's social intelligence about their own and others' feelings. What is interesting is that emotional intelligence subsumes Gardner's (1983) inter- and intra-personal intelligences. Although the idea has generated great interest from practitioners, little research has been reported to indicate its criterion-related validity within an occupational setting. Indeed, Dulewicz and Higgs (1999) have suggested that part of this difficulty may be due to the largely derivative and anecdotal nature of the original theory which is based on the internal introspection of a semi-transient dimension, termed a 'meta mood'. Thus, the theory on which these tools are derived may be questionable. While this new measure has enjoyed some commercial success, it is clear that there are ongoing concerns about the weakness of the underpinning model.

## 6 Culture-free testing

A key issue that many of these models of intelligence and ability fail to address is the value placed on particular skills within a particular culture (Kline, 1993, p.172). For instance, inherent to Sternberg's model of intelligence are environmental and experiential components. Intelligence emerges as a concept which is culturally specific, and, as a result, any measurement will be inseparable from the social and political factors that dominate that particular context. These findings are significant for psychometricians and test-users, and suggest a research agenda for those interested in examining whether measurement of mental ability can cross cultural borders. This is important for global organizations who want to know if they can select employees who will be able to operate effectively and efficiently in any location (see Dilemma box 7.2).

> ## *Dilemma box 7.2*
>
> You are an HR consultant for a multinational oil company and have been asked by the HR vice-president to review the criteria for leadership selection across the business. There are five key business areas: Europe, America, Africa, South East Asia and Antarctica. There are four business operations: exploration, drilling, refining and marketing. Where do you start? What issues do you need to be sensitive to?

A key challenge to the application of testing on a global basis is how can we devise instruments that can be used fairly to assess candidates from across different cultures? On one hand, as we have seen, intelligence has a cultural component, $g_c$, suggesting that those who succeed within a given environment understand the significant conventions, artefacts and symbols of that context. Indeed, in some organizations all assessments are undertaken in English as it is regarded as the language of business and therefore successful applicants must be able to speak and read it well. On the other hand, the growing multicultural character of societies and the requirements of multinationals to recruit staff from across the world to work in any of their operations has increased the demand for a 'pure' measure of intelligence. Most of the measures however, reported earlier in this chapter and in Chapter 6 reflect a dominant Western view of intelligence and its implicit values. These include ordering items from left to right, orientating the test from top to bottom, or completing the test under a time constraint as well as more explicit content issues.

One of the most well-known ' culture-free' ability tests is Raven's Progressive Matrices (1965). This test comprises three distinct ability levels, suitable for children and people with learning difficulties through to the upper 20 per cent of the ability distribution. Based on the assessment of more culture-free fluid intelligence, the test's items involve abstract reasoning as measured through the presentation of a pattern, or matrix, in which a part is missing. In this test, the test-taker has to select from the options supplied one that completes the pattern.

The tests claim to transcend diverse linguistic and cultural differences and those based on physical ability as it is an entirely non-verbal instrument (as Figure 7.8 shows). Even the instructions can be provided in a mime if necessary to avoid the use of language. The only category of applicants that it does not suit are candidates with visual impairments. It has high administrative and scoring ease and so training of assessors can be kept to a minimum. The test is flexible and can be used in both individual or group administration contexts.

Nonetheless, it is not without problems for test-users. The materials can be rather confusing to follow and the norm tables are difficult to use (Hogan, 2003). Disappointingly, there is limited evidence that this instrument actually removes the bias towards majority groups. More attention is required in this area in order to enable us to answer whether it is possible to create an instrument that is culture-free and how far a test containing purely spatial items is free from cultural bias.

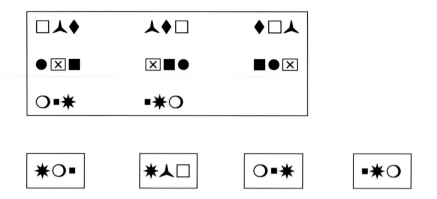

*Figure 7.9   Example of simulated Raven's progressive matrices item*

This is a growing market for an instrument that transcends cultures. Test-developers are increasingly turning their attentions to devising similar tools. It is clear that all of these types of culture-free instruments share a focus on figural or spatial reasoning, but often deploy insufficiently broad definitions of 'intelligence' to be of much use in an occupational setting. Whilst a simple inspection of any test will show how far it is non-verbal, it will not reveal whether it is actually free from cultural bias.

Some researchers have suggested that spatial ability is an inferior measure of intelligence to verbal ability. The predictive power of spatial ability is restricted in its application for higher level jobs. Instead, a more robust measure might be to use a verbal test developed within the candidate's own language and context. There is certainly increased attention amongst test-developers to translating their tests, or devising instruments from scratch for use in a different context, thereby trying to ensure comparability between their instruments across different cultures.

Another response to this dilemma that re-emerged in the 1980s was the attempt to identify alternative biological measures as a substitute for psychometric ability tests. It was argued that this type of measure could provide culturally free psychometric ability measures. Researchers in this area, such as Eysenk, have long argued that intelligence is confined to the speed of neuron signals and so attention has focused on cognitive processes, rather than on exploring effects of thinking. This area has received a significant boost over recent years through the development of new brain imaging techniques, such as Computed Axial Tomography (CAT) scans. Earlier studies of brain activity using electroencephalography (EEGs) measured average evoked potential and found correlations (0.83) between biological measures of brain-wave complexity and the Weschler intelligence test (Eysenck and Barrett, 1985). Another finding identified the more rapid habituation of EEG 'neural adaptability indexes' amongst the highly intelligent (Shafer, 1982, 1985). However, it is clear that there are problems with these tests if the psychometric measures that are used to calibrate these biological measures are themselves culturally biased.

Culture-free psychometric testing is an area of concern for organizations, test-developers and applicants. It is evident that more research will need to be undertaken in the area over the next few years if we are to ensure equality in the measurement of cognitive ability. It could be argued that there is no such thing as a culture-free multinational: most show implicit sets of values and norms. As a result, we must ask how far the question of cultural equality in testing is possible? Alternatively, we could ask how desirable is the notion of culture-free testing if the sole users of these instruments are multinational organizations? On the face of it, this may appear very politically incorrect, but it is possible that testing *should* reflect the abilities that a culture deems as significant and therefore creating a generic instrument is simply not viable or important. Rather, it is about the identification and accurate measurement of the abilities that that culture identifies as of significance in work performance.

In order to take this debate further we need to examine and understand further two important issues: to what degree are differences in test performance produced by different geographic contexts or produced by different organizational contexts? As a result of the answers to these questions, it may emerge as more valid to devise specific organizational tools, which would transcend geographical areas, but retain their predictive properties for different roles within one multinational. Alternatively, it may emerge that we need different tests for different parts of the world. The likelihood is that the answer will vary with the level of the specific job role; nonetheless, this type of research agenda will enable us to explore in more detail the value of culture-free testing within selection and recruitment.

### Dilemma box 7.3

You are asked to develop an assessment programme for a power-generating company who want to appoint an international manager to work mainly in their South American and Dutch generating businesses. The company's main language is English but you know that local languages are spoken. The job analysis suggests that numerical and verbal reasoning are important in this role, but also the ability to communicate with key workers is a main safety consideration. The managerial test battery that you have used in the past is available in English, Dutch and South American Spanish. There is also a spatial test in this battery that claims to predict logical reasoning in a culture-free way. What do you choose? Why?

## 7   Summary

Ability testing offers organizations high predictive validity and a relatively low-cost means of assessment. Research evidence suggests that it can be one of the most valuable measurement tools for those involved in selection and recruitment. However (as indicated in Chapter 6), this tool still only accounts for 50 per cent of the variance in job performance. I will return to a more fundamental critique of this approach to selection in the final chapter. It is clear, however, that the development of instruments in this area tends to reflect a particular theoretical perspective derived from a narrow band of specifically Western populations, comprising of mainly military or student samples. As a result, it is a *partial* view and one which is increasingly open for reappraisal. Despite some theoretical advances, practitioners tend to focus on the measurement of distinct abilities, whilst researchers are more concerned with the assessment of general ability. This creates an important gap between research and practice. In addition, new approaches to ability testing are deflecting attention from maximal towards typical performance and challenging the artificial separation of ability, personality and motivation within selection measurement tools.

A key problem, noted in Chapter 6 and here, is the ongoing discrimination against minority ethnic groups by ability instruments. Limited attention has been paid to devising culture-free alternatives, with their emphasis on fluid intelligence measurement. There is some debate regarding the power of non-verbal assessment tools for higher job levels. Some organizations use English as their preferred language of testing, reflecting its dominance in the world of business, but the increasingly multicultural character of many societies and the global selection requirements of multinationals are requiring a re-think. While it may be important to assess more experiential aspects, which relates to the assessment of crystallized intelligence, here problems of cultural difference re-emerge.

The continual separation of crystallized and fluid intelligence results in the ongoing division of knowledge and process, and does little to increase our understanding of individual differences. This is an area of selection where both researchers and practitioners are requiring change, but I wonder whether a more fundamental change is required?

---

## Exercise

Take the person and job description outlined in Chapter 2. Consider what psychometric tests could be used to compare candidates. Get details of tests from publishers' catalogues to show you the range of different measures available at this level. Consider how far the same measures could be utilized for jobs at higher and lower levels within the organization. Make special note of any cultural specific issues with each test. Highlight the level of diversity available in the norm tables for the different tests.

---

# CHAPTER 8

# Selection tools 5: personality assessment

## 1 Overview

There has been a renewal of interest in the topic of personality since the 1990s. The use of personality instruments has been increasing since the 1970s – not just in the selection of new employees or in the development of those currently employed, but as an increasingly popular tool within business and political communities. Personality has become an important variable in both the applied and academic fields of psychology and marketing, helping to provide an insight into decisions from whether to buy a particular product through to the selection of an employee. Practitioners find that personality instruments are comparatively easy to use and allow comparisons between different individuals. In addition, they provide a powerful linguistic and semantic tool to facilitate the conceptualization, understanding and valuing of differences between individuals. This in fact gives them a much wider role than recruitment and selection, extending to training, development and change management applications.

The history of the development of personality-assessment techniques has been dogged by controversy between lay practitioners and psychologists. There has been an ongoing debate concerning the theoretical basis for such tools, and long-standing questions regarding their reliability and validity. While reliable tests are arguably relatively easy to devise, it is in their validity that enduring problems can be found. In Chapter 8 I will consider five major topics concerning personality tools: (1) their internal and temporal stability, (2) their predictive validity, (3) the ease with which they can be faked, (4) the ethical aspects of their global application and (5) their use in team selection. Although it is argued that personality tools may help to reduce ethnic biases in other selection processes, we will examine the limited concrete evidence that supports this claim. I will also explore the development and application of these tools within an applied business context. We begin by reviewing the historical application of personality within selection and then, through identifying six distinct theoretical perspectives on personality, move on to explore the development of different approaches on how to measure personality.

## 2 Introduction

The topic of personality produces a divergence of views between the lay public and psychologists. To the lay person personality has been a 'central, salient, critical and interesting' topic (Furnham, 1992, p.15) concerning an individual's public reputation. Indeed, the public seem fascinated with personality assessment – happy to complete personality assessments in magazines at leisure where the results are within their control but with more concern when they are used in selection. Anxiety is created when control of their result shifts. For psychologists, the concept of 'personality' is useful as it enables predictions to be made about behaviour. The measurement of personality is considered by some to be valuable in selection and recruitment, where through administering a questionnaire, inferences can be made concerning the candidate's suitability for the role. Others, as we shall see, challenge the reliability and validity of these data.

Organizations are increasingly using personality assessment as part of their selection process [64 per cent report its use in the UK (Anderson and Shackleton, 1993)], yet its predictive validity remains around 0.21 (Schmitt *et al.*, 1984) to 0.40 (Robertson and Smith, 2001). These low validity measures imply that personality tests are not measuring what they claim to. For example, although purporting to measure 'leadership' or 'sociability', there is not a relationship between the score a candidate receives for these criteria and the leadership or sociability they would demonstrate at work.

As a result of these major concerns, personality measurement tools were not popular in selection and recruitment until the 1960s and their use has risen most dramatically throughout the 1990s. Their increase in popularity for practitioners as a selection tool has been matched by an increase in researchers interested in exploring and evaluating the role of personality (Barrick and Mount, 1991; Barrick *et al.*, 2003; Salgado, 1999). Despite their growing use, there is a mismatch between their popularity amongst practitioners and the scientific evidence of their actual value as a selection decision-making tool (Robertson, 1994) (see Table 6.1).

## 3   How do we define personality?

### Box 8.1 Different definitions of personality

- Allport (1937, p.24) 'The dynamic organization within the individual of those psychophysical systems that determine his unique adjustment to his environment.'

- Cattell (1965, p.63) 'that which permits a prediction of what a person will do in a given situation.'

- Cronbach (1984, p.17) 'One's habits and usual style, but also... ability to play roles.'

- Kline (1993, p.217) Personality measurement consists of 'a set of items, usually questions or statements about feelings or behaviour, to which subjects have to respond by answering the question, or agreeing or disagreeing with the statements.'

- Moynihan and Peterson (2001, p.328) 'personality traits are the key antecedent of an individual's cognitions and affective states that may influence his or her task and interpersonal or socio-emotional role behaviour (in teams).'

(wide)

The previous list highlights the wise spectrum of definitions of personality that have been devised – from the specific to the general. Depending on the theoretical perspective being applied, personality has been defined in a number of different ways. The list emphasizes the relationship between individuals and their context, their predictive value in terms of future behaviour, the format and the breadth of measurement domain. In this way, personality assessment is regarded as a measure of both *internal* dimensions, or feelings, and *external* dimensions, or behaviours.

Some researchers have argued *against* the use of personality instruments in selection, suggesting that it is 'impossible to catch the rich subtlety of human feelings in brief statements' (Kline, 1993, p.218). Others have been more concerned with their impact on test-takers, suggesting such tools are an affront to their intelligence and sensibilities (Heim, 1975). As noted in Chapter 6, humans have long sought a means of categorizing themselves and others in terms of their temperaments in order to understand and predict behaviour. I will now briefly review the historical development of personality assessment and reveal some enduring conflicts and controversies that are still much in evidence in assessment practices today.

## 4   Historical development of personality as a selection tool

The First World War saw advances in ability testing and also provided a prototype personality test through Woodworth's (1918) 'personal data sheet'. This was used to assist in screening out seriously disturbed would-be soldiers. It was the Second World War which allowed psychologists to make their greatest advances in personality measurement (Rose, 1989). Because war-time situations were unique, they provided psychologists with the 'incentive, status and population' to allow them to calibrate dimensions of personality (*ibid.*, p.231). Personality assessment was seen as a solution to one of the army recruiters' key problems: they faced unacceptably high levels of mental breakdown amongst the officer grade. This was clearly a problem as officers were regarded as pivotal in ensuring the motivation, welfare and effectiveness of their fighting units. Officer selection was regarded primarily as an issue of character and personality and the failure of the upper classes to provide the necessary volume of stable and effective leadership created the need for new assessment techniques designed to identify the desired qualities across all the social classes. Involved with this attempt to identify officer temperaments were those from the Tavistock Institute, like Rees and Wittkower, and Eysenck from the Mill Hill Emergency Hospital.

There were differences in the development of personality research between the UK and the USA. In the USA, the focus was on standardizing measurement, and a plethora of questionnaire-based tools were devised. (Most were self-report instruments.) In contrast, attention in the UK was on the development of ingenious assessment processes that were designed to mirror real life and enable the direct observation of behaviour. At the heart of these distinctions lay fundamental differences in how personality was being conceptualized – as either a robust internal trait, or a changing state dependent on the individual and the external context in which they found themselves. In the UK, the personality traits being measured were not regarded as constant, context-free dimensions. Instead, personality was seen in more gestalt terms – as a system of tensions and needs that were dynamic in their interaction and varied according to their context. Thus, an officer was seen as a leader within a group context, not as someone with a distinct set of stable traits that could be simply identified from a questionnaire. This person–situation debate remains at the heart of different conceptions of personality and its functioning today.

Bion (1946, p.79) pioneered UK personality assessment through the 'leaderless group test'; this involved setting up situations that reflected real life. The purpose of this tool was to provide the context in which the 'temptation to give full reign to his personal ambitions was already there' for the candidate. The task itself provided a 'cloak of invisibility for testing officers' as the candidates were so immersed in the task.

Increasingly, psychologists began to recognize the influence of both genetic and situational influences on personality. For instance, studies of identical twins who had been raised apart suggested a genetic component to personality (Bouchard, 1997). There are, however, a number of other influences that have been identified as playing a part in the development of our personality. Contemporary views of personality regard it as a composite of the following influences: age, genetics, constitution, education, family, socio-cultural environment, situational, life experiences and physiological influences. What is important to note here is that many of these aspects are dynamic – for instance, age, situation and life experiences. In a work situation, the organization's culture and structure can also be seen as influencing personality. Like ability, personality is regarded as a function of genetic and environmental factors, and the two appear to affect each other (see Figure 8.1).

Traditional approaches to personality, as you will see later, have tended to emerge from a clinical context and so have limited application in the world of work. Modern conceptions of personality in selection have risen out of the criticism of the applications of personality tools in the 1970s and 1980s and the topic now enjoys a flurry of renewed interest in the occupational sphere. This growth has arisen for two reasons: first, through the prominence of the concept of individual differences which lies at the heart of US personality theory and, second, the flexibility of personality assessment where it has become easy to include it in studies as either independent, dependent, or a moderating variable (Weiss and Adler, 1984). Arguably, the more widespread application of personality measurement has been achieved through the adoption of a piecemeal approach to the topic, due to the convenience and commercial availability of some personality tests, rather than through more theoretical development (Furnham, 1992).

Indeed, in some cases particular tools – such as the clinical instrument, the Minnesota Multiphasic Personality Inventory (MMPI, 1951) – are used completely inappropriately in a selection context. Thus, Furnham concluded that it has been commercial availability rather than the quality of the tools *per se* that has driven the growth of particular measures, resulting

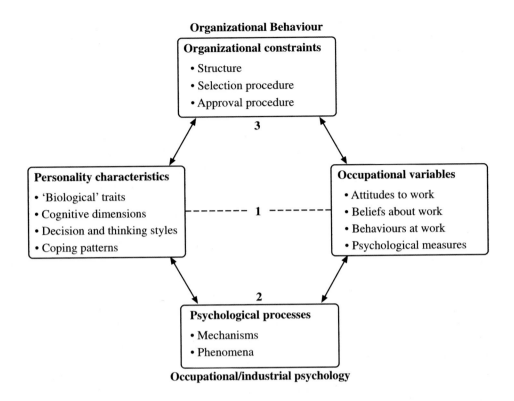

**Figure 8.1**   *Relationship between personality and work*

(Furnham 1992, p.11)

in the use of simplistic and naïve statistical procedures in order to identify relationships between personality variables and health- or work-related factors. Studies of personality have tended to concentrate on four major work-related areas: leadership, motivation, 'employee withdrawal' behaviour (for example, turnover, absenteeism and lateness) and goal-setting behaviour (Weiss and Adler, 1984). We will be concentrating on results as they relate to selection and recruitment. Let us now turn our attention to the theoretical underpinnings of personality.

## 5   Approaches to personality and its measurement

There are six approaches to personality theory and its measurement: the **psychodynamic, biological, behavioural, phenomenological,** social-cognitive and **trait** approaches (Table 8.1 gives a summary). Each has a distinctive philosophical and psychological conception of personality and can be categorized according to the emphasis that it places on situational (or external) forces as opposed to internal (or personal) forces. Over time, new theories have shifted their focus from the external (for example, the behavioural emphasis on punishment or reward) towards more internal psychological drives. Each theory lends itself to distinct ways of assessing or measuring personality.

**Table 8.1 Summary of the six main approaches to personality theory and their study**

| Type of approach | Focus | Central concern | Type of method |
|---|---|---|---|
| Psychodynamic | Internal | Unconscious | Psychoanalysis, MBTI™ preferences |
| Biological | Internal | Brain trait link | Specific dimensions – EPQ |
| Behavioural | External | Habits and reinforced responses | Behavioural assessment |
| Phenomenological | Internal | Individual interpretation of events | FIRO |
| Cognitive–social | Both external and internal | Context and cognition | No unique measurement system |
| Trait-based | Internal | Values, behaviour and relationship with performance | 16PF™ OPQ™ IPI™ etc. |

## 5.1 The psychodynamic approach

The psychodynamic models of personality were developed from a clinical population, and so are derived from insights into a particular group. Psychoanalysis set out to explain human behaviour in terms of people's unconscious and underlying motives. Freud (1856–1939) emphasized unconscious processes as a way of trying to account for the many aspects of behaviour that are not successfully governed by conscious intention. He understood the mind (and therefore personality) as being a product of anxiety-provoking mental conflicts. He also showed how influential early experiences of care were in forming personality.

Another major contributor to this perspective was Jung (1875–1961), who introduced two terms: **introversion**, which concerned an orientation toward the internal world, and **extraversion**, which was more outwardly focused. These terms were later developed by Eysenck to form the basis of his three-factor model of personality which I will discuss in more detail later. Drawing upon Jung's theoretical work in the 1920s, Isabel Myers and her daughter Katherine Briggs developed a personality tool as a way of promoting future harmony in the world as a direct response to the carnage of the First World War. They saw their tool as developing greater understanding of individual differences. Their test, the 'Myers Briggs Type Indicator'™, is still in frequent use today for development purposes.

## 5.2 The biological approach

Biologically based theories of personality emphasized the role of heredity and biology in personality formation and development. Eysenck's (1967) model, which is one of the most commonly used, was concerned with understanding individual temperament and not personality *per se*. Eysenck had been trained by Burt in the 1930s in the application of psychometric techniques and he led the development of new personality measurement in the UK. The model Eysenck devised initially focused on two dimensions: 'neuroticism' and 'introversion/extraversion'. In 1952 he added 'psychoticism' as a result of his post-war work from the Maudsley Hospital and the Eysenck Personality Questionnaire (EPQ) emerged. Based on his field research Eysenck assumed a biological basis for personality and in 1967 he claimed that introversion and extraversion were related to the brain's reticular activating system (RAS) and emotional stability to the visceral brain (Figure 8.3).

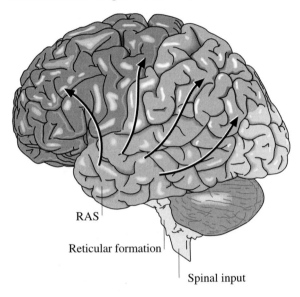

Figure 8.2   *Biological areas associated with aspects of personality. RAS (reticular activating system).*

His model was based on access to the British army soldiers in the Mill Hill Emergency Hospital who could not adjust to the army life of routine and discipline. This enabled him to undertake two distinct types of study. The first were large-scale factorial studies using questionnaires and rating scales. The second were experimentally based studies that focused on specific aspects of temperament – such as persistence, irritability and sense of humour. These two complementary designs enabled dimensions that were identified through the large-scale studies to be refined by the more focused experimental research. These factor models grouped together particular acts into habitual responses which were then organized into more general personality factors.

Eysenck's EPQ model located an individual in a space called 'personality' by virtue of their scores on two axes – 'introversion/extraversion and 'neuroticism'. Their location within this space determined the kind of behavioural disorders they would have (Rose, 1987). The model made assumptions about the links between environmental adaptation and dispositional aspects; as a result he suggested personality influenced individuals' propensity to learn and their responses to stressful situations.

These biological theories also consider *how* we learn, but in terms of our biological propensity to learn, and link brain function to maximum performance levels. There is a plethora of empirical confirmation of the differences in biological functioning in relation to our temperament (Cook, 1998). However, it has been argued (Furnham, 1992) that these theories tend to be over-simplistic, because they reduce personality to a small number of variables, and in doing so also simplify brain activity. There has been an ongoing debate in medical and psychological circles concerning how far brain anatomy shapes behaviour. A simplified question emerges: is there a biological basis for personality, or instead does an individual's personality shape their brain? However, this assumes an unsophisticated one-way causality, rather than considering how chemical brain pathways are necessarily an effect of our experiences in a current, past and anticipated future environment. What is important is to acknowledge this dual influence.

## 5.3 The behavioural approach

The behaviourist movement, which had a profound impact on psychology in the USA in the 1950s and 1960s, abolished the dichotomy between internal and external determinants of behaviour. This predominantly American school of thought dominated psychology through the work of Dollard, Miller and Skinner. They emphasized the role of learning in shaping behaviour, and criticized the belief that internal predisposition and tendencies caused behaviour. They argued that external factors were paramount. The behaviourist perspective challenged the term 'personality', arguing that it was superfluous as overt behaviour was completely comprehensible as a response to the world an individual found themselves in. It was not that internal states did not exist; merely that they were not important for understanding how an individual behaves.

The importance of rigorous scientific method was emphasized: much of the early work in the field was on animals (rats and pigeons) and experimental settings with detailed observations were used. The work focused on the role of 'habitual responses', 'reinforcers' and the 'conditioning' and 'shaping' of behaviour. They distinguished between primary physiological drives and secondary drives, such as money. Topics like 'frustration' and 'incompatible responses' that created conflict were identified. Behaviourism has been both refined and superseded – in particular by cognitive paradigms which dominate contemporary academic psychology.

## 5.4 Phenomenological and humanistic approaches

The phenomenological and humanistic models arose from criticisms of two of the psychoanalytical and behaviourist models. The psychoanalytical model was regarded as being too concerned with dysfunctional and neurotic behaviours, while the behavioural models were seen as too focused on directly observable behaviours. They were influenced by the growth of individualism in the USA and emphasized the importance of subjective experience and subjective reality. The approach stems from Lewin's lifespace and Snygg and Comb's work in the 1930s, followed in the

1950s by Kelley's personal construct theory, the humanistic work of Maslow's self-actualization theory, and Roger's new therapeutic views on unconditional positive regard.

The phenomenological and humanist approaches regard people as creative and actively engaged in their experiences, with humanists emphasizing the importance of interpersonal relations. These theories are concerned with how people's experiences and perceptions shape behaviour at any given moment. Interpretation is therefore key. The emphasis is on trying to understand the self and on comprehending how a person sees him/herself in order to understand the meaning and predictability of their behaviour. The humanistic emphasis is more focused on the interpersonal and stresses the therapeutic relationship. Because it celebrates individual change, it is inherently sceptical about the notion of personality as consistent over time. As a result, it is explicitly critical of personality measurement because of the notion of stability.

Their alternative phenomenological approach concerned the importance of self and the development of this self, identifying higher human motives and the need to experience life in a unique way. The psychometric tool developed by Schultz (1978) – Fundamental Interpersonal Relations Orientation (FIRO) – emerges from the phenomenological tradition and examines three needs: 'inclusion', 'control' and 'affection'. A key problem for this approach is methodological: it is notoriously difficult to create tools that make it possible to capture adequately one person's conceptualization of their world in a way that allows comparison with others. Validity is therefore difficult and theorists in these domains tend to be fiercely anti-reductionist.

## 5.5 The social-cognitive approach

The social-cognitive approach encompasses cognitive and social behaviour approaches and learning approaches to personality. It built directly on the foundations of behaviourism and learning theory in its emphasis on the importance of *situation*, but added other factors, such as cognition, which drew attention back to internal processes (Engler, 1995). At the same time, behaviourism was being revised in a cognitive direction in the sense that inferred mental processes were again acknowledged as important in understanding behaviour. Social-learning models are based predominantly on the work of Albert Bandura and Robert Walters from the early 1970s. The social-learning theory they proposed focuses on the role of observation and imitation in personality development. They argue that individuals mimic others who are models for them. Bandura (1986) suggests that there is a 'reciprocal determinism' linking a person's disposition and their situation to their behaviour. Each aspect, he argues, is a function of the other two.

This approach has highlighted the influence of *context* on behaviour and focuses attention on the issue of stability. Work in this domain has shown that some people are more consistent than others in terms of both specific and general personality traits (Pervin, 2002). As a result, researchers have argued that it is possible to devise a stable situational-behavioural profile, rather than a stable individual behaviour profile (Shoda *et al.*, 1994). A problem for researchers in this area is that they are limited as to the kinds of phenomena they can assess and the ways in which these can be examined. Their concern with 'power, precision and predictability' restrict the topics and insights that are possible, deflecting away from a more holistic understanding of human nature (Engler, 1995, p.252).

## 5.6 Trait-based approaches

This final group of theories predominates today – particularly in selection and recruitment. Evidence indicates that all human languages contain terms used to characterize personality traits (Dixon, 1977). Personality trait theorists derived their models from statistical procedures, predominantly factor analysis, to identify clusters of components which are predictive of individual difference. For example, Eysenck and Eysenck (1967) found that within English-speaking cultures a cluster of terms around the trait 'sociability', that include 'energetic' and 'cheerfulness', could be found. Using this factor-based approach, in theory anything can be measured. For example, the components of personality that are assessed can include how we think, feel, our attitudes or behaviours. The differences between traits can be assessed in terms of performance effectiveness within a particular job role, or task.

Eysenck was the first to adopt a trait-based approach, but the foremost trait-based instrument for use in a work setting is Cattell's (1953) sixteen personality factor questionnaire (or '16PF'™ as it is commonly referred to). (Many other instruments have subsequently emerged, such as the California Personality Inventory (ICP), the NEO Personality Inventory and the Occupational Personality Questionnaire (OPQ). Cattell's (1950) 16PF™ was developed too late to have a military application. However, it enabled personality to be more finely described by distinguishing between the 'surface' (the overt behaviour) and 'source' (the underlying variable) behind a trait. Rose (1989, p.47) argues that this development was important as it enabled personality to be 'visualized, materialized, inscribed, calculated and administered'.

A question that many trait-based researchers have sought to examine is whether there is a universal structure of traits that applies across all cultures. McCrea and Costa (1997) have argued that their **'big five model'** transcends different cultures, but others suggest that there may be inherent cultural and gender biases in many trait-based tools. I will return to the problem of culture later in this chapter .

A chief criticism of many of the instruments on which this perspective is based is that they are atheoretical. Trait-based researchers aggregate individual data which conceals the variability and stability issue on which social-cognitive researchers have focused their attention. There has been limited work to reconcile these two opposing perspectives.

> ## *Dilemma box 8.1   Trait vs. behaviour*
>
> You are in charge of running a selection programme for a new business director in a housing association, a job which is crucially important for the firm. There are four potential applicants for this job and you decide to use a personality test as part of the selection process. One candidate, Jane, has scored high for extraversion. During the final decision-making session with all of the assessors, however, a concern arises about a discrepancy in Jane's results: although her personality score was high for extraversion, the assessors of the group exercise did not find that she was particularly outgoing. They ask you to explain how someone's score can be high, but the behaviour seen is different. What do you say?

## 5.7  Application of theory: types vs. traits

A key distinction in the different approaches to personality lies in the use of the terms 'trait' and 'type'. Type theories are the oldest and the simplest means of classifying people. They are concerned with identifying broad categories and syndromes. Type theories classify individuals into a particular group who show the same preferred behaviours. Hippocrate's initial model of temperament is a typology, as is the Myers–Briggs Type Indicator, or Belbin's Team Types (see Figure 8.3).

| Extraversion | ⟷ | Introversion |
| Sensing | ⟷ | Intuition |
| Thinking | ⟷ | Feeling |
| Judging | ⟷ | Perceiving |

*Figure 8.3   Myers–Briggs typology*

There can be difficulties in fitting an individual into one distinct category, as opposed to another. For example, in the MBTI™ a person might be high on extraversion and sensing, low on thinking and in the middle on the final preference dimension. In this personality tool, individuals are asked, on the basis of additional material, to indicate whether their personality preferences are ESTJ or ENTP. Typologies can be the most rigid of all approaches: a person is identified as a 'type', as in the proceeding example, and the last letter in the sequence cannot be omitted.

In contrast, the trait approach is concerned with identifying differences between people. Traits can be identified at a number of levels, so hierarchies can be developed that cluster different groups of related components through the use of factor-analytical procedures. Theoretically, anything can be a trait and can be measured provided it shows an underlying statistically significant difference between individuals. For example, innovation is a trait from the OPQ™. Examples of trait-based models of personality include Eysenck's EPQ model, Cattell's 16PF or Saville and Holdsworth's Occupational Personality Questionnaire (OQP).

Whilst trait- and type-based theories are distinct, they do complement one another (see Figure 8.4). For example, Eysenck used the type terms 'extraversion–introversion' to identify those individuals that fell above or below the mean on a trait. Similarly, a combination of particular traits might relate to a specific type.

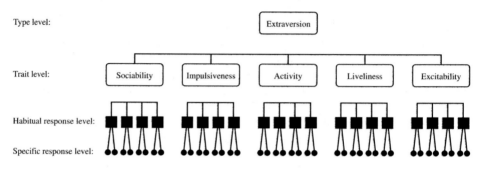

*Figure 8.4   An example of type and trait in the same model*

Traits are considered highly stable aspects of personality. Arguably, measurement can be made for more transient aspects (termed 'states'). These include the measurement of mood and are considered to change with the context. This is an area of increasing interest given the current vogue to assess emotion at work.

# 6   Applying personality tools

Interest in personality in occupational settings has not been without controversy. Four major issues emerge concerning the application of these tools in recruitment and selection: stability, predictive validity, faking and ethical issues.

## 6.1 Stability

Longitudinal studies play a valuable role in personality measurement for assessing the key issue of stability (Furnham, 1992). Some personality assessment models already account for this. For instance, the MBTI™ is based on several bi-polar dimensions, and suggests that as people get older they either become more entrenched at one end of the four bi-polar dimensions, or they recognize the need to be more flexible and change behaviour as the situation dictates, and as a result tend towards the mid-point.

Research using longitudinal methods is inherently problematic for a number of reasons. Cohorts shrink over the years, the use of unreliable tools renders initial work obsolete (which results in low validities), and, all too often, a sample is insufficiently broad, tending to comprise of students as opposed to a more generic population. Finally, as we saw in Chapter 3, there can also be inbuilt restrictions-of-range issues.

Other researchers have taken a more theoretically informed view and have argued that how someone behaves is dependent on the situation (Mischel, 1969) and that inconsistencies in behaviour across time or situation render the construct of personality invalid. For example, a person may be extravert at a disco and more introvert at a funeral. What does this tell us about their temperament? Which is the 'real' person? Thus, there was a dilemma in personality assessment: whilst we can measure personality, without stripping out all questions of context it might not necessarily be possible to predict future behaviour based on it.

It is only recently that the topic of stability has received the attention it deserves as a key problem that will arise with any attempt to measure personality. Looking at the whole issue of instability, Hampson (1997, 1998), distinguished between three different types of inconsistency which are at the heart of stability: temporal, cross-situational and internal (which focuses on the inconsistency that might arise where the applicant completes the questions with an idealized self in mind, as opposed to a more realistic self).

While the inconsistency dilemma has led to much debate, there have relatively recently been attempts to resolve it through a reconceptualization of personality to focus on behavioural coherence and not consistency *per se* (Davis and Million, 1994; Hampson, 1997). This is an attempt to accommodate both temporal and situational variations and confounds simplistic trait theories of personality. For example, using Peabody's (1967) distinctions between evaluative and descriptive components of traits, Hampson (1997) explored how inconsistencies arise as we seek to describe ourselves and others. She claimed that it is simplistic to argue, as Goldberg and Kilowski (1985) do that inconsistency arises from those with low verbal intellect; instead she found that inconsistencies are a product of social conditioning, and in particular concerning social desirability, so questions such as those concerning an individual's propensity to gossip might be answered in a different way if the individual had a strong religious faith, or lived in a culture where such behaviour was frowned upon.

Hampson's study identified that individuals, particularly from a Western culture, tend to see their personalities in positive terms. It also found considerable inconsistency in terms of how people see themselves, which emerges as richer and more multifaceted than the way they view others. Perhaps this is because people imagine themselves in different situations and see the variety of their behavioural responses. This is in part because instead of excluding traits that might create inconsistencies, people tend to include contradictions as a means of trying to show more fully the complexity of who they are. There are, however, some underlying conventions that individuals use, for example in preferring to create inconsistencies through overlapping descriptive traits (for instance, describing oneself as 'outgoing' *and* 'shy') rather than contradicting their evaluations of how much, or how little, of these aspects they possess. In addition, there are common trait factors in which such inconsistency arises. For example, more inconsistency is found surrounding traits concerning 'emotional stability', while least variation is found for 'openness/intellect' traits.

Other researchers have undertaken studies of ageing people and twins to examine the longitudinal stability of personality measurement. These studies suggest that as people age so their traits become more conventional (Ackerman, 1994).

The question of stability in personality assessment is an important concern for the users of these tools in selection and recruitment as it underlies the reliability and validity of personality measurement tools. Without consistency of results over time, personality measurement would be rendered useless. Stability is also a significant issue which enhances our understanding of distortion and faking behaviour in completing these instruments and reveals that whilst our reporting of personality may be inconsistent, there are patterns to these inconsistencies.

## 6.2 Predictive validity

An increasing body of research evidence supports the application of personality measurement as a useful tool in selection because it argues that it shows a statistically predictive relationship with job performance (Furnham and Heaven, 1999). Studies from insurance-claim examiners (Arneson *et al.*, 1993), sewing machine operators (Krilowicz and Lowery, 1996), sales representatives (Barrick *et al.*, 2002) and military service personnel (Bartram and Dale, 1982; Bartram, 1995) have shown relationships between job performance and personality variables. Some have identified an incremental validity that personality assessment can offer in enhancing other selection tools. For example, commercial airline pilot success can be predicted with 73.8 per cent accuracy by gathering information about flying experience and through the use of check flights. This figure is enhanced by 5.5 percent when personality assessment is included (Hörman and Mascke, 1996). In an occupation such as flying, the cost of a single mistake can be devastating, if not fatal. Personality research into successful military pilots revealed that they are more likely to have stable and extravert personalities than those who failed their training (Bartram and Dale, 1982). Subsequent data from 528 male fight training applicants suggested a strong self-selection bias into such occupations, with this group showing higher emotional stability and extraversion than the general population as assessed on the 16PF$^{™}$ and Eysenck's measure (Bartram, 1995). For example, the study below reveals the relationship between the personality of bus drivers and the safety of their bus (see Figure 8.5).

A key issue that underlies the predictive power of personality in selection is **bandwidth.** This is the varying breadth of coverage offered by each personality assessment questionnaire.

### 6.2.1  Bandwidth and the big five solution?

Despite the enduring popularity of different categorization systems for personality, historically, psychologists have been unable to agree on a single unifying theory of personality, or on the precise number of dimensions. A key issue for those studying personality concerns the breadth of the factors, with models ranging from 3 to over 30 different dimensions.

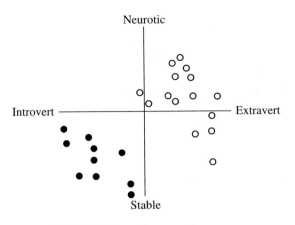

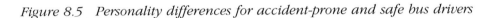

○ Individual with bad accident record
● Individual with good accident record

*Figure 8.5   Personality differences for accident-prone and safe bus drivers*

(adapted by Shaw and Sichel, 1970, from Furnham and Heaven, 1999, p.195)

The two most prominent researchers in the trait field have identified models ranging from either 3 factors to 16. Eysenck (1952; with Eysenck, 1985) proposed three broad dimensions of personality:

1   Extraversion–Introversion

2   Stability–Neuroticism

3   Tough–Tender-mindedness.

While Cattell (1953), in contrast, proposed 16 distinct, or narrow, factors of personality (see Table 8.2).

## Table 8.2 The primary source traits covered by the 16PF test

| Factor | Low sten score description (1–3) | High sten score description (8–10) |
|--------|----------------------------------|-------------------------------------|
| A | *Cool*: reserved, impersonal, detached, formal, aloof. Sizothymia* | *Warm*: outgoing, kindly, easygoing, participating, likes people. Affectothymia |
| B | *Concrete-thinking*: less intelligent. Lower scholastic mental capacity | *Abstract-thinking*: more intelligent, bright. Higher scholastic mental capacity |
| C | *Affected by feelings*: emotionally less stable, easily annoyed Lower ego strength | *Emotionally stable*: mature, faces reality, calm. Higher ego strength |
| E | *Submissive*: humble, mild, easily led, accommodating Submissiveness | *Dominant*: assertive, aggressive, stubborn, competitive, bossy. Dominance |

| F | *Sober*: restrained, prudent, taciturn, serious<br>Desurgency | *Enthusiastic*: spontaneous, heedless, expressive, cheerful.<br>Surgency |
|---|---|---|
| G | *Expedient*: disregards rules, self-indulgent<br>Weaker superego strength | *Conscientious*: conforming, moralistic, staid, rule-bound.<br>Stronger superego strength |
| H | *Shy*: threat-sensitive, timid, hesitant, intimidated.<br>Threctia | *Bold*: venturesome, uninhibited, can take stress.<br>Parmia |
| I | *Tough-minded*: self-reliant, no-nonsense, rough, realistic.<br>Harria | *Tender-minded*: sensitive, overprotected, intuitive, refined.<br>Premsia |
| L | *Trusting*: accepting conditions, easy to get on with.<br>Alaxia | *Suspicious*: hard to fool, distrustful, sceptical.<br>Protension |
| M | *Practical*: concerned with 'down-to-earth' issues, steady.<br>Praxernia | *Imaginative*: absent-minded, absorbed in thought, impractical.<br>Autia |
| N | *Forthright*: unpretentious, open, genuine, artless.<br>Artlessness | *Shrewd*: polished, socially aware, diplomatic, calculating.<br>Shrewdness |
| O | *Self-assured*: secure, feels free of guilt, untroubled, self-satisfied.<br>Untroubled adequacy | *Apprehensive*: self-blaming, guilt-prone, insecure, worrying.<br>Guilt proneness |
| $Q_1$ | *Conservative*: respecting traditional ideas.<br>Conservatism of temperament | *Experimenting*: liberal, critical, open to change.<br>Radicalism |
| $Q_2$ | *Group-oriented*: a 'joiner' and sound follower, listens to others.<br>Group adherence | *Self-sufficient*: resourceful, prefers own decisions.<br>Self-sufficiency |
| $Q_3$ | *Undisciplined self-conflict*: tax, careless of social rules.<br>Low integration | *Following self-image*: socially precise, compulsive.<br>High self-concept control |
| $Q_4$ | *Relaxed*: tranquil, composed, has low drive, unfrustrated.<br>Low ergic tension | *Tense*: frustrated, overwrought, has high drive.<br>High ergic tension |

\* Titles in roman type are the technical names for the factors and are explained more fully in the *Handbook* © 1993 by the Institute for Personality and Ability Testing, Inc., Champaign, Illinois, USA. All rights reserved. Reproduced from 16PF fifth edition from the *Administrator's Manual*.

The quest for a consensus as to how the optimum number of personality traits has been further hampered by the so-called **jangle fallacy**. This is when the same trait name is used by two or more questionnaires, but the trait is distinctively different (Block, 1995). Thus unnecessary confusion enters an already complicated situation.

In trying to work out a potential solution, Norman (1963) built on McDougall's (1932) work to create a broad five-factor model to account for the variance in personality. This so-called 'big five model' was later developed by Digman (1990) into its present form where openness, agreeableness and 'conscieentiousness' have been added to neuroticism and extraversion. Costa and McCrea (1985) are responsible for devising the most widely used test of these five constructs: the NEO (see Box 8.2).

## Box 8.2 Descriptor of the 'big five' personality factors

### Factor 1   Neuroticism

This measure is concerned with emotional stability. Those scoring high on this measure have tendencies to experience negative emotions, like fear, anger, guilt, sadness, embarrassment. They are more susceptible to psychological distress. Those with low scores tend to be more emotionally stable. They are usually calm and even-tempered, relaxed and able to face stressful situations without becoming upset, or unnerved.

### Factor 2   Extraversion

Extraverts are sociable people. They tend to prefer large groups and gatherings, in which they are more talkative, assertive, and socially active. They are enlivened and stimulated by social contact and tend to have a cheerful and optimistic disposition. Introverts are less easy to characterize, tending to be more reserved (as opposed to unfriendly), independent of thought, and even-paced. They prefer to spend time alone, which others may regard as shyness. Although not given to the exuberant high spirits of extraverts, they cannot be considered necessarily as unhappy, or pessimistic.

### Factor 3   Openness to experience

Openness is characterized by attentiveness to the inner world of thoughts and feelings. Those who score high on this dimension tend to be intellectually curious and show independence of judgement. They are willing to entertain novel and uncontroversial values and views, hence there is a link suggested with creativity. They experience both positive and negative emotions far more than closed people. In contrast, those with low scores on this factor tend to be more conservative and conventional. They prefer the traditional to the novel, and their emotional responses tend to be somewhat muted. They are more intensive in their scope and depth of interests.

### Factor 4   Agreeableness

An agreeable person is an altruistic person. They tend to be sympathetic to others and are, as such, eager to assist people. They may, therefore, give up their own ideas too quickly, whilst those scoring low on this dimension tend to be more sceptical of others' intentions and are competitive as opposed to co-operative. They prefer to fight for their own interest and are far more critical in their thinking style.

## Factor 5 Conscientiousness'

'Conscientiousness' is primarily concerned with the control of impulses. This self-control is characterized by, in addition to emotional control, more active attention towards planning, organizing and punctuality. Those scoring high tend to be strong-willed individuals, who are purposeful and determined in their actions. There is an association with occupational or academic achievement. Lower scores on 'conscientiousness' tend to be less exacting in their application to work and more lackadaisical in their focus on tasks. There is also evidence of having more hedonistic interests.

The 'big five model' is not without critics. Criticisms centre on two main problems. First, it has been argued that five factors are insufficient to cover all the complexities of human personality (Waller and Ben-Porath, 1987). Thus, the model is not comprehensive, and alternatives such as a seven-factor model have been suggested (Tellegen, 1993). There has, however, been very limited support for such a move to expand from five broad traits. The second issue is a lexical measurement conundrum, concerning how far it is possible to condense the complexities of human personality into the single words that are commonly found in many of the big five personality assessment instruments (Block, 1993, 1995).

The decision concerning whether to use a broad or narrow personality assessment relates to the complexity, or 'bandwidth', of constructs by which personality is inferred. A broad focus, for example on extraversion, might only identify 'social confidence', whereas a narrower focused instrument might include 'sociability', 'assertiveness', 'impulsivity' and 'task preferences' as aspects of extraversion. As a result, there is thus a need for care when applying labels to any trait. This can become more significant, as you will see, when recruiting for specific roles. For example, if selecting for a sales role where high attention to the quality of service offered to customers is important, a broad bandwidth measure of the trait 'extraversion' would not be sensitive to the distinctions between 'warmth' and 'excitement-seeking'. Both are, arguably, dimensions of 'extraversion', but only one is of value within this selection context. The test-users must therefore examine in detail the personality tools they wish to use.

Part of the difficulty that has faced those who want to research personality is how quickly even the most simple study designs can produce an unwieldy complexity of data that renders computation difficult. For example, as Robertson (1994) notes, if personality is restricted to five broad dimensions, and three levels are considered – low, medium or high – then 125 (5*5*5) possible combinations of personality emerge. A commonly used scoring system is the 10-point sten score which relates to the underlying normal distribution of the results (see Figure 8.6). Through using such a scoring system, nearly ten million possible combinations emerge. Imagine then the problems for researchers using a narrow, and arguably more sensitive, personality tool which assesses many more dimensions of personality, such as the 16PF™ or the 32-factor OPQ™, where many million more possibilities emerge.

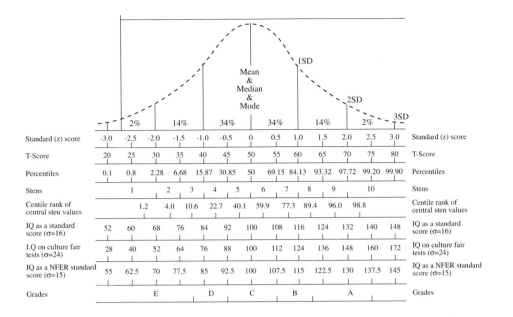

*Figure 8.6   Normal distribution curve and sten scores*

There is an ongoing debate between researchers as to what the most appropriate level of personality trait is. Ones and Visweveran (1996) argue that five broad typologies are best, as they are most predictive of overall job performance. Others dispute this view (Schneider *et al.*, 1996; Paunonen and Ashton, 2001) and suggest that a narrower approach is more appropriate when trying to identify and study the relationship between specific aspects of personality and performance. It is only by adopting a hypothesis-based research design in which specific facets of personality are assessed in relation to particular aspects of behaviour that we will be able to gain more insight and understanding into the inferred relationship between temperament and behaviour. As part of this, researchers have sought to identify which of the five factors is most important in a given selection context.

### 6.2.2   *Most predictive factor?*

The debate concerning which is the most predictive factor in personality measurement is akin to the debate in ability testing between 'g' and other specific measures that we encountered in Chapter 7. There is similar controversy here between researchers as to which is the most important personality factor. Do note that the focus of their debate concerns the impact of personality in enhancing the predictive power of selection tools for organizations, not about enhancing personality theory in general.

In reviewing the research evidence, most support has been found for 'conscientiousness' (Barrick and Mount, 1991; Barrick *et al.*, 2003; Ree *et al.*, 1994; Salgado, 1997). 'Conscientiousness' has been identified, along with a 'g' cognitive ability measure, as showing the best predictive validity for job performance (Robertson and Kinder, 1993). Indeed, Behling (1998) goes so far as to argue that it is one of the most valid predictors of work performance next to general intelligence, while in their meta-analysis, Hurtz and Donovan (2000) reveal that it has the highest validity of any of the big five dimensions: they identified correlations between this trait and overall performance and three other distinct aspects of performance, from training outcomes through to job role performance of around 0.22 (adjusted for true validity of 0.20).

An opposing view is taken by some researchers who argue in favour of using a more multifaceted big five approach and thus maintaining the complexity of human behaviour, rather than reducing it to a few simple dimensions (Ones and Visweveran, 1996).

There are five criticisms which can be levied at studies focused on the identification of the most predictive personality factor. The first problem is the focus on very broad aggregation of job performance and this throws into question the adequacy of the assessment. As I noted earlier (in Chapters 1 and 2), there are inherent difficulties in using an aggregate measure – such as overall performance – because the measure can be so broad as to become meaningless when trying to understand the relationship between distinct aspects of personality and their influence on job performance.

Second, many studies have considered the most predictive trait across multiple occupational groups. Initial studies have shown a consistent relationship between 'conscientiousness' and job-performance measures, including job and training proficiency, across many occupational groups, for instance, professionals, police, managers, sales staff and semi-skilled workers (Barrick and Mount, 1991; Salgado, 1997). There has also been support for dimensions such as 'integrity' and 'conscientiousness' as being valid predictors of performance. However, in examining a specific occupational group, such as managers, lower validity coefficients with performance job and training were found. For instance, a group such as 'managers' share little other than a job title in common. Thus, the use of broad aggregations is relatively meaningless.

A third concern is due to the level of analysis undertaken. Barrick et al. (2003) found that when looking at overall work performance 'extraversion', 'openness' and 'agreeableness' were not predictive of work performance, unless they were applied to certain occupations, or certain criteria. Nonetheless, studies that have examined specific occupational groups and particular facets of job performance have found support for narrowly defined personality factors rather than the broad big five (Robertson et al., 2000; Hurtz and Donovan, 2000). It is only through more focused research designs that researchers can hope to gain more understanding of the impact of certain aspects of personality on particular work roles (Weiss and Adler, 1984). One potential way forward is for studies to be undertaken on the basis of clear designs concerning which personality factors researchers are interested in and what specific aspects of occupational behaviour. All too often, such research fails to include precise independent behavioural measures.

Fourth, although studies concerning which trait is the most predictive have confirmed 'conscientiousness', on closer examination a range of different definitions emerge, all labelled the same, but actually comprising of a number of different sub-factors. For example, Costa and McCrea (1985) include the sub-factors of 'competence', 'order', 'dutifulness', 'achievement', 'striving', 'self-discipline' and 'deliberation' in their measure of 'conscientiousness', whilst Hogan (1991) excluded 'achievement' (see Figure 8.7). Barrick and Mount's (1991) definition reveals further differences, with a broader definition including both 'dependability' and 'achievement' (as in the will to achieve). Some have argued that it is important to distinguish between these subcomponents of 'dependability' and 'achievement' (Hough, 1992; Robertson *et al.*, 2000), whilst others dispute this (Barrick and Mount, 1991). Thus, there is no consensus amongst researchers as to what this 'conscientiousness' trait actually is.

Finally, this type of research has been plagued by the over use of meta-analytical studies. Many of the studies that are included in meta-analysis are based on personality measurement instruments which were not originally designed explicitly to assess the big five; instead they were designed to measure a diverse group of traits. Meta-analytical researchers amend these original measures by using a post hoc system, where expert raters re-classify the measures using the big five. There is evidence of further contamination of the process with low inter-rater agreement levels (Hurtz and Donovan, 2000). Indeed, Barrick *et al.* (2003, p.9) called for a moratorium on meta-analytical studies of personality in order to enable researchers to commence new research into the link between personality and performance.

As a result of the research, evidence which points to the importance of 'conscientiousness' is fraught with problems. However, a more complex picture is beginning to emerge which points to the importance of combined traits, rather than a single personality trait, as being significant in predicting and understanding the influence of personality on job performance. For example, Witt *et al.* (2002) recently suggested, based on reanalysing large samples from multiple occupational groups, that job performance ratings are highest for those with a combination of 'conscientiousness' and 'agreeableness'. Those with high 'conscientiousness', but with lower interpersonal sensitivity, received lower ratings than those with high 'agreeableness'.

Barrick and Mount (1991) have shown that for both sales and managerial jobs, 'extraversion' is a valid predictor of both training and job proficiency. Other studies of managers, however, have revealed that too much of one factor (such as 'conscientiousness') can have a significant and detrimental impact on creativity or change (Goldberg, 1992). Hogan and Ones (1997) argue that too much 'conscientiousness' may be just as undesirable as too little in specific occupational populations. It is easy to speculate about how a particular dimension might combine. For example, in a sales environment, 'extraversion' might be considered an advantage, but coupled with high 'agreeableness', it may result in lower sales as the individual may have difficulty closing their deals.

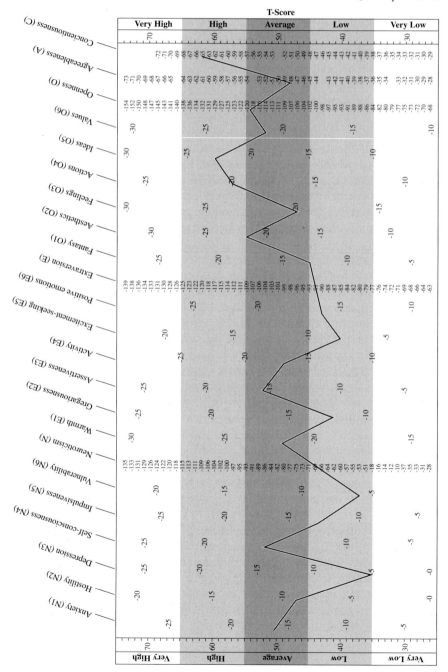

Figure 8.7   Neo personality profile showing trait sub-factors

(Kaplan and Saccuzzo, p.437)

In some occupational groups, the qualities of 'conformity', 'detail', 'conscientiousness', 'purposefulness' and 'organization' may be desirable, but not always. Robertson *et al.* (2000) found that in managerial populations, 'conscientiousness' was not desirable, did not significantly predict current performance ($r = 0.09$) and was negatively correlated with promotability (–0.2). This finding shows how broad-based personality measures reduce validity. As a result, the inclusion of all dimensions within a particular personality test, rather than just those where there might be a theoretical link to job performance, may well weaken the relationships researchers find. Therefore, it is important that researchers utilize a more specific focus and consider the relationship between specific personality dimensions and specific types of occupational and job outcomes.

Through adopting a more conceptually rigorous approach to the study of personality and performance, researchers will expand the variation in performance away from one single aggregated criterion measure and a meaningless broad occupational grouping which, some have argued, has masked the specific relationship between personality and performance and resulted in the production of misleadingly low results (Dunnette, 1963; Salgado, 1997). Nicholson (1996, p.199) argues that such reductionist approaches 'throw away ... the essential value and sophistication of current thinking about the structure of personality' through attempting to examine predictive validity in terms of a single variable.

Unfortunately, two further levels of complexity remain omitted from research in the personality field. The ongoing view of the individual as a component of a system, or organization, fails to examine in more detail the interaction between the psychological function of work for the individual with the demands and the constraints that a particular organization places on work output. An individual's expression of their personality is not independent of the context in which they work. This ongoing removal of the context restricts psychologists' understanding of how personality predicts work behaviour (Furnham and Heaven, 1999).

Second, there is little acknowledgement of the additional influence that dimensions such as ability, or motivation, play in the complex interaction between personality and the context (Ackerman, 1997; Barrick *et al.*, 2002). Beginning to understand this interaction is vital for occupational psychologists to see how motivated and conscientious workers would rapidly lose their commitment and determination if they are never acknowledged or rewarded by the organization. These personality traits, coupled with intelligence, might result in candidates with such profiles rapidly choosing to take their skills and work-attitudes elsewhere and leave the organization in search of greener pastures.

Thus, there is a two-way dynamic whereby organizational structure influences personality, which in turn affects organizational structure. Few organizations recognize this potential influence and all too often selection processes are seen in isolation from the culture and other systems (see Dilemma boxes 8.2 and 8.3).

### Dilemma box 8.2 In with the new?

A previously very successful and risk-averse bank approaches you and asks you to develop a new selection system for their graduate recruitment programme. They want to become more innovative in the services they offer customers as they are starting to see that their services are no longer as attractive as their competitors. They see this group of new young people as the key to get the level of change they require. What do you advise them?

### Dilemma box 8.3 Changing politics

A previously successful political party approaches you and asks you to develop a new selection system for them to assist in the short-listing of Parliamentary candidates. They are keen to be seen as the party with more women MPs. The new process they want will provide all-woman lists from which constituencies will choose their candidate. They see this junior grade as being the main place that women can enhance the appeal of the party to the electorate. Will this be sufficient enough change for them? What advice do you offer?

## 6.3 Distortion and faking

A key concern for psychometricians is the issue of distortion or **faking** in tests. They are particularly concerned with distortion of results in selection settings (Hough, 1998; Stark *et al.*, 2001). Many personality questionnaires involve self-report and so two distinct aspects of distortion can emerge. Both are important as they have an impact on the reliability and validity of the assessment results. The first is unintentional distortion, either by someone with limited self-insight or an individual who is eager to please and be seen in a good light. The desire to be 'seen in a positive light' can be considered as a personality trait, as it varies between individuals. Indeed, this trait and other personality dimensions, such as 'high self-esteem', 'caution' or 'indecisiveness', produce more positive responses. Self-deception, or lack of self-insight, can be an obvious reason for distortion. Those with high '**social desirability**' results have been found to be unself-critical and to have little insight into themselves.

The second effect concerns conscious, or *deliberate*, impression management and faking by test-takers. This can arise for a number of reasons. At the most benign, distortion occurs due to 'central response tendency', where the test-taker opts for a safe, middle response option when completing a rating scale. This distortion reduces the variability of the responses. It also can affect standardization across groups as one person's 'agree' might be another's 'uncertain' (see Figure 8.8).

Choose between two statements, for example

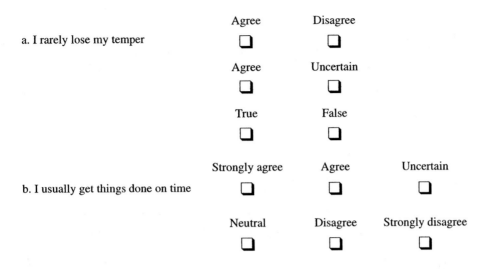

*Figure 8.8   Response formats in personality questionnaires*

It can be countered by using the forced-choice or **ipsative response format**, which I will discuss shortly, or by using the simple response format 'Yes/No', which Guildford (1959) argued was the best format to prevent the adoption of acquiescence.

Individuals who are particularly acquiescent are more inclined to respond affirmatively rather than negatively to any question that they are posed. In order to counter this tendency, items are reversed and scored in a negative way. For example, if assessing the trait 'self-confidence', a reversed item might ask 'I sometimes feel uncomfortable in social situations'.

In addition, distortion can occur due to a bias towards the social desirability response, where individuals respond in the most socially acceptable or socially desirable way. It can occur both as a subconscious process where the person's focus is on fitting in and pleasing others, or it can be a more deliberate act of manipulation by the test-taker to appear either much better or much worse. This is particularly the case when there is a lot at stake, such as in a selection situation, or where a plea of criminal insanity is being lodged in a murder trial.

### 6.3.1   Minimizing faking

#### 6.3.1.1   Instructions

In order to safeguard against the practices of faking or distortion, six different recommendations have been identified. The first concerns the instructions provided to the test-taker. These should be clear and it is suggested they should include a warning of the consequences of distortion, such as removal from the selection process (see Chapter 3).

### 6.3.1.2   Pacing

Second, although tests of typical performance, in contrast to ability tests, do not have time constraints, instructions normally include suggestions about the pacing of responses. For example, the test-taker is asked 'not to think too hard about each response'. The assumption is that by asking the respondents to move more quickly through the questionnaire, they do not ponder and try to identify a 'perfect' response from the possible responses in front of them. Holden *et al.* (2001, p.160) support this view, arguing that 'lying takes time'.

### 6.3.1.3   Inclusion of social desirability scales

The third control is the inclusion of a 'social desirability' scale in the personality tool. Scales are designed to identify those who have set out to manage the impression they make in the test, either by appearing more positive, termed 'faking good', or by trying to position themselves as worse, termed 'faking bad'. The MMPI was the first test to incorporate a 'lie' scale and most instruments now include such scales.

All of the items that comprise these measures have been selected on the basis that most people respond in a particular way. Standard social desirability scales have emerged, for example the Marlowe–Crowne scale. With these scales there can be wider issues of transportability into different cultures. For example, the Marlowe–Crowne scale includes items such as: 'I'm always willing to admit when I make a mistake' or 'I like to gossip at times'. Whilst these are items that might have a socially conventional response in Western societies, there is no clear absolute level for social desirability. These sub-scales do not necessarily transfer successfully across certain cultures: honesty is socially constructed. For example, in Japan or Italy honesty does not appear to be valued in the same way as in other cultures and so faking has emerged as an important consideration for test-users. As a result, practitioners are often advised to use an ipsative format to try and reduce this behaviour. The ipsative format forces the applicant to choose between a number of aspects of personality, all of which are desirable. The applicant has to choose only the one that is most and least like them and therefore they cannot choose them all.

Some questionnaires go further. The 16PF©, for example, includes a re-calculation which can be undertaken across a number of scales if high faking has been identified. This is an extreme tactic, but indicative of the impact of such behaviour on the reliability of the scores.

### 6.3.1.4   Response format

The presentation of items plays a critical role in reducing and controlling faking. There are two types of questions that can be used in personality tests: first, there are **normative items**. These ask the test-taker to rate how far they 'agree' or 'disagree' with a particular statement on a rating scale. Some have argued that normative version for the response format is superior as it is a more precise measure of psychological characteristics (Kline, 1993). However, normative formats are more open to particular patterns of distortions such as centralist tendencies, acquiescence, or deliberate distortion (Martin *et al., 2002*). Underlying the response issue is the type of questions that are used in each test. Inevitably, responses are a product of the questions asked (Guildford, 1959). The phrasing of items can cause distortion and produce positive responses that are not indicative of how the individual would typically respond (Kline, 1993). This problem stems from the face validity of items. It is self-evident that the vaguer the item, the more likely one is to agree with it. For example, there is a difference between 'I like sport' and 'I swim three times a week'.

The second and most widely used alternative format is the ipsative format. Ipsative questions involve a forced choice where the test-taker has to select one from a number of different responses (see Figure 8.9). Each of the possible responses is usually matched for social desirability so that all are equally attractive options. Although not a faking scale *per se*, it is concerned with measuring the consistency of response. There is, however, a high interdependence between the scales on these types of test, so that the final score can represent only the relative strength of answer provided by the individual. This is due to the negative correlation between some of the scores so that choosing one response precludes being able to choose another. For example, in Figure 8.9 a simple ipsative item is included so that you cannot choose to be both social and organized. In ipsative-response personality tools, the choice is often more complex between three and five mutually exclusive statements. It is important that the test-user keeps in mind the version of the instrument that has been used in a particular situation to aid both their interpretation of the results and in feeding back the results to the test-taker.

It is recommended that test-users only use ipsative versions in highly competitive situations as they produce other aspects of distortion, such as central tendency, where the applicant consistently chooses the middle ranked response and acquiescent response formats. However, this format does have its critics. Many argue that ipsative items are inferior as they distort the instrument (Johnson *et al.*, 1988). It is argued that this type of format cannot be used to compare individuals as the reliabilities are exaggerated and they have limited predictive validity. Saville and Wilson (1991) have challenged and attempted to refute these claims.

In evaluating the ipsative approach, recent evidence has indicated that test-takers – provided they have a good insight into the specific job role – can create a realistic fake response (Martin *et al.*, 2002). (This extends Mahar *et al.*'s (1995) earlier work on faking.) This study compared the impact of normative and ipsative versions of the OPQ tool on faking behaviour and found that there was a significant difference on the ipsative version, but not on the normative version, between groups who set out to fake and the honest groups. This suggests that forced choice tools may have more impact in moderating faking behaviour.

### 6.3.1.5  Item opacity

A fifth suggestion to reduce faking is to conceal the purpose of the questionnaire so that the test-taker is unaware of which trait is being assessed (Guildford, 1959). This, of course, assumes a level of naïvety in the test-tester that may be misplaced, given the increasing exposure of individuals to such instruments. The ever more sophisticated lengths to

Normative format

| | Strongly disagree | Disagree | Unsure | Agree | Strongly agree |
|---|---|---|---|---|---|
| | 1 | 2 | 3 | 4 | 5 |
| I enjoy talking to people | ☐ | ☐ | ☐ | ☐ | ☐ |

Ipsative version

Pick from the statements presented below which is most and least like you

| | Most | Least |
|---|---|---|
| I enjoy talking to people | ☐ | ☐ |
| I worry about deadlines | ☐ | ☐ |
| I can keep things tidy | ☐ | ☐ |
| I dislike helping others | ☐ | ☐ |

*Figure 8.9   Normative and ipsative example of the same item*

which they are willing to go to obtain the right answer can be seen in the growth of self-help books in this area. A variation on this is to conceal the purpose at an individual item level through using opaque questions, such as: 'Would you rather have been Jack the Ripper or Dr. Crippen?'

The idea behind this question is that faking consistently is easier for the more obvious items. It is not clear, however, what impact on the content, or face, validity such items produce. One view is that they may actually have the opposite effect and inadvertently make deliberate fakers more defensive and evasive in the response patterns they adopt. In that case, such items may prove redundant.

### 6.3.1.6   Results feedback

The final deterrent to distortion is through providing feedback to the test-taker. This is recommended as best practice for any organization using tools, with feedback of results occurring during an assessment centre. The feeding-back of personality test results provides an opportunity to gain clarification and gather further examples of behaviour from the test-taker. Through the inclusion of this checking process it is possible that faking will be identified.

### 6.3.2   Is faking important?

Despite concerns about the danger of distortion, evidence suggests that faking and distortion have a negligible impact on psychometric outcome, revealing no detrimental impact on validity (Barrick and Mount, 1996; Christiansen et al., 1994). More importantly, however, the use of 'faking good' responses may either be a reflection of wider personality issues, such as 'conventionalism', or as Cattell identified, due to a combination of other traits. He found that high 'social desirability' scores correlated positively with high 'extravert' and low 'anxiety' factors. As a result, it could be argued that 'faked' responses merely reflect the individual's outlook on the world. Indeed, some researchers have argued that high faking may actually be a quality that is required in particular occupations, for example airline stewards and stewardesses who score high on social desirability have been identified as better at their jobs (SHL, 1989).

Distortion is an issue that test-users and -developers need to be aware of, but there are likely to be variations in the patterns of distortion between individuals, which change depending on the situation or on the job role the individual is attempting to play. This is an interesting emergent issue which has caused some researchers to focus on the motivational issues that underlie faking behaviour in order both to understand it and to explore its potential impact. Far more attention needs to be given to the influence of distortion behaviour on the predictive validity of personality assessment tools. My concern is that in response to the perceived deviance of faking behaviour, assessment items become more intrusive and less relevant to the world of work. There is anecdotal evidence of clinical instruments, such as the MMIP being misapplied in a selection context in the USA. How would an applicant for a job as a bus driver feel when asked to respond to a question from the commonly utilized MMPI about the consistency of their bowel movements, or if they thought they were Jesus Christ? Personality instruments are by their very nature intrusive. It is important that test-developers and -users ensure that the instruments they use have high content- and face-validity if they want to ensure that their selection processes are not challenged by applicants.

## *Dilemma box 8.4 Faking?*

Prudence Brown has got through to the last round for a job as the accountancy administrator in a printing company. Prudence is very excited about the job, not only for the opportunities it will present, but also because of the atmosphere created by the people she might be working with. The firm emphasizes teamwork and is keen to ensure balance in all of its departments. As part of this initiative the letter inviting her to the final part of the selection process clearly states she will be asked to complete a personality inventory. Prudence is quite a shy person who is happy to work on her own, or with a small group of people. She comes to ask your advice as she believes you know something about recruitment and she really wants to do well and get this job. Her question is simple: should she change her answers on the personality test to try and reflect a more team-oriented extravert person? What do you advise her to do and why?

## 6.4  Ethics

Ethical concerns also arise in the use of personality tools. There are two central themes I wish to highlight – both about the tools' application. The first concerns the use of personality instruments to support de-selection, or redundancy; the second is concerned with the development and application of tools based on a Western context for multi-ethnic groups, whether from that culture, or another.

### 6.4.1  Use in de-selection

Personality instruments are increasingly entering the wider toolkit of the human resources practitioner. A consequence of this is that their application has extended from selection into redundancy situations. There are ethical considerations which arose from the decision in the early 1990s by a UK utility company to de-select employees on the grounds of their personality profiles. In this case, the test-takers were not aware of the eventual use of the data they were asked to provide and the test was not designed for use in this context. Although an out-of-court settlement was reached, there are other anecdotal cases of these instruments being misused and redundancies being given based on the grounds of personality, and not work performance.

Personality tests in these contexts are misused in three ways. First, the basis of de-selection rests on some arbitrary notion of there being a preferred personality type for a particular role. This view is suspect as it assumes there is one best way of 'being' in the role and involves a very simplistic view of work and how it is done, instead of identifying the infinite variety of ways that work can be undertaken and performed. As I suggested in Chapter 1, this is a dangerous view that, taken further, could result in the stereotyping of job functions and the atrophy of departments in which these identical people work. Diversity is important in ensuring the stimulation of different ways of performing roles and in bringing in new perspectives and challenging existing views thereby ensuring the on-going viability of companies. (Maybe the dominance of one personality type is the reason the firm is in trouble anyway!)

The second misuse lay in the use of the personality tool's expert system which was used to provide personality reports for each applicant. In many cases, the redundancy process involves the individual being left with a report that is designed to show them their profile, highlighting areas of concerns. This abuse involves providing a cheap and easy substitute for personal feedback. The individual has worked for the organization and therefore evidence must exist of their on-the-job behaviour: it is this, and not personality, that should form the basis of the decision to sack them. This is a far more ethical approach to redundancy as behaviour is something the individual can choose to change. Some personality tools have pejorative labels that alienate people. It is an abuse to tell an individual that they are being made redundant as they have too little 'conscientiousness'. It merely presents them with a label to carry away, which they might find difficult to remove.

Finally, given the low predictive validity of personality tests, it is unethical to act on the basis that they can reliably predict a given individual's job performance. It is questionable what value these might have in both selection and de-selection. It is an abuse of the tool to attempt to hide behind a veneer of scientific rigour when making redundancies. There are predictive validity and reliability concerns, due to the stability and faking, that make their inclusion in such processes contentious. The lay

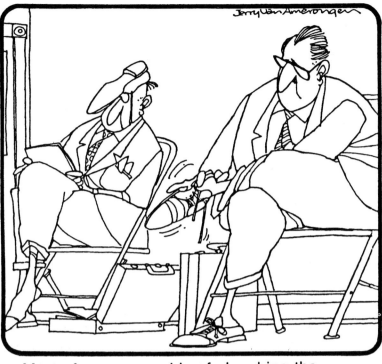

Most of us are capable of absorbing the
negative suggestions of others.

*Figure 8.10 The impact of labels?*

person is probably not aware of these concerns and instead regards these
tools as a reliable and valid measure; thus the labelling of individuals
through these tools is important. Many test-developers are concerned with
how the tools they develop might be misused in this way. It is the
responsibility of users not to abuse both the test-taker and -developer.

### 6.4.2   *Reducing discrimination?*

Some researchers have argued that personality tools should be included in
selection due to the lower unfair and racist discrimination of these tools
compared with cognitive assessment instruments (Hough *et al.*, 1990). This,
however, is a claim which has been refuted by Ryan *et al.* (1998), who
looked at the impact on validity and discrimination between different ethnic
groups using a combination of ability and cognitive tests.

Some support for the lower discrimination effects of these tools has been indicated by test-developers. A study in 1991 for the Occupational Personality Questionnaire (OPQ), involving a sample of 3,000 people and reported in their manual, deliberately included UK-based Afro-Caribbeans and Asians in order to identify whether there were cultural differences in test performance. This study found more within-group differences than between-group effects. Using the same tool, Nyfield *et al.* (1992) found significant differences between UK, US and Turkish managers, but again within-group differences predominated. This suggests that there are cultural differences, but that there were more differences within a particular cultural group than were found across different cultures.

A more recent UK-based study, however, suggested small but significant minority ethnic differences (Ones and Anderson, 2002). This study used the same tool (OPQ) and two other personality tools (Hogan Personality Inventory [HPI] and the Business Personality Indicator [BPI]) and compared Asian, Black, Chinese and White applicants' personality test results. The study found similarities between White and Chinese means but differences between Black–White means and Asian–White means for the OPQ and HPI instruments (*ibid.*). While these differences were insufficiently large to warrant a call for the use of specific ethnic-group norm tables in the UK, they do indicate differences. The study showed that different measures of the same construct do not assess exactly the same trait, suggesting that choice of instrument is important in measuring personality. Moreover, the study suggested important implications for test construction. During test construction, items tend to be removed based on large subgroup response differences; however, this assumes that there are no group differences in the construct/trait being measured, and that any differences in the test scores are a reflection of the cultural bias of the items. In this research, higher effect sizes for ethnic-group differences were found compared to other studies. In order to gain a better understanding of these differences, two areas of future study are suggested: the first involves examining the impact of different item selection strategies on subgroup (gender and ethnicity) differences; the second requires more multiple-country research be undertaken exploring subgroup differences for personality measures.

Higgs (2001) argued that there is a weakness in research examining both the development and application of tests for multicultural populations. This is a growing concern as practitioners are increasingly looking to use instruments which they can apply right across the globe in their recruitment programmes. Indeed some organizations are so concerned about the partiality of these tools that they do not use them for recruiting staff from developing countries.

In addition to ethnic differences, some research has suggested certain gender differences in personality traits. Costa *et al.* (2001), in a large ($n$ = 23,031) multicultural (26 countries) and mixed-gender study, found small gender differences: women scored higher in 'neuroticism', 'agreeableness', 'warmth' and 'openness to feelings' than men, who were higher in 'assertiveness' and 'openness to ideas'. These differences varied across different cultures and were most pronounced for the European and American samples where it could be argued that traditional sex roles are minimized. Ones and Anderson's (2002) aforementioned study also examined gender differences, but their UK-based study did not find they were significant.

A more promising technique to reduce unfair discrimination is the assessment of temperament using observational techniques and by assessing candidates in realistic job contexts. The application of assessment-centre techniques, which I will consider in the next chapter, shows the most promise in removing the kind of contaminating influences that have been built into test items.

## 6.5 Teams

Many of the measures I have examined focus on the selection of individuals who are isolated from the social context in which they typically perform their work. Increasingly, however, work is undertaken in a *team* context. Nonetheless, there has been limited attention paid to the assessment and measurement of both personality and ability on a team basis. Traditionally, methods of assessment have not conceptualized knowledge and ability as a 'collective' or social construction that resides not with one individual but through the interaction of a group. In this way, how work is performed is rarely based on an individual's endeavours and is more likely to be shared across the efforts of their colleagues too.

There is a paucity of research that has looked at group or team composition. This is in part due to the added complexity of measuring personality variables at an aggregated level. Researchers in this area are concerned with average team personality profiles, as well as the range (maximum to minimum) and the variance (standard deviation) of the team members' profiles. A further complication is the nature of the task itself. Increasingly, teams are being deployed without adequate consideration of whether a team is the best way for the work to be achieved.

Some researchers (Moynihan and Peterson, 2001; Barry and Stewart, 1997; Van Vianen and De Dreu, 2001) have identified a relationship between high-performing teams and the personality factors of 'agreeableness' and 'conscientiousness'. Others have only found contrary results for 'conscientiousness' when applied to team level, suggesting that having a member with low conscientiousness predicts success in top teams (Searle and Stern, 2003). In addition, Barrick *et al.* (1998) found that teams with moderate levels of emotional stability and *without* introvert members performed better. This is an interesting finding but may relate more to the task than the team itself. Barry and Stewart (1997) suggest that in an interdependent task, a minimum level of extraversion is required.

Teams are an increasingly important aspect of organizations and the selection of stable and productive team members who can co-operate and create synergies together is likely to be a key to differentiating successful companies from their competitors in the future. The methodological and analytical problems of work in this area need to be overcome if academics are to assist practitioners in the application of personality tools to team work.

# 7 Summary

An individual's personality cannot be measured directly: instead, it has to be inferred based on their behaviour. Six different, and at time opposing, approaches emerge with distinct views about the importance of situational as opposed to internal drivers for our behaviour. The differences between these models and the approach they take to personality assessment were examined. In the main, the tools used in selection and recruitment focus on the atheoretical trait-based approach.

Since the 1980s, the topic of 'personality' has received an increasing amount of attention both from practitioners and researchers. The resurgence in the use of these instruments has in part been based on the results of meta-analytic studies that have boosted their predictive validity. Researchers have tried to solve key problems in the field: namely consistency, bandwidth and fakeability. In so doing they have created new understandings and, despite the obstinacy of these serious concerns, raised confidence in personality tools for both test-developers and -users.

The field continues to be dominated by self-report questionnaires, and these continue to produce problems of faking and distortion. Earlier in the development of personality assessment, the UK focus was on observation by others (Bion, 1946), and not on the self-report by individuals of their feelings, attitudes, thoughts and behaviours. There has been limited attention given to this alternative context-dependent view of personality. Self-report instruments superseded the unstructured projective processes, such as Rorschach's ink blot test or the Thematic Apperception Test (TAT) common in the 1920s and 1930s, where the aim was to reveal *unconscious* preoccupations. In contrast, modern personality self-report tools are designed to offer a standardized, objective and structured assessment that allows for ease of construction, comparison and measurement. They assume the honesty of individuals and they also assume that each test-taker also has sufficient and accurate insight into their own behaviour. Few, indeed, consider whether self-knowledge exists for everyone. Studies have in fact suggested that it may be more reliable to get others to assess personality rather than using candidates themselves.

The predictive accuracy of personality tools is low, and despite the rising popularity of these instruments, concerns remain about their value in a selection and recruitment context. In part, the resurgence of interest in this form of measurement has been achieved by a focus on the assessment of specific traits – such as 'innovation potential' – which has allowed organizations to regard personality tools as a panacea to ameliorate, what are in reality, structural factors. This has enabled organizations to create and deploy temperament measures to identify those with a suitable disposition to work for them. There is, however, an inherent tension here that organizations have been unwilling to address. Those organizations who seek to change their fortunes, for example by boosting their innovation levels through changing the tools they use for selection, may potentially exacerbate their problems; instead, organizations need to look at their structure and culture in conjunction with their recruiting policies if they are to create successful and lasting change. It is no good attempting to just change part of the problem.

All too often, the impact of personality measurement in selection may reduce the diversity of new employees through the identification of whether an individual fits a specific 'personality profile'. There is little recognition of the variety of ways that a task can be approached, or of how the individual's personality will blend with those they will have to work with. Team assessment remains an under-explored topic. These personality measures are often used as a simplistic fit/misfit screening device, instead of enabling applicants to reveal their full potential.

Finally, test-developers have taken a particular view of cultural difference that permeates both their choice of items and how such differences are measured. There are increasing calls not only for developers, but also for researchers to widen the range of cultural contexts they study, and to look again at within- and between-groups divergence data and to examine how it is used. More sophistication is required in our interpretation of such differences than is currently found.

The study of personality at work is beginning to change: more attention is now paid to trying to understand which traits are important for which aspects of particular jobs. Through examining the evidence, it is clear that without this fundamental review, we cannot begin to understand the relationship between inner states and outer work performance. In addition, without an appreciation of the influence of other dimensions – such as intelligence, motivation and organizational context – we will not fully recognize and value the role that personality assessment can play in selection.

---

## *Exercise*

Using the job analysis you have completed earlier, suggest personality traits that may be important for selection. Are they mutually exclusive?
Taking some well-known personality instruments, consider how far these tests could help a recruiter identify volitional and customer-care aspects of a candidate.

# CHAPTER 9

# Selection tools 6: work samples – simple and multiple method tools

## 1  Overview

Work sample assessment is an approach to selection and recruitment that looks at the hands-on performance in a test designed to simulate what is actually required to perform a task on the job. This type of assessment falls into two distinct categories: the first is used to assess current skill and ability levels, such as job-knowledge tests or situational judgement tests; the second predicts future work-related skills, such as trainability tests and assessment centre exercises. These processes can vary enormously in their complexity, sophistication and in the number of assessments included – from a simple one-criterion job-knowledge test to an 'assessment centre' (where a number of individual and group exercises and psychometrics tools are combined and where multiple methods, criteria and assessors are used to enhance the selection decision).

Work-related sampling methods were first introduced in the 1920s and their application has dramatically increased since the 1960s across a wider range of job levels, particularly for managerial posts (Hollway, 1991). They have become increasingly popular with human resources practitioners because of evidence of higher face validity and greater fairness for non-traditional candidates (Lievens and Klimosky, 2001; Schmitt and Mills, 2001). It can also be argued that they provide candidates with a more realistic preview of the job. In addition, the validity of these different approaches ranges from 0.37 to 0.54 – the predictive validity of assessment centres is the highest of any selection process.

From a psychological perspective, however, there are some important outstanding questions: what precisely are these tests measuring? Why might they show less unfair discrimination for minority ethnic groups and female applicants?

The advancing popularity of work-based testing reflects a move towards a more complex approach to assessment procedures. This trend identifies not just job skills *per se*, but wider characteristics regarded as important in providing organizations with their future competitive advantage, such as how a task is undertaken. It could be said that the use of these tools reflects an increasing sophistication and confidence among human resources professionals, who see the adoption of more complex and rigorous assessment and development practices as demonstrating this professional group's pivotal place in helping to shape organizations for the future.

The growth of these new work-based assessment processes also reflects wider societal and organizational changes in structures and practices. Changes in the demographics of workforces have led to a reduction in the dominance of the traditional White male group within the workforce and have forced organizations to reconsider their selection processes. Evidence indicates that these non-cognitive tools increase the fairness of assessment processes, particularly for previously under-represented groups in the workforce – namely minority ethnic groups and women (McDaniel and Nguyen, 2001; Schmitt and Mills, 2001). This demographic change in the UK and USA, coupled with the reduction of staff through de-layering and downsizing during the 1990s, have forced organizations to reconsider the contributions of all their employees. Work sample methods can be used for both selecting new recruits and identifying existing staff with potential to develop (Spychalski *et al.*, 1997).

On closer examination, a cultural dimension emerges in the adoption of these tools across the world. They are used more widely in countries such as Germany, the Netherlands, the UK and USA, where an intellectual perspective rooted in the natural sciences can be found and where the focus is on the collection and assessment of objectively verifiable information, rather than on a person's family connections, as in Poland or China (Newell and Tansley, 2001). Many of the foremost group of countries have also seen public and legal challenges mounted against paper-and-pencil-based ability tests in the 1960s and 1970s on grounds of discrimination and have thus sought to adopt a more 'holistic' approach to assessing candidates (Highhouse, 2002).

These new assessment methods have allowed a more systematic identification of those who not only have the relevant, or potentially, relevant skills within an organization but also those who fit into the organizational culture. The added benefit of assessing both work-related skills and fit is that staff turnover is reduced, resulting in considerable potential savings to an organization's training and development budget. The utility (benefit minus the cost) of non-cognitive techniques can be high for organizations. Firms cannot afford to continue to carry those who do not contribute, or to support and train those who cannot pass final professional examinations.

In addition, these methods frequently require multiple assessors and therefore increase the number of stakeholders involved in the selection process. These stakeholders can include the candidate, the multiple assessors, human resource professionals, the local user (that is the department/unit seeking new staff) and the wider organization. The use of multiple stakeholders assists and supports the integration of non-traditional employees, particularly to senior roles, by providing more widespread endorsement of their appointment; and it can also help embed change programmes across the wider organization for both new recruits and amongst existing staff.

The application of work sample methods is also growing outside these selection and development contexts. Increasingly, they are used to assess individuals for wider professional and other training and development purposes. There are three reasons for this. First, there have been significant changes since the 1980s in adult training. National and EU government impetus has changed the process of skilled and semi-skilled training, increasing access through modularized competency-based training. Second, organizational changes have reduced the possibility of 'jobs-for-life' and, coupled with the creation of wider global opportunities, this has led to a requirement for standardized and portable recognition for training at every level. Third, the advance in information systems and technology has resulted in a renaissance in assessment methods. Professional bodies, such as national medical and architectural institutes in the USA, are recognizing that it is not the technical knowledge *per se* that is important for their members, but how they carry out the task. Task simulations are therefore becoming a popular part of formal accreditation and assessment.

On the other hand, critics of work sample tools argue that they are atheoretical and related to an empirical, socio-technical and predominantly Western view of the individual, the organization and work. As a result, it is argued that they fail to consider other less objectively based aspects which different cultures regard as important, such as the candidate's social and economic standing, or their more holistic match with the organization. These alternative views are significant and underlie the resistance to the adoption of these processes in different parts of the world. Nevertheless, they are rarely discussed within HR literatures. Despite attempts to explore the correlations between these non-cognitive tools and cognitive ability, there is little insight into how they actually work; there is simply evidence that they do (Klimoski and Brickner, 1987; Lievens and Klimoski, 2001).

In Chapter 9, I shall explore these non-cognitive work-based selection techniques and distinguish between those concerned with current skills and abilities and those concerned with identifying future potential. I will also differentiate between those using simple criteria and those which are more complex and utilize multiple criteria, exercises and assessors. Much of the research that has been undertaken in this area concerns assessment centres used to select higher level employees, and the latter part of the chapter is devoted to this form of work sampling. I will also review the evidence as to their value for organizations, question whether they offer new insights into job performance, and ask whether this form of assessment is contaminated. I will highlight improvements that can be made to this form of assessment process and consider its potential for application on a global basis.

## 2   Introduction

Work sample assessments are tests based on sampling the judgements, work-based abilities and behaviours of applicants. These tests assess an individual's *practical* work habits, and they are based on gathering actual samples of applicants' behaviours rather than 'signs or indicators', such as those found in personality or ability tests (Callinan and Robertson, 2000, p.251). Some researchers argue that they assess tacit knowledge (Sternberg, 1997); others define them as a test of what a person can *do*, rather than what a person *knows* (Smith, 1991). Therefore, they can be viewed as an assessment of the interaction between skills and abilities rather than individual components (Callinan and Robertson, 2000).

As a result of this relationship, they show high 'fidelity', that is a strong link between the assessment and the actual work. Fidelity is a form of validity.

There are five types of tests that can be included in the category of work sample: (1) job-knowledge tests, (2) hands-on performance assessment, (3) situational judgement tests, (4) trainability tests and (5) assessment centre exercises (Callinan and Robertson, 2000). I will use this taxonomy to discuss the differences between these types of tests shortly.

The techniques of work sampling grew dramatically in popularity during the 1980s, with the need of organizations for accurate tests which reduce the potential adverse impact often found in cognitive ability tests (see Chapters 6 and 7). This is important for all roles, but particularly in public service jobs (such as the police), where, for instance, representation from all ethnic groups is a key policy for effective working within local communities. These tools have a transparency which appeals to HR practitioners given the increasingly litigious nature of candidates, who may resort to legal challenge if they perceive that the assessment has unfairly disadvantaged them. There is also a demand from organizations for tools that address a broader range of work-related characteristics identified as important in job performance, including social competence, self-discipline, motivation, customer service characteristics and practical knowledge (Landy, 2000). It is argued that such approaches are significant in broadening the predictor space: they widen the range of criteria to include other factors that differentiate performance between individuals, and focus on gathering actual evidence for each criterion. This leads to improvements in validity and the identification of components that do not adversely discriminate against candidates from minority ethnic groups.

Weijerman and Born (1995) found that there was no unfair discrimination from work sample processes in terms of gender. Other researchers, such as Schmidt (1992) and Shore (1992), went further and suggested that some senior management exercises actually favoured women. Hoffman and Thornton (1997) found limited impact from 'race' on test performance. They did find, nonetheless, that in some tests – such as in-tray exercises which include a high cognitive component – ethnic performance differences were still present. It would be inaccurate then to argue that unfair discrimination is eliminated entirely by such tests. In Chapters 6 and 7, I have indicated that assessments that provide a transparent link between the task being assessed and the final job performance can appear to reduce the differences in performance between candidates from minority ethnic groups and those of Caucasian origin. These tests do have high face validity (Steiner and Gilliland, 1996), and they are often designed to include both job content and context aspects in the assessment; they therefore provide elements of a good job preview.

Some of these techniques have shown high predictive validity (0.54) (Robertson and Smith, 2001). Indeed, it has been argued that they have the highest validity of any selection tool, with an incremental validity above general mental ability tests of 0.12 (Schmidt and Hunter, 1998). In simple terms, this represents a 24 per cent increase in predictive validity through using the two tests together. Work sample tools, it is claimed, boost validity as they are tapping into a different range of performance-related factors.

Nevertheless, work sampling has limitations. First, a critical issue is that this type of test often requires more in-depth job knowledge than other selection instruments. Evidence indicates correlations between work experience and job performance, with individuals' experience affecting their work sample performance above and beyond their previously accrued task-specific knowledge (Quinones et al., 1995). As a result, they may disadvantage inexperienced applicants, such as graduates. It can be argued that some tests are measures of current, and not potential, work-related ability. Care must therefore be taken in interpreting the results as they may be a reflection of initial skill, and not potential levels.

Second, research shows that over time these validities shrink, or attenuate, more than other instruments (Robertson and Kandola, 1982) – for instance, cognitive ability tests. This suggests that the abilities assessed in work sample tests are not necessarily those required to perform the role over time. When a comparison was made between traditional paper-and-pencil tests and work sample assessment used for US Naval recruitment into a machinist role, it was found that, despite the initially high validity for work sample methods, after 18 months the performance predicted by the paper-based test was far better (Siegel and Bergman, 1975).

Moreover, the attenuation of work sample validity may be a product of an increasingly erroneous assumption that job roles are static and stable (see Chapter 2). Rapid changes in both the content of job roles and in organizational context create a dynamic that work sample techniques are unable to incorporate. As a result, when change is an issue, it may be more appropriate to use a tool that assesses underlying abilities, such as a verbal ability test.

Finally, the process of developing and delivering these instruments is often very costly and time consuming. As with other selection instruments, each test must be developed separately and validated for that particular population and particular role. The very nature of these tests often means that access is required to specific equipment that can only be found in the workplace, and this adds an additional constraint to the flexibility of the assessment.

A critical distinction between many, but arguably not all, work sample tests and cognitive and personality assessments is that these tools are concerned with collecting evidence of the candidate's behaviour, through an actual sample. Exercises would be designed to allow information about this social behaviour to be observed and collected. For instance, if the criterion 'social confidence' was being measured, the candidate would be expected to be seen at ease with new people and able to communicate freely. In contrast, other tests, such as personality and ability tests, are concerned with assessing potential. As a result, the relationship between their criteria and the actual job performance is more opaque: the data collected is used is an indication, or a sign, of the individual's potential. An example is the differences found in Dilemma box 8.1, where the candidate's behaviour suggested they were shy, yet they scored 'extravert' in a self-report measure.

Let us briefly recap on the history of work sample tools before turning attention to their theoretical underpinning.

## 3   Historical dimension

The first application of the technique that we would now call work sampling can be found in the USA where it was applied to tram drivers in Boston around 1913. Using Munsterberg's judgement tests, candidates were asked to make distance and speed estimates. Those selected on the basis of these tests were found to have fewer accidents.

Exercises that incorporated both multiple candidates and assessors were first used at a senior organizational level, as I indicated in Chapter 9, for the selection of officers in the Second World War. Bion's (1946) leaderless group test is a work sample test in the sense that as:

> the actual task of the test is merely a cloak of invisibility for the testing officers who are present ... it is not an artificial test, but the real-life situation that has to be watched – that is, the way in which a man's capacity for personal relationships stands up under the strain of his own and other men's fear of failure and desire for personal successes.
>
> (Bion, 1946, p.80)

It was not, however, until the mid-1950s that work sampling evolved into the sophisticated multiple exercise/multiple candidate approach we see deployed in organizations today. American Telephone and Telegraph (AT&T) was the first company to devise a new system – the Managerial Progress Study – for development purposes to help identify potential future leaders. This was the first application of attention being given to managers', rather than workers', assessment (Hollway, 1991). Since this was the group expected to lead the organization and be committed to the future, new resources went into finding and nurturing them. Assessment centres have been a stalwart of managerial selection practices ever since.

## 4   Theoretical perspective

The theoretical background to work sample techniques is based on the underlying premise of *behavioural consistency*. This assumes that past behaviour predicts future performance. Such theory focuses on the relationship between the identified performance criterion and the predictor and is termed 'point–to–point' correspondence (Asher and Sciarrion, 1974). In this form of assessment, the central premise involves an equivalence between the behaviour required to complete the test and that required for successful performance in the job.

The lower validity found for other non-work sample tests may be due to the distinction between signs and samples. Assessors have to make an inference between the performance predictor and the performance criterion, without objective verifiable evidence of it. As a result, this lack of transparency contaminates the assessment. In supporting this view, Anderson *et al.* (1994) found that assessors pay more attention to observed data than that collected from self-report tools, such as personality, ability and biodata tests. Robertson and Kandola (1982) argue, however, that in reality there may be a gap between these two aspects for everything but the most simple hands-on task. Therefore, this assumed point-to-point correspondence might not be as clear in practice as is claimed in theory.

A key means by which distortion can arise in work sample tests is due to an over-reliance on face validity. Many test developers confuse face validity with its more robust counterpart – content validity (which we explored in Chapter 3). This fault has particularly been found in exercises commonly used in senior assessment programmes, which involve multiple criteria, such as the leaderless group discussions and in-tray measures (Lowry, 1993; Schippman *et al.*, 1990). These tests might appear to assess a particular work-related skill, and so no further data are gathered regarding their correlation with other work-related performance. Accurate identification of assessment criteria is critical for the development of reliable tools.

A second aspect of contamination occurs where this technique does not include sufficient breadth, so that a test may not be representative of all aspects of the job. This breadth is termed test 'bandwidth' (Callinan and Robertson, 2000, p.256). As I indicated in Chapter 6, test-developers must ensure that their tests comprehensively assess the domain. For example, a test of a psychometrician's job knowledge that failed to test knowledge of reliability would be inadequate in terms of bandwidth. By its very nature, the process of work sample testing involves artificially dividing the job into distinct aspects. What is important is that in determining the final content of a test, both the representativeness of the task and those aspects which are critical to successful task performance are included. Work sample tests are scored by assessing performance, not against other novices, but against experts in the job. Therefore, the level achieved in this type of test equates with the candidates' actual job level. Thus, someone who gets 95 per cent of the test right should be able to complete 95 per cent of the job. There is, however, one further important criterion of validity. This is criticality: imagine a test of an electrical engineer that had sufficient breadth, but omitted a crucial issue such as whether the person was colour blind. This illustrates the importance of including both representativeness and criticality in work sample testing.

There is some debate between researchers as to how far these instruments are context and content relevant. These features are termed a test's **'fidelity'** and **'specificity'**, respectively (Callinan and Robertson, 2000, p.256). Robertson and Kandola (1982) argue that context is not significant, whilst Smith (1991) disagrees, stating that the creation of realistic and standardized conditions are an integral part of work sample testing. Both of these issues have important implications for the job preview dimensions inherent in this type of assessment. Some argue that the more abstract the measure used to represent the job role, the lower the potential predicative validity (Callinan and Robertson, 2000). However, others suggest that the time and costs involved in creating high fidelity tools may not be justified (Motowidlo *et al.*, 1990). Given the speed of changes in technology, this is a problem that is developing rapidly and on which more research is currently being undertaken. Evidence does indicate that low fidelity paper-and-pencil versions of work sample tests do have effects – reducing applicants' positive reactions, the job preview elements and creating unfair discrimination. We need to see if the same is also true for low fidelity computer-based versions.

Work sample assessment relies on the ability of the test to enable the objective observation of work-related behaviours and skills. It assumes that there is a *correct* way of performing a task. As I noted earlier, an inherent problem of the 'one correct' view of work is that it may result in stagnation of the workforce by reducing diversity. This approach places objective observation and categorization at the forefront of the assessment, thus ignoring the importance of the individual relationship between the applicant and the assessor. The candidate is assessed against objectively discernable behavioural criteria by a trained assessor. This view reflects a dominant reductionist social science paradigm that is found in the USA, the UK, Germany and the Netherlands. It is challenged in other countries within Europe such as Italy and France, and across the world, such as in China.

Those adopting a socio-technical view of work have suggested that often it is the structure of the work that requires more scrutiny (Klein, 1976). Myopic attention on the selection of candidates diverts attention away from a more fundamental examination of the job. It results in facets of the job (such as the structure, content and dominant approach to the tasks that comprise a job) becoming taken for granted. It takes no account of how these facets of the task influence the behaviour of job-holders, or the appropriateness of their behaviour. The approach adopted by work sample techniques views the individual as fitting into an existing system – a cog in the wheel – rather than changing or making an impact on it in any way.

I will now review the different types of approaches to work sample testing by dividing them into current assessment tests and future-focused assessment processes.

# 5   Current level

## 5.1 Job-knowledge tests

A job-knowledge test is the most obvious type of work sample test and concerns *current* levels of performance. This type of test often concentrates on a specific dimension or content. An example of this type of test is the Highway Code assessment found in most countries' driving tests. In their review of such tools, Robertson and Kandola (1982) identified that paper-and-pencil versions had a median predictive validity of 0.40. This is an area, however, in which computer-based testing is having a dramatic impact. Initially, the paper-and-pencil tests were translated into computer versions, but subsequent research indicated that performance on these tests was affected by the medium. As a result, time and resources have been devoted to generating new computer-based job-knowledge assessment formats. An example of this type of test can be found in the UK Highway Code assessment which is part of the driving test.

This form of testing is increasingly being used where the pass or fail will have a significant impact on the livelihood of the test-taker. This is termed 'high stakes testing'. Computer-based work sample testing is increasing in the US professional licensing organizations, such as architecture and medicine. The introduction of this new medium has a number of advantages for such organizations. First, it allows them to increase the number of test sessions held throughout the year. This appeases applicants who may have to wait long periods of time to sit, or re-sit, assessments without which they cannot practise professionally. It evens out the organization's workload, spreading the examinations process into smaller, more manageable units throughout the year.

This type of testing can also be more cost-effective. Through the use of computer-mediated testing, large item banks can be developed. Further, as we saw in Chapter 6, the advent of item response theory has allowed the interrogation and analysis of single items, rather than complete tests. As a result, families of items can be cloned so that the same concept can be tested, with small alterations to the question content, the data used, or the right answer in the multiple-choice order. With an exponential increase in the number of potential permutations for each question, this improves the chances of reducing cheating as an applicant is less able to memorize the test items. In addition, data can be gathered from computer-based testing for item completion rates. This is useful for two distinct applications. First, it reveals those who cheat since their response times are quicker, and, second, it identifies item-difficulty levels.

Computer-based testing creates new protocols regarding interruptions and stoppages. For example, due to problems with keeping telephone lines open, most organizations choose to download the entire test to each site at the start of each session and send back results on completion rather than testing live online. This makes the issue of test re-starting much more straightforward if there is a problem as the computer can simply take the test-taker back to the item they had stopped at, whereas in paper-and-pencil tests the test administrator must reply on the answer sheet to indicate where the applicant has got to. The software also ensures test-takers have limited options open to them: for example, they cannot use other functions such as e-mail whilst the test is live and it reduces the number of keys they can press.

In addition, the application of computer-based testing changes security arrangements. It would be naïve to suggest that computer-based testing has eradicated security issues. As with any high stakes situation the benefits of cheating are massive. These systems merely change the types of security problems. At each test session, for instance, test-takers may be doing the same questions in a different order, or taking different questions assessing the same concept. This alters the way that the venue is patrolled, or '**proctored**' to use the US term, thus administrators do not have to be so concerned about test-takers looking at each other's work as they will be doing different items. As the tests are delivered on the day down the telephone line to each venue, storage security issues are replaced by potential hacker and firewall issues. Another concern is server security: this is important not only for ensuring the safety of test items, but also for results. Complex firewall systems need to be in place to prevent hackers entering the systems and causing damage.

What is likely is that this type of testing will become increasingly common for all types of knowledge-based testing in the future. While I have focused on professional testing here, similar concerns apply to any form of knowledge testing. The costs of setting up and developing such items can be prohibitive. The application of such new mediums for testing fundamentally changes the relationship between three key stakeholders – the test-taker, the test-developer and the test-user. It could be argued that in the past the power lay with the test-user who bought the test and the scoring system and then kept their results. Computerized testing increases the power of test-developers to protect their intellectual property, and creates a new form of dependency amongst test-users. Test-developers now need to provide versions of the test for candidates and to score and interpret the results. In addition, test-users must trust the developer that the results they receive are accurate as they will not be able to check for themselves. Issues of personal security and access become more prominent (Searle, 2003): test-takers' positions weaken as their results are now held by two organization – the test developer and the user. Organizations must provide test-takers with more information regarding the purpose and process of assessment, including who will be able to gain access to these sensitive data.

## 5.2  Hands-on performance tests

The most traditional form of test in this domain is the psychomotor test, which is characterized by manual dexterity tests (see Figure 9.1). In this type of test, the job role is broken down into key behavioural components that can be reproduced as a behavioural checklist. As a result, assessment is easier. Robertson and Kandola (1982) reported median validity for this type of tool of 0.39. This type of test has a wider application than selection, as it can also be used to diagnose training needs and quality assessment. In his study of military tests in this category, Carey (1991) identified their application in quality auditing processes for the US Marine Corps and examined a range of different tests, finding that the actual performance of many military tasks was not necessary for valid selection and training. Work sample testing offered a more valid and cheaper system where expensive ordinance is involved.

Other applications for this type of test include telephone skills. Gael *et al.* (1972; 1975) produced a series of such tests during the 1970s, which sampled how operators handled telephone calls and assessed their record preparation and filing skills. Using a simple scoring system of 'right', 'wrong' and 'not performed', they tested telephonists handling a sample one hour of calls.

The inherent problem for many tests in this area is the requirement of previous job experience, including on identical or similar equipment. This is likely to reduce their application in selection for novice groups of applicants.

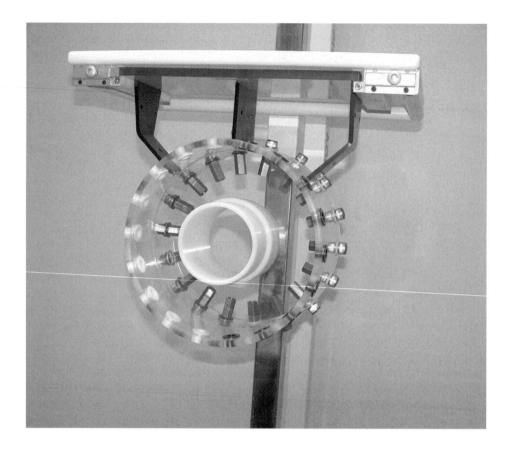

*Figure 9.1   Layette instrument hand tool dexterity test*

## 5.3  Situational judgement tests

A situational judgement test does not include actual performance of the task, but asks the candidate to indicate how they would behave (we discussed this briefly in Chapter 7, section 5.1). So it does not strictly provide a sample of the applicant's behaviour, only their approach (see Box 9.1 below). Some researchers have categorized this as a job simulation (Motowidlo *et al.*, 1997).

Situational judgement tests assess the candidate's application of their job knowledge through presenting a situation and a number of potential responses or choices (see Box 9.1). In some cases, the response format asks them to indicate the best and also the worst response to the scenario given. This approach is more akin to the situational interview process outlined in Chapter 5. Many argue that this form of testing is merely a surrogate job-knowledge test (Schmidt, 1994), but one not necessarily based on direct experience *per se*. However, there is some dispute about this latter issue, as research indicates that scores on situational tests do increase with the amount of job experience (McDaniel and Nguyen, 2001). The test may not be understood sufficiently by those without experience.

## Box 9.1   Example of item from a situational judgement test assessing customer-relations skills for a tele-banking organization

You answer a call from a customer who wants to find out about the location of some funds they have transferred from their internet account. This type of account is designed to be supported in the main by a computer interface. You know that you cannot answer their query directly and would have to call another department to find out more.

Do you:

- Say that you cannot help and suggest they log on to their account and search themselves?
- Offer to contact the other department for them and find out what has happened?
- Say that you cannot help and suggest they call the other department who might be able to help?

Increasingly, assessors for professional qualifications are becoming aware that it is insufficient for professions, such as medicine or architecture, to merely have the relevant job knowledge, but that assessment should also include how this knowledge is applied. As a result, situational testing which examines complex problem-solving situations, such as diagnosing patients' illnesses and identification of a relevant treatment plan, can be included. This drive for new assessment formats has occurred at the same time as advances in information technology make it possible to provide assessment simulations. For example, the US Medical Licencing Examination (USMLE™) has spent more than twenty years trying to develop assessment tests that contain situational assessments in order to examine doctors' diagnostic skills. (Visit their website [www.usmle.org] to see an example: go to 'test materials' and 'step 3' for the situational simulations.)

Situational tests have also been used to select those applying for roles requiring leadership or team skills. Paper-and-pencil versions of situational tests were developed to assess a range of skills including teamwork, conflict resolution and leadership. Stevens and Campion (1999) reported good correlations between these tests and actual team-work performance of around 0.32; however, on closer examination the test was also found to correlate highly with general mental ability tests (0.91). Paper-and-pencil formats may constrain the complexity of the scenarios, and the potential responses, that can be used in these tests. The length, complexity and comprehensibility of written formats appear to be inextricably linked (McDaniel and Nguyen, 2001).

Advances in video- and computer-based testing have improved the fidelity of the situational judgement test, enhancing their context and content sensitivity (for example, Chan and Schmitt, 1997). These new formats can provide more complexity, offering competing scenarios requiring the applicant to identify priorities. Situational tests are already showing good results in industries such as air-traffic control (Burke, 2000) and for selecting airline pilots (Carey, 1991). In these cases, the tests provide a useful surrogate for assessment where the cost or damage of a full simulation would be prohibitive. However, more research needs to be undertaken in order to help us understand the impact of the new computer-based medium on the results. The *format* of a test, whether it is paper-and-pencil or computer-mediated, creates a new test, and so they are not interchangeable, but subtly different. More work is required to ensure their substitutability.

One question that has emerged is precisely what is being measured by these tests and is it different from other psychometric tools. Significant correlations have been found between this form of assessment and cognitive ability tests, with results of 0.53 and criterion-related validity of 0.56 (McDaniel *et al.*, 1997). Situational tests have been found to correlate with other variables including personality dimensions, such as 'emotional stability', 'conscientiousness' and 'agreeableness' (McDaniel and Nguyen, 2001), and also cognitive ability and job-knowledge tests (Motowildo *et al.*, 1997). Recent work suggests a predictive validity for job performance of 0.34 (McDaniel *et al.*, 2001). In its defence, some argue that it is a more complex multi-faceted measure and so it may be difficult to identify precisely what is being assessed (Chan and Schmitt, 1997; McDaniel and Nguyen, 2001).

Research evidence does suggest that these instruments have a beneficial effect in reducing unfair discrimination for both minority ethnic groups and female applicants (McDaniel and Nguyen, 2001; Schmitt and Mills, 2001; Weekley and Jones, 1997). The reason for this is unclear, with some arguing it is because non-job related cognitive load factors are removed (Callinan and Robertson, 2000). Weekley and Jones (1997) found that merely using a video medium alone does not reduce such discrimination. Schmitt and Mills (2001), in their study for a customer service role, compared paper-and-pencil tests with a telephone simulation, and found smaller group differences between White and Afro-American applicants. They suggest that simulations can reduce unfair discrimination in some contexts, although discrimination would occur against minority ethnic groups where the selection ratio was low and where only top-scoring applicants were chosen.

The cost of elaborate simulations can constrain their adoption by firms, but the aforementioned simulation study indicates that cheaper options can be created with a little thought. A concern remains, however, that because of improvements offered by this type of test in reducing discrimination and evidence of their face validity, less rigorous evaluation will be undertaken to examine how they work. McDaniel and Nguyen (2001, p.109) call for more attention to be paid to how item characteristics influence validity and their potential fake resistance.

The main, and as yet unresolved, question is why do these simulations reduce discrimination for minority groups? Chan and Schmitt (1997) suggest a number of potential reasons for this. First is the implicit assessment of reading comprehension required by paper-based tests. The candidate is required to understand and follow a more abstract form of assessment. Simulation tests minimize the necessity for reading and verbal material (as we saw with culture-free testing in Chapter 7). A second factor that has been suggested concerns the higher face validity of job-based situations and simulations, which is linked to candidates' motivation and expectations. The candidate can see the link between the assessment and the job they are trying to get more clearly. To support this view, Gilliland (1994) has suggested a relationship between assessment performance and the perceived procedural justice of a test.

Part of the difficulty in enhancing our understanding of discrimination lies in the prevailing view concerning the measurement of subgroup differences, which treats the differences which are found as a product of error, rather than a discernible difference between culturally-diverse groups. The development of psychometrics and other assessment tools has been hampered from the onset by this issue, beginning, as we saw in Chapter 6, with Terman's early view at the start of the twentieth century. Perhaps the problem lies in the failure of assessment-process developers to consider the people that lie behind these data. We need to take more interest in why these differences arise and whether they are the product of the test, or related to cultural and gender differences. We will never be able to create equality of access while we retain this partial view of individual differences in the data. (This concern is given more discussion in Chapter 10.)

## 6   Assessment of future potential skills

The second type of work sample assessment differs from the three techniques I have just outlined because it does not require work-related experience. There are two techniques that fall into this category – trainability tests and assessment centre exercises – and both are concerned with the identification of *potential* work-related abilities. As there is a huge volume of research on assessment centres, I will discuss these in their own section, but it is worth highlighting now that assessment centres look at *future* potential and not current ability.

### 6.1  Trainability tests

Trainability tests measure not the current level of work-related ability, but how quickly the test-taker will assimilate and accommodate new knowledge or skills. They are distinct from all other forms of test that I have previously mentioned as they include guidelines as to what training should be provided. Both the structure and content of a trainability test are included and the time period strictly limited. This is to ensure that all test-takers have a standardized experience. This central focus on trainability rather than ultimate performance is an important feature that differentiates this type of instrument from situational judgement tests. In their meta-analysis of tests in this area, Robertson and Downs (1989) found validity of 0.48 between tests that involved the identification of errors and actual performance.

This type of tool is important as it enables skill assessment of those with no prior experience. It can play a critical role for organizations who are recruiting trainees to positions where long and costly periods of training are involved, representing a substantial investment on the part of both the test-taker and the organization. This would include professions such as accountancy, computer-programming and insurance actuaries.

One difficulty of developing tests of this type is that the measure must sample not only the content of the job, but also the learning context. The validity of such instruments is dependent both on aspects of the learning and the outcome. Research suggests that this is far easier to achieve in structured learning environments, for example in information-technology training (Reilly and Israelski, 1988).

## 7   Assessment centres

The assessment centre is not a place, but a *process* designed to measure multiple criteria. This process comprises a sophisticated assessment of work-related skills by creating a forum designed to allow a candidate to exhibit a range of work-related behaviours. The assessment centre comprises of exercises that are work samples, and includes additional selection tools, such as personality and ability tests. Assessment centres typically comprise a number of different selection tools. They frequently include cognitive ability tests, personality assessment tools and structured interviews. Multiple candidates undertake a range of different exercises, some on an individual basis and some in a group. In addition, work sample based exercises include individual-focused techniques which are designed to mirror more closely the job role, such as managing an in-tray or giving a presentation. Candidates are also involved in group-based exercises which may include role plays, leaderless group discussions or business simulations.

The exercises that make up an assessment centre involve a number of assessors; some are specialists – for example, occupational psychologists with skills in using psychometric tests. The final selection decision is made on the basis of the 'wash-up'. This is a discussion (involving all of the assessors) which compares the performance of the candidates on all of the different exercises. Typically, such an in-depth assessment lasts a day or so with candidates undertaking each of the exercises at different times (see Table 9.1). The whole process is expensive both to develop and to run.

This form of assessment has grown rapidly in popularity and is usually used for management selection. UK studies show that whereas 7 per cent of organizations used this approach in 1973 (Gil *et al.*, 1973), it had risen to 20 per cent by the mid-1980s (Robertson and Makin, 1985) and to around 65 per cent in the 1990s (Shackleton and Newell, 1997). AT&T was the first organization to use management assessment centres; the original included nine components: (1) a business game, (2) leaderless group discussion, (3) in-tray exercise, (4) two-hour interview, (5) projective test, (6) personality test, (7) 'q sort', (8) intelligence tests and (9) an autobiographical essay and questionnaire. Many of these components have been mentioned in earlier chapters, but some were opportunities to sample work-based abilities and skills.

**Table 9.1 Assessment centre programme**

| Time | Cognitive and personality psychometric tests | Structured interview | Presentation | Group business simulation | Customer service role play |
|---|---|---|---|---|---|
| 9.30 | 1,2,3 | 4 | 5 | | 6 |
| 10.30 | 1,2,3 | 5 | 6 | | 4 |
| 11.00 | 1,2,3 | 6 | 4 | | 5 |
| 11.30 | 4,5,6 | 1 | 2 | | 3 |
| 12.00 | 4,5,6 | 3 | 1 | | 2 |
| 12.30 | 4,5,6 | 2 | 3 | | 1 |
| 1.00–1.45 | L | U | N | C | H |
| 1.45 | | | | 1,2,3,4,5,6 | |
| 3.30 | WA | S | H | U | P |

Because all the exercises in assessment centres are developed based on a job analysis and designed around the particular components of a role, the whole process has high face validity. As a result, it is seen by candidates and organizations to be a more thorough and fair way of selection. Studies of incremental validity have raised concerns by suggesting that the primary construct being measured is often cognitive ability. However, other work-related skills are being assessed. Researchers remain perplexed as to precisely what is being measured by these sophisticated work sample exercises. Let us now examine in more detail what is involved.

Assessment centres are distinct from other forms of work sample techniques for three key reasons. First, they offer the opportunity of assessing potential skill, and therefore the process can be used for selecting new recruits, but also can be valuable in identifying the talents of existing staff. The technique involves assessors making inferences based on a sample of the candidates' behaviour, such as their decision-making skills or approach to leadership, and rating their underlying qualities. This is in contrast to the more straightforward observing and recording of other work sample tests. As a result of these inferences, assessment centres stretch the 'point-to-point' correspondence between the criteria of assessment and satisfactory performance that underlies work-sampling techniques.

Second, this type of exercise enables a wider range of criteria to be assessed. For example, in a group-based exercise, criteria such as 'organization skills', 'directing and leading others', 'teamworking', 'creative problem-solving' and 'effective communication' might be simultaneously measured. The hallmark of a good assessment centre is the use of dimensions that accurately reflect successful managerial abilities. This is, however, difficult to achieve through one exercise and so the process involves using a number of distinct work sample exercises to provide multiple opportunities to assess each dimension (see Table 9.2). Limited attention, however, has been paid to the value of each of the individual assessment components to see whether the in-tray exercise, for example, accounts for the biggest variance in performance, or whether the interview was the best predictor.

**Table 9.2 Criteria and exercise matrix**

| Criteria | Personality psychometric tests | Structured interview | Presentation | Group business simulation | Customer service role play |
|---|---|---|---|---|---|
| 'organization skills' | ✓ | ✓ | ✓ | ✓ | |
| 'directing and leading others' | ✓ | ✓ | | ✓ | ✓ |
| 'teamworking' | ✓ | ✓ | | ✓ | |
| 'creative problem-solving' | ✓ | ✓ | ✓ | ✓ | ✓ |
| 'effective communication' | ✓ | ✓ | ✓ | | ✓ |

Third, the assessment centre is most frequently aimed at assessing an aggregation of higher level (managerial) competence, rather than a specific work-related skill. In this way, assessment centres are not a work sample in the strict sense but a process providing a forum for the expression of specific work-related behaviours (Lowry, 1993). These issues, especially the latter two, may be critical in accounting for the low validity (0.37) reported for some assessment centres in comparison with the values reported earlier, which are commonly found in single work sample tools (0.54) (Robertson and Smith, 2001).

Work sample exercises that are typically used in an assessment centre can be divided into three distinct categories: individual, one-to-one, and group-based assessment processes. I will now examine the different exercises used in assessment centres and then move on to look in more detail at how assessment centres are planned and administered, validity and reliability issues, problems of contamination and, finally, how the assessment centre process can be improved.

## 7.1 Individual exercises

First are exercises based solely on individual performance. These include in-basket/in-tray, planning exercises, and case analysis. In-tray exercises are designed to simulate important aspects of management jobs and focus on the organizing, prioritizing, decision-making, and indication of actions required. The tasks are based on information found in a range of sources, including memos, emails, letters, records and other documentary items. In much the same way, 'planning' and 'case analysis' exercises involve the candidate analysing data from a range of different sources and writing a report discussing and offering support for their opinions.

Research indicates that the in-tray exercise is one of the most common found in assessment centres (occurring in 95 per cent of cases) (Thornton and Byham, 1982). It is also the one for which most research has been undertaken. The exercise permits the direct observation in a standardized problem situation of an individual's behaviour in a highly job-relevant context. It can often be supplemented with an interview which probes in more detail how the candidate made their decisions. Significant correlations have been found between this test and cognitive ability tests (Lievens and Klimoski, 2001).

There can, however, be large variations in the content and assessment of in-tray tasks. Schippman *et al.* (1990) argued that although they have high face validity, this may often be their only virtue. Many test-publishers have created generic versions of these exercises that can be purchased for use in selection and development. Unsurprisingly, these off-the-shelf exercises show lower validity than bespoke tools devised for a particular job and context. More contentiously, this may be a result not of a lower contextual fit for the tool, but symptomatic of an underlying low level of skill from local human resource professionals (Callinan and Robertson, 2000). The purchase of generic items may merely reflect inadequate expertise or limited familiarity with the assessment centre process.

Early studies from the AT&T data suggested that individual exercises were a good discriminator between different types of candidates, accounting for 16 per cent of the variance in assessment centre performance. Lopez (1966) compared the performance of trainees with experienced managers and found that trainees tended to produce wordier responses, were less likely to take action on the basis of the importance of a problem, and often did not see the implications of their actions. Therefore, although it is suggested that no prior expertise is required, there does appear to be a difference in performance on these exercises as a result of job experience.

## 7.2 One-to-one exercises

One-to-one exercises are the second type of exercise undertaken in assessment centres. The constructs typically measured in a role play include communication, listening and interpersonal skills, whilst a presentation is more concerned with candidates' challenging and persuasion skills. These include role-playing, fact-finding interviews, and making presentations. Variations can emerge in candidates' performance during role plays because of inconsistent responses by the other parties: it is therefore advisable to have dedicated role players to ensure some standardization in the exercise (Lievens and Klimoski, 2001). This is an example of where administration factors can affect the candidate's outcome.

There can be huge variations in the instructions given for these tasks. For example, details can either be given to candidates on their arrival at the assessment centre, which gives all applicants the same amount of time and resources, or they can be prepared in advance, which makes it harder to assess how far the work is actually that of the candidate. The issue of passing other's work off as one's own is rarely considered in this context. However, senior staff rarely create their own presentations and so perhaps this is a further way in which a presentation mimics real life.

## 7.3 Group exercises

The final category of exercise is the group exercise. These include leaderless group discussions and business simulations. The content of these varies greatly, with face validity being enhanced by the use of topics related to the work context. Bion (1946) argued in his earlier version of a group-based exercise that they assess candidates' tolerance of uncertainty, stress and flexibility.

Two variants exist of the leaderless discussion exercises. First are those that assign roles to each candidate, providing them with a brief that other candidates are unaware of. This type of test is typically assessing candidates' negotiation and persuasion skills, teamwork, planning and organization, quality of decision and leadership in the form of managerial control and delegation abilities. Test-publishers provide generic versions of this exercise. The second type assigns no roles, merely the topic. Similar aspects will be assessed but often this type of test offers little other than face validity.

Kleinmann (1993) conducted an unusual study of this type of exercise, providing candidates with information regarding what they were being measured on. He found that the quality of the assessors' rating improved as candidates sought to demonstrate the desired behaviours. Paradoxically, this assisted assessors, enabling them to provide more distinct ratings (within exercises) and consistent rating (between exercises). However, they resulted in lower criterion-related validity. In another study, Schneider and Schmidt (1992) manipulated the content and form of this type of task from an open group to more of a role play, and identified that the form of the task was the most important factor in changing the ratings that candidates received.

Studies examining the reliability of group exercises have indicated high inter-rater reliability of around 0.82 and test–re-test results of 0.72 (Bass, 1954). A key issue for these group exercises is termed the 'ipsativity factor', as each candidate's performance is dependent on the others. For example, research has found that a poor candidate in a poor group is rated more highly than a poor candidate in a good group (Gaugler and Rudolph, 1992). Limited research has been undertaken to assess how far applicants' behaviour is modified by their experience of these selection exercises. This is particularly important in the case of graduate applicants who may attend a series of these assessment centres as part of the main graduate selection period, termed 'the milk round'.

## 7.4  Self-assessment exercises

Although behavioural data are collected from each of the aforementioned exercises, another important source of data can be gathered from the candidates themselves. Self-assessment data can be collected in the form of a rating by the candidate of their performance following each exercise. These data sources have received limited attention from practitioners until now. Hunter and Schmidt (1998) argue that self-rating can make a valuable contribution to assessment centres. They claim that the limited research into this area tended to be marred by some additional problems, for example, the inclusion of self-assessment often replaced ineffective assessor training or was a substitute for poor exercise construction.

Recent studies indicate high correlations between participants' self-rating and those of their assessors, but not with overall job ratings (Nowack, 1997). Hogan (1991) disputes their value, arguing that external assessment is better than self-assessment. Blach (1992) argues that part of the problem is that those who tend to be less able also tend to over-estimate their ability, resulting in a skew between their self-ratings and those provided by the assessors. This overestimation is a consistent finding, especially in studies from a selection context (Anderson *et al.* 1984; Nilsen and Campbell, 1993; Saal *et al.* 1980). A recent study identified improvements that could be made to self-assessment to boost their value to selection (Jones and Fletcher, 2002). These changes included: increasing the length of the assessment form by including behavioural dimensions based on the selection competencies; changing the instructions to promote a more realistic appraisal by the applicant of their skills; and implying that the candidate would be held accountable where a discrepancy was found between their rating and that of the assessors.

By applying these self-insights in a development context, such as in a promotion-development centre, a valuable contribution can be made to individuals' learning and development process, encouraging candidates to reflect on their behaviour in the light of the behavioural competencies the organization is looking for at a senior level. Those with low self-assessment accuracy have been shown to find behavioural modification and adaptation difficult, suggesting a significant link between reflection and successful performance (Fletcher and Kerslake, 1992; Schmidt *et al.*, 1986). Studies have found that those with high self-insight are more likely to succeed in organizations, gaining greater levels of promotion (Fletcher and Kerslake, 1992; Thornton, 1980). In addition, self-insight appears to be linked to organizational fit. Russell (1985) found that successful candidates chose behaviour that demonstrated greater organizational congruence than their less successful counterparts. This was confirmed by later studies (Klimoski and Brickner, 1987; Lievens, 2001a). Snyder (1974) termed this skill 'self-management' and argued that successful candidates were able to use this ability to gain attention and make favourable impressions. Some might suggest that this is beneficial, as the candidate is selecting the most appropriate behaviour for that context and thus reflection is important. There is a paucity of research examining the sustainability of behaviour found within an assessment centre context in order to explore in more detail the possibility of faking.

## 7.5 Planning and administration

Planning and administering an assessment centre is complex. Each criterion identified by the job analysis must be measured a number of times through different exercises. It can be a difficult task to decide which is the most appropriate exercise for each criterion as some behaviours change based on the context. In order to ensure that each criterion is adequately assessed, a matrix is constructed (as we saw in Table 9.2).

In addition, each participant may be undertaking different exercises at different times (see aforementioned Table 9.1). Frequently, each exercise has different assessors. Assessors consider the samples of behaviour before them and rate the candidates on the given criteria. Training therefore is a critical issue to ensure standardization, both in terms of the ratings between assessors and also *across* exercises, and to guarantee that evidence is treated in the same way regardless of exercise or assessor. I shall return to the topic of training in section 7.9.

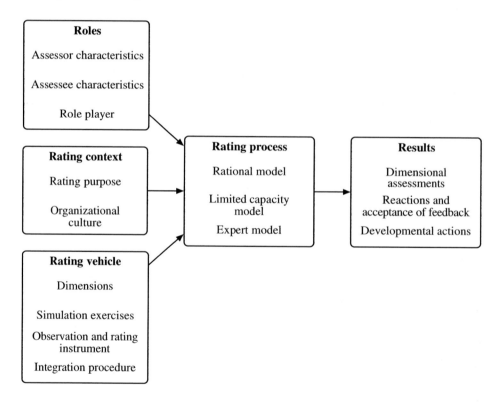

*Figure 9.2   Component model of assessment centres*

(Lievens and Klimoski, 2001, p.247)

## Dilemma box 9.1   Cost versus the benefits of an assessment centre

You are HR director, and the chief executive asks to see you. She is concerned at the amount of money your department spends on selections. The file that the Accounts Department has produced shows that the two-day assessment centre you organize for graduates and the three-day management development and promotion programmes costs the firm £7,500 and £10,000, respectively, per appointment. There were 70 graduates and 50 managers selected using these methods last year. She points out that these costs could be reduced to under £1,000 by only using psychometric tests. Why do you use assessment centres?

Note to help you: Benefit = (quality*quantity) – cost

Your evidence indicates that the quality of the process can be measured by multiplying together three figures: the predictive validity coefficient for these two different processes, 0.5 for the assessment centres and 0.25 for the paper-and-pencil version respectively; the selection ratio, or the mean Z score, for those candidates selected which is 2.1; and the standard deviation of the applicant pool, which is the amount of variation in the value of the work performed by those who are successful compared to those who fail. This is £3,316 for the graduates and £9,756 for the managers.

Quantity involves the number selected multiplied by their tenure with the firm, which has been 20 years.

Cost is the number selected multiplied by the cost of a successful candidate.

## 7.6 Reliability and validity

The reliability and validity of assessment centres are complex issues. Since the process comprises many different and distinct parts, it is necessary to ask whether reliability or validity is an effect of the whole or the composite parts. Lievens and Klimoski (2001) lament the paucity of attention given to examining the construct validation of assessment centres. Insufficient studies have been undertaken to look at the separate exercises that comprise assessment centres, with the result that it still remains unclear precisely what assessment centres are measuring (Klimoski and Brickner, 1987; Lievens and Klimoski, 2001).

Bray and Grant (1966) conducted the first evaluation into an assessment centre by following up on 400 AT&T candidates after between five and seven years. They reported high predictive validity for the method in identifying middle managers, with 0.44 for college graduates and 0.71 for those who had not attended tertiary education. The process was also successful in identifying the 88 per cent of college applicants and 95 per cent of non-college applicants who did not reach middle management. However, there are some problems with this study. Promotions to management were always done with knowledge of the assessment centre results and this brings a criterion contamination issue into play (Klimoske and Brickner, 1987). Second are concerns about false-negative results. Campbell and Bray (1967) argued that 46 per cent of those who were not accepted could have succeeded in the first tier of management. They argue that assessment forums are more important as a promotion tool than as a selection one, as those who did not succeed often chose to leave the company, increasing the sample's restriction of range for later validity studies.

Part of the rise in the popularity of assessment centres is due to their lower adverse impact than other assessment tools, such as cognitive ability tests. Evidence suggests they have lower adverse impact on candidates from minority ethnic groups (Hoffman and Thornton, 1997), although this does vary somewhat and is not found in exercises, such as in-trays, which have a high cognitive component. There are also good results in terms of gender fairness (Weijerman and Born, 1995). It has been suggested, however, that assessment centres do not completely eliminate all unfair discrimination. Interestingly, male candidates have received lower evaluations than female candidates, suggesting a reversal in the potential impact of these processes (Schmidt, 1993; Shore, 1992). No evidence has been found of age discrimination.

Meta-analytic research and individual validation studies do give cause for concern as they reveal disappointingly low predictive validity. The average cost of an assessment centre for the UK civil service was recently put at around £10,000 per appointment (Feltham, 1988). Scholz and Schuler (1993), in their meta-analysis of assessment centres, found high concurrent validities between rating and cognitive and personality aspects. They revealed corrected correlations between assessment centre rating and general intelligence (0.43), dominance (0.23), achievement motivation (0.30), social competence (0.31) and self-confidence (0.26). This research suggests that cheaper more valid tools are available.

Part of the difficulty for those evaluating assessment centres concerns the dynamics of the criteria being assessed. Although the individuals are being measured at one point in time, some of their behavioural skills are important for current progression, whilst the importance of others does not emerge until much later in their careers. In this way, the predictive power of certain behavioural criteria has different gestation periods. For example, Jansen and Stoop (2001) found that academic ability and written communication predicted early career success, whereas self-confidence and oral communication were more indicative of long-range success. As a result, the predictive validity of criteria changed. They found that the most predictive criterion for success (measured using salary growth over a seven-year period) was 'interpersonal effectiveness', but this only emerged after a number of years. This suggests that it is through appropriate networking and communication that an individual is first noticed, and then admitted into the possibility of being considered for a senior role.

Validity studies of assessment centres have been plagued with two additional changes at work that have significantly affected their measurement. First, the manager's role has changed to reflect wider organizational structural issues, such as down-sizing or de-layering, and wider societal changes, such as demographic and technology-based change.

Second, the way in which most jobs are performed today has changed dramatically with the advent of new information and technology systems. Therefore, those selected then as suitable in a senior post may not be suitable now if chosen on the basis of work-sampling exercises.

There are five keys issues which in different ways potentially contaminate the reliability and validity of the assessment centre process. These include: (1) the choice of assessor, (2) rating behaviour, (3) processual aspects such as administrative issues, (4) problems of incremental validity and (5) criterion contamination.

## 7.7 Contamination of the assessment centre process

### 7.7.1 Assessors

The choice of assessor is a critical factor in ensuring the value of an assessment centre. Research examining which factors affected the assessor-rating process identified that gender was not important but that age and rank significantly affected ratings. These, however, accounted for only 2 per cent of the variance in ratings (Lowry, 1993).

There have been attempts to identify the qualities assessors should possess. In a study using the 16PF® instrument, those scoring high on intelligence, sensitivity and poise were found to be the best candidates (Bartels and Doverspike, 1997). Other studies have underlined the pivotal role that motivation plays not only for a candidate's performance, but also for assessors (Frink and Klimoski, 1998; Lerner and Tetlick, 1998). These studies indicate that accountability is an important motivator for assessors. This can be achieved in two ways: first, by making assessors responsible for providing feedback to candidates regarding their performance. This ensures that they keep details and relevant notes. Second, the accountability of assessors to the wider organization for their selection decisions needs to be increased. Assessment centres are highly visible organizational processes that can enhance the motivation and the status of those picked to assist in selecting future leaders.

### 7.7.2 Rating behaviour and criteria difficulties

Early research identified problems arising in the way that assessors make their ratings, and deviate from the given predictive criteria. Byman (cited in Mayes *et al.*, 1997) argued that assessors become distracted by exercises which are too realistic: the assessors appear to be trying to reach their own conclusions rather than observing the candidates. A view which has gained more support suggests that instead of rating each of the given criteria in an exercise, assessors should focus on candidates' overall performance level and not separate their assessment into the different criteria (Sackett and Dreher, 1982; Jones, 1992). Looking in more detail at their rating behaviour reveals worrying trends. A study of four assessment centres with 222 participants found no significant correlations of the same criteria across different exercises, but large positive correlations of different criteria on the same exercise (Robertson *et al.*, 1987). This supports the view of criteria reduction, with assessors collapsing the criteria into one generic performance measure. Studies have emulated these findings across different countries for selection assessment centres, including the UK, Australia, the Netherlands, Belgium, Germany, France and Singapore (see Lievens and Klimoski, 2001). Development centres, it was assumed, could offer better discriminant validity because the detailed feedback required for candidates based on each criterion would motivate assessors to perform differently. Research did not corroborate this view and found them just as poor in this respect (Joyce et al., 1994).

Part of the reason for this problem lies in the cognitive processing of these behavioural data. Evidence suggests that assessors become overburdened by the task of having to keep in mind more than four or five predictive criteria per exercise (Maher, 1990). As a result, the distinctions between each criterion become blurred due to the decision heuristics employed by assessors. Howard (1997, p.22) found that ratings were frequently a muddled collection of 'traits (e.g. energy), learned skills (e.g. planning), readily demonstrable behaviours (e.g. oral communication), basic abilities (e.g. mental ability), attitudes (e.g. social objectivity), motives (e.g. need for achievement) or knowledge (e.g. industry knowledge)'. A solution to this is to simplify the criteria, thereby creating an unintended set of super-ordinate criteria by which to measure the candidates' performance. Some studies indicate that two underlying criteria are used (Sackett and Hakel, 1979), whilst others suggest three factors dominate, including interpersonal factors and problem-solving elements (Russell, 1985). No gains have been found through introducing criteria that are easier to observe than others (Kleinmann et al., 1995).

At a simple level, the cognitive complexity of an assessor's task is increased if they are required to *record* the evidence. The traditional method of assessment developed by Bray and Grant (1966) involves assessors following four distinct stages: observation, long-hand recording of data, classifying behaviour in terms of it providing evidence of a particular criterion, and rating each criterion. Studies indicate that 80 per cent of assessors record their observations using long hand, in line with traditional methods (Boyle et al., 1995; Spychalski et al., 1997).

In order to prevent the blurring of criteria and reduce the burden on assessors, different means of recording observational data have been suggested. These include behavioural checklists to provide an additional structure to the assessors' task by giving them lists of behaviours to guide their post-observation evaluations (see Table 9.3). These lists are designed to help assessors in three ways: by providing operational definitions of the rating criteria; by standardizing the types of behaviours they are paying particular attention to and assisting retrieval by providing cues.

Reilly et al. (1990) compared the convergence of ratings across exercises for assessors who were provided with behavioural checklists versus those who used the traditional method. They found increased convergence of criteria across the exercises, but not within exercises. This finding indicates lower discrimination between the separate criteria. A third device, based on Bales' (1970) group observation studies, is a 'behavioural coding' system. This differs from the others as it can be used directly during the observation of an exercise, speeding up one-stage recording and classification by the use of simple frequency counts. The assessors work from pre-prepared data-gathering sheets that standardize the behaviour being recorded between assessors and reduces their cognitive load. Hennessy *et al.* (1998) compared all three methods, traditional observation, behavioural coding and behavioural checklists, and found little difference in terms of the accuracy of judgement, accuracy of written information and correlation between ratings and assessors' attitudes toward the process. Assessors favoured the behavioural coding as it provided an additional structure to the process and reduced the cognitive demands made on them.

**Table 9.3 Example of a behavioural checklist for the criterion 'innovation'**

| Positive indicators | Negative indicators |
| --- | --- |
| Generates original solutions to problems | Prefers to use well-tried out solutions to problems |
| Suggests ideas of his/her own | Rarely puts forward own ideas |
| Is willing to consider others' views | Not willing to listen to others' input |
| Encourages challenges from others | Avoids asking for others' feedback |
| Challenges own thinking and perspectives | Raises faults and objections to others' ideas, but does not do same to own |
| Has a positive view of change | Prefers the status quo. Sees change as destabilizing and to be avoided |

In addition to concerns about rating behaviour, studies have revealed that assessors treat information in different ways. Lichtenstein and Srull (1987) found that assessors process information differently depending on the purpose it is to be used for. They found differences between data depending on whether it was for selection or development purposes. There has been limited work undertaken to explore this behaviour in more detail. In addition, Anderson *et al.* (1994) found that assessors treat data from different sources in different ways. They found more attention was given to direct observations of candidates, such as those found in group exercises, than written evidence provided from in-trays, or biographical data. This maybe a by-product of ill- or undefined assessment criteria (Kaufmann *et al.*, 1993), but more commonly relates to inadequate levels of assessor training, which should include attention to the consistency of interpretation from the same criteria over each exercise.

Research has revealed that discrimination between criteria and criteria convergence can be reduced by changing the assessment process. Sackett and Dreher (1982) found higher correlations between different criteria on the same exercise than on the same criteria across different exercises. Therefore, assessors were measuring candidates' general performance as a whole and not a specific criterion. In order to control this behaviour, researchers have suggested that assessors measure all the candidates across one or two criteria instead of assessing a candidate across them all. This has been found to improve ratings (Lievens and Klimoski, 2001).

A more subtle form of criteria contamination is also evident. Klimoski and Brickner (1987) suggest that assessors include wider criteria than those provided in their observation processes. Evidence suggests that they are looking not just at performance, but also at organizational fit (Staufenbiel and Kleinmann, 1999). This has a subtle but significant effect on results. Paradoxically, Lievens and Klimoski (2001) suggest that such additional criteria may enhance the predictive validity of the assessment centre process.

In addition, assessors are prone to the same forms of errors as those found in the interview process, such as halo and horns (which we discussed in Chapter 5). These can be important contaminants to the final rating given to candidates.

### 7.7.3   Processes of assessment centres

There is no 'one' process for assessment centres: they vary widely in terms of their length and complexity. In reviewing the literature, three processual aspects emerge which can have an important impact on the final decision. These relate to the exercises, the other participants and the final decision-making process.

The assessment centre consists of a number of different exercises, and choice of exercises is critical in ensuring adequate depth and range of criteria assessment. There is frequently confusion between face and content validity in assessment centre exercises (Craik et al., 2002). Limited attention has been paid to the effect of exercise order on candidates' performance, although Bycio and Zoogah (2002) indicated a very small impact, accounting for only one per cent of the variation.

Limited attention has been paid to the impact of other participants' behaviour on the final outcome. Many of the exercises are designed to simulate group activity. The behaviour of each candidate in these exercises is contingent on the behaviour of others. Gaugler and Randolph (1992) noted that in group exercises domination by one person significantly affects the performance of all.

A further change in candidates' performance results from previous experience, favourably affecting their performance across a range of exercises. Nothing is really known about how candidates' strategies and approaches to the assessment process change as a result of exposure to the assessment process. There is a paucity of research regarding which factors are at work. Possible tactics include tips, use of the grapevine, feedback or use of behavioural modelling techniques (see Lievens and Klimoski, 2001, p.252).

The final 'wash-up' decision-making process gathers together all the assessors to review the data they have gathered. Limited research has considered the influence of this final process on the quality of decisions made. Evidence from the UK and the USA suggests that organizations commonly use a consensual system (Spychalski et al., 1997; Boyle et al., 1995). This approach has the advantage of ensuring that all the assessors contribute to the process. However, evidence suggests that a mechanical process of adding the ratings actually produces better results (Lievens and Klimoski, 2001). A key role is therefore played by HR professionals who are involved in collating ratings data and focusing the discussion. It would be naïve to ignore that assessment centres are a political process. It is therefore desirable that all assessors support the final decision and that evidence of behaviours which are of concern is adequately aired. Group influences can affect the decision-making and either enhance or contaminate the quality of the final decision. Limited attention has been paid to how group dynamics or organizational culture influence the discussion.

### 7.7.4 Incremental validity

The assessment centre produces a cumulative measurement that is useful in situations where a decision is high risk, such as in the leadership of organizations, or where performance involves complexity, such as in managerial roles. Some researchers have sought to assess the incremental value of these combined processes over and above that of a single assessment tool. This is an important question given the high costs incurred in developing and running these multiple exercises, multiple criteria and multiple assessor processes. Klimoski and Strickland (1977) argue that assessment centres outperform any other selection tool and that their value lies in breadth of tools used, so that each exercise contributes independently to prediction (Goffin *et al.* 1996). However, Scholz and Schuler (1993) found disappointing results, identifying their high correlation with standard measures of $g$ of 0.43. This was later corroborated by Ree *et al.* (1994). Schmidt and Hunter (1998) argue that the incremental validity of these complex processes over and above cognitive ability tests is as low as 0.02. Therefore they suggested that there are far cheaper tools available that achieve the same outcome (Klimoski and Brickner, 1987).

This view is perhaps a little simplistic and negates the broader role of assessment centres, in serving many functions for different stakeholders. For candidates, if well developed, they provide a unique job preview, which can assist them in confirming or changing career decisions. For organizations, they are a marketing tool, particularly those that have to compete for the best candidates. Second, assessment is a political process within organizations, especially for those experiencing large changes. The process can create support for non-traditional appointments and promotion decisions, giving successful candidates added legitimacy from those respected in the organization. In addition, the process can reinforce new behavioural values that have been identified as important by the organization. These effects, however, can be diminished if the process is perceived to favour particular applicants. Indeed, evidence suggests that internal development centres used for promotion are often deliberately tested by managers, who knowingly put forward poor applicants to test the system. Clearly, assessment centres operate at a complex political and social level as well as at an individual assessment level.

### 7.7.5 Criterion contamination

The outcome of assessment centres involves a decision regarding someone's future in the organization. Researchers argue that the problem with many of the predictive validity studies is that there are significant contamination problems. The assessment decision creates a self-fulfilling prophesy, as candidates who are rejected by promotion-focused development centres find it difficult to progress in the organization and perhaps leave, restricting the sample range. Early work has indicated that this problem becomes further exacerbated when the rejected applicant's face is perceived as no longer fitting so they are almost forced out, regardless of whether in fact they do have the necessary skills (Klimoski and Strickland, 1977). Measurement contamination has also been found to be a more subtle problem where global or summary ratings of later performance effectiveness are used, so inflating ratings (*ibid.*). These are inherent weaknesses of many of the predictive validity studies for assessment tools. In addition, much of the evidence supporting assessment centres is based on a narrow database derived from a few large organizations. The range of organizations using these complex assessment practices is growing, but without further validation studies of these new ones we must question their value in assessing candidates and in giving value for money to organizations. Several researchers have considered how assessment centres can be improved in order to retain their advantages in limiting unfair discrimination in comparison to other traditional forms of assessment.

## 7.8 Improvements to the process

Wernimont and Campbell (1968) provide the grounding for several recommendations about improving assessment centres. There is no one overarching way to improve assessment centres as they vary depending on their function in terms of design, content, administrative complexity and cost. There are three distinct areas in which clear improvements can be made. However, for each improvement, additional concerns and issues arise. The three areas include: those focusing on the assessment criterion, those concerned with the exercises and those aimed at improving the assessment.

### 7.8.1 Assessment criterion

There are three changes that can be made to the measurement criteria for assessment centres in order to improve their construct validity. The evidence for these has already been aired in this chapter and they include: reducing the number of criteria being measured to a maximum of five; ensuring the identification of distinct, conceptually independent criteria in order to avoid confusion; and the provision of behavioural definitions for each criterion to aid their transparency for assessors.

The purpose of an assessment centre is, however, to enable conditions for a representative and comprehensive sample of behaviour to be provided by the candidate. Many of these suggestions could erode the bandwidth of the assessment centre, thus improving the construct validity at the expense of its predictive power.

### 7.8.2 Exercises

The second area concerns factors affecting exercises. Assessment centres are often a deluxe version of work samples. Exercises which are more realistic have been found to enhance criterion-related validity. Research indicates that different forms of exercise create subtle distinctions in the display of particular criteria, for example the demonstration of leadership in a written exercise versus a group discussion. Neidig and Neidig (1984) found that candidates do often perform differently on exercises, so that convergence around a particular criterion can neither be guaranteed, nor should be welcomed. Without understanding why such disparity emerges we cannot reliably state that performance differences are the product of inadequate exercise design rather than emanating from real individual variance. Well-constructed exercises are capable of measuring subtle differences (Lance *et al.*, 1995). Indeed, candidates who fluctuate in their performance across different criteria are easier for assessors to rate than those for whom no differences emerge, where ratings can become blurred (Lievens, 2001b).

In addition to the exercises themselves, two peripheral concerns can have an important impact. First, the content and use of instructions can significantly change a candidate's performance. As with ability and personality tests, clear guidelines are vital for candidates. Second, the addition of trained role players improves the construct validity of role play exercises (Lievens and Klimoski, 2001). As with the instructions, this reduces the variance in the exercises, limiting it to the candidates' behaviour.

In order to ensure that behaviours are comprehensively measured, behavioural data should be collected from across a variety of exercises. This enables the data to be triangulated, so that opportunities for both confirmatory and disconfirmatory evidence can be sought. Thus, the selection of exercises plays a crucial role in creating reliable and valid work samples for senior and complex positions. The pivotal role of exercises is neatly summarized by Lievens and Klimoski (2001, p.270), who stated that, 'unless the exercises provide an opportunity to observe enough behaviours and to do so under (assessor) favourable conditions, it is difficult to infer traits or dispositions'.

### 7.8.3 *Assessor rating processes*

The third area for improvement concerns the process whereby ratings are arrived at. Significant advances can be made to reduce the convergence of ratings by basing the assessment on the criteria, not on individual participants, so that the assessor observers a criterion, such as 'innovation' across all of the applicants. This simple change can reduce the cognitive overload of assessors and change the final review process to focus assessors on understanding the whole criteria picture rather than on merely championing those individuals they have observed. Thus, the process becomes more collective, with assessors becoming engaged in identifying differences in criteria across exercises, and internal rater reliabilities improve.

Much research has considered the assessors themselves, and focused on the key issues of assessor selection and training. Organizations vary as to whether they use a pool of assessors or use a small number of individuals constantly. There are advantages from both, depending on wider organizational concerns. Repeatedly using the same assessors increases internal consistency within and between assessors through their prolonged experience. On the other hand, having a pool diffuses decision-making throughout the organization and enables wider acceptance for those identified.

In terms of the selection of assessors, Klimoski and Brickner (1987) and Lievens (2001b) concur that there is a value in using management assessors who are aware of organizational norms and values, and can take these into account in their assessment. Lievens (2001b) found this created more accurate ratings, and ensured a greater degree of fit between the new appointee and the organization. The organizational level of such assessors is also important. In a development and promotion context, support has been found for assessors who are at least two job levels removed, who are therefore familiar enough with the job, and are less likely to know candidates (Cascio and Silbey, 1987). This may be a problem in organizations with flat hierarchies. In addition, good qualities for assessors include those who have high self-insight, who are sensitive, mature and interested in their perception of human behaviour.

It has been argued that it is better to have assessors chosen for their specific expertise, for example psychologists. This may be particularly important in the development setting where detailed feedback needs to be provided and an action plan developed. However, whilst this suggestion might provide an assessor with highly honed observation and assessment skills, it can undermine some of the aforementioned wider political aspects and create problems of ownership and responsibility for the results. As an alternative, a blend of those with specific organizational skills and assessment expertise will ensure both aspects are attended to.

## 7.9 Training

Training plays a key role in boosting assessor skills and in creating a consensus frame of reference for assessors. Lievens (2001b) compared different approaches to data-gathering and evaluation in order to assess different models of assessment. He compared traditional assessor practices (observe, record, classify and evaluate) with more schema-based approaches. The latter provides assessors with examples of poor, average and good performance on each criterion and encourages them to scan the exercises (*ibid.*, p.258). In this process, there was no separation between the evaluation and observation stages. The result indicated that both forms of assessor training provide improved rating skills, but that schema-driven techniques showed higher inter-rater reliability between assessors and more differentiation and accuracy in criteria assessment. The use of schema-based approaches makes it more difficult to check for manipulations as the ratings are based on written behavioural descriptions.

Other research has concentrated on the form of training provided, and revealed wide discrepancies in terms of the length and thoroughness of events ranging from one day to one week. Maher (1995) concluded that two days' training was better than one. Training should provide insights into the exercises and into the criteria, identifying how they should be used, and provide opportunities to ensure standardization between assessors. In addition, Lievens and Klimoski (2001) argue for the inclusion of theory about social information processing, interpersonal judgement, social cognition and decision-making theory in order to provide assessors with an insight into potential pitfalls in their individual and joint decision-making processes (see Figure 9.3).

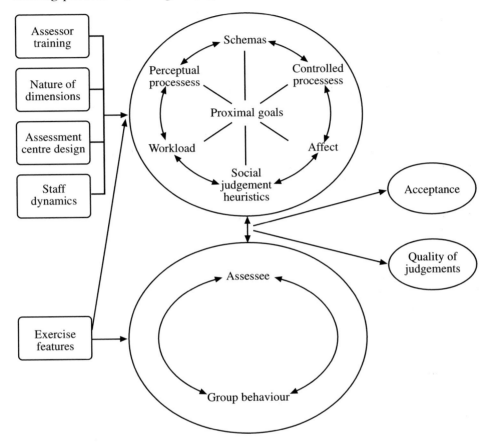

*Figure 9.3   Assessment centres and the social judgement process*

(Lievens and Klimoski, 2001, p.277)

Although limited research is available, it is clear that a candidate's performance can be enhanced by coaching across a range of exercises. Attention therefore needs to be paid, particularly in graduate assessment programmes, to gaining information about how much experience candidates have had.

## 8   Summary

This chapter has considered the evidence for five main varieties of work sample testing: job-knowledge testing, hands-on performance testing, situational tests, trainability tests and assessment centres. Each varies in its approach but all share, to a greater or lesser extent, an emphasis on equivalence between the criteria of assessment and those of job performance. Through this process, work sampling appears to enhance the performance of candidates from minority ethnic groups and female candidates. There are key questions as to how far the criteria being assessed are samples of current behaviour, or signs of potential. Evidence suggests that the more inferences assessors make regarding what they see, the lower their predictive power. However, it is clear that selection decisions based on work sample approaches are more affected by attenuation than other selection tools. Therefore. although high predictive validities are common, the long-term value of such results may be open to question. We need to ensure that these techniques are not just measuring surface level individual differences, which erode as organizations and roles change. Instead we need tests which offer the robust measurement of underlying criteria, and not tests that merely look as if they do so.

As with other assessment techniques, the assessors play a pivotal role in the value of these measures. As a result, care must be taken in selecting and training them adequately. Steps can be taken to assist their task through the use of pre-prepared coding sheets, and in ensuring distinct, relevant and focused assessment criteria. In addition to the given criteria, assessors may paradoxically introduce more context indicators that in the long run will boost the predictive power of these techniques. While researchers in the field do not understand how these tools work, it is clear they provide additional job-performance-related data.

The whole field of work sampling is undergoing major changes with the advent of new computer-mediated work sample tests. Our understanding is greatly improving as to how this medium can help reduce costs and raise the value, fairness, security and consistency of testing. Computer-based simulations will develop rapidly over the next few years and, provided work sample tests are based on reliable job analysis, evidence suggests that their use will further reduce the disparity found in the performance on other tests of female applicants and candidates from minority ethnic groups. This is important for organizations as they seek assessment tools that do not discriminate against any category of employee.

## *Exercise*

Construct an assessment centre for the job description given to you in Chapter 2. Identify the criteria and the types of method you will use. Outline their contribution to the process. Construct rating tools for each instrument and discuss with your tutor the problems you might face and how you would get round them.

# Critiques and future focus

## 1   Overview

While in the preceding chapters, recruitment and selection practices have been placed in their current and historical context, in Chapter 10 we move on to examine two competing perspectives: the psychometric view and the critical view. The psychometric view has dominated research and therefore warranted most of our attention so far. This takes a rationalistic, positive, scientific, increasingly questionnaire-based approach to recruitment and selection and its proponents argue that organizations can benefit considerably by using these more structured methods. Through focusing on the results of incremental validity studies, they suggest that different tools can be combined to optimize the effectiveness of recruitment and selection.

The second is a more critical view and includes the social-interactionist perspective, which disputes the whole premise of measurement that underlies the psychometric view. Critical approaches, which have gained limited attention from researchers and organizations, regard current methods as flawed and limited. They expand the number of factors that can be involved in recruitment and selection, and point to the difficulties with the assumptions (particularly regarding criteria development) that can underlie data-gathering and decision-making. For example, the role of meta-analysis is analysed: while it might appear to have boosted confidence in the value of recruitment and selection techniques, on closer examination significant inconsistencies are revealed. I discuss the problems of this technique and then go on to examine more fundamental challenges to the psychometric view. Three distinct criticisms emerge. First, I look at the notion that it is a simplistic, partial and biased view of individual differences which does not in fact measure mental processes, but mental productivity. Second, and related to this, is that the temporal and cultural context of the techniques limit their wider and future application in dynamic situations. Third, I argue that recruitment and selection processes are contaminated and flawed by a lack of rationality, and as a result fail to reflect on the impact of power and self-reflection in data-gathering and decision-making.

I outline these concerns to reveal the variation in their severity and complexity because I believe that they pose major challenges to the plausibility of many current recruitment and selection practices. They are currently marginalized, but without attending to some of these concerns, we may never fully understand and appreciate the failure of recruitment and selection processes to achieve their initial promise.

## 2   Introduction

The historical perspective outlined in each chapter has given an insight into how the dominant positive scientific, psychometric perspective emerged in today's selection and recruitment practices. Two main approaches are used within the psychometric view. The first relies on a notion of the applicant's capacity for self-reflection and ability to accurately self-report on characteristics identified as relevant to the job role. This is usually done either by an easily administered self-completion questionnaire (such as biodata, personality, ability or work sample instruments) or through a structured interview. The second approach relies on an external expert to observe the applicant, gathering and analysing the applicant's behaviour by means of scenarios aligned to the job. Both of these approaches are psychometric and data are often regarded as facts, implying that they provide objective answers. In practice, psychometric tools require inferences to be made and significantly distorted by faking and other less obvious processes.

A more critical perspective has only been integrated to any degree in research on interviews, where a social interactionist perspective has emerged. It questions whether the positivist scientific model can ever be appropriately applied to the power-saturated world of selection interviewing. Further, it challenges the usefulness of breaking down and qualifying social exchange and the claim by assessors that they are able to make objective decisions. Other critical concerns regarding individual difference measurement can be found in Chapters 6 and 7 on cognitive testing. Although these critiques were present at the outset in 1911 and again in the 1950s, they have received limited attention from academic researchers. Transition in workforces – through the expansion of the numbers of women, minority ethnic groups and the pressure to select applicants on a global basis – have all created a fresh impetus for this critique to be re-visited. This critical voice has been important within organizational sociology (for example Callaghan and Thompson, 2002) and is finding increasing resonance within occupational psychology.

This chapter begins by examining the psychometric approach and from that paradigm offers some best-practice guidelines in order to improve the various techniques. I then examine meta-analysis, which has underpinned the resurgence in confidence in many of these tools, by exploring critically how meta-analysis works and by identifying key problems. Attention then turns towards more fundamental challenges to this dominant psychometric perspective.

## 3   Improving the psychometric approach?

### 3.1 Best-practice guidelines

A review of evidence related to the prevailing psychometric approach to recruitment and selection suggests that a number of improvements can be made to current techniques. Each of the previous chapters has been dominated by this psychometric view and so the following suggestions emerge from within this perspective rather than from its critique. The best practices outlined below represent a summary of the evidence from each of the preceding chapters; they would of course vary depending on the specific job role and context.

- Application of job analysis to identify the knowledge, skills and abilities required for successful job performance within a given context and culture. (This would include attention to minority ethnic groups and gender aspects as appropriate.) (Chapter 2)

- Ongoing criterion-related validation of the process to monitor and ensure fairness and suitability. (This would include the identification of relevant performance data.) (Chapter 3)

- Standardization of the process to ensure that candidates can be compared. This process should comply with local legal and other regulatory practices. It should also be sensitive to candidate's expectations of the process. (Chapters 3 and 9)

- Job previews to enable candidates to make an informed choice and provide information on the recruitment and selection process itself. (Chapter 4)

- Focused application form to gather data on the identified criteria. (Chapter 4)

- Previously piloted biodata form that is specific to the job and context. (Chapter 4)

- Structured references that help referees focus on providing information on job-specific criteria. (Chapter 4)

- Structured interviews to enhance reliability. (Chapter 5)

- Appropriate choice of psychometrics, including provision of relevant psychometric norms which reflect the sample population. (Chapters 6, 7, 8)

- Training for assessors to provide familiarity with the process and consistency to their evaluations. (Chapters 2, 5, 6 and 9)

- Triangulation of data to provide confirmatory and disconfirmatory evidence for each criterion, with opportunity to clarify where questions arise. (Chapter 9)

- Feedback provided to all candidates on the process that, if unsuccessful, includes mention of their strengths that might be relevant in applying for other jobs by noting the context specificity of the process they have been through. (Chapter 1, 5, 6, 8 and 9)

- Focused criteria to reduce the burden on assessors typically between five and eight criteria. (Chapter 9)

- Examination of the genralizability of results by exploring how far they are an occupation-, organization- or country- specific outcome.

In the above guidelines, it is important to consider how far specific organizational practices might generalize across different continents. Attention should be paid to local candidates' expectations in order to ensure that their anxiety levels about the process do not increase. Regardless of the location they are operating in, it is appropriate to ensure that organizations apply good and fair practice. Reflecting on the evidence supporting each of the different techniques, it has been clear that trade-offs emerge between the reliability of each technique and its fairness. The type of recruitment and selection process chosen should be appropriate to the job and context and therefore it is questionable whether a generic system can be both fair and valid.

I now want to highlight critiques of meta-analysis, a technique that has been important in raising supporting evidence for many of these tools. I will then turn attention towards drawing together more fundamental criticisms of the dominant psychometric approach.

## 3.2 Problems of meta-analysis

Since the 1980s, the popularity and technical sophistication of recruitment and selection methods have undergone a renaissance. This has been led in part by the support offered by meta-analytic studies which have enhanced the credibility of tools (such as personality tests) for use in recruitment and selection. Nonetheless, meta-analysis, which involves the aggregation of data derived from many similar studies, cannot compensate for the weaknesses of the original studies. Looking back at Figure 1.4, you can see that the predictive validity of the different techniques for overall job performance or training outcomes do not rise above 0.65. Thus, a considerable amount of variance in job and training performance remains unaccounted for. Despite the sophistication of these techniques, they still only offer partial information regarding the criteria for successful job performance.

The dominance of meta-analysis in providing the justification for recruitment and selection processes can mask a series of problems. The over-emphasis on the meta-analytical method is coming under increasing attack from some quarters (Bobko et al., 1999). A key concern is the weakness of the outcome measures that are used in validity studies. As I indicated earlier, outcome measures used in many studies are often inadequate, and so the meta-analysis simply compounds and disguises poor studies.

Second, these studies may have gathered subtly different data. For example, in Chapter 8, the problem of aggregating personality factors with the same label but distinctly different sub-factors was highlighted. In order to improve this situation, Bobko et al. (1999) advocated that where a composite variable – such as aggregating biodata items – is involved a composite outcome measure must also be used.

A third problem with meta-analytic research arises where inconsistent correction procedures are used by the initial researchers. There needs to be an improvement in the reporting of meta-analytic studies to ensure that reports include details such as type and size of sample, which values have been removed from each primary study and whether any of these values have been corrected.

Meta-analysis has enhanced the argument for the inclusion of various recruitment and selection techniques by enabling smaller studies to be aggregated. However, the aggregation of weak initial studies, which are limited, for example, in terms of the sample populations, or in the type of assessment measures used, or the sophistication of their outcome measures, does not make the findings more robust. These problems can be compounded through the removal of significant details and in the aggregation decisions that later researchers make.

# 4   Critiques of the psychometric perspectives

More fundamental challenges can be levied at the psychometric perspective. It could be argued that the psychometric approach reflects a Western context, which is based on a capitalistic premise of the dominance of profit and the market-place as a regulator. Recruitment and selection processes are only useful where the organization has more applicants than vacancies. In this context, discrimination concerns the identification of the best applicant for the job through fair, and therefore valid, methods. Even when it is critical to choose a suitable person, this is only possible when there are sufficient applicants. Where there is not a surfeit of applicants, training becomes more significant to organizations. Western countries and many of their organizations have long had the luxury of being able to choose their workers, for their own countries, or elsewhere. Full employment has not been the goal of these societies, and, as I discussed in Chapter 6, for some countries these systems have provided the tools to legitimize the exclusion of particular groups of emigrants.

Three critiques emerge that will now be discussed: first is a challenge to individual differences (a concept that lies at the heart of psychometrics). The second issue is the relevance of these systems in predicting future job success in a complex and rapidly changing world of work. Finally, I explore more fundamental concern that calls into question one of the central assumptions underpinning the psychometric view – namely, rationality. Inherent to the idea of rationality is the omission of an adequate discussion of power and self-reflection. These issues are addressed in turn and opportunities for alternative perspectives highlighted.

## 4.1  Individual differences?

One of the most fundamental critiques to be levied at the psychometric approach to recruitment and selection is its misconception of individual differences. Selection practices emerged to provide organizations with administrative simplicity (Rose, 1985). They are based on a conception of discernible and stable differences between individuals. Statistical models, such as the normal distribution model, provide assumptions of regularity amongst populations that enable the formulation of laws, or norms. Psychometrics is the method underpinning the theory of individual difference. However, what must be noted is that the theory emerged *after* the method (Hollway, 1991).

Four issues emerge from under the banner of individual difference that starts with an examination of what these processes are actually measuring. These include: (1) the problems of measurement in psychometrics (2) the domination and irrelevance of a quest for the best measure, which results in the reduction of assessment to a simplistic view of maximal cognitive capacity and fails to capture candidate's typical behaviour; (3) the inherent bias in the field which has been driven by pragmatic considerations rather than theoretical rigour; and (4) the inadequacy of the other measures used to validate different recruitment and selection practices. I now turn to each of these concerns individually.

### 4.1.1  *What is being measured?*

For many of the pioneers of this field, such as Binet (1904) and Burt (1925), psychometrics was the measurement of mental capacities that enabled differences between individuals to be identified. As many early psychometricians were eugenicists, the models of fit they created reinforced the prevailing notion of the fixed place of a given individual with society and thus the central role of heredity in determining levels of intelligence. To this end, psychometrics was heralded as the means of measuring the 'skeleton of the mind' (Burt, 1925, p.74).

The problem with this view lay in the opportunistic operationalization of the psychometric method, which resulted in the exultation of a few measures 'chosen almost by accident from the tester's stock as the ruling forces of the mental universe' (Cronbach, 1957, p.675). These mental tests, and the claims which were being made for them, were treated with caution by some who argued that 'they give us only a very blurred and often inaccurate picture of the factors which really underlie the problem under investigation' (Myers, 1911, p.196). Critics argue that these were not measures of mental process, but assessments of a subtly different factor – mental efficiency. This distinction and the critical debate it leads to has lost much of its voice in psychology today.

Psychometricians appear to regard every aspect of human behaviour as open to measurement. Many researchers have questioned the viability of such a view (Michell, 1997; Stevens, 1951). In many of the preceding chapters I have highlighted the expansion of atheoretical tools by the arbitrary assignment of a numerical value to any event or object, regardless of its scientific rationale. The inference these approaches make regarding internal attributes and concepts, such as personality, are often based on questionable and tautologous grounds, stemming from the items themselves rather than a discernible psychological phenomena (Kline, 1998). Moreover, the façade of objectivity that psychometrics creates can deceive test-users and test-takers into failing to question or challenge the results produced by psychometric assessment.

As a result of the notion that all aspects of human behaviour can be measured, many organizations have expanded the breadth of criteria and attributes they use in recruitment and selection. For example, a new direction in testing that has moved away from measuring the actual or potential skills required to do the job towards selecting on the basis of other criteria, such as 'inner commitment', or 'organizational fit', has emerged. On the one hand, the assessment of these attributes can be seen as offering organizations the means to identify staff with similar values and goals, and thereby increase their productivity, performance, job satisfaction, and reduce stress levels and turnover (Kristof, 1996; Schneider, 1987). On the other hand, the efficacy of such an approach is questionable: first, can these elements actually be measured? Second, how desirable is it to select on the basis of such factors? Through the recruitment of like-minded individuals, it is likely that the diversity and adaptability of a firm will be reduced. In addition, it is unclear what organizations give their staff in return for their 'enhanced commitment' – some would argue that commitment to an organization has to be earned through compliance with the psychological contract, meeting or exceeding employee's expectations (Rousseau, 2001). A further concern is that this new focus on the development of psychological measures could result in the potential exploitation of an individual's predispositions, such as their 'loyalty', 'compliance to authority' or 'quality of work ethic', to  maximize the organization's advantage for minimum effort. It is interesting to speculate what type of organization would see these qualities as a prerequisite.

### 4.1.2   *The one best measure?*

Researchers and organizations appear to be fixated on identifying the *single most important* selection tool. This myopic view of selection techniques frequently results in a simplistic reduction to the role of cognitive ability as the best predictor of job performance (see Figure 1.4). In contrast, some researchers argue that although offering the highest validity of all the recruitment and selection processes, the use of cognitive tools is still problematic as they focus on the measurement of maximal fluid intelligence ($g_f$) approaches, whereas job performance is based on a measure of typical and culturally related factors ($g_c$) (Ackermann, 1999).

Increasingly, there is a call for more sophisticated conceptions of mental process to be devised which include attention on both the cognitive processes involved in processing information and the precise content of a test. To date, the impact of test content on test performance has been largely ignored, but this issue is beginning to experience a resurgence of interest within occupational-attainment and work-sample testing where content knowledge is the prime focus of the assessment. However, attention towards test content still provides a partial view of individual capability as these tests implicitly involve culturally entwined abilities, such as reading.

Attempts to eliminate culturally specific knowledge from tests have focused on fluid intelligence ($g_f$), but it is entirely artificial to separate process from the content of knowledge. In using simple information-processing tasks, relatively low predictions of task performance are found, especially where the task requires knowledge, effort and persistence over time. Ackerman (1999, p.443) argues 'it is impossible to eliminate all content from ability tests'. For example, culturalization provides familiarity with a testing environment and practice taking tests results in changes between simple $g_f$ and general factors of intelligence. As a result of these concerns, cognitive measures may not in fact provide an actual measure of an individual's abilities.

One response to these difficulties has been to propose an assessment that includes a holistic picture of individual potential by including elements of intelligence, personality and motivation in the measure. Evidence suggests that there are clear correlations between personality and ability (Ackerman, 1997; Barrick *et al.*, 2002). For example, Ackerman and Heggestad (1997) studied Holland's Interest Typology, which identifies three distinct vocational choices, and found that those with realistic interests were likely to be good at jobs that included physical strength, aggressive action, and motor co-ordination and skill. People with an investigative or intellectual interest preferred tasks that involved thinking things through rather than action, preferring to organize and understand their world. Finally, those with an artistic interest preferred to interact indirectly with others, showing a lack of sociability and introspectiveness. Research in this area is important as it reveals the naïvety of trying to identify one simplistic measure (see Figure 10.1).

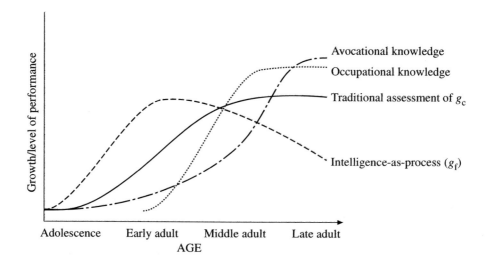

*Figure 10.1: Holland's Interest Typology*

(Ackermann, 1999, p.446)

Few researchers have adopted this more sophisticated view of cognitive measurement that attempts to link together ability, personality and motivation and focuses on typical, and not maximal performance. After all, people at work can rarely sustain their maximal level of performance for long. This work represents a new way of understanding and measuring individuals, which may also offer fresh insight into individual difference across different cultures.

### 4.1.3 Inherent bias

A central problem within psychometrics lies in the partial treatment of variance, which creates an inherent bias. Identifying and quantifying variance between individuals is at the heart of psychometrics, but the way variance has been viewed has confounded the possibility of gaining a more complete picture of individual differences. Part of the problem stems from the lack of representativeness of the populations which were used to establish the yardsticks for 'normal' and 'abnormal' that underlie individual difference measures. Instead of studying the whole population, psychometricians tend to use particular groups who are convenient for them and they therefore become over-represented. These groups include people who are mentally ill, students and military personnel. Measurers derived from the military, for example, were skewed towards younger, more physically fit, White males. Similarly, the study of the manager has dominated the occupational setting, but this group is also more likely to be White and male.

The identification of deviation from the norm is therefore inevitably compromised by the inadequacy of the sampling. However, a further concern lies in how such findings were treated. The most obvious problem of norms derived from over-represented groups (for example, White males) is the danger of rendering as 'abnormal' marginalized groups, such as women or black people. However, we can see a more subtle exclusion effect as well. The data that deviated from the established norms became 'cast into the outer darkness' to become known as 'error variance' (Cronbach, 1957, p.674). Continually in earlier chapters of this book we have seen examples of differences in performance across different ethnic groups or genders which have been treated as indicative of a defective item or instrument, rather than as offering more profound insight into human mental capacity and group or cultural differences.

As a result of this treatment of variation, many of the selection tools show an inequality of opportunity on gender, 'racial', economic or educational grounds. In part, the unfair discrimination of these groups stems from the failure to identify and understand '**consistent group difference effect**', which psychometricians use to discern test item performance differences (Baron *et al.*, 2003, p.6). **Differential item functioning (DTI) analysis**, which is used to examine aggregated group differences, rarely reveals any consistent patterns to these differences, but it does appear to increase the potential fairness of a test's items. This lack of appreciation of group differences has resulted in the ongoing use of selection tools that continue to de-select disproportionately high numbers of members of minority ethnic groups. However, there are other factors which appear to affect the performance of some individuals.

Evidence suggests that there are consistent relationships between 'race', socioeconomic status, educational attainment, motivation, anxiety, perceptions of tests and test performance (Baron *et al.*, 2003; Chan *et al.*, 1997; Mains-Smith and Abram, 2000). Those groups who perform worst on tests typically come from non-Western cultural traditions and these instruments disproportionately deselect those from minority ethnic groups. The aforementioned research indicates that White test-takers show more motivation to do well in these situations than Black test-takers. Helms (1992) reflected that despite some attempts to achieve culturally equivalent cognitive assessment, it remains elusive. This may be because, as I noted earlier, little attention has been paid to test content and to the influence of motivation on test outcome.

Similarly, research has revealed significant differences in test performance in the speed and accuracy levels amongst different ethnic groups. The critical question, however, of whether this reflects real differences in potential job performance or is an artefact of the psychometric tool has been largely ignored. This failure is another example of the pragmatism and lack of theoretical rigour that has driven the field of psychometric research. As a result, most intelligence tests adopt a White-centric approach in terms of their definition of intelligence, the cultural assumptions and the linguistic patterns that are used – all of which favour the majority White group. Although alternative assessment techniques have at times revealed promising initial findings, they have unfortunately been found to measure different constructs, and where care is taken to match the cognitive constructs being measured, the reduction in group differences typically disappears (Baron *et al.*, 2003). For example, differences between White, Black and Hispanic test-takers have been reduced where interactive, behavioural and aurally oriented tests were used, and standard deviations between the White and the minority ethnic groups have been reduced from 1.03 to 0.45 (Pulakos and Schmitt, 1996). However, despite its improved fairness, this type of assessment remains a less valid measure of performance than traditional verbal-ability testing. Problems with attenuation can also be found, so that the validity of the scores reduces with time in the job.

A second approach to improving the test results for minority ethnic groups has centred on the use of coaching. The research findings here are incomplete; in one case, they revealed that, despite the willingness of these groups to participate in the coaching, it had a limited impact on test results (Ryan *et al.*, 1998). In another study, although improvements were found, the sample size was too small and no adequate comparison group was used (Fletcher and Wood, 1993). The paucity of research concerning equity for minority ethnic groups mirrors the lack of interest in lower socio-economic groups and educational under-achievers within our society (Hunt, 1999).

### 4.1.4   *Inadequate predictive measures*

Another difficulty related to the approach taken to establishing individual differences stems from the type of predictive outcome data used in the development of selection tools. Assessment has frequently focused on US-based student samples in which simplistic outcomes have been used that show little differentiation between individuals. Indeed, as I noted in Chapter 1, the overall job performance measure frequently used by many organization-based validity studies is the performance-appraisal system, which can consist of a politically motivated measure used by management to provide evaluations of their own performance, rather than that of their subordinates. These performance assessments are often positively skewed, and fail to reflect adequately the real performance of the individual, their department or the organization. Indeed, frequently the appraiser has not actually seen the individual at their work and so is unable to meaningfully comment. In addition, few validity studies consider how far the individual has had any control over their performance. They do not take into account the context in which the individual is operating. For example, as noted in Chapter 8, those selecting staff for 'innovation' rarely consider how far the organization may actually stifle the desired criterion.

At the heart of the predictive measurement problem lies the frequently overlooked distinction between an individual's performance and the outcome. Performance is a behaviour: 'it is something that people do and is reflected in the actions that people take ... performance is *not* [my emphasis] the consequence or the result of action' (Campbell, 1990, p.704). As a result, in any job there will be a number of performance components. In contrast, an outcome is a context-based indication of effectiveness of that performance. It is naïve not to recognize the temporal and contextual parameters that underlie such outcomes. An outcome can be regarded as an evaluation of the results of performance, within a particular time-frame and context. A poor outcome could be achieved by doing the right thing in the wrong context, or in the wrong time-frame. For example, in product or service innovation it may take time for the success to be either realized or adequately measured by the organization. Thus, the final achievement of an outcome may lie outside the control of the individual.

In a work setting it is unlikely to be appropriate to posit a concept such as 'overall performance' and then reduce it to a simplistic assessment. Increasingly, researchers are arguing for a more complex approach to performance measurement akin to the **balanced score card**' that has been adopted by some organizations. Through this more sophisticated approach, differences within and between individuals' effectiveness can be more easily identified. For example, Bartram *et al.* (2002) advocate the classification of four effectiveness measures: (1) economic, (2) technological, (3) commercial and (4) social. This system would also increase measurement complexity by using particular groups of stakeholders to assess the breadth and level of impact for each effectiveness measure. Although an improvement on previous attempts, this system is still constrained by prevailing political, temporal and contextual elements which may render it of limited use.

Individual difference is at the heart of assessment and yet it is clear that problems arise in what is actually being measured by recruitment and selection tools. There have long been questions raised about the relationship between the label given to a test and what can actually be measured. At one level, those within the field are pragmatic, calling for more complexity in the measurement by arguing that performance in ability tests also comprises of personality and motivational factors. There is also attention being given to reviewing the type of measures used to validate these tools. However, for those outside the field the whole premise of occupational measurement can be seen as fatally flawed through its failure to provide theoretical rigour to assessment and by the inadequate exploration of differences. This results in a lack of real insight into individual differences and also perpetuates an inequality in the opportunities for those who were previously in a minority at work. The increasing numbers of women and minority ethnic groups within the work place could provide an impetus for change. However, how radical will this revisiting be? A concern is that existing models will be kept in place rather than creating an opportunity to start afresh in considering what can be meaningfully measured.

Let us now turn our attention towards two other critiques: the first looks at how these tools can be applied in a changing world; the second examines the notions of rationality, power and reflexivity.

## 4.2 Application of the tools in a dynamic world

A central premise underlying the processes of recruitment and selection is the fitting of the worker to the job. Job analysis rests on the view that there is only one way to do the job and that using these methods allows the characteristics required for successful job performance to be revealed. As noted in Chapter 2, it is debatable that there is only one, or one best, way of performing a job. Indeed, the transition of the working population to include more women, minority ethnic groups and part-time workers challenges many previous working practices. In many organizations, there is often no consideration, for instance, of how those who are not able-bodied might perform a job. The result is that a job analysis can reveal only a partial view of how the job can be performed that conforms with the prevailing context and dominant employee group.

The application of scientific management techniques has resulted in the standardization of many tasks for semi-skilled and unskilled workers. However, standardization is difficult to achieve in a truly team-based working environment. With the escalation of team-working in many organizations, job analysis becomes harder to undertake as the division of labour reflects the skills, talents and interests of individual team members, making simple standardization impossible, but also undesirable. There have been attempts to introduce standardized processes into previously skilled jobs, such as banking and insurance. Whilst these practices might have reduced the salary bill, they have also eroded workers' job satisfaction and increased staff turnover. This, in turn, can increase costs through the selection and training of new staff and may reduce the quality of service that existing staff provide (Collinson and Collinson, 1996).

In addition, as we have seen in Chapter 2, job analysis concerns successful performance within a particular time-frame and market-place. More and more, stability is eroded for organizations as they are expected to react with increased speed in order to maintain their position. Although attempts have been used to deploy job-analysis techniques to form the basis of future-orientated job profiles, as we have seen (Chapter 2) this is fundamentally at odds with the process.

## 4.3 Rationality? Power and reflexivity

A more profound criticism of the psychometric approach emerges from challenges to the ability of human beings to be 'rational', that is to make reliable and consistent decisions. This issue has received little attention. In the 1960s the inadequacies of humans' decision-making processes were revealed (Simon, 1960), and recent evidence has revealed similar issues in the paucity of applicants' decision-making processes when choosing jobs

(Highhouse and Hoffman, 2001). The problem is that there is little attention paid to the link between rationality and the validity of recruitment and selection systems. Researchers know little about the decision-making processes that are involved in crucial HR practices. For example, in her studies of interviews, Dose (2003) shows that assessors spend more time discussing information which is common knowledge to all of the assessors rather than that known to only a few, and Zedeck (1986) identified the significance of group dynamics in influencing assessors' decision-making in assessment centres. Similarly, Silvester *et al.* (2003) showed how researchers have tended to focus on the equity of ratings' applicants for interviews, than on considering assessor's decision-making processes.

These studies have revealed that while applicants might receive the same rating, by researching the attributions recruiters use it is clear that the basis of their decisions is entirely different. As a result, they suggest that the previous view of fairness is misleading and in fact results in the condoning of tools that mask discriminatory decision-making processes. Few researchers have considered the necessity of exploring and improving our understanding of the *processes* applicants and assessors use. For instance, attention towards processes would enable the identification of the cultural context for the speed/accuracy trade-off found in testing and a more detailed exploration of how assessors actually make their selection decisions.

At the centre of the psychometric view, the assessor – whether involved in identifying a new recruit or in appraisal systems used to validate the recruitment process – is seen as impartial and capable of making rational decisions. Increasingly, this view is challenged and re-visited.

A related issue is that of the role of *power*. This challenges the notion of objectivity in selection and recruitment decisions. Brooks-Gordon (2002), in her brief look at academic referees, identified the influence of gender on references. She found that male referees wrote in impersonal and absolute terms, and focused on technical and factual details. Their statements were confident, declamatory and wide-ranging about the applicant's abilities. In contrast, female referees tended to base their references on their personal interactions with the individual. As a result, though less formulaic and more creative, they offered less direct and more personal support for the applicant. She speculates how far, through their use of language, female referees were perpetuating the low numbers of senior female academics. This illustrates the subtle action of power in assessment processes, which has also emerged in the proceeding chapters.

Many of the recruitment and selection processes outlined in this book rely on candidates having sufficient self-reflectivity and self-insight to be able to discern and articulate accurately their skills and abilities. Yet there are many reasons why this should not be assumed. For example, someone may not see themselves as being particularly introverted in their social exchanges and yet others would regard them as being so. Research has shown that there is limited coherence in the personality attributes applicants identify and in the value data obtained from third parties. Frequently, interviews require the applicant to be able to identify their influence in changing a situation, and research has suggested that there are gender differences in the type of impact individuals regard themselves as having on their environment. For example, early studies indicated that women were much more likely to ascribe success to an *external* and *uncontrollable* factor (such as luck), whereas men attributed events to *internal* and *controllable* factors, such as their ability (Deaux and Emswiller, 1974). Although research based on UK students during interview-training found no difference in the attributes made by men and women (Silvester *et al.*, 2003), it is interesting to speculate how far gender and culture might affect candidates' views of themselves, so that they may regard it as immodest to take all the credit for something and therefore give only a partial view of their talents which in turn influences their success in job applications.

In contrast to the limited attention on different influences in how applicants identify and articulate their skills and effectiveness, faking is a topic that has received a lot of attention from researchers and organizations. Recent speculation has considered whether faking might actually be a desirable behavioural characteristic as it demonstrates contextual sensitivity. Miles *et al.* (2003) examined two forms of what might be considered deviant behaviour, including 'cheating', which involved performing better in an unsupervised test than a supervised one, and 'faking', which involved high self-reporting of numerical competence, but low numerical ability test results. The results in Figure 10.2 show the distinct personality profiles of each distinct type of behaviour, with fakers showing organizationally desirable attributes such as 'ambition', 'organizational ability' and 'emotional control'. In contrast, cheaters were shown to be less 'self-confident' and 'socially bold', with lower 'sense of duty'. Whilst these results are interesting, the lack of a control group mars their reliability.

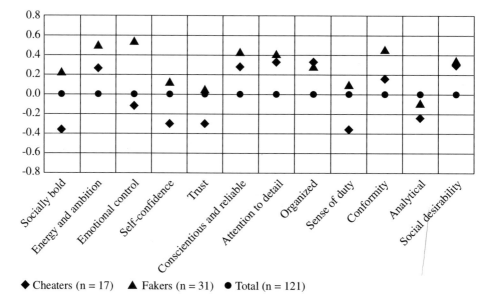

*Figure 10.2 Cheaters' and fakers' personality*

There is a growing use of candidates' self-assessment in selection and recruitment, either when first applying for the job through the use of job-fit questionnaires, or in assessment centres, where the individual is encouraged to consider how they performed in each exercise (Fletcher *et al.*, 2002). This process requires the individual to become actively involved in evaluating his or her competence for the job. Whilst the inclusion of such instruments might represent a welcome departure from the passive role of the applicant in the recruitment process, more cynically the role of these tools may be to ensure that applicants are more willing to accept their rejection from the organization. As with any self-completion instrument, an implicit assumption underpinning such assessment tools is that the individual has sufficient self-insight and a desire to answer honestly. Limited attention has been given to examining how far this is the case.

Research in this area is important as it shows differences in terms of gender, culture and status that affect the reliability of the information on which many recruitment and selection decisions are made. It challenges the claims of rationality and objectivity which are key assumptions underpinning the psychometric perspective. Studies in this area reveal the importance of looking in more detail not at the outcome *per se*, but the processes involved in the use of these tools. Through such work, fundamental problems with the psychometric view begin to be revealed and the importance of looking more closely at social exchanges between assessors and applicants.

## 5   Contrasting perspectives

In reflecting on the two competing perspectives on selection and recruitment (between the dominant psychometric approach and its critics), fundamental differences emerge. It is difficult to see how they might be reconciled. The concerns raised by those adopting a more critical stance have largely been unheeded by the dominant psychometric approach. Some important considerations, particularly regarding different processes and the treatment of group differences, have been revealed, which, if explored in more detail, could enhance the reliability and fairness of recruitment and selection systems. To ignore these concerns is to the detriment of organizations, applicants, recruiters and researchers. Increasing attention needs to be paid to the challenges they offer if the development of assessment is to be enhanced. For others, however, the application of these processes is fundamentally flawed. Given the increasingly global application of recruitment and selection practices within many large organizations it is important that equality of opportunity is at their heart and so it is essential that attention turns towards exploring differences. Without this refocusing, unfair discrimination will merely be perpetuated.

Let us now turn our attention to three important future factors that are directly influencing selection and recruitment: technology change, globalization and the changing nature of work.

## 5.1 Technology-led revolution

The technology-based transition in recruitment and selection is driven by US organizations and researchers. This is occurring for five main reasons. First, the internet is increasingly being used to administer selection processes. This enhances the flexibility of recruitment and selection processes, enabling applicants to have easier access at times and places to suit themselves, provided they can access a computer and the internet. The flexibility of *who* can apply for a vacancy is also opened up, regardless of the country applicants live in, expanding the pool of applicants. The use of technology has also altered how individuals are informed about vacancies. This transition offers flexibility for those who work abroad to stay in touch with job opportunities back home, or in other countries. Through the email and other web-based communication tools, the job of head-hunters and specialist recruiters has been made far easier.

The second reason that technology is changing recruitment and selection practice is through the development of new tools. Technology is altering the initial applicant attraction process, affecting how candidates are identified through both legal and illegal means. Passive job changers (those not actively looking to change jobs) can be identified with increasing ease, and using covert techniques, passive specialist applicants can be more easily recognized and approached. Thus, technology is making access to this group easier for recruiters, providing information about new potential opportunities for speculative and more active job seekers.

Technology has also created more sophisticated job previews which allow applicants a more comprehensive insight into the actual job they might be doing. Whilst providing more information, there is an increasing use of self-assessment fit questionnaires, so that candidates might be forgiven for thinking that *they* are the ones doing the evaluation, given the requests to reflect and consider how far their skills and abilities match the demands of the new job. Through these questionnaires, the cost of processing an ultimately unsuccessful candidate is saved and individuals deterred in a way that maintains, and at times enhances, the reputation of the firm; the firm is seen as doing the applicant a favour rather than wasting their time.

Third, psychometric assessment is shifting away from more abstract paper and pencil-based tests to the use of more sophisticated materials that might include video clips, simulations and scenarios. These content and format developments can be seen as enhancing the realism of the assessment, and, as we have seen, potentially reduce unfair discrimination for minority groups. In addition, on-line ability testing is likely to have a major impact in shaping our understanding of cognitive processes in the future. Through the collection of additional information, such as response rates for individual questions, more insight into faking behaviour is likely. The expansion of bespoke assessments will also grow, helping to create new models of intelligence. The expansion of tests with a global application might result in the development of more insights into cultural and gender differences. However, concerns about dominance of particular populations and Western-based models remain.

A fourth transition that has resulted from this technology-led transition is a change in where the power lies in the selection and recruitment process. In the past, paper and pencil-based testing placed test-users in control of the psychometrics tools. They bought the test batteries they required and controlled access to the materials and the results. Internet-based testing and the use of item response theory have fundamentally shifted this control back to the developer. The user may be unaware what types of items the applicants are being assessed on and may be provided with a result that they have no means of checking and validating without the test-developer. The applicants taking the test may at times be unaware that a third party is now handling their assessment.

A final way that technology is changing recruitment and selection is in job analysis through enabling the collection of more explicit performance data. This area has received less attention in the literature, but it is likely that practice is ahead of research. The advent of electronic performance monitoring and control systems (EPMCSs) enables organizations to covertly collect, store, analyse and report the actions and performance of their employees. These systems allow detailed data to be gathered, such as the contents of computer screens as they are being used for a particular task, the number of key strokes in a given period, monitoring file access, communication activities, such as email and web browsing. In addition, work spaces can also be video recorded. Whilst this level of data would provide a unique and detailed insight into job performance, it would have serious privacy implications for employees (Searle, 2003; Stone, 1995). This may be an area in which practice is ahead of research.

Technology offers the potential for us to expand and revise our understanding about cognitive processes and to gather data from wider sample groups. The question remains how far the adoption of new technology will create an equality of opportunity or a perpetuation of existing bias.

## 5.2  Global selection?

The second transition is the globalization of recruitment and selection practices. This transition is in part linked to technological changes, but its impetus is economic, with the increased expansion of large organizations onto a global trading platform and the opportunities to recruit staff more cheaply outside traditional and local labour pools. This raises the question about how far psychometric selection should become global.

Job analysis techniques can assist HR professionals to develop a picture of the same job role across different contexts. This might also assist managers operating internationally to gain an understanding about how specific jobs differ. These techniques offer job-holders a way of reviewing and reflecting on their practices in order to be able to share and improve on job performance. It is unlikely that a global job analysis would be meaningful in creating generic criteria. What is more likely is that in some contexts similar parts of a particular job go together, whereas in others the same title disguises a completely different job.

In some multinational organizations, there may be a requirement for a senior manager to operate on a transnational basis and in such cases this is likely to be recruited as a central function. When undertaking job analysis for such a position, differences may be found between previous employees who were successful in one type of context, but not in another. This would represent a significant difference and suggest that distinct profiles for jobs exist in different contexts. If so, it is questionable how helpful and feasible the use of generic criteria for such transnational positions would be. Instead we need to explore how far role, context and organization each shape job requirements in distinct ways.

The best practice for organizations is to ensure a standardization in the processes they adopt, thus enabling applicants to be compared fairly, for example using a structured interview. This standardized approach to the assessment process assumes that applicants are given the same advantages. However, it is not clear how far the questions that comprise a structured interview in one context would necessarily be appropriate in another. As with psychometric tests, there may be assumptions in an interview question which do not transcend different cultural contexts.

Evidence suggests that where training is provided for assessors, evaluations of applicants are more consistent. However, this view assumes that assessors are consistent in the evaluations they make. Research indicates that different assumptions and attributions are made of women and men (Silvester et al., 2003). It is important that more attention is paid to examining the decision-making process in order that we understand how far recruitment and selection can become proceduralized. Training allows assessors to reflect on the attributions and assessments they make of others, and this is a valuable process for them, especially if working in different contexts.

As suggested earlier, the traditional approach taken towards psychometric tools reveals an inherent bias towards a Western view of intelligence, imbued with a mono-cultural attitude towards assessment and using a particular linguistic repertoire which may be at odds with culturally diverse populations. Cognitive ability and personality tests clearly show culturally specific approaches to evaluating mental processes. The increasing application of the internet to administer such tests may merely compound their bias towards White males from higher socio-economic backgrounds. This might be the very population an organization is seeking to recruit from; however, few would acknowledge this openly. Despite attempts to reduce cultural bias in tests, they remain a problem. It is therefore difficult to consider how appropriate it would be to develop a psychometric test for use on a global basis. A key question that concerns those involved in recruitment and selection is: how appropriate is it to adopt a global system?

There are also culturally determined variations in recruitment and selection practices that reflect different candidates' expectations and different organizational requirements (Iles and Robertson, 1994). However, for organizations there are several factors which suggest that the global adoption of these practices may be likely in the future. Culture influences the structure and networks of organizations, and as noted in Chapter 1, recruitment and selection tools reflect a Westernized context which may enhance their attraction within some organizations. There is an increasing diffusion of knowledge of HR recruitment and selection systems – either through the management education based on Western business schools or by mergers and takeovers of local firms by multinational organizations. This may create a tension between the maintenance of current local practice and the need to adopt consistent systems across the organization. There may, however, be additional pressures from headquarters to achieve economies of scale in the recruitment and selection systems they use.

Different legal and regulatory environments can enhance the requirement for more transparency in HR processes, such as in the USA. The example posed in Dilemma box 1.2 outlined the legal problems recruitment can create as it crosses national borders. The escalation of these practices may have an impact on regulation, changing local requirements. An example of control can be clearly seen in the strict regulations in the UK on the purchase of psychometric tests. In many countries, they can easily be obtained without any prior training and are thus open to misuse. This situation will only change with regulation to restrict access to these instruments and to provide some quality control for applicants. Such a view is however at odds with the prevailing view of the market as a regulator, but without such controls all the main stakeholders are potentially harmed. This presents a challenge to the users and takers of psychometric tests.

Depending on the national culture, support varies for the prevailing psychometric approach, with countries that have an intellectual tradition that favours the natural sciences, such as the UK or Germany, more readily accepting this approach (Shackleton and Newell, 1994). Cultural variance can also be found regarding uncertainty avoidance and this can result in an increasing reliance on few selection methods, with a tendency to use psychometric tests and interviews, but with more attention given to auditing and validation of these processes. In contrast, in countries such as China, psychometric tools are seen as removing the importance of the candidate–assessor relationship, with a strong emphasis on getting to know the individual. Family connection is regarded as more significant than cognitive testing in Poland, whereas in Japan educational background is crucial. Given these distinctions it must be questioned how feasible, without imposition, a generic approach to recruitment and selection would be.

Although some organizations appear to adopt more Western approaches to selection and recruitment, it would be naïve to assume that these techniques are being applied in an identical way. Attention might focus on the outcomes of these tools, but it is far more likely that differences will lie in the selection decision-making processes. Silvester *et al.* (2003) have revealed the distinctions in the processes that assessors from the same culture use, making different attributions of applicants on the basis of the same information. We can only speculate how differently the same response to a structured interview question would be evaluated by those from different cultures.

The demand for valid reliable and fair recruitment and selection processes should increase the pressure on psychometric test-developers, and developers and users of other tools, to ensure that discrimination is minimized. However, this requires applicants to be aware of fairness and discrimination issues, and the possibility of creating standardized global recruitment practices remains remote without a fundamental revisiting of the field of individual differences and an understanding of the influence of group differences in psychometric testing. This presents an interesting challenge to organizations, psychologists and all those involved in recruitment and selection and influences current conceptions of differences.

## 5.3 The changing nature of work

The third area affecting recruitment and selection policy and practice is the changing nature of work. In several chapters in this book attention has been drawn away from input, that is selecting employees, towards achieving the output or displaying the required behaviours, such as a customer service ethos. Increasingly, employees are working in self-organizing teams in which it is difficult to determine the boundaries between different job-holders' responsibilities. The team undertakes the task and members co-operate and work together to achieve it. Recruitment and selection practices focus on identifying a suitable person for the job, but as we have seen with job analysis, isolating a job's roles and responsibilities may be difficult to do in fast-changing and team-based situations.

Recruitment and selection practices consider the potential employee at one period of time. There is limited consideration given to dynamic elements. The nature and type of work is evolving all the time. New recruits may have potential skills which the organization has not yet recognized; their addition to an existing team may create novel resources and ways of doing the job that enhance everyone in the team. Alternatively, the reality of the organization's culture may be at odds with the selection criteria and stifle the new employee. These are dynamic aspects that reveal the need to pay attention towards integration between the employees and their working context.

In the literature in this area, limited attention, other than in the interview field, has been given to the social-interactionist perspective. This perspective offers researchers and practitioners new insights into recruitment and selection by revealing the complexity behind the search and assessment of new employees, but, may be more importantly, this approach reminds us that selection is a social process. Recruitment and selection processes should not be considered in isolation but instead more attention is required to reveal the interaction between different actors and the integration of new employees into the firm.

A further change to recruitment and selection stems from the escalating accountability and pressure to deliver being placed on employees, often in return for reduced job security and variety, and this has seen some skilled individuals choosing to work for themselves rather than for large organizations. This shift toward self-employed status is particularly acute amongst women and within highly skilled technology-based jobs. It represents a potential challenge for recruiters away from the psychological psychometric-based approach which assesses individuals' capabilities towards a less psychological, more quality-focused performance measurement of a contracting entity. The expansion of the self-employed market may push psychologists and HR professions out of a role unless they can show their skills in this new area of selection. Should the focus for such selection be on outcome or performance for these outsourced workers?

# 6   Summary

This chapter has summarized the dominant and critical perspectives in selection and recruitment. Through suggesting improvements in the application of current techniques the difficulties of devising a generic selection system were exposed. The expectations of candidates and recruiters, local legal and regulatory requirements and the specific job and context were all seen to play a part in determining what is appropriate in any given situation.

The dominant psychometric perspective was outlined and an initial critique regarding the use of meta-analysis raised before three key concerns were identified – individual difference, static analysis and rationality power and self-reflectivity. These included fundamental problems with the underlying theory of individual differences. These were the partiality of what was actually being measured and the lack of complexity which excludes broader elements of motivation and personality within intelligence test performance. In addition, there is clearly an over-emphasis on maximal performance in testing, which is at odds with the typical performance requirements found in work. The inherent discrimination of the approach in terms of its treatment of variance was raised, and the dominance of a specific Western conception of intelligence, which reveals underlying cultural and linguistic influences that affect the ability of such instruments to be applied on a global basis.

The confusion between outcome and performance was also discussed by highlighting the potential biases in the simplistic measures commonly being used. The building blocks of recruitment and selection were criticized due to their limited temporal and contextual focus. A tension between the flexibility required by organizations and their employees and these criterion-generating techniques emerged. A further problem was identified which challenged the rationality of human decision-makers. The influences of power and self-reflection were discussed, which called into question the reliability of these tools.

Attention then turned to three emerging issues concerning the role of technology, globalization and the changing nature of work, and their influence on recruitment and selection were discussed. The danger for the first two aspects is that through the adoption of an almost mechanistic and standardized approach to recruitment and selection many of the aforementioned criticisms are compounded. More recognition is called for of the importance of the social interaction process of recruitment and selection and the necessity to look at the inter-relationship between these processes and the local and wider organizational context, and also to try and incorporate a dynamic element. Researchers need to examine how far validity generalizations emerge at job level, organizational level or the country level. Without an appreciation of these critical distinctions our insights will remain partial and potentially biased. The future offers researchers an opportunity to reassess their conceptions of individual differences and to think afresh about how best to measure current and future human potential. As the applicant pool increases, the potential to ensure equality of opportunity must be a priority and enable us to look again at our processes and gain new insights.

# Glossary

**ability test**   timed tool designed to measure maximal cognitive capacity or potential, regardless of the prior experience of the test-taker.

**adverse impact**   American term used to refer to the effect of a selection process that discriminates unfairly against applicants from particular groups, such as minority ethnic groups.

**affirmative action**   American term to refer to an organizational initiative designed to actively promote an under-represented group within the organization (*see* positive discrimination).

**alpha ability**   level of the specific skill a psychometric test is designed to measure (*see* beta ability).

**Americanization**   term used to define the adoption of practices originally used within American organizations by organizations elsewhere around the world, such as the individualization of work contracts and remuneration.

**appraisal**   organization-based assessment of an individual's work performance.

**aptitude test**   tool designed to measure what a person has a propensity or aptitude for, such as special interests or abilities, personality traits.

**assessment**   measurement of an individual's work-related skills and aptitudes.

**astrology**   analysis based on birth dates and location claimed to predict, among other things, job performance and personality.

**atheoretical**   lacking any theoretical basis.

**attainment test**   instrument designed to measure the effects on individual's performance following a programme of study (also termed achievement test).

**attenuation**   reduction in the relationship between two variables that results from imperfect reliability and/or group homogeneity.

**attraction**   the process by which an applicant is informed about, and becomes interested in, applying for a position within an organization.

**attrition**   the process of leaving an organization. Also called turnover.

**autobiographical application blank (biodata)**   questionnaire developed for a specific work role based on the biographical profiles of those who have been successful in that role.

**balanced score card**   outcome measurement process where results for a range of different aspects of performance are used (rather than just one), for example efficiency and environmental impact.

**bandwidth**   breadth of coverage offered by a given personality assessment questionnaire. Relates to the complexity of the dimension.

**behavioural anchored rating scale**   hierarchical scale of behaviours used to assess the quality of applicants' responses in situational interview questions.

**behavioural approach to personality**   an approach which focuses on the role of learning and experience in shaping behaviour.

**bespoke tool**   an instrument developed specifically for that organization, and/or a specific job.

**beta ability**   generic skill of test completion, for example, time management, that is enhanced through the test experience and results in improvements to the result obtained.

**bias**   systematic over- or under-estimation of a true value. Can result from a skew in the content or interpretation of candidates' results.

**big five model of personality**   model that reduces personality to five key factors: extraversion, conscientiousness, agreeableness, neuroticism, openness.

**biologically based theory of personality**   approach which focuses on the role of heredity and biology more generally in personality formation and development.

**bloated specific**   a scale or test with high co-efficient alphas, which results from the limited variation in the items used, so that it is as if the same item were being used.

**British Psychological Society**   the statutory body within the UK that regulates psychologists.

**career path**   types of jobs and experience followed by an individual in the course of their working life as they pursue an occupation.

**carry-over effect**   where there is insufficient gap between the completion of two tests such that the result obtained on the second session is artificially raised through the experiences of the first.

**classical test theory**   a theory which posits that any test result obtained consists of a true score + an error.

**co-efficient Alpha**   technique used to assess the internal reliability of the items that comprise a particular test or scale. Psychometricians argue alphas of 0.7 and above are desirable (also known as Kuder-Richardson reliability).

**cognitive-social approach to personality**   an approach to personality which encompasses both cognitive-behavioural and environmental factors in explaining personality.

**Commission for Racial Equality**   UK-based, government-funded organization which aims to promote and protect the equality of treatment for workers regardless of their race or ethnicity.

**competence**   an underlying skill, body of knowledge or behavioural pattern that predicts successful performance.

**concurrent validity**   a form of validity based on the relationship between the test-taker's performance in two forms of assessment completed at the same time, for example an ability test and a job sample test.

**consistent group difference effect** a statistical technique used to ensure the fairness of a test for minority groups in which items are examined to see how far they consistently differentiate between different sample groups.

**construct validity** a form of validity based on establishing support for the hypothetical construct which a test is measuring.

**construct-irrelevant variance** where an item is included in a test that is not relevant to the domain of interest.

**content under-representation** where an important component relevant to the conceptual domain is omitted from a test.

**content validity** a form of validity based on the adequacy with which a conceptual domain is covered by a test.

**correlation coefficient** a Pearson product-moment correlation coefficient is a numerical index of the strength of relationship between two variables. It ranges from +1.00 to -1.00. 0 indicates there is no relationship.

**criterion** an organizationally relevant measure or estimate of success in a job.

**criterion-keyed** test construction method where the items in the test correspond to an external domain or criterion.

**criterion-related** a scoring method which interprets the raw score based on the likelihood of the applicant achieving some external criterion.

**critical incident technique** a technique developed by Flanagan (1954) and used in job analysis by asking a job expert to identify effective and ineffective job behaviour which are then used to outline the most important parts of a task.

**crystallized intelligence** level of reasoning that reflects culturally specific and learned components.

**curriculum vitae (CV)** a summary of work experience, qualifications, skills, and competencies prepared by an individual making a job application.

**development, training or rehabilitation plans** future-focused organizational documents that indicate goals and the strategy for an individual's future development.

**differential item functioning (DTI) analysis** an analysis used to examine aggregated group differences in psychometric testing in order to increase the potential fairness of a test.

**domain-referenced** a scoring method which interprets the raw score obtained on a test based on the likelihood that those obtaining this score would have a level of skill and ability in terms of a particular criterion.

**efficacy** a term used in social psychology to refer to a person's perception of how effective they are at influencing matters which are of importance to them.

**entitlement statement** claiming credit for positive events.

**Equal Opportunities Commission**   UK-based organization that aims to promote and protect the fairness of work opportunities for all regardless of ethnicity and gender.

**error**   factor affecting the reliability of the measurement obtained for an individual. This can be either random or systematic.

**extra-role behaviour**   job criterion referring to behaviours that lie outside those task-specific expectations of a work role, such as citizenship behaviours.

**extraversion**   a personality dimension defined by a person's orientation toward the external world.

**Eysenck personality questionnaire**   a three-dimension trait questionnaire measuring personality.

**factor analysis**   a statistical technique used to identify clusters (or linear combinations) of items.

**faking**   distortion of information by an individual during a selection and recruitment process that may or may not be deliberate.

**faking good**   an American term referring to the distortion of results to appear better than would be the case in reality.

**fidelity**   a term used in testing to refer to a form of validity which assesses the relationship between the assessment given and the actual work.

**fit**   a match between an individual and organization.

**fluid intelligence**   level of reasoning skills applied to novel situations and argued to be cultural free.

**general intelligence factor ('g')**   a measure of generic mental ability developed by Spearman.

**generalizability theory**   a method for studying reliability that allows several sources of unreliability to be examined simultaneously.

**globalization**   adoption of generic recruitment and selection processes regardless of local context.

**grade point average (GPA)**   American term used to identify the average mark achieved during undergraduate study. It is used as an indication of intelligence.

**graphology**   an analysis of handwriting claimed to predict job performance and personality. This is commonly utilized in France.

**group dynamics**   a term coined by social psychologists to describe the continuous interplay among individuals within a group setting.

**Guttman scale**   test construction method where items are placed in a hierarchy of difficulty, so completing a more difficult item successfully *ipso facto* would mean that all of the preceding items would also be correct.

**halo effect**   the positive influence from one aspect of a candidate that boosts the ratings they receive from assessors, for example, their physical attractiveness.

**hard items** a term used in biographical data to refer to easily verifiable data, e.g. age, sex and qualifications.

**horns effect** the negative influence from one aspect of a candidate (typically physical appearance) that lowers the ratings the applicant receives from assessors.

**HR processes** the enactment of an organization-based human resource policy and practice.

**HR strategy** a high-level organizational management process and practice that focuses on future strategies for the enhanced use of human resources.

**impression management** an attempt by an individual to actively manage the image others have of them.

**in-role behaviour** job criterion traditionally expected from that role.

**intelligence** the various definitions of this theoretical construct, including the measurement of human cognitive functioning to indicate the amount of knowledge available, the speed with which new knowledge is acquired and the ability to adapt successfully to a new environment.

**Intelligence Quotient (IQ)** a score gained by test-taker which is compared with scores of those based on whom the test is normed.

**interview** a dialogue between the candidate and representative(s) of the organization with a view to establishing job or promotion suitability or job performance.

**introversion** personality dimension defined by a person's orientation toward their internal world.

**ipsative response format** a response format where candidate has to pick one true statement about themselves from a choice of several equally desirable responses.

**item analytic method** a test-construction method where the items in the test are selected on the basis of their relationship to the overall test result.

**Item Response Theory (IRT)** a technique for developing tests that identifies both the difficulty of an item and the ability of the test-taker. Thus, it is possible to differentiate between experts and novices using the same scale.

**jangle fallacy** where the same trait name is used by two or more psychometric questionnaires but the actual trait is distinctly different (Block, 1995).

**Japanization** term used to define the adoption of practices originally used within Japanese organizations by companies around the world. These include standard operations, team-work and total quality management.

**job analysis** a range of different techniques designed to collect information about the job role.

**KSA** knowledge skills and abilities (American version), or knowledge skills and attitudes (British version).

**Kuder-Richardson reliability** a technique used to assess the internal reliability of the items that comprise a particular test or scale. Psychometricians argue that alphas of 0.7 and above are desirable. (Also known as co-efficient Alpha.)

**media** a term used to cover range of different means by which selection and recruitment systems can be delivered to the candidate. These include: internet-, computer-, video- and telephone-based interfaces.

**middle manager** a person occupying a position in the middle tier of management within an organization.

**norm group** the specific population sample used to compare and interpret results from a psychometric test. Raw scores of applicants are interpreted on the basis of this comparison group.

**normative item** a psychometric response format where candidates are asked whether they agree or disagree with a particular statement.

**norm-referenced scoring** a scoring method which interprets the raw score obtained on a test against a comparable group from a specific population who are performing that job well.

**null hypothesis** a term devised by experimental psychology to describe the goal of an experiment which involves the rejection of the null hypothesis by proving that the experimental treatment did produce a significant effect.

**occupational psychology** an area of psychology that focuses on individuals, teams and organizations in relation to work.

**online multiple-choice test** an internet-delivered test where test-takers must select the correct answer from a number of choices provided.

**parallel versions** a reliability measure used in test development where two versions of the test are devised and a comparison made of the results obtained.

**performance dimension** the range of behaviours provided by a job expert and used in a behaviourally patterned description interview to indicate effective job performance.

**personality psychometric test** a test designed to measure enduring and stable elements in individuals' preferred way of behaving.

**personality type** identifies broad categories and syndromes which classify individuals into a particular group who show the same typical behaviours.

**phenomenological approach to personality** concerned with how people's experiences and perceptions shape behaviour.

**point-to-point correspondence** a direct relationship between a performance criterion on the assessment and successful completion of the job.

**position analysis questionnaire (PAQ)** verbally delivered job analysis checklist devised by McCormick, Jeanneret and Mecham (1972).

**positive discrimination** a British term used to refer to an organizational initiative designed to actively promote an under-represented group within the organization.

**practice effect** the improvement of a test score as a result of earlier test experience.

**predictive validity** a form of validity based on the relationship between the test taker's performance in two forms of assessment completed at the different times.

**proctored** American term for a supervised assessment process.

**promotion routes** types of jobs and experience expected from an individual if they are to get promotion within an occupation or organization.

**psychodynamic model of personality** based on clinical experience, this model understands human behaviour and relationships in terms of people's unconscious processes and inner conflicts.

**psychological construct** an abstract theoretical variable that is devised in order to explain some phenomenon which is of interest to psychologists.

**random error** an unsystematic error obtained by test-taker on a psychometric test which reduces the reliability of the measure obtained.

**recruitment** the filling a post from a pool of applicants who do not currently work for the organization.

**references** comments, evaluations and endorsements obtained from third parties who know the applicant well.

**reliability** measurements made to assess the accuracy of a test.

**reperotory grid** a technique developed for use in clinical psychology by Kelly (1954), which involves the generation of bi-polar constructs obtained from an ongoing and exhaustive comparison of elements belonging to the same family, such as people or job roles.

**restricting of range** reduced variability in one or more variables, which will affect the correlation. This is particularly found where unsuccessful candidates are removed from the sample population.

**scoring keys** used in psychometric tests to aid marking and interpretation of raw scores.

**selection** an applicant chosen for a post from a pool of candidates who currently work for the firm.

**self-report** the process by which the applicant reflects on and indicates their own skills and competencies.

**situational specificity** result or measurement that is pertinent only within a specific context.

**social constructionism** a theoretical approach to how knowledge is generated that emphasizes how people's understanding is constrained by their social world, in particular by language. In this view, knowledge is not a simple reflection of reality and therefore cannot claim to be objective or universal.

**social desirability** a response mode where individual selects a conventionally acceptable answer.

**social processes** social interactions, as opposed to task-related behaviours, which play a role in effective job performance.

**soft item** a term used in biographical data to categorize less easily verifiable data, such as a person's values or attitudes.

**Spearman-Brown's formula** a calculation that corrects for the deflated reliability obtained from split-half testing. It enables a correlation to be done on each half test as if each were a full-length test.

**specificity** a term used in testing to assess the specific content covered by a test.

**split-half testing** used in test development for reliability purposes, involving the division of test items into two mini-tests, which are completed and a comparison made of the results.

**stability** enduring quality that will be replicated over time.

**standard error of measurement** a technique used to correct for systematic error.

**stereotyping** an oversimplified perception of individuals and groups, frequently related to prejudice.

**systematic error** a predictable error in the score obtained by test-takers that can be corrected for.

**test manual** a specific report for every test that indicates how the test was developed, how it is to be administered and containing norm tables for interpretation.

**test-developer** the designer and developer of a psychometric test.

**test-retest reliability** the stability of a test assessed by having the same person complete the test on two separate occasions, usually separated by several months. The reliability is the difference between the two scores over the period.

**test-taker** a job applicant who completes a psychometric test as part of a recruitment or selection process.

**test-user** someone who uses psychometric tests. In this context it usually applies to an organization.

**Thurstone scales** a test construction method used for attitudinal assessment where both the items in the test and their relative weighting are identified by a panel of judges.

**trait approaches** personality theory-derived statistical procedures based on the identification of clusters of components which are predictive of individual difference.

**transportability** the movement of criteria from one job role or organization to another.

**turnover**   employees leaving an organization.

**two-way power relationship**   a term used to identify the power of both the organization and the candidate in a recruitment and selection situation.

**typical performance tests**   an un-timed psychometric assessment based on how an applicant typically behaves.

**utility**   the analysis of the cost–benefits of a selection process.

**validity**   concerned with the appropriateness of what is being measured in a test or instrument.

**volition**   the motivation and drive to achieve a desire outcome.

**Wechsler scale for intelligence**   test for intelligence. Available in either adult or child versions.

**worker-oriented analysis**   job analysis focusing on what the worker brings to the task as demonstrated in how the job is undertaken.

**work-orientated analysis**   job analysis focusing on the job tasks.

**work-profiling system**   job analysis tool devised by SHL that collects data on the main tasks of the job, training and qualifications requirements, the responsibility given, the physical environment and the remuneration package.

**work-sample method**   an assessment that focuses on tasks associated with the specific job role.

# Bibliography

Aamodt, M.G., Kimbrough, W.W., Keller, R.J. and Crawford, K.J. (1982) 'The relationship between sex, race, and job performance level and the generation of critical incidence', *Educational and Psychological Research*, vol.2, pp.227–34.

Ackerman, P.L. (1987) 'Individual difference in skills learning. An integration of psychometric and information processing perspective', *Psychological Bulletin*, vol.102, pp.3–7.

Ackerman, P.L. (1988) 'Determinants of individual differences during skill acquisition: cognitive abilities and information processing', *Journal of Experimental Psychology: General*, no.117, pp.288–318.

Ackerman, P.L. (1994) 'Intelligence, attention and learning: Maximal and typical performance' in Detterman, D.K. (ed.) *Current Topics in Human Intelligence. Vol. 4: Theories of Intelligence*, Norwood, NJ, Ablex, pp.1–27.

Ackerman, P.L. (1997) 'Personality, self-concept, interests and intelligence: Which construct doesn't fit?', *Journal of Personality*, vol.65, no.2, pp.171–204.

Ackerman, P.L. (1999) 'Traits and knowledge as determinants of learning and individual difference: Putting it together' in Ackerman, P.L., Kyllonen, P.C. and Roberts, R.D. (eds) *Learning and Individual Difference: Process, Trait and Content Determinants*, Washington, American Psychological Association pp.437–60.

Ackerman, P.L. and Heggestad, E.D. (1997) 'Intelligence, personality and interest: evidence for overlapping traits', *Psychological Bulletin*, vol.121, pp.219–45.

Ackerman, P.L. and Kanfer, R. (1993) 'Integrating laboratory and field study for improving selection: Development of a battery for predicting air traffic controller success', *Journal of Applied Psychology*, vol.78, pp.413–32.

Adams, R. (2002) 'Certified Checks. Big Brother: Someone somewhere is watching over you', Part One, *The Guardian*, 7 September, p.15.

Agor, W. (1986) 'The logic of intuition: How top executives make important decisions', *Organizational Dynamics*, Winter, nos 5–15.

Alimo-Metcalfe, B.M. and Alban-Metcalfe, R.J. (2003) 'Leadership: A masculine past, but a feminine future'. Paper presented at the Division of Occupational Psychology Annual Conference, Bournemouth, January.

Allport, G.W. (1937) *Personality: A Psychological Interpretation*, New York, Holt Press.

Allworth, E. and Hesketh, B. (1999) 'Construct-oriented biodata: capturing change-related and contextually relevant future performance', *International Journal of Selection and Assessment*, vol.7, pp.97–111.

Anastasi, A. (1990) *Psychological Testing*, 6th edn, New York, Macmillan.

Ancona, D.G. and Caldwell, D.F. (1992) 'Bridging the boundary: External activity and performance in organisational teams', *Administrative Science Quarterly*, vol.34, no.3, pp.634–65.

Anderson, C.D., Warner, J.L. and Spencer, C.C. (1984) 'Inflation bias in self-assessment employment examinations: Implications for valid employee selection', *Journal of Applied Psychology*, vol.69, no.4, pp.574–80.

Anderson, N. and Shackleton, V. (1993) *Successful Selection Interviewing*, Oxford, Blackwell.

Anderson, N., Payne, T., Ferguson, E. and Smith, T. (1994) 'Assessor decision making, information processing and assessor decision strategies in a British Assessment centre', *Personnel Review*, vol.23, pp.52–62.

Anderson, N.R., Silvester, J., Cunningham-Snell, N. and Haddleton, E. (1999) 'Relationships between candidate self-monitoring, perceived personality and selection interview outcomes', *Human Relations*, vol.52, pp.1115–31.

Annett, J. and Duncan, K.D. (1967) 'Task analysis and training design', *Occupational Psychology*, vol.41, pp.211–21.

Arneson, S., Millikin-Davies, M. and Hogan, J. (1993) 'Validation of personality and cognitive measures for insurance claims examiners', *Journal of Business and Psychology*, vol.7, pp.459–73.

Arnold, J., Cooper, C. and Robertson, I. (1997) *Work Psychology: Understanding Human Behaviour in the Workplace*, London, Financial Times/Pitman Publishing.

Arthur, J. (1998) 'Laparoscopic surgery training: Reform or reformation? How well can the research and advice of occupational psychology be heard?' Paper presented at the West Midlands British Psychological Society Conference.

Arthur, W., Doverspike, D. and Barrett, G.V. (1996) 'Development of job analysis-based procedure fore weighting and combining content-related tests into a single test battery score', *Personnel Psychology*, vol.49, pp.971–85.

Arvey, R.D. (1979) 'Unfair discrimination in the employment interview: Legal and psychological aspects', *Psychology Bulletin*, vol.86, pp.736–65.

Ash, R.A. and Edgell, S.L. (1975) 'A note on the readability of the position analysis questionnaire', *Journal of Applied Psychology*, vol.60, pp.765–6.

Asher, J.J. and Sciarrion, J.A. (1974) 'Realistic work sample tests: A review', *Personnel Psychology*, vol.27, pp.519–33.

Avery, R.D. and Campion, J.E. (1982) 'The employment interview: a summary and review of research', *Personnel Psychology*, vol.35, pp.281–322.

Avery, R.D., Maxwell, S.E. and Abraham, L.M. (1982) 'Reliability artefacts in comparable work procedures', *Journal of Applied Psychology*, vol.70, pp.695–705.

Axtmann, L. and Jablin, F.M. (1986) 'Distributional and sequential interaction structure in the employment screening interview'. Paper presented at the Annual Meeting of the International Communication Association, Chicago, May.

Badagliacco, J. M. (1990) 'Gender and race differences in computing attitudes and experience', *Social Science Computer Review*, vol.8, pp.42–63.

Bales, R.F. (1970) *Personality and Interpersonal Behavior*, New York, Holt, Rinehart and Winston.

Ball, K.S. and Searle, R.H. (2002) 'The institutionalisation of HR management practice in a UK manufacturing firm: power, politics and process'. Paper presented at the European Group of Organisation Studies, Barcelona, July.

Bandura, A. (1986) *Social Foundations of Thought and Actions: A social cognitive theory*, Englewood Cliffs, NJ, Prentice Hall.

Barber, A. (1998) *Recruiting Employees: Individual and Organisational Perspectives*, Thousand Oaks, CA, Sage.

Baron, H. and Austin, (2000) *Measuring Ability via the Internet: Opportunities and Issues*. Paper presented at the Annual Conference of the Society for Industrial & Organizational Psychology, New Orleans, LA.

Baron, H. and Miles, A. (2002) 'Schema based generation: The online numerical reasoning testing system'. Paper presented at The International Conference on Computer-based Testing and the Internet: Building Guidelines for Best Practice, Winchester.

Baron, H., Martin, T., Proud, A., Weston, K. and Elshaw, C. (2003) 'Ethnic group difference and measuring of cognitive ability'. Paper presented at the British Psychological Society Division of Occupational Psychology Conference, Bournemouth, January.

Baron, R.A. (1989) 'Impression management by applicants during employment interviews: The "too much of a good thing" effect' in Eder, R.W. and Harris, M.M. (eds) *The Employment Interview Handbook* London, Sage, pp.204–15.

Barrick, M.R. and Mount, M.K. (1996) 'Effects of impression management and self-deception on the predictive validity of personality constructs', *Journal of Applied Psychology*, vol.81, pp.261–72.

Barrick, M.R. and Mount, M.K. (1991) 'The Big Five personality dimensions and job performance: a meta-analysis', *Personnel Psychology*, vol.44, pp.1–26.

Barrick, M.R., Mount, M.K. and Judge, T.A. (2003) 'Personality and performance at the beginning of the new Millennium: What do we know and where do we go next?', *International Journal of Selection and Assessment,* vol.9, pp.9–30.

Barrick, M.R., Stewart, G.L. and Piotrowski, M. (2002) 'Personality and job performance: Test of the mediating effects of motivation among sales representative', *Journal of Applied Psychology*, vol.87, no.1, pp.43–51.

Barrick, M.R., Stewart, G.L., Neubert, M.J. and Mount, M.K. (1998) 'Relating member ability and personality to work–team processes and team effectiveness', *Journal of Applied Psychology*, vol.83, pp.377–92.

Barritz, L. (1965) *Servants of Power,* Middletown, CT, Wesleyan University Press.

Barry, B. and Stewart, G.L. (1997) 'Composition, process and performance in self-managed groups, the role of personality', *Journal of Applied Psychology*, vol.82, pp.62–78.

Bartels, L.K. and Doverspike, D. (1997) 'Assessing the assessor, the relationship of assessor personality to leniency in assessment centre ratings', *Journal of Social Behavior and Personality*, vol.12, pp.179–90.

Bartram, D. (1995) 'The predictive validity of the EPI and 16PF for military flying training', *Journal of Occupational and Organisational Psychology*, vol.68, pp.219–30.

Bartram, D. (2002) 'The impact of the internet on testing: Issues that need to be addressed by a code of goods practice'. Paper presented at The International Conference on Computer-based Testing and the Internet: Building Guidelines for Best Practice, Winchester.

Bartram, D. and Dale, H. (1982) 'The Eysenck Personality Inventory as a selection test for military pilots', *Journal of Occupational Psychology*, vol.55, pp.287–96.

Bartram, D., Baron, H. and Kurz, R. (2003) 'Let us turn validation on its head'. Paper presented at the British Psychological Society Division of Occupational Psychology Conference, Bournemouth, January.

Bass, B.M. (1954) 'The leaderless group discussion technique', *Personnel Psychology*, vol.3, pp.17–32.

Bayley, N. (1968) 'Behavioural correlates of mental growth: Birth to thirty-six years', *American Psychologists*, vol.23, pp.1–17.

Becker, T. and Colquitt, A. (1992) 'Potential versus actual faking of bio data form: An analysis along several dimensions of item type', *Personnel Psychology*, vol.45, pp.389–406.

Beer, M., Spector, B., Lawerence, P., Mills, D. and Walton, R. (1984) *Human Resource Management: A General Manager's Perspective*, New York, Free Press.

Behling, O. (1998) 'Employee selection: will intelligence and conscientiousness do the job?', *Academy of Management Executive*, vol.12, pp.77–86.

Belbin, M. (1981) *Management Teams: Why They Succeed or Fail*, Oxford, Helimann.

Bennet, G.K., Seashore, H.G. and Wesman, A.G. (1962) *Differential Aptitude Tests*, 2nd edn, New York, Psychological Corporation.

Benson, P.G. and Hornsby, J.S. (1988) 'The use of influence tactics in job evaluation committees', *Group and Organization Studies*, vol.13, pp.208–24.

Berkson, H.M., Harris, M.M. and Ferris, G.R. (1999) 'Enhancing organisational reputation to attract applicants' in Eder, R.W. and Harris, M.M. (eds) *The Employment Interview Handbook*, London, Sage, pp.83–98.

BeVier, C., Roth, P., Bobko, P., Switzer F. and Tyler, P. (1998) 'Racial differences in cognitive abilities: A meta-analysis'. Unpublished manuscript, Clemson University, cited in Bobko *et al.* (1999).

Bion, W.R. (1946) 'The leaderless group project', *Bulletin of the Menninger Clinic*, vol.10, pp.77–81.

Blach, W. (1992) 'Effects of class standing on students' predictions of their final exam scores', *Teaching of Psychology*, vol.19, pp.136–41.

Bliesener, T. (1996) 'Methodological moderators in validating biographical data in personnel selection', *Journal of Occupational and Organizational Psychology*, vol.69, pp.107–20.

Block, J. (1993) 'Studying personality the long way' in Funder, D.C., Payne, R.D., Tomlinson-Keasey, C. and Widaman, K. (eds) *Studying Lives through Time*, Washington, DC, American Psychological Association, pp.9–41.

Block, J. (1995) 'A contrarian view of the five factor approach to personality description', *Psychological Bulletin*, vol.117, pp.187–215.

Bobko, P., Roth, P.L. and Potosky, D. (1999) 'Derivation and implications of a meta-analytic matrix incorporating cognitive ability, alternative predictors, and job performance', *Personnel Psychology*, vol.52, no.3, pp.561–90.

Bolster, B.I. and Sprinbett, B.M. (1961) 'The reaction of interviewers to favourable and unfavourable information', *Journal of Applied Psychology*, vol.45, pp.97–103.

Borman, W.C. and Motowidlo, S.J. (1993) 'Expanding the criterion domain to include elements of contextual performance' in Schmitt, N. and Borman, W.C. (eds) *Personnel selection in organizations*, San Francisco, CA, Jossey-Bass.

Borman, W.C., Dorsey, D. and Ackerman, L. (1992) 'Time spent responses as time allocation strategies: Relations with sales performance in a stockbroker sample', *Personnel Psychology*, vol.45, pp.763–77.

Bouchard, T.J. (1997) 'The genetics of personality' in Blum, K. and Nobel, E.P. (eds) *Handbook of Psychiatric Genetics*, Boca Raton, FL, Circle Press Ltd, pp.279–96.

Boyatzis, R.E. (1982) *The Competent Manager*, New York, Wiley.

Boyle, S., Fullerton, J. and Wood, R. (1995) 'Do assessment/development centres use optimum evaluation procedures? A survey of practice in UK organizations', *International Journal of Selection and Assessment*, vol.3, pp.132–40.

Brand, C.R. and Deary, I.J. (1982) 'Intelligence and inspection time' in Eysenck, H.J. *A Model for Intelligence*, New York, Springer, ch.5.

Bray, D.W. and Grant, D.L. (1966) 'The assessment centre in the measurement of potential for business management', *Psychological Monographs*, vol.80, (17 whole no. 625).

Bridges, W. (1994) *Jobshift*, Reading, MA, Addison-Wesley.

Bright, J.E.H. and Davies, F.(1999) 'You did WHAT in 1983?!: The effects of explained and unexplained gaps in career history presented in resumes', *Australian Journal of Career Development*, vol.8, no.1, pp.12–17.

Bright, J.E.H. and Hutton, S. (2000) 'The impact of competences statements on resumes for short-listing decisions', *International Journal of Selection and Assessment*, vol.8, pp.41–53.

Brooks-Gordon, B. (2002) 'An exploration of academic culture and the unintentional queen bee', *Psychology of Women Section Review*, vol.4, no.2, pp.18–20.

Brown, B.K. and Campion, M.A. (1994) 'Biodata phenomenology: recruiters' perceptions and the use of biographical information in resume screening', *Journal of Applied Psychology*, vol.79, pp.897–908.

Burke, E. (2000) 'Assessing and selecting decision-makers for risk critical roles'. Paper presented at the British Psychological Society Division of Occupational Psychology Conference, Brighton, January.

Burnham, P.S. (1965) 'Prediction and performance' in *From High School to College: Readings for Counsellors*, New York, College Entrance Examination Board, pp.65–71.

Burt, C. (1924) 'The mental differences between individuals', *Journal of the National Institute of Industrial Psychology*, vol.11, no.2, pp.67–74.

Butler, S.K. and Harvey, R.J. (1988) 'A comparison of holistic versus decomposed rating of position analysis questionnaire work dimensions', *Personnel Psychology*, vol.41, pp.761–71.

Bycio, P. and Zoogah, B. (2002) 'Exercise order and assessment centre performance', *Journal of Occupational and Organizational Psychology*, vol.75, no.1, pp.109–15.

Byman, cited in Mayes *et al.*, 1997.

Cahn, D.D. (1976) 'The employment interview: A self-validation model', *Journal of Employment Counselling*, vol.13, pp.150–5.

California Personality Inventory (CIP) Palo Alto, CA, Consulting Psychologist Press.

Callaghan, G. and Thompson, P. (2002) '"We recruit attitude": the selection and shaping of routine call centre labour', *Journal of Management Studies*, vol.39, no.2, pp.233–54.

Callinan, M. and Robertson, I.T. (2000) 'Work sample testing', *International Journal of Selection and Assessment*, vol.8, no.4, pp.248-60.

Campbell, J.P. (1990) 'Modelling the performance prediction problem in industrial and organisational psychology' in Dunnette, M.D. and Hough, L.M. (eds) *Handbook of Industrial and Organisational Psychology*, vol.1, Palo Alto, CA, Consulting Psychologists Press, pp.687–732.

Campbell, J.P. (1994) 'Alternative models of job performance and the implications for selection and classification' in Rumsey, M.G., Walker, C.B. and Harris, J.H. (eds), *Personnel Selection and Classification*, Hillsdale, NJ, Erlbaum.

Campbell, J.P., McCoy, R.A., Oppler, S.H. and Sager, C.E. (1993) 'A theory of performance' in Schmitt, N. and Borman, W.C. (eds.), *Personnel Selection in Organisations*, San Francisco, CA, Jossey-Bass, pp.35–70.

Campbell, R.J. and Bray, D.W. (1967) 'Assessment centres: an aid in management selection', *Personnel Administration*, vol.30, pp.6–13.

Campion, M.A., Campion, J.E. and Hudson J.P. (1984) 'Structured interviewing: A note on incremental ability and alternative question types', *Journal of Applied Psychology*, vol.79, pp.998–1002.

Campion, M.A., Pursell, E.D. and Brown, B.K. (1988) 'Structured interviewing: Raising the psychometric properties of the employment interview', *Personnel Psychology*, vol.41, pp.25–42.

Campion, M.A., Pursell, E.D. and Brown, B.K. (1988) 'Structured interviews: raising the psychometric properties of the employment interview', *Journal of Applied Psychology*, vol.79, pp.998–1002.

Carey, N.B. (1991) 'Setting standards and diagnosing training needs with surrogate job performance measures', *Military Psychology*, vol.3, pp.135–50.

Carlson, K.D., Scullen, S.E., Schmidt, F.L., Rothstein, H. and Erwin, F. (1999) 'Generalisable biographical data validity can be achieved without multi-organizational development and keying', *Personnel Psychology*, vol.52, pp.731–55.

Carroll, J.B. (1993) *Human Cognitive Abilities: A Survey of Factor-analytic Studies*, Cambridge, Cambridge University Press.

Cartell, R.B. (1973) *Personality and Mood by Questionnaire*, San Francisco, CA, Jossey-Bass.

Cartell, R.B. (1978) *The Scientific Use of Factor Analysis*, New York, Springer.

Cascio, W.F. (1976) 'Turnover, biographical data and fair employment practice', *Journal of Applied Psychology*, vol.61, pp.575–80.

Cascio, W.F. and Silbey, V. (1987) 'Utility of the assessment centre as a selection devise', *Journal of Applied Psychology*, vol.56, pp.40–4.

Cattell, R.B. (1950) *Personality: A Systematic, Theoretical and Factual Study*, New York, McGraw-Hill.

Cattell, R.B. (1953) *A Guide to Mental Testing*, 3rd edn, London, London University Press

Cattell, R.B. (1965) *The Scientific Analysis of Personality*, Baltimore, MD, Penguin.

Cattell, R.B., Eber, H.W. and Tatsuoka M.M. (1970) *The 16 Personality Factor Questionnaire*, Champaign, IL, IPAT.

Chan, D. and Schmitt, N. (1997) 'Video-based versus paper-and-pencil method of assessment in situational judgement tests: Subgroup differences in test performance and face validity perceptions', *Journal of Applied Psychology*, vol.82, pp.143–59.

Chan, D., Schmitt, N., de Shin, R.P., Clause, C.S and Delbridge, K. (1997) 'Can racial difference in cognitive test performance be reduced by presenting problems in a social context?', *Journal of Applied Psychology*, vol.82, no.2, pp.300–10.

Chan, K.Y., Drasgow, F. and Sawin, L.L. (1999) 'What is the shelf life of a test? The effects of time on the psychometrics of a cognitive ability test battery', *Journal of Applied Psychology*, vol.84, no.4, pp.610–19.

Chandler, A.D. (1962) *Strategy and Structure*, Cambridge, MA, MIT Press.

Chapman, D.S. and Rowe, P.M. (2001) 'The impact of videoconference technology, interview structure and interviewer gender on interview evaluations in the employment interview: A field experiment', *Journal of Occupational and Organisational Psychology*, vol.74, no.3, pp.279–98.

Cheepan, C. (1988). *The Predictability of Informal Conversation*, New York, Pinter.

Christiansen, N.D., Gothin, R.D., Johnson, N.G. and Rothstein, M.G. (1994) 'Correcting the 16PF for faking: Effects of criterion-related validity and individual hiring decisions', *Personnel Psychology*, vol.47, pp.847–60.

Christmas, L.A. and Branson, D.H. (1990) 'Influence of physical disability and dress of female job applicants on interviewees', *Clothing and Textile Research Journal*, vol.8, pp.51–7.

Clevenger, J., Pereira, G.M., Wiechmann, D., Schmitt, N. and Harvey, V.S. (2001) 'Incremental validity of situational judgment tests', *Journal of Applied Psychology*, vol.86, no.3, pp.410–17.

Coleman, V. and Borman, W. (2000) 'Investigating the underlying structure of the citizenship performance domain', *Human Resources Research Review*.

Collinson, D.L. and Collinson, M. (1997) 'Delayering managers: time–space surveillance and its gendered effects', *Organization*, no.4, pp.375–408.

Cook, M. (ed.) (1998) *Personnel Selection: Adding Value Through People*, 3rd edn, Chichester, Wiley.

Cordery, J.L. and Servastos, P.P. (1993) 'Response to the original and revised job diagnostic survey: Is education a factor in responses to negatively worded items?', *Journal of Applied Psychology.* vol.78, pp.141–3.

Cortina, J.M., Goldstein, N.B., Payne, S.C., Davison, H.K. and Gilliland, S.W. (2000) 'The incremental validity of interview scores over and above cognitive ability and conscientiousness scores', *Personnel Psychology*, vol.53, pp.325–51.

Costa, P., Terracciano, A. and McCrea, R.R. (2001) 'Gender differences in personality traits across cultures: robust and surprising findings', *Journal of Personality and Social Psychology*, vol.81, no.2, pp.322–31.

Costa, P. and McCrea, R.R. (1985) *The NEO Personality Inventory Manual*, Odessa, FL, Psychological Assessment Resources.

Craik, K.H., Ware, A.P., Kamp, J., O'Reilly III, C., Staw, B. and Zedeck, S. (2002) 'Explorations of construct validity in a combined managerial and personality assessment programme', *Journal of Occupational and Organizational Psychology*, vol.75, no.2, pp.171–93.

Cronbach, L.J. (1949) 'Response sets and test validity', *Educational and Psychological Measurement*, vol.6, pp.475–94.

Cronbach, L.J. (1951) 'Coefficient alpha and the internal structure of tests', *Psychometrika,* vol.16, pp.297–334.

Cronbach, L.J. (1957) 'The two disciplines of scientific psychology', *American Psychologist*, vol.12, pp.671–84.

Cronbach, L.J. (1984) *Essentials of Psychological Testing*, 4th edn, New York, Harper Row.

Cronbach, L.J. and Meehl, P.E. (1955) 'Construct validity in personality tests', *Psychological Bulletin*, vol.52, pp.281–302.

Czaja, S. and Sharit, J. (1998) 'Age differences in attitudes toward computers', *Journal of Gerontology: Series B: Psychological Sciences and Social Sciences*, vol.53, pp.329–40.

Davis, R.D. and Million, T. (1994) 'Personality change: Metatheories and alternatives' in Heatherton, T.F. and Weinberg, J.L. (eds) *Can Personality Change?*, Washington, DC, American Psychological Association, pp.856–919.

Delbridge, R. and Turnbull, P. (1992) 'Human resource maximization: The management of labour under just-in-time manufacturing systems' in Blyton, P. and Turnbull, P. (eds) *Reassessing Human Resource Management*, London, Sage.

Delery, J.E. and Kacmar, K.M. (1995) 'The use of impression management tactics in the employment interview: An investigation of the influence of applicant and interviewer characteristic'. Paper present at the annual meeting of the Society for Industrial and Organizational Psychology, Orlando, FL.

Detterman, D.K. and Daniels, M.H. (1989) 'Correlations of mental tests with each other and cognitive variables are highest in low IQ groups', *Intelligence*, vol.13, pp.349–60.

Deutsch, M. and Gerard, H.B. (1955) 'A study of normative and informational social influences upon individual judgement', *Journal of Abnormal and Social Psychology*, vol.51, pp.629–36.

Dewberry, C. (2001) 'Performance disparities between white and ethnic minorities: real differences or assessment bias?', *Journal of Occupational and Organisational Psychology*, vol.74, no.5, pp.659–74.

Digman, J.M. (1990) 'Personality structure: emergence of the five-factor model', *Annual Review of Psychology*, vol.41, pp.417–40.

Dipboye, R.L. (1994) 'Structured and unstructured selection interviews: Beyond the job-fit model' in Ferris, G.R. (ed.) *Research in Personnel Selection and Human Resource Management*, vol.12, Greenwich, CT, JAI, pp.79–123.

Dipboye, R.L. and Wiley, J.W. (1978) 'Reactions of male raters to interviewee self-presentation style and sex', *Journal of Vocational Behaviour*, vol.10, pp.1–12.

Dixon, R.M.W. (1977) 'Where have all the adjectives gone?', *Studies in Language*, vol.1, pp.19–80.

Dose, J.J. (2003) 'Information exchange in personnel decision making', *Applied Psychology: An International Review*, vol.52, no.2, pp.237–52.

Dougherty, T.W., Ebert, R.J. and Callender, J.C. (1986) 'Policy capture in the employment interview', *Journal of Applied Psychology*, vol.71, pp.9–15.

Dougherty, T.W., Turban, D.B. and Callender, J.C. (1994) 'Confirming first impressions in the employment interview: A field study of interviewer behaviour', *Journal of Applied Psychology*, pp.659–65.

Douthitt, S.S., Eby, L.T. and Simon, S.A. (1999) 'Diversity of life experiences: the development and validation of graphical measures of receptiveness to dissimilar others', *International Journal of Selection and Assessment*, vol.7, pp.112–25.

Drakeley, R.J. (1989) 'Biographical data' in Herriot, P. (ed.) *Assessment and Selection in Organizations*, Chichester, Wiley, pp.439–53.

Drakeley, R.J., Herriot, P. and Jones, A. (1988) 'Biographical data, training success and turnover', *Journal of Occupational and Organisational Psychology*, vol.61, pp.145–52.

Drasgow, F. (2002) 'New Items and New Tests: Opportunities and Issues'. Paper presented at The International Conference on Computer-based Testing and the Internet: Building Guidelines for Best Practice, Winchester.

Dreher, G.F. and Sackett, P.R. (1983) *Perspectives on Staffing and Selection*, Homewood, IL, Irwin.

DuBois, P.H. (1970) *A History of Psychological Testing*, Boston, MA, Allyn and Bacon.

DuBois, P.H. (1972) 'Increase in educational opportunity through measurement', *Proceedings of 1971 Invitational conference on testing problems*, Princeton, NJ, Education Testing Service.

Dulewicz, V. and Higgs, M. (1999) 'Can emotional intelligence be measured and developed?', *Leadership and Organization Development Journal*, vol.20, no.5, pp.242–53.

Dunnette, M.D. (1963) 'A note on the criterion', *Journal of Applied Psychology*, vol.47, pp.251–4.

Dunnette, M.D. (1966) *Personnel Selection and Placement*, London, Tavistock.

Dunnette, M.D. (1967) 'The assessment of managerial talent' in Wiockert, F.R. and McFarland, D.E. (eds) *Measuring Executive Effectiveness*, New York, Appleton-Century-Crofts.

Earl, J., Bright, J.E.H.R. and Adams, A. (1998) 'In my opinion: what gets graduates resumes short-listed?', *Australian Journal of Career Development*, vol.7, pp.15–19.

Eder, R.W. (1999) 'Contextual effects on interview decisions' in Eder. R.W. and Ferris, G.R. (eds) *The Employment Interview: Theory, Research and Practice* pp.113—26, Newbury Park, CA, Sage.

Eder, R.W. and Harris, M.M. (1999) *The Employment Interview Handbook*, London, Sage.

Edwards, A.L. (1957) *The Social Desirability Variable in Personality Research*, New York, Dryden.

Elkins, T.J. and Phillips, J.S. (2000) 'Job context, selection decision outcome, and perceived fairness of selection tests: Biodata as an illustrative case', *Journal of Applied Psychology*, vol.85, pp.479–84.

Engler, B. (1995) *Personality Theories*, 4th edn, Boston, MA, Houghton Mifflin.

Engler-Parish, P.G. and Millan, F.E. (1989) 'An exploratory relation control analysis of the employment screening interview', *Western Journal of Speech Communication*, vol.53, pp.30–51.

Evans, R. (2002) 'Base Invader, Big Brother: Someone somewhere is watching over you. Part one', *The Guardian,* 7 September, pp.16–18.

Eysenck, H. J. and Barrett, P. (1985) 'Psychophysiology and the measurement of intelligence' in Reynolds, C.R. and Wilson, P.C. (eds) *Methodological and Statistical Advances in the Study of Individual Differences*, New York, Plenum Press, pp.1–49.

Eysenck, H.J. (1952) *The Scientific Study of Personality*, London, Routledge.

Eysenck, H.J. (1967) *The Biological Basis for Personality*, Springfield, IL, Charles C. Thomas.

Eysenck, H.J. and Eysenck, M.J. (1985) *Personality and Individual Differences: A Natural Science Approach*, New York, Plenum Press.

Eysenck, H.J. and Eysenck, S.B.G. (1967) 'On the unitary nature of extraversion', *Acta Psychologica,* vol.26, pp.383–90.

Farrell, J.N. and McDaniel, M.A. (2001) 'The stability coefficients over time: Ackerman's' (1988) model and the general aptitude test battery', *Journal of Applied Psychology*, vol.86, no.1, pp.60–79.

Feltham, R. (1988) 'Utility analysis of the Civil Service Commission (CSC)', cited in Nelson, N., ASE psychometric (1995) notes validity section page 101.

Ferris, G.R. and Judge, T.A. (1991) 'Personnel/human resource management: A political influence perspective', *Journal of Management*, no.17, pp.447–88.

Fischer, C.S., Hout, M., Jankowski, M.S., Lucas, S.R., Swindler, A. and Voss, K. (1996) *Inequality by Design*, Princeton, NJ, Princeton University Press.

Fisher, R.A. (1925) *Statistical Methods for Research Workers*, London, Oliver and Boyd.

Fiske, D.W. and Butler, J. M. (1963) 'The experimental conditions for measuring individual differences', *Educational And Psychological Measurement*, vol.23, pp.249–344.

Flanagan, J.C. (1954) 'The critical incident technique', *Psychological Bulletin,* vol.51, pp.327–58.

Fletcher, C. (1981) 'Candidates' beliefs and self-presentation strategies in selection interviews', *Personnel Psychology*, vol.10, pp.14–17.

Fletcher, C. (1990) 'The relationship between candidate personality, self-presentation strategies, and interviewer assessment in selection interviews: An empirical study', *Human Relations*, vol.43, pp.739–49.

Fletcher, C. and Kerslake, C. (1992) 'The impact of assessment centres and their outcomes on participants' self-assessments', *Human Relations*, vol.45, pp.73–81.

Fletcher, C. and Spencer, A. (1984) 'Sex of candidate and sex of interviewer as determinants of self-presentation orientation in interviews?: An experimental study', *International Review of Applied Psychology*, vol.33, pp.305–13.

Fletcher, S. and Wood, R. (1993) 'The efficacy of coaching in test-taking behaviour: A preliminary investigation'.

Forrester, R.H. (1994) 'Implications of lean manufacturing for human resource strategy', *Work Study*, vol.33, no.3, pp.20–4.

Forrester, R.H. (2000) 'Capturing learning and applying knowledge: An investigation of the use of innovation teams between Japanese and American automotive firms', *Journal of Business Research*, no.47, no.1, 35–46.

Forsyth, S., Drake, M.F. and Cox, C.E. (1985) 'Influence of applicant's dress on interviewer's selection decisions', *Journal of Applied Psychology*, vol.70, pp.374–8.

Frink, D. and Klimoski, R. (1998) 'Toward a theory of accountability in organisations and human resource management' in Ferris, G.R. (ed.) *Research in Personnel and Human Resource Management*, vol.16, Greenwich, CT, JAI Press.

Furnham, A. (1992) *Personality at Work*, London, Routledge.

Furnham, A. and Heaven, P. (1999) *Personality and Social Behaviour,* London, Arnold.

Gael, S. and Grant, D.L. (1972) 'Employment test validation for minority and nonminority telephone company service representatives', *Journal of Applied Psychology*, vol.56, pp.135–9.

Gael, S., Grant, D.L. and Ritchie, R.J. (1975) 'Employment test validation for minority and nonminority telephone operators', *Journal of Applied Psychology*, vol.60, pp.411–19.

Gardner, H. (1983) *Frames of the Mind: The Theory of Multiple Intelligences*, New York, Basic Books.

Gaugler, B.B. and Randolph, A.S. (1992) 'The influence of assessee performance variation on assessors' judgements', *Personnel Psychology*, vol.45, pp.77–98.

Ghiselli, E.E. (1966) *The Validity of Occupational Aptitude Tests*, New York, Wiley.

Gil *et al.*, (1973) cited in Shackleton and Newell (1997).

Gilliland, S.W. (1993) 'The perceived fairness of selection systems: An organisational justice perspective', *Academy of Management Review*, vol.18, pp.694–734.

Gilliland, S.W. (1994) 'Effects of procedural and distributive justice on reactions to a selection system', *Journal of Applied Psychology*, vol.79, pp.691–701.

Gilmore, D.C. and Ferris, G.R. (1989) 'The effects of applied impression management on interviewer judgements', *Journal of Management*, vol.15, pp.557–64.

Gilmore, D.C., Stevens, C.K., Harrell-Cook, G. and Ferris, G.R. (1999) 'Impression management tactics' in Eder, R.W. and Harris, M.M. (eds) *The Employment Interview Handbook*, London, Sage, pp.321–36.

Goff, M. and Ackerman, P.L. (1992) 'Typical intellectual engagement', *Journal of Educational Psychology*, vol.84, no.4, pp.537–52.

Goffin, R.D., Rothstein, M.G. and Johnson, N.G. (1996) 'Personality testing and the assessment centre', *Journal of Applied Psychology*, vol.81, pp.746–56.

Goffman, E. (1959) *The Presentation of Self in Every Day Life*, Garden City, NJ, Doubleday.

Goldberg, L.R. (1992) 'The development of markers for the Big Five factor structure', *Psychological Assessment*, vol.4, pp.26–42.

Goldberg, L.R. and Kilowski, J.M. (1985) 'The prediction of semantic consistency in self-descriptions: Characteristics of persons and terms that affect the consistency of response to synonym and antonym pairs', *Journal of Personality and Social Psychology*, vol.48, pp.82–98.

Goldsmith, D.B. (1922) 'The use of a personal history blank as a salesmanship test', *Journal of Applied Psychology*, vol.6, pp.149–55.

Goldstein, I.L., Zedeck, S. and Schneider, B. (1993) 'An exploration of the job analysis-content validity process' in Schmitt, N. and Borman, W.C. (eds.), *Personnel Selection in Organisations*, San Francisco, CA, Jossey Bass, pp.3–34.

Goleman, D. (1996) *Emotional Intelligence*, London, Bloomsbury.

Gordon, R.A. (1997) 'Everyday life as an intelligence test: effects of intelligence, and intelligence context', *Intelligence*, vol.24, pp.203–30.

Graves, L.M. and Karren, R.J. (1999) 'Are some interviewers better than others?' in Eder, R.W. and Harris, M.M. (eds) *The Employment Interview Handbook*, pp.243–59, London, Sage.

Graves, L.M. and Powel, G.N. (1995) 'The effects of sex similarity on recruiters evaluations of actual applicants: A test of the similarity-attraction paradigm', *Personnel Psychology*, vol.48, pp.85–98.

Green, P.C., Alter, P. and Carr, A.E. (1993) 'Development of standard anchors for scoring generic past-behavior questions in structured interviews', *International Journal of Selection and Assessment*, vol.1, pp.203–12.

Guildford, J.P. (1956) 'The structure of intellect', *Psychological Bulletin*, vol.53, pp.267–93.

Guildford, J.P. (1959) 'Three facets of intellect', *American Psychologist*, vol.14, pp.469–79.

Guildford, J.P. (1959) 'Traits of creativity' in Anderson, H.H. (ed.) *Creativity and its Cultivation*, New York, Wiley.

Guildford, J.P. (1959) *Personality*, New York, McGraw-Hill.

Gustafsson, J.E. (1984) 'A unifying model for the structure of intellectual abilities', *Intelligence*, vol.8, pp.179–203.

Hackman, J.R. (1992) 'Group influences on individuals in organisations' in Dunnette, M.D. and Hough, L.M. (eds) *Handbook of Industrial and Organizational Psychology*, 2nd edn, vol.2, Palo Alto, CA, Consulting Psychologists Press.

Hakel, M.D., Dobmeyer, T.W. and Dunnette, M.D. (1970) 'Relative importance of three content dimensions in overall suitability ratings of job applicants' resumes', *Journal of Applied Psychology*, vol.54, pp.65–71.

Hambleton, R.K., Swaminathan, H. and Rogers, H.J. (1991) *Fundamentals of Item Response Theory*, London, Sage.

Hammer, E.G. and Kleinman, L.S. (1988) 'Getting to know you', *Personnel Administrator*, vol.34, pp.86–92.

Hampson, S.E. (1997) 'Determinants of inconsistent personality descriptions: Trait and target effect', *Journal of Personality*, vol.65, no.2, pp.249–90.

Hampson, S.E. (1998) 'When is an inconsistency not an inconsistency? Trait reconciliation in personality description and impression formation', *Journal of Personality and Social Psychology*, vol.74, no.1, pp.102–17.

Harris, M.M. (1998) 'Reconsidering the employment interview: a review of recent literature and suggestions for future research', *Personnel Psychology*, vol.42, pp.691–726.

Harris, M.M. (1998) 'The structured interview: what constructs are being measured?' in Eder, R. and Harris, M. (eds) *The Employment Interview: Theory, Research and Practice*, Thousand Oaks, CA, Sage Publications.

Harris, M.M. (1999) 'What is being measured?' in Eder, R.W. and Harris, M.M. (eds) *The Employment Interview Handbook*, London, Sage, pp.143–57.

Hartigan, J.A. and Wigdor, A.K. (1989) *Fairness in Employment Testing*, Washington, DC, National Academy Press.

Harvey, R.J. (1991) 'Job analysis' in Dunnette, M.D. and Hough, L.M. (eds) *Handbook of Industrial and Organizational Psychology*, 2nd edn, vol.2, Palo Alto, CA, Consulting Psychologists Press.

Harvey-Cook, J.E. and Taffler, R.J. (2000) 'Biodata in professional entry-level selection: statistical scoring of common format applications', *Journal of Occupational and Organizational Psychology*, vol.73, pp.103–18.

Hathaway, S.R. and McKinley, J.C. (1951) *The Minnesota Multiphasic Personality Inventory Manual*, New York, Psychological Corporation, revised.

Heilman, M.E. and Saruwatari, L.R. (1979) 'When beauty is beastly: The effects of appearance and sex on evaluations of job applicants for managerial and non-managerial jobs', *Organizational Behavior and Human Performance*, no.23, pp.360–72.

Heilman, M.E., Block, C.J. and Lucas, J.A. (1992) 'Presumed incompetent? Stigmatization and affirmative action efforts', *Journal of Applied Psychology*, vol.77, no.4, pp.536–44.

Heim, A. (1975) *Psychological Testing*, London, Oxford University Press.

Helms, J. (1992) 'Why is there no study of cultural equivalence in standardised cognitive ability testing?', *American Psychologist*, vol.47, no.9, pp.1083–101.

Hennessy, J., Mabey, B. and Warr, P. (1998) 'Assessment centre observation procedures: An experimental comparison of traditional checklist and coding methods', *International Journal of Selection and Assessment*, vol.6, no.4, pp.222–31.

Herriot, P. (1987) 'The selection interview' in Warr, P. (ed.) *Psychology at Work*, Harmondsworth, Penguin, pp.139–60.

Herriot, P. (1989) 'Selection as a social process' in Smith, M. and Robertson, I.T. (eds) *Advances in Selection and Assessment*, Chichester, Wiley, pp.171–87.

Herrnstein, R.J. and Murray, C. (1994) *The Bell Curve: Intelligence and Class Structure in American Life*, New York, Free Press.

Higgs, M. (2001) 'Book review of *Personality in the Workplace*', *Journal of General Management*, vol.26, no.3, pp.92–4.

Highhouse, S. (2002) 'Assessing the candidate as a whole: A historical and critical analysis of individual psychology assessment for personnel decision making', *Personnel Psychology*, vol.55, no.2, pp.363–97.

Highhouse, S. and Hoffman, J.R. (2001) 'Organisational attraction and job choice' in Cooper, C.L. and Robertson, I.T. (eds) *International Review of Industrial and Organisational Psychology*, vol.10, Chichester, Wiley, pp.36–64.

Hoffman, C.C. and Thornton, G.C. (1997) 'Examining selection utility where competing predictors differ in adverse impact', *Personnel Psychology*, vol.50, pp.455–70.

Hogan, J. and Rybicki, S.L. (1998) *Performance Improvement Characteristics Job Analysis*, Tulsa, OK, Hogan Assessment Systems.

Hogan, R. and Ones, D.S. (1997) 'Conscientiousness and integrity at work' in Hogan, R., Johnson, J. and Briggs, S. (eds) *Handbook of Personality Psychology*, San Diego, CA, Academic Press, pp.849–70.

Hogan, R.T. (1991) 'Personality and personality measurement' in Dunnette, M.D. and Hough, L.M. (eds) *Handbook of Industrial and Organisational Psychology*, 2nd edn, vol.2, Palo Alto, CA, Consulting Psychologist Press, pp.873–919.

Hogan, T.P. (2003) *Psychological Testing: A Practical Introduction*, New York, Wiley.

Holden, R.R., Wood, L.L. and Tomashewski, L. (2001) 'Do response time limitations counteract the effect of faking on personality inventory validity?', *Journal of Personality and Social Psychology*, vol.81, no.1, pp.160–9.

Hollway, W. (1991) *Work Psychology and Organisational Behaviour: Managing the Individual at Work*, London, Sage.

Hörman, H.L. and Mascke, P. (1996) 'On the relation between personality and job performance of airline pilots', *International Journal of Aviation Psychology*, vol.6, pp.171–8.

Horn, J.L. and Cattell, R.B. (1966) 'Refinement and test of the theory of fluid and crystallised general intelligences', *Journal of Educational Psychology*, vol.57, pp.235–70.

Horn, J.L. and Noll, J. (1994) 'A system for understanding cognitive capabilities: A theory and the evidence on which it is based' in Detterman, D. (ed.) *Current Topics in Human Intelligence. Vol.4. Theories in Intelligence,* Norwood, NJ, Ablex, pp.151–204.

Hough, L.M. (1992) 'The Big Five personality variables – construct confusion: Description versus prediction', *Human Performance,* vol.5, pp.139–55.

Hough, L.M. (1998) 'Effects of intentional distortion in personality measurement and evaluation of suggested palliatives', *Human Performance,* vol.11, pp.209–44.

Hough, L.M. and Oswald, F.L. (2000) 'Personnel selection: looking toward the future – remembering the past', *Annual Review of Psychology,* vol.51, pp.631–64.

Hough, L.M., Eaton, N.K., Dunnette, M.D., Kamp, J.D. and McCloy, R.A. (1990) 'Criterion-related validities of personality constructs and the effect of response distortion on those validities', *Journal of Applied Psychology,* vol.75, pp.581–95.

Howard, A. (1997) 'A reassessment of assessment centres, challenges for the 21st century', *Journal of Social Behavior and Personality,* vol.12, pp.13–52.

Huebert, J.P. and Hauser, R.M. (eds). (1999). *High stakes: Testing for tracking, promotion, and graduation,* Washington, DC, National Academy Press.

Huffcutt, A.I., Roth, P.L. and McDaniel, M.A. (1996) 'A meta-analytic investigation of cognitive ability employment interview evaluations: moderating characteristics and implications for incremental validity', *Journal of Applied Psychology,* vol.81, no.5, pp.459–73.

Huffcutt, A.I., Weekley, J.A., Wiesner, W.H., Groot, T.G. and Jones, C. (2001) 'Comparison of situational and behavioural description interview questions for higher-level positions', *Personnel Psychology,* vol.54, no.3, pp.619–54.

Hull, C.L. (1928) *Aptitude Testing,* London, Harrap.

Hunt, E. (1999) 'Intelligence and human resources: Past, present and future' in Ackerman, P.L., Kyllonen, P.C. and Roberts, R.D. (eds) *Learning and Individual Difference: Process, Trait and Content Determinants,* Washington, DC, American Psychological Association, pp.3–31.

Hunter, J.E. and Hirsh, H.R. (1987) 'Applications of meta-analysis' in Cooper, C.L. and Robertson, I.T. (eds) *International Review of Industrial and Organizational Psychology,* Chichester, Wiley, pp.321–57.

Hunter, J.E. and Hunter, R.F. (1984) 'Validity and utility of alternate predictors of job performance', *Psychological Bulletin,* vol.96, pp.72–98.

Hunter, J.R. and Schmidt, F.L. (1981) 'Fitting people into jobs: The impact of personnel selection on national productivity' in Dunnette, M.A. and Fleischman, E.A. (eds) *Human Performance and Productivity: Vol. 1 Human Capability Assessment,* Hillsdale, NJ, Erlbaum, pp.233–84.

Hunter, J.R. and Schmidt, F.L. (1983) 'Quantifying the effects of psychological interventions on employee job performance and work force productivity', *American Psychologist,* vol.38, pp.473–8.

Hunter, J.R. and Schmidt, F.L. (1990) *Methods of Meta-analysis: Correcting Error and Bias in Research Findings,* Newbury Park, CA, Sage.

Hunter, Schmidt, F.L. and Judiesch, M.K. (1990) 'Individual differences in output variability as a function of job complexity', *Journal of Applied Psychology*, vol.75, pp.28–42.

Hunter, J.R., Schmidt, F.L. and Rauschenberger, J.M. (1977) 'Fairness of psychological tests: Implications of four definitions for selection utility and minority hiring', *Journal of Applied Psychology*, vol.62, pp.245–60.

Hurtz, G.M. and Donovan, J.J. (2000) 'Personality and job performance: The big five revisited', *Journal of Applied Psychology*, vol.85, no.6, pp.869–79.

Iles, P. and Salaman, G. (1995) 'Recruitment, selection and assessment' in Storey, J. (ed.) *Human Resource Management: A Critical Text*, London, Routledge, pp.209–34.

Jablin, F.M. and McComb, K.B. (1984) 'The employment screening interview: An organizational assimilation and communication perspective' in Bostrom, R.N. (ed.) *Communication Yearbook 8,* Beverley Hill, CA, Sage, pp.137–63.

Jablin, F.M., Miller, V.D. and Sias, P.M. (1999) 'Communication and interaction processes' in Eder, R.W. and Harris, M.M. (eds) *The Employment Interview Handbook*, London, Sage, pp.297–30.

James, L. R., Demaree, R.G., Mulaik, S.A. and Ladd, R.T. (1992) 'Validity generalisation in the context of situational models', *Journal of Applied Psychology*, vol.77, pp.3–14.

James, O. (2002) *They f\*\*\* you up: How to Survive Family Life*, London, Bloomsbury.

Janis, I.L. (1972) *Victims of Group Think: A Psychological Study of Foreign Policy Decisions*, Boston, MA, Houghton Mifflin.

Jansen, P.G.W. and Stoop, B.A.M. (2001) 'The dynamics of assessment centre validity: Results of a seven-year study', *Journal of Applied Psychology*, vol.86, no.4, pp.741–53.

Janz, J.T. (1982) 'Initial comparisons of patterned behavior description interviewing versus unstructured interviews', *Journal of Applied Psychology*, vol.67, pp.557–80.

Janz, J.T., Hellervik, L. and Guilmore, D.C. (1986) *Behavior Description Interviewing: New, Accurate, Cost effective*, Newton, MA, Allyn and Bacon.

Jawahar, I.M. and Williams, C.R. (1997) 'Where all the children are above average: The performance appraisal purpose effect', *Personnel Psychology*, vol.50, pp.905–26.

Jencks, C. (1992) *Rethinking Social Policy: Race, poverty and the underclass*, Cambridge, MA, Harvard University Press.

Johnson, C.E., Wood, R. and Blinkhorn, S.F. (1988) 'Spuriouser and spuriouser: The use of ipsative personality tests', *Journal of Occupational Psychology*, vol.61, pp.153–62.

Jones, E.E. and Pittman, T.S. (1982) 'Toward a general theory of strategic self-presentation' in Suls, J. (ed.) *Psychological Perspectives on the Shelf*, vol.1, pp.231–62, Hillsdale, NJ, Lawrence Erlbaum.

Jones, L. and Fletcher, C. (2002) 'Self-assessment in a selection situation: an evaluation of different measurement approaches', *Journal of Occupational and Organizational Psychology*, vol.75, no.2, pp.145–62.

Jones, R.G. (1992) 'Construct validation of assessment centre final dimensions ratings: Definition and measurement issues', *Human Resource Management Review*, vol.2, pp.195–220.

Joyce, L.W., Thayer, P.W. and Pond, S.B. (1994) 'Managerial function: An alternative to traditional assessment centre dimensions?', *Personnel Psychology*, vol.47, pp.109–21.

Judge, T.A. (2000) 'The employment interview: A review of recent research and recommendations for future research', *Human Resource Management Review*, vol.10, no.4, pp.383–407.

Kacmar, K.M. and Hockwanter, W.A. (1995) 'The interview as a communication event: a field examination of demographic effects on interview outcome', *Journal of Business Communication*, vol.32, pp.207–32.

Kacmar, K.M., Delery, J.E. and Ferris, G.R. (1992) 'Differential effectiveness of applicant impression management tactics on employment interview decisions', *Journal of Applied Social Psychology*, no.22, pp.1250–72.

Kalin, R. and Rayko, D.S. (1978) 'Discrimination in evaluative judgements against foreign-accented job candidates', *Psychological Reports*, no.43, pp.1203–9.

Kamin, J.L. (1974) *The Science and Politics of IQ*, Harmondsworth, Penguin.

Kandola, R. (1995) 'Managing diversity: New broom or old hat' in Cooper, C.L. and Robertson, I.T. (eds) *International Review of Industrial and Organisational Psychology*, vol.10, Chichester, Wiley, p.3–35.

Kandola, R. and Fullerton, J. (1994) *Managing the Mosaic*, London, IPD.

Kanfer, R. and Ackerman, P. L. (1989) 'Motivation and cognitive abilities: An integrative/aptitude-treatment interaction approach to skill acquisition', *Journal of Applied Psychology*, vol.74, pp.657–90.

Kaplan, M.F. and Miller, C.E. (1987) 'Group decision making and normative versus informative influence: Effects of type of issue and assigned decision rule', *Journal of Personality and Social Psychology*, vol.53, pp.306–13.

Kaplan, R.M. and Saccuzzo, D.P. (2001) *Psychological Testing: Principle, Applications and Issues*, 5th edn, Belmont, CA, Wadsworth.

Karas, M. and West, J. (1999) 'Construct-oriented biodata development for a selection to a differentiated performance domain', *International Journal of Selection and Assessment*, vol.7, pp.86–96.

Kaufmann, J.R., Jex, S.M., Love, K.G. and Libkuman, T.M. (1993) 'The construct validity of assessment centre performance dimensions', *International Journal of Selection and Assessment*, vol.1, pp.213–23.

Kelly, G.A. (1954) *The Psychology of Personal Constructs Vols 1 and 2*, New York, Norton.

Kerr Brown Consulting (1992) 'Test exposure'. Paper presented at the annual conference of the BPS Division of Occupational Psychology, Cumbria.

Kirton, M.J. (1967) 'Some notes on the dynamics of resistance to change. The defender role' in Watson, G. (ed.) *Concepts for Social Change*, Washington, DC, National Training Laboratories.

Kleges, R.C., Klem, M.L., Hanson, C.L., Eck, L.H., Ernst, J., O'Laughlin, D., Garrot, A. and Rife, R. (1989) 'The effects of applicant's health status and qualifications on simulated hiring decisions', *Journal of Obesity*, vol.14, pp.527–35.

Klein, L. (1976) *A Social Scientist in Industry*, Aldershot, Gower.

Kleinmann, M. (1993) 'Are rating dimensions in assessment centres transparent for participants? Consequences for criterion and construct validity', *Journal of Applied Psychology*, vol.78, pp.988–93.

Kleinmann, M., Exler, C., Kuptsch, C. and Köller, O. (1995) *Zeitschrift für Arbeits- und Organisationpsychologie*, vol.39, pp.22–8.

Klimoski, R. and Brickner, M. (1987) 'Why do assessment centres work: The puzzle of assessment centre validity', *Personnel Psychology*, vol.40, pp.243–60.

Klimoski, R. and Strickland, W.J. (1977) 'Assessment centres: Valid or merely prescient?', *Personnel Journal*, vol.30, pp.353–61.

Klinch, D. (2002) 'Equivalence for computerised and traditional ability tests: Test fairness and construct validity'. Paper presented at The International Conference on Computer-based Testing and the Internet: Building Guidelines for Best Practice, Winchester.

Kline, P. (1993) *The Handbook of Psychological Testing*, London, Routledge.

Kline, P. (1998) *The New Psychometrics: Science, Psychology and Measurement*, London, Routledge.

Kluger and Rothstein (1993) 'The influence of selection test type of applicant reactions to employment testing', *Journal of Business and Psychology*, vol.8, pp.3–25.

Koczwara, A. and Silvester (2003) 'Hearing men and seeing women: Success in the selection interview'. Paper presented at the British Psychological Society Division of Occupational Psychology Conference, Bournemouth, January.

Krilowicz, T. and Lowery, C. (1996) 'Evaluation of personality measures for the selection of textile employees', *Journal of Business and Psychology*, vol.11, pp.55–61.

Kristof, A.L. (1996) 'Person–organization fit: An integrative review of item conceptualizations, measurement and implications', *Personnel Psychology*, vol.49, pp.1–49.

Krzystofiak, F., Newman, J.M. and Anderson, G. (1979) 'A quantified approach to measurement of job content: procedures and payoffs', *Personnel Psychology*, vol.32, pp.341–57.

Laming, D. (1997) 'A critique of a measurement-theoretical critique: Commentary on Michell "Quantitative science and the definition of measurement in psychology"', *British Journal of Psychology*, no.88, pp.389–91.

Lance, C.E., Newbolt, W.H., Gatewood, R.D. and Smith, D.E. (1995) 'Assessment centre exercise factors represent cross-situational specificity, not method bias'. Paper presented at the Annual Conference of the Society for Industrial and Organisational Psychology, Orlando, FL.

Landis, R.S., Fogli, L. and Goldberg, E. (1998) 'Future-oriented job analysis: a description of the process and its organizational implications', *International Journal of Selection and Assessment*, vol.6, no.3, pp.192–7.

Landy, F. (2000) 'Public policy and assessment: Which is the cart and which is the horse?'. Paper presented at the British Psychological Society Occupational Psychology Conference, Brighton, January.

Langdale, J.A. and Weitz, J. (1973) 'Estimating the influence of job information on interview agreement', *Journal of Applied Psychology*, vol.57, pp.23–7.

Latham, G.P. and Finnegan, B.J. (1993) 'Perceived practicality of structured, patterned, and situational interviews' in Schuler, H., Farr, J.L. and Smith, M. (eds) *Personnel Selection and Assessment: Individual and Organisational Perspectives*, Hillsdale, NJ, Lawrence Erlbaum, pp.41–55.

Latham, G.P. and Saari, L.M. (1984) 'Do people do what they say? further studies on the situational interview', *Journal of Applied Psychology*, vol.79, pp.599–616.

Latham, G.P., Saari, L.M., Pursell, E.D. and Campion, M.A. (1980) 'The situational interview', *Journal of Applied Psychology*, vol.65, pp.422–7.

Lecznar, W.B. and Dailey, J.T. (1950) 'Keying biographical inventories in classification test batteries', *American Psychologist*, no.5, p.279

Ledvinka, J. (1971) 'Race of interviewer and the language elaboration of black interviewees', *Journal of Social Issues*, vol.27, pp.185–97.

Legge, K. (1995) *Human Resource Management: Rhetorics and Realities*, London, Macmillian Business Press.

Lerner, J.S. and Tetlick, T.E. (1998) 'Accounting for the effects of accountability', *Psychological Bulletin*, vol.125, pp.225–75.

Lichtenstein, M. and Srull, T.K. (1987) 'Processing objectives as a determinant of the relationship between recall and judgement', *Journal of Experimental Social Psychology*, vol.23, pp.93–118.

Liden, R.C., Wayne, S.J. and Stilwell, D. (1993) 'A longitudinal study on the early development of leader-member exchanges', *Journal of Applied Psychology*, vol.78, pp.662–74.

Lievens, F. (2001a) 'Assessors' training strategies and their effects on accuracy, interrater reliability and discriminate validity', *Journal of Applied Psychology*, vol.86, no.2, pp.255–64.

Lievens, F. (2001b) 'Assessors and the use of assessment centre dimensions: A fresh look at a troubling issue', *Journal of Organizational Behavior*, vol.22, no.3, pp.203–21.

Lievens, F. and Harris, M.M. (2003) 'Research on Internet Recruitment and Testing: Current Status and Future Directions' in Robertson, I. and Cooper, C. (eds) *The International Review of Industrial and Organizational Psychology*, Chichester, Wiley.

Lievens, F. and Klimoski, R.J. (2001) 'Understanding the assessment centre process: where are we now?' in Cooper, C.L. and Robertson, I.T. (eds) *International Review of Industrial and Organisational Psychology*, vol.16, Chichester, Wiley, ch.8.

Lin, T.R, Dobbins, G.H. and Farh, J.L. (1992) 'A field study of race and age similarity effects in interview ratings in conventional and situational interviews', *Journal of Applied Psychology*, no.77, pp.363–71.

Lopez, F.M. (1966) *Evaluating Executive Decision Making: The In-basket Technique*, New York, American Management Association.

Lowry, P.E. (1993) 'The assessment centre: An examination of the effects of assessor characteristics on assessor scores', *Public Personnel Management*, vol.22, pp.487–501.

Madden, J.M. (1962) 'The effect of varying the degree of rater familiarity in job evaluation', *Personnel Administrator*, vol.25, pp.42–6.

Mael, F.A. (1991) 'A conceptual rational for the domain and attributes of biodata items', *Personnel Psychology*, vol.44, pp.736–92.

Mahar, D., Cologon, J. and Duck, J. (1995) 'Response strategies when faking personality questionnaires in a vocational selection setting', *Personality and Individual differences*, vol.18, pp.605–9.

Maher, P.T. (1990) 'How many dimensions are enough?'. Paper presented at the International Congress on the Assessment Centre Method, Orange, CA.

Maher, P.T. (1995). 'An Analysis of the Impact of the Length of Assessor Training on Assessor Competency', Paper presented at the International Congress on the Assessment Centre Method, Kansas City, MO.

Mains-Smith, N.E. and Abram, C.M. (2000) *Evaluation of Item Bias and Test-taking Attitudes concerning the Royal Navy Recruitment Test*, DERA/CHS/CR00547/1.0.

Marchese, M.C. and Machinsky, P.M. (1993) 'The validity of the employment interview: A meta-analysis', *International Review of Selection and Assessment*, no.1, pp.18–26.

Martin, B.A., Bowen, C.C. and Hunt, S.T. (2002) 'How effective are people at faking on personality questionnaires?', *Personality and Individual differences*, vol.32, pp.247–56.

Maurer, S.D. and Lee, T.W. (1994) 'Towards a resolution of contrast error in the employment interview: A test of the situational interview' in Moore, D.P. (ed.) *Best Paper Proceedings: Academy of Management*, Madison, WI, Omnipress, pp.132–6.

Maurer, T.J., Solamon, J.M., Andrews, K.D. and Troxtel, D.D. (2001) 'Interviewee coaching, preparation strategies and response strategies in relation to performance in situational; employment interviews: an extension of Maurer, Solamon and Troxtel (1998)', *Journal of Applied Psychology*, vol.86, no.4, pp.709–17.

Mayes, B.T., Belloli, C.A., Riggio, R.E. and Aguirre, M. (1997) 'Assessment centres for course evaluations: A demonstration', *Journal of Social Behavior and Personality*, vol.12, pp.303–20.

McComb, K.B. and Jablin, F.M. (1984) 'Verbal correlates of interviewer empathic listening and employment interview outcomes', *Communications Monographs*, vol.51, pp.353–71.

McCormick, E.J., Jeanneret, P.R. and Mecham, R.C. (1972) 'A study of job characteristics and job dimensions as based on the position analysis questionnaire (PAQ)', *Journal of Applied Psychology*, vol.56, pp.347–68.

McCrea, R.R. and Costa, P. T. (1997) 'Personality trait structure as a human universal', *American Psychologist*, vol.52, no.5, pp.509–16.

McDaniel, M.A., Whetzel, D.L., Schmidt, F.L. and Maurer, S.D. (1994) 'The validity of employment interviews: A comprehensive review and meta-analysis', *Journal of Applied Psychology*, vol.79, no.4, pp.599–616.

McDaniel, M.A., Finnegan, E.B., Morgeson, F.P., Campion, M.A. and Braverman, E.P. (1997) 'Predicting job performance from common sense'. Paper presented at the 12th Annual Conference of the Society for Industrial and Organizational Psychology, St Louis, MO, April.

McDaniel, M.A., Morgeson, F.P., Finnegan, E.B., Campion, M.A. and Braverman, E.P. (2001) 'Use of situational judgement tests to predict job performance: A clarification of the literature', *Journal of Applied Psychology*, vol.86, no.4, pp.730–40.

McDaniel, M.A. and Nguyen, N.T. (2001) 'Situational judgement tests: A review of practice and constructs assessed', *International Journal of Selection and Assessment*, vol.9, pp.103–13.

McDaniel, M.A., Finnegan, E.B., Morgeson, F.P., Campion, M.A. and Braverman, E.P. (2001) 'Use of situational judgement tests to predict job performance: A clarification of the literature', *Journal of Applied Psychology*, vol.86, no.4, pp.730–40.

McDougall, W. (1932) 'Of the words character and personality', *Character Personality*, vol.1, pp.3–16.

McGrath, J.E. (1984) *Groups: Interaction and Performance*, Englewood Cliffs, NJ, Prentice Hall.

Michell, J. (1997) 'Quantitative science and the definition of measurement in psychology', *British Journal of Psychology*, vol.88, pp.389–91.

Miles, A., Keeley, S., Newcombe, I. and Williams, R. (2003) 'On-line testing: Is cheating a problem?'. Paper presented at the British Psychological Society Division of Occupational Psychology Conference, Bournemouth, January.

Milkowich, G.T., and Bourdreau, J.W. (1994) '"Reference checking gets creative', *Personnel Journal Supplement*, August, pp.22–4.

Miller, D.T. and Ross. M. (1975) 'Self-serving bias in the attribution of causality: fact or fiction', *Psychological Bulletin*, vol.82, pp.213–25.

Minnesota Multiphasic Personality Inventory (MMPI) (see Hathaway and McKinley, 1951).

Mischel, W. (1969) *Personality and Assessment*, New York, Wiley.

Mitchell, T.W. and Klimoski, R.J. (1982) 'Is it rational or empirical? A test of methods for scoring biographical data', *Journal of Applied Psychology*, vol.67, pp.411–8.

Morgeson, F.P. and Campion, M.A. (1997) 'Social and cognitive sources of potential inaccuracy in job analysis', *Journal of Applied Psychology*, vol.82, no.5, pp.627–55.

Mosel, J.N. (1952) 'Prediction of department stores sales performance from personal data', *Journal of Applied Psychology*, vol.36, pp.8–10.

Motowidlo, S.L. (1999) 'Asking about past behaviour versus hypothetical behaviour' in Eder, R.W. and Harris, M.M. (eds) *The Employment Interview Handbook*, London, Sage, pp.179–90.

Motowidlo, S.J., Dunnette, M.D. and Carter, G.W. (1990) 'An alternative selection procedure: The low-fidelity simulation', *Journal of Applied Psychology*, vol.75, pp.640–7.

Motowidlo, S.J., Hanson, M.A. and Crafts, J.L. (1997) 'Low-fidelity simulations' in Whetzel, D.L. and Wheaton, G.R. (eds) *Applied Measurement Methods in Industrial Psychology*, Palo Alto, CA, Davies-Black.

Mount, M.K., Barrick, M.R. and Strauss, J.P. (1994) 'Validity of observer ratings of the big five personality factors', *Journal of Applied Psychology*, vol.79, no.2, pp.272–80.

Mount, M.K., Witt, L.A. and Barrick, M.R. (2000) 'Incremental validity of empirically keyed Biodata scales over GMA and the five factor personality constructs', *Personnel Psychology*, vol.53, pp.299–323.

Moynihan, L.M. and Peterson, R.S. (2001) 'A contingent configuration approach to understanding the role of personality in organisational groups', *Research in Organisational Research*, vol.23, pp.327–78.

Mumford, M.D. and Owens, W.A. (1987) 'Methodology review: principles, procedure and findings in the application of background data measures', *Applied Psychology Measures*, vol.11, pp.1–31.

Murphy, K.R. (1989) 'Is the relationship between cognitive ability and job performance stable over time?', *Human Performance*, vol.2, pp.183–200.

Murphy, K.R. (1994) 'Advances in meta-analysis and validity generalisation' in Anderson, N.R. and Herriot, P. (eds.), *International Handbook of Selection and Appraisal*, 2nd edn, Chichester, Wiley, pp.322–42.

Murphy, K.R. (2000) 'Impact of assessments of validity generalisation and situational specifically on the science and practice of personnel selection', *International Journal of Selection and Assessment*, vol.8, pp.194–215.

Myers Briggs Type Indicator™, Palo Alto, CA, Consulting Psychologist Press.

Myers, C.S. (1911) 'The pitfalls of mental testing', *British Medical Journal*, January, pp.195–6.

Neidig, R.D. and Neidig, P.J. (1984) 'Multiple assessment centre exercises and job relatedness', *Journal of Applied Psychology*, vol.69, pp.182–6.

Newell, S. (2000) 'Selection and assessment in the Knowledge Era', *International Journal of Selection and Assessment*, vol.8, pp.1–6.

Newell, S. and Shackleton, V. (2001) 'Selection and assessment as an interactive decision-action process' in Redman, T. and Wilkinson, A. (eds) *Contemporary HRM: Texts and Cases*, London, Prentice Hall, pp.24–44.

Newell, S. and Tansley, C. (2001) 'International uses of selection methods' in Cooper, C.L. and Robertson, I.T. (eds) *International Review of Industrial and Organisational Psychology*, vol.16, Chichester, Wiley, pp.195–213.

Nicholson, N. (1996) 'Towards a new agenda for work and personality', *Applied Psychology: An International Review*, vol.45, pp.189–215.

Nilsen, D. and Campbell, D.P. (1993) 'Self-observer rating discrepancies: Once an overrater, always an overrater?', *Human Resource Management*, vol.32, nos.2–3, pp.265–81.

Norman, W.T. (1963) 'Towards an adequate taxonomy of personality attributes. Replicated factor structure in peer nominated personality ratings', *Journal of Abnormal and Social Psychology*, vol.66, pp.574–83.

Nowack, K.M. (1997) 'Congruence between self-other ratings and assessment centre performance', *Journal of Social Behavior and Personality*, vol.12, pp.145–66.

Nunnally, J.O. (1978) *Psychometric Theory*, New York, McGraw-Hill.

Nunnally, J.O. and Bernstein, A. (1994) *Psychometric Theory*, New York, McGraw-Hill.

Nyfield *et al.* (1992), as cited in the *Occupational Personality Questionnaire Manual*, SHL Ltd, Surrey, Thames Ditton.

Olea, M.M. and Ree, M.J. (1994) 'Predicting pilot and navigator criteria: not much more than g', *Journal of Applied Psychology*, vol.79, pp.845–51.

Ones, D.S. and Anderson, N. (2002) 'Gender and ethnic group differences on personality scales in selection: Some British data', *Journal of Occupational and Organizational Psychology*, vol.75, no.3, pp.255–77.

Ones, D.S. and Visweveran, C. (1996) 'What do pre-employment customer service scales measure? Explorations in construct validity and implications for personnel selection'. Paper presented at Annual Meeting Society Industrial and Organizational Psychology, San Diego, CA.

Owen, W.A. (1976) 'Background data' in Dunnette, M.D. (ed.) *Handbook of Organisational Psychology*, Chicago, IL, Rand McNally.

Palmer, D.K., Campion, M.A. and Green, P.C. (1999) 'Interviewing training for both applicant and interviewer' in Eder, R.W. and Harris, M.M. (eds) *The Employment Interview Handbook*, London, Sage, pp.337–51.

Park's Guide (1999) *Graduates in the Eyes of Employers*, London, Park HR and The Guardian.

Parsons, C.K., Cable, D.M. and Liden, R.C. (1999) 'Establishing person–organisation fit' in Eder, R.W. and Harris, M.M. (eds) *The Employment Interview Handbook*, London, Sage, pp.125–41.

Patterson, F.C. (2000) *The Team Potential Indicator Manual*, Oxford, Oxford Psychologist Press.

Patterson, M., West, M.A., Lawthom, R. and Nickell, S. (1997) *Impact of People Management Practices on Business Performance*, London, Institute of Personnel and Development, Issues in People Management.

Paunonen, S.V. and Ashton, M.C. (2001) 'Big five factors and facets and the prediction of behaviour', *Journal of Personality and Social Psychology*, vol.81, no.3, pp.524–39.

Peabody, D. (1967) 'Trait inferences: Evaluation and descriptive aspects', *Journal of Personality and Social Psychology Monographs*, vol.7, no.4 (whole no. 644).

Pearn, M. and Kandola, R. (1993) *Job Analysis: A Manager's Guide*, London, Institute of Personnel Management.

Pervin, L.A. (2002) *Current Controversies and Issues in Personality*, 3rd edn, New York, Wiley.

Peters, L.H. and Terbury, J.R. (1975) 'The effects of temporal placement of unfavourable information and of attitude similarity on personnel decision making', *Organizational Behaviour and Human Performance*, vol.13, pp.279–93.

Peterson, N.G., Mumford, M.D., Borman, W.C., Jeanneret, P.R. and Fleishman, E.A. (1999) *An Occupational Information System for the 21st Century: the Development of O\*NET*, Washington, DC, American Psychological Association.

Pingitore, R., Dugoni, B.L., Tindale, R.S., and Spring, B. (1994) 'Bias against overweight job applicants in a simulated employment interview', *Journal of Applied Psychology*, no.79, pp.909–17.

Prewett-Livingstone, A.M. and Field, H.S. (1999) 'The employment interview and race: a review' in Memon, A. and Bull, R. (eds) *Handbook of the Psychology of Interviewing*, Chichester, Wiley, pp.239–52.

Price, R. and Patterson, F. (2003 forthcoming) *On-line Application Forms: Psychological Impact on Applicants and Implications for Recruiter. Selection and Development Review*.

Prien, E.P. and Saleh, S.D. (1963) 'A study of bias in job analysis and evaluation', *Journal of Industrial Psychology*, vol.1, pp.113–7.

Pulakos, E.D. and Schmitt, N. (1995) 'Experienced-based and situational interview questions', *Studies of Validity*, vol.48, pp.289–303.

Pulakos, E.D. and Schmitt, N. (1996) 'An evaluation of two strategies for reducing adverse impact and their effect on criterion-related validity', *Human Performance*, vol.9, pp.241–58.

Purcell, J. (1989) 'The impact of corporate strategy on human resource management' in Storey, J. (ed.) *New Perspectives on Human Resource Management*, London, Routledge, pp.67–91.

Quinones, M.A., Ford, J.K. and Teachout, M.S. (1995) 'The relationship between work experience and job performance: A conceptual and meta-analytic review', *Personnel Psychology*, vol.48, pp.887–910.

Raven, J.C. (1965) *Advanced Progressive Matrices: Sets I and II*, London, H.K. Lewis.

Raymark, P.H., Schmit, M.J. and Guion, R.M. (1997) 'Identifying potentially useful personality constructs for employees' selection', *Personnel Psychology*, vol.50, pp.723–36.

Ree, M.J. and Carretta, T.R. (1994) 'The correlation of general cognitive ability and psychomotor tracking tests', *International Journal of Selection and Assessment,* vol.2, pp.209–16.

Ree, M.J., Earles, J.A. and Teachout, M.S. (1994) 'Predicting job performance: not much more than g', *Journal of Applied Psychology*, vol.79, pp.518–24.

Reed Executive PLC. (25 March 2002) http://www.reed.co.uk/ www.milkround.com *Paper Prejudice hits Job Seekers*, available from http:// cws.huginonline.com/R/132089/PR/200203/853957_10.html (accessed 14 May 2002).

Reilly, R. and Israelski, E.W. (1988) 'Development and validation of minicourses in the telecommunications industry', *Journal of Applied Psychology*, vol.73, pp.721–6.

Reilly, R., Henry, S. and Smither, J. (1990) 'An examination of the effects of using behaviour checklists on the construct validity of assessment centre dimensions', *Personnel Psychology*, vol.43, pp.71–84.

Reilly, R.R. and Chao, G.T. (1982) 'Validity and fairness for some alternative employee selection procedure', *Personnel Psychology*, vol.35, pp.1–62.

Robertson, I.T. (1994) 'Personality and personnel selection' in Cooper, C.L. and Rosseau, D.M. (eds) *Trends in Organisational Behaviour*, vol.1, Chichester, Wiley, pp.75–89.

Robertson, I.T. and Kinder, A. (1993) 'Personality and job competences: the criterion-related validity of some personality variables', *Journal of Occupational and Organizational Psychology*, vol.66, pp.225–44.

Robertson, I.T., Baron, H., Gibbons, P., MacIver, R. and Nyfield, G. (2000) 'Conscientiousness and managerial performance', *Journal of Occupational and Organizational Psychology*, vol.73, pp.171–80.

Robertson, I.T. and Downs, (1989) 'Work sample tests of trainability. A meta-analysis', *Journal of Applied Psychology*, vol.74, no.1 pp.402–10.

Robertson, I.T. and Kandola, R.S. (1982) 'Work sample tests: Validity, adverse impact and applicant reaction', *Journal of Occupational Psychology*, vol.55, pp.171–83.

Robertson, I.T. and Makin, P. (1985) 'Management selection in Britain: A survey and critique', *Journal of Occupational Psychology*, vol.59, pp.45–57.

Robertson, I.T. and Smith, M. (2001) 'Personnel Selection', *Journal of Occupational and Organizational Psychology*, vol.74, no.4, pp.441–72.

Robertson, I.T., Gratton, L. and Stukts, D. (1987) 'The psychometric properties of managerial assessment centres: dimension into exercises won't go', *Journal of Occupational Psychology*, vol.60, pp.187–95.

Robertson, I.T., Iles, P.A., Gratton, L. and Sharpley, D. (1991) 'The impact of personnel selection and assessment methods on candidates', *Human Relations*, vol.44, pp.963–82.

Robertson, L. and Block, C.J. (2001) 'Racioethnicity and job performance: a review and critique of theoretical perspectives on the causes of group differences', *Research in Organisational Behaviour*, vol.23, pp.247–325.

Rolland, J.P. and Mogenet, J.L. (1994) *Manuel d'application.Systeme D5D d'aide à l'évaluation des personnes*, Paris, Les Editiones du Centre de Psychologie Applique.

Rose, M. (1975) *Industrial Behaviour: Theoretical Development since Taylor*, Harmondsworth, Penguin.

Rose, N. (1985) *The Psychological Complex: Psychology, Politics and Society in England 1969–1939*, London, Routledge.

Rose, N. (1989) *Governing the Soul: The Shaping of the Private Self*, London, Routledge.

Roth, P.L. and Bobko, P. (2000) 'College grade point average as a personnel selection device: Ethnic group difference and potential adverse impact', *Journal of Applied Psychology*, vol.85, no.3, pp.339–406.

Rothstein, H.R., Schmidt, F.L., Erwin, F.W., Owens, W.A. and Sparks, C.P. (1990) 'Biographical data in employment selection: Can validities be generalizable?', *Journal of Applied Psychology*, vol.75, no.7, pp.175–84.

Rousseau, D.M. (2001) 'Schema, promise and mutuality: The building blocks of the psychological contract', *Journal of Occupational and Organizational Psychology*, vol.74, no.4, pp.511–42.

Russell, C.J. (1985) 'Individual decision processes in an assessment centre', *Journal of Applied Psychology*, vol.70, pp.737–46.

Rust, J. and Golombok, S. (1989) *Modern Psychometrics: The Science of Psychological Assessment*, London, Routledge.

Ryan A., Ployhart, R. and Friedel L. (1998) 'Using personality testing to reduce adverse impact: A cautionary note', *Journal of Applied Psychology*, vol.83, pp.298–307.

Ryan, A.M., McFarland, L., Bacon, H. and Page, R. (1999) An international look at selection practices: Nation and culture as explanations for variability in practice', *Personnel Psychology*, vol.52, no.2, pp.359–91.

Saal, F.E., Downey, R.G. and Lahey, M.A. (1980) 'Rating the ratings: Assessing the psychometric quality of rating data', *Psychological Bulletin*, vol.88, pp.413–28.

Sackett, P.R. and Dreher, G.F. (1982) 'Constructs and assessment centre dimensions: Some troubling empirical findings', *Journal of Applied Psychology*, vol.67, pp.401–10.

Sackett, P.R. and Hakel, M.D. (1979) 'Temporal stability and individual differences in using assessment information to form overall ratings', *Organizational Behavior and Human Performance*, vol.23, pp.120–37.

Salgado, J. F. and Moscoso, S. (2000) 'Construct validity of employment interview. Under review', cited in Moscoso, S. (2000) 'Selection interview: a review of validity evidence, adverse impact and applicant reactions', *International Journal of Selection and Assessment*, no.8, pp.237–47.

Salgado, J.F. (1997) 'The five factor model of personality and job performance in the European Community', *Journal of Applied Psychology*, vol.82, pp.30–43.

Salgado, J.F. (1999) 'Personnel selection methods' in Cooper, C.L. and Robertson, I.T. (eds) *International Review of Industrial & Organizational Psychology*, New York, Wiley.

Sanchez, J.I. (2000) 'Adapting work analysis to a fast-paced and electronic business world', *International Journal of Selection and Assessment*, vol.8, pp.207–15.

Sanchez, J.I. and Fraser, S.L. (1992) 'On the choice of scales in task analysis', *Journal of Applied Psychology*, vol.77, no.4, pp.454–553.

Sanchez, J.I. and Levine, E.L. (1999) 'The impact of raters' cognition on judgement accuracy: An extension to the job analysis domain', *Journal of Business and Psychology*, vol.9, pp.309–25.

Sandberg, J. (2000) 'Understanding human competence at work: An interpretative approach', *The Academy of Management Journal*, vol.43, no.1, pp.9–26.

Saville, P. and Wilson, E. (1991) 'The reliability and validity of normative and ipsative approaches in the measurement of personality', *Journal of Occupational Psychology*, vol.64, pp.219–38.

Schein, E.H. (1980) *Organisational Psychology*, 3rd edn, Englewood Cliffs, NJ, Prentice Hall.

Schippmann, J.S., Prien, E.P. and Katz, J.A. (1990) 'Reliability and validity of in-basket performance measures', *Personnel Psychology*, vol.43, pp.837–59.

Schlenker, B.R. and Weigold, M.F. (1990) 'Self-consciousness and self-presentation: Being autonomous versus appearing autonomous', *Journal of Personality and Social Psychology*, vol.59, pp.820–8.

Schmidt, F.L. (1988) 'The problems of group difference in ability test scores in employment selection', *Journal of Vocational Behaviour*, vol.33, pp.272–92.

Schmidt, F.L. (1992) 'What do data really mean? Research findings, meta-analysis and cumulative knowledge in psychology', *American Psychologist*, vol.47, pp.1173–81.

Schmidt, F.L. (1994) 'The future of personnel selection in the US army' in Rumsey, M.G., Walker, C.B. and J.H. Harris (eds) *Personnel Selection and Classification*, Hillsdale, NJ, Erlbaum.

Schmidt, F.L. and Hunter, J.E. (1996) 'Measurement error in psychological research: Lessons from 26 research scenarios', *Psychological Methods,* vol.1, pp.199–223.

Schmidt, F.L. and Hunter, J.E. (1998) 'The validity and utility of selection methods in personnel psychology: practical and theoretical implications of 85 years of research findings', *Psychological Bulletin*, vol.124, pp.262–74.

Schmidt, F.L. and Hunter, J.E. (1999) 'Theory testing and measurement error', *Intelligence*, vol.27, pp.183–98.

Schmidt, F.L. and Rader, M. (1999) 'Exploring the boundary conditions for interview validity: meta-analytic findings for a new interview type', *Personnel Psychology*, vol.52, no.2, pp.445–65.

Schmidt, F.L., Hunter, J.E., McKenzie, R.C. and Muldrow, T. W. (1979) 'Impact of valid selection procedures on work-force productivity', *Journal of Applied Psychology*, vol.64, pp.609–26.

Schmidt, F.L., Ones, D.S. and Hunter, J.E. (1992) 'Personnel Selection', *Annual Review of Psychology*, vol.43, pp.671–710.

Schmidt, F.L., Viswesvaran, C. and Ones, D.S. (2000) 'Reliability is not validity and validity is not reliability', *Personnel Psychology*, vol.53, no.4, pp.901–3.

Schmitt, N. (1993) 'Group compositions, gender and race effects on assessment centre ratings' in Schuler, H., Farr, J.L. and Smith, M. (eds) *Personnel Selection and Assessment: Individual and Organisational Perspectives*, Hillsdale, NJ, Erlbaum, pp.315–32.

Schmitt, N. and Chan, D. (1998) *Personnel Selection: a Theoretical Approach*, Thousand Oaks, CA, Sage Publications.

Schmitt, N. and Mills, A.E. (2001) 'Traditional tests and job simulations: minority and majority performance and test validities', *Journal of Applied Psychology*, vol.86, no.3, pp.451–8.

Schmitt, N., Clause, C. and Pulakos, E. (1996) 'Subgroup differences associated with different measures of some common job relevant constructs' in Cooper, C. and Robertson, I. (eds) *International Review of Industrial and Organizational Psychology*, New York, Wiley, pp.115–40.

Schmitt, N., Ford, J.K. and Stulzt, D.M. (1986) 'Changes in the self-perceived ability as a function of performance in an assessment centre', *Journal of Occupational Psychology*, vol.59, pp.327–35.

Schmitt, N., Gooding, R.Z., Noe, R.A. and Kirsch, M. (1984) 'Meta-analysis of validity studies published between 1964 and 1982 and the investigation of study characteristics', *Personnel Psychology*, vol.37, pp.407–22.

Schneider, B. (1987) 'The people make the place', *Personnel Psychology*, vol.40, no.3, pp.437–53.

Schneider, B. and Kinz, A.M. (1989) 'Strategic job analysis', *Human Resource Management*, vol.28, pp.51–63.

Schneider, J. (1991) 'Look to the future: Generating information about jobs and job requirements to meet future organisational needs'. Presented at the 6th Annual Conference of the Society for Industrial and Organizational Psychologists, St Louis, MO.

Schneider, J.R. and Schmidt, N. (1992) 'An exercise design approach to understanding assessment centre dimensions and exercise constructs', *Journal of Applied Psychology*, vol.77, pp.32–41.

Schneider, R.J., Hough, L.M. and Dunnette, M.D. (1996) 'Broadsided by broad traits, or how to sink science in five dimensions or less', *Journal of Organizational Behavior*, vol.17, pp.639–55.

Scholz, G. and Schuler, H. (1993) 'The nomological network of the assessment centre: A meta-analysis' [in German], *Zeitschrift für Arbeits- und Organisationpsychologie*, vol.37, pp.73–85.

Schultz, William C. (1978) *The Firo Scales: Firo-B*, Palto Alto, CA, Consulting Psychologists Press.

Searle, R.H. and Ball, K.S. (forthcoming) 'Strategy, human resource policy and innovation practice: Evidence from the UK', *Journal of Creativity and Innovation Management*.

Searle, R.H. and Stern, P. (2003) 'Team composition and performance', European Association of Work and Organisational Psychology Conference, May, Portugal.

Searle. R.H. (2003) 'Organizational justice in E-recruiting: issues and controversies', *Surveillance and Society*, vol.1, no.2, pp.227–31.

Shackleton, V. and Newell, S. (1991) 'Management selection: A comparative study survey of methods used in top British and French companies', *Journal of Occupational and Organisational Psychology*, vol.64, pp.23–36.

Shackleton, V. and Newell, S. (1994) 'European management selection methods: A comparison of five countries', *International Journal of Selection and Assessment*. vol.2, pp.91–102.

Shackleton, V. and Newell, S. (1997) 'International assessment and selection' in Anderson, N. and Herriot, P. (eds) *International Handbook of Selection and Assessment*, Chichester, Wiley.

Shafer, E.W.P. (1982) 'Neural adaptability: a biological determinant of behavioural intelligence', *International Journal of Neuroscience*, vol.17, pp.183–91.

Shafer, E.W.P. (1985) 'Neural adaptability: a biological determinant of g factor intelligence', *Behavioural and Brain Sciences*, vol.8, pp.240–1.

Shahani, C., Dipboye, R.L. and Gehrlein, T.M. (1991) 'The incremental validity of an interview to college admissions', *Educational and Psychological Measurement*, vol.51, pp.1049–61.

Sharf, J. (2000) 'As if "g-loaded" adverse impact isn't bad enough, Internet recruiters can expect to be accused of "e-loaded" impact', *The Industrial-Organizational Psychologist*, vol.38, p.156.

Shaw, L. and Sichel, H. (1970) *Accident Proneness*, Oxford, Pergamon.

Shaw, M.R. (1983) 'Taken-for-granted assumptions of applicants in simulated selection interviews', *Western Journal of Speech Communication*, vol.47, pp.138–56.

SHL (1989) *Occupational Personality Questionnaire – OPQ32 Manual and User's Guide*, Thames Ditton, SHL Group.

SHL (1990) *The Work Profiling System – Manual and User Guide*, Thames Ditton, SHL Group.

Shoda, Y., Mischel, W. and Wright, J.C. (1994) 'Intraindividual stability in the organisation and patterning of behaviour: Incorporating psychological situations into the idiographic analysis of personality', *Journal of Personality and Social Psychology*, vol.67, pp.674–87.

Shore, T.H. (1992) 'Subtle gender bias in the assessment of managerial potential', *Sex Roles*, vol.27, pp.499–515.

Siegel, A.I. and Bergman, B.A. (1975) 'A job learning approach to performance prediction', *Personnel Psychology*, vol.28, pp.352–9.

Silvester, J. (1997) 'Spoken attributions and candidate success in the graduate recruitment interview', *Journal of Occupational and Organizational Psychology*, vol.70, pp.61–73.

Silvester, J., Anderson, N.R., Gibb, A., Haddleton, E. and Cunningham-Snell, N. (2000) 'A cross-modal comparison of the predictive validity of telephone and face-to-face selection interviews', *International Journal of Selection and Assessment*, vol.8, pp.16–21.

Silvester, J., Mohammed, A., Anderson-Gough, F.M. and Anderson, N.R. (2002) 'Locus of control and impression management in the selection interview', *Journal of Occupational and Organizational Psychology*, vol.75, no.1, pp.59–77.

Silvester, J., Patterson, F. and Ferguson, E. (2003) 'Attributional style as a predictor of customer care and sales performance in retail sales assistants', *Journal of Occupational and Organizational Psychology*, p.76.

Simon, H.A. (1960) *The New Science of Management Decisions*, New York, Harper and Row.

Smith, B.N., Hornsby, J.S., Benson, P.G. and Wesolowski, M. (1989) 'What is in a name? The impact of job titles on job evaluation results', *Journal of Business and Psychology*, vol.3, pp.341–51.

Smith, C., Organ, D. and Near, J. (1983) 'Organizational citizenship behavior: Its nature and antecedents', *Journal of Applied Psychology*, vol.68, pp.653–63.

Smith, F. (1991) 'Work sample testing' in Wigdor, A.K. and Green, B.F. (eds) *Performance Assessment for the Workplace*, Washington, DC, National Academy Press.

Smith, J.E. and Hakel, M.D. (1979) 'Convergence among data sources, response bias, and reliability and validity of a structured job analysis questionnaire', *Personnel Psychology*, vol.32, pp.677–92.

Smith, M. (1994) 'A theory of the validity of predictors in selection', *Journal of Occupational and Organizational Psychology*, vol.67, pp.13–31.

Snyder, M. (1974) 'Self-monitoring of expressive behavior', *Journal of Social Behavior and Personality,* vol.30, pp.526–37.

Spearman, C. (1904) '"General intelligence", objectively determined and measured', *American Journal of Psychology*, vol.15, pp.210–93.

Spearman, C. (1923) *The Nature of 'Intelligence' and the Principles of Cognition*, London, Macmillan.

Spearman, C. (1927) *The Abilities of Man*, London, Macmillan.

Spencer, L.M. and Spencer, S.M. (1993) *Competence at Work: Models for Superior Performance*, New York, Wiley.

Springbett, B.M. (1958) 'Factors affecting the final decision in the employment interview', *Canadian Journal of Psychology*, vol.12, pp.13–22.

Spychalski, A.C., Quinones, M.A., Gaughler, B.B. and Pohley, K.A. (1997) 'A survey of assessment centre practices in organisations in the United States', *Personnel Psychology*, vol.50, pp.71–90.

Stammers, R.B. and Patrick, J. (1975) *The Psychology of Training*, London, Methuen.

Stark, S., Chernyshenko, O.S., Chan, K., Lee, W.C. and Drasgow, F. (2001) 'Effects of the testing situation on item responding: cause for concern', *Journal of Applied Psychology*, vol.86, no.5, pp.943–53.

Statt, D. (1981) *The Concise Dictionary of Psychology*, London, Routledge.

Staufenbiel, T. and Kleinmann, M. (1999) 'Does P-O fit influence the judgements ion assessment centres?'. Paper presented at the European Congress of Work and Organisational Psychology, Espoo-Helsinki, Finland.

Steiner, D.D. and Gilliland, S.W. (1996) 'Fairness reactions to personnel selection techniques in France and the United States', *Journal of Applied Psychology*, vol.81, pp.134–47.

Steiner, I.D. (1972) *Group Processes and Productivity*, New York, Academic Press.

Sternberg, R.J. (1997) 'Tacit knowledge and job success' in Anderson, N. and Herriot, P. (eds) *International Handbook of Selection and Assessment* London, Wiley, pp.201–13.

Sternberg, R.J. and Wagner, R.K. (1986) *Practical Intelligence,* Cambridge, Cambridge University Press.

Sternberg, R.J. and Wagner, R.K. (1995) 'Testing common sense', *American Psychologist,* vol.50, pp.912–27.

Stevens, C.K., Mitchell, T.R. and Tripp, T.M. (1990) 'Order of presentation and verbal recruitment strategy effectiveness', *Journal of Applied Social Psychology*, vol.20, pp.1076–92.

Stevens, M.J. and Campion, M.A. (1999) 'Staffing work teams: Development and validation of a selection tests for teamwork settings', *Journal of Management*, vol.25, pp.207–28.

Stevens, S.S. (1946) 'On the theory of scales of measurement', *Science*, vol.103, pp.421–57.

Stevens, S.S. (1951) 'Mathematics, measurement and psychophysics' in Stevens, S.S. (ed.) *Handbook of Experimental Psychology*, New York, Wiley.

Stohr-Gilmore, M.K., Stohr-Gilmore, M.W. and Kistler, N. (1990). 'Improving selection outcomes with the use of situational interviews: Empirical evidence from a study of correction officers for new generation jails', *Review of Public Personnel Administration*, vol.10, no.2, pp.1–18.

Stokes, G.S. and Reddy, S. (1992) 'Use of background data in organisational decisions' in Cooper, C.L. and Robertson, I.T. (eds) *International Review of Industrial and Organizational Psychology*–, Chichester, Wiley, pp.285–321.

Stokes, G.S. and Searcy, C.A. (1999) 'Specification of scales in Biodata from development: rational versus empirical and global versus specific', *International Journal of Selection and Assessment*, vol.7, pp.72–96.

Stone, D.L. (1995) 'The perceived fairness of drug testing and honesty testing'. Paper presented at the meeting of the Academy of Management, Vancouver, British Columbia, Canada.

Sue-Chan, C., Latham, M.G., Evans, M.G. and Rotman, J.L. (1997) 'The construct validity of the situation and patterned behaviour description interviews: cognitive ability, tacit knowledge and self-efficacy as correlates'. Unpublished manuscript, Faculty Management, University of Toronto, Canada, cited in Robertson and Smith (2001).

Taylor, F.W. (1911) *The Principles of Scientific Management*, New York, Free Press.

Taylor, P. and Small, B. (2000) 'A meta-analytic comparison of situational and behavioural description interview question'. Paper presented at the 15th Annual Conference of the Society of industrial and organizational psychology, New Orleans, LA.

Tellegen, A. (1993) *Folk Concepts and Psychological Concepts of Personality and Personality Disorder*.

Terman, L.M. (1916) *The Measurement of Intelligence*, Boston, MA, Houghton Mifflin.

Terman, L.M. (1924) 'The mental test as a psychological method', *Psychological Review*, vol.38, pp.406–27.

Tetlock, P.E. (1985) 'Accountability: The neglected social text of judgement and choice' in Cummings, L.L. and Staw, B.M. (eds) *Research in Organisational Behaviour*, vol.7, Greenwich, CT, JAI Press.

Thayer, P.W. (1977) 'Something old, something new', *Personnel Psychology*, vol.30, pp.513–24.

Thornton, G.C. (1980) 'Psychometric properties of self-appraisals of job performances', *Personnel Psychology*, vol.33, pp.263–71.

Thornton, G.C. and Byham, W.C. (1982) *Assessment Centres and Managerial Performance*, New York, Academic Press.

Thurstone, L.L. (1938) 'Primary mental abilities', *Psychological Monographs*, p.1.

Tullar, W.I. (1989) 'The employment interview as a cognitive performing script'. in Eder, R.W and Ferris, G.R. (eds) *The Employment Interview: Theory, Research and Practice*, Newbury Park, CA, Sage, pp.233–46.

Van Vianen, A.E.M. and De Dreu, C.K.W. (2001) 'Personality in teams: Its relationship to social cohesion, task cohesion and team performance', *European Journal of Work and Organizational Psychology*, vol.10, no.2, pp.97–121.

Van Vianen, A.E.M. and Willemsen, T.M. (1992) 'The employment interview: The role of sex stereotypes in the evaluation of male and female job applicants in the Netherlands', *Journal of Applied Social Psychology*, vol.22, pp.471–91.

Veres III, J.G., Locklear, T.S. and Sims, R.R. (1990) 'Job analysis in practice: A brief review of the role of job analysis in human resource management' in Ferris, G.R., Roland, K.M. and Buckley, R.M. (eds) *Human Resource Management: Perspective and Issues*, pp.79–103. Boston, MA, Allyn and Bacon.

Veres, J.G., Green, S.B. and Boyles, W.R. (1991) 'Racial differences on job analysis questionnaires: An empirical study', *Public Personnel Management*, vol.20, pp.135–44.

Vernon, P.E. (1950) *The Structure of Human Abilities*, London, Methuen.

Vernon, P.E. (1961). *The Structure of Human Abilities*, 2nd edn, London, Methuen.

Vernon, P.E. (1963) *Personality Assessment*, London, Methuen.

Vernon, P.E. and Parry, J.B. (1949) *Personality Selection in the British Forces*, London, University of London Press.

Viswesvaran, C. and Ones, D. S. (2000) 'Perspectives of models of job performance', *International Journal of Selection and Assessment*, vol.8, pp.216–25.

Viswesvaran C., Ones, D.S. and Schmidt, F.L. (1996) 'Comparative analysis of the reliability of job performance ratings', *Journal of Applied Psychology*, vol.81, pp.557–74.

Waller, N.G. and Ben-Porath, Y.S. (1987) 'Is it time for clinical psychology to embrace the five factor model of personality?', *American Psychologist*, vol.42, pp.887–9.

Walters, L.C., Miller, M.R. and Ree, M.R. (1993) 'Structured interviews for pilot selection: No incremental validity', *The International Journal of Aviation Psychology*, vol.3, no.1, pp.25–38.

Wason, P.C. (1966) 'Reasoning' in Foss, B. (ed.) *New Horizons in Psychology*, Harmondsworth, Penguin.

Watkins, L.M. and Johnston, L. (2000) 'Screening of job applicants: the impact of physical attractiveness and application quality', *International Journal of Selection and Assessment*, vol.8, pp.77–84.

Weekley, J.A. and Gier, J.A. (1987) 'Reliability and validity of situational interviews for sales positions', *Journal of Applied Psychology*, vol.72, pp.484–7.

Weekley, J.A. and Jones, C. (1997) 'Further studies of situational tests', *Personnel Psychology*, vol.52, pp.679–701.

Weijerman, E.A.P. and Born, M.P. (1995) 'The relationship between gender and assessment centre scores' [in Dutch], *Gedrag en Organisatie*, vol.8, pp.284–92.

Weiss, E.M. and Barbeite, G.F. (2001) 'Internet as a job source and job site preference'. Paper presented at the 16th Annual Conference of the Society for Industrial and Organizational Psychology, San Diego, CA.

Weiss, H.M. and Adler, S. (1984) 'Personality and organisational behaviour' in Staw, B.M. and Cummings, L.L. (eds) *Research in Organisational Behaviour*, vol.6, Greenwich, CT, JAI Press, pp.1–50.

Wernimont, P.R. and Campbell, J.P. (1968) 'Signs, samples and criteria', *Journal of Applied Psychology*, vol.52, pp.372–6.

Westoby, J.B. and Smith, J.M. (2000) *The 16PFS Job Spec.*, Windsor, Assessment and Selection in Employment (ASE).

Wiesner, W.H. and Cronshaw, S.F. (1988) 'A meta-analytic investigation of the impact of interview format and degree of structure on the validity of the employment interview', *Journal of Organizational Psychology*, vol.61, pp.275–90.

Wilkinson, L.J. (1997) 'Generalisable biodata? An application to the vocational interests of managers', *Journal of Occupational and Organizational Psychology*, vol.70, pp.49–60.

Witt, L.A., Burke, L.A., Barrick, M.A. and Mount, M.K. (2002) 'The interactive effects of conscientiousness and agreeableness on job performance', *Journal of Applied Psychology*, vol.87, no.1, pp.164–9.

Wolf, T.H. (1973) *Alfred Binet*, Chicago, IL, University of Chicago Press.

Wood, R. and Payne, T. (1998) *Competency Based Recruitment and Selection: A practical Guide*, Chichester, Wiley.

Woodworth, R.S (1918) *Dynamic Psychology*, New York, Columbia University Press.

Wright, D.E. and Dennis, I. (1999) 'Exploring the speed-accuracy trade-off' in Ackerman, P.L., Kyllonen, P.C. and Roberts, R.D. (eds) *Learning and Individual Difference: Process, Trait and Content Determinants*, Washington, DC, American Psychological Association, pp.231–50.

Zedeck, S. (1986) 'A process analysis of the assessment centre method' in Staw, N.B. and Cummings, L.L. (eds) *Research in Organisational Behavior*, vol.8, pp.259–96.

Zuckerman, M. (1991) *Psychobiology of Personality*, Cambridge, Cambridge University Press.

# Acknowledgements

Grateful acknowledgment is made to the following sources for permission to reproduce material in this book:

### Figures

*Figure 1.2:* Storey, J. (1989) *New Perspectives on Human Resource Management*, Thomson Learning UK; *Figure 1.3:* Beer, M. and Spector, B. (1984) *Managing Human Assets*. By kind permission of the authors; *Figure 1.4:* Robertson, I.T. and Smith, M. (2001) 'Personnel selection', *Journal of Occupational and Organizational Psychology*, Vol.74, Part 4, p.443. Reproduced with permission from the Journal of Occupational and Organizational Psychology, © The British Psychological Society; Anderson, N. and Shackleton, V. (1993) *Successful Selection Interviewing*, Blackwell Publishing Ltd; *Figure 2.1:* Van Amerongen, J. (1993) *The Neighbourhood*. Reprinted with special permission of Cowles Syndicate; *Figure 2.2:* © O*NET Online – Occupational Information Network; *Figure 2.3:* From Roethlisberger, F.J., *Management and the Worker*, Harvard University Press, 1966; *Figure 2.4:* Stammers, R. and Patrick, J. (1975) 'Analysis for training', Herriott, P. (ed.) *Essential Psychology: The Psychology of Training*. Thomson Publishing Services; *Figure 2.5:* © SHL Group Plc 2003 – reproduced with permission; *Figure 3.1:* Cook, M. (1990) *Personnel, Selection and Productivity*. Reproduced by permission of John Wiley & Sons Limited; *Figure 3.2:* PSYCHOLOGICAL TESTING 6/E by Anastasi, © 1990, by Anne Anastasi. Reprinted by permission of Pearson Education, Inc., Upper Saddle River, NJ; *Figure 5.1:* Parsons, C.K. *et al.* (1999) 'Establishing person–organisation fit', p.127, (eds) Eder, R.W. and Harris, M.M., *The Employment Interview Handbook*. Copyright © 1999. Reprinted by permission of Sage Publications, Inc.; *Figure 5.2:* Anderson, N. and Shackleton, V. (1993) *Successful Selection Interviewing*, Blackwell Publishing Ltd; *Figure 5.3:* Anderson, N. and Shackleton, V. (1993) *Successful Selection Interviewing*, Blackwell Publishing Ltd; *Figure 7.1:* Courtesy of the Museum of Questionable Medical Devices; *Figure 7.7:* Saville, P. (1997) *Occupational Testing Course Notes*. © SHL Group Plc, 2003 – reproduced with permission; *Figure 8.4:* Eysenck, H.J. (1967) *The Biological Basis of Personality*, Charles C Thomas, Publisher, Springfield, Illinois, USA; *Figure 8.6:* © SHL Group Plc, 2003 – reproduced with permission; *Figure 8.7:* Reproduced by special permission of the Publisher, Psychological Assessment Resources, Inc., 16204 North Florida Avenue, Lutz, Florida 335549, from the *NEO Personality Inventory Manual*, by Paul Costa and Robert McCrae, Copyright 1985 by PAR, Inc. Further reproduction is prohibited without permission of PAR, Inc.; *Figure 8.10:* Van Amerongen, J. (1993) *The Neighbourhood*. Reprinted with special permission of Cowles Syndicate; *Table 8.2:* Copyright © 1993 by the Institute for Personality and Ability Testing, Inc, Champaign, Illinois, USA. All rights reserved. Reproduced from 16PF Fifth Edition Administrator's Manual.

### Tables

*Tables 2.1, 2.2 and 2.3:* This material is taken from *Job Analysis: A Managers' Guide* by Pearn & Kandola 1993, with the permission of the publisher the Chartered Institute of Personnel and Development, London; *Figure 9.1:* © Courtesy of Lafayette Instruments, www.licmef.com; *Figure 9.2:* adapted from Cooper, C.L. and Robertson, I.T. (2001) *International Review of Industrial and Organizational Psychology*, John Wiley and Sons Ltd; *Figure 9.3:* Adapted from Cooper, C. L. and Robertson, I.T. (2001) *International Review of Industrial and Organizational Psychology*, John Wiley and Sons Ltd.

### Boxes

*Boxes 4.2 and 4.3:* Courtesy of Ford Motor Co Ltd; *Box 4.5:* Business Awareness Questionnaire, KPMG.

Every effort has been made to locate all copyright holders, but if any have been overlooked the publishers will make the necessary arrangements at the first opportunity.

# Index